AUDIO DESIGN

AUDIO DESIGN
Sound Recording Techniques for Film and Video

Tony Zaza

PRENTICE-HALL, INC.

Englewood Cliffs, New Jersey 07632

Library of Congress Cataloging-in-Publication Data

Zaza, Tony
   Audio design : sound recording techniques for film and video /
Tony Zaza.
     p. cm.
   Includes bibliographical references.
   ISBN 0–13–050733–4
   1. Sound—Recording and reproducing. 2. Video tape recorders and
   recording. 3. Sound motion pictures. I. Title.
   TK7871.4.Z39 1990
   621.389′3—dc20   90–6971
                                         CIP

Editorial/production supervision
  and interior design: LAURA A. HUBER
Cover design: BEN SANTORA
Manufacturing buyers: KELLY BEHR/SUSAN BRUNKE

The publisher offers discounts on this book when ordered
in bulk quantities. For more information, write:

  Special Sales/College Marketing
  College Technical and Reference Division
  Prentice Hall
  Englewood Cliffs, New Jersey 07632

Printed in the United States of America

10 9 8 7 6 5 4 3 2 1

ISBN 0-13-050733-4

PRENTICE-HALL INTERNATIONAL (UK) LIMITED, *London*
PRENTICE-HALL OF AUSTRALIA PTY. LIMITED, *Sydney*
PRENTICE-HALL CANADA INC., *Toronto*
PRENTICE-HALL HISPANOAMERICANA, S.A., *Mexico*
PRENTICE-HALL OF INDIA PRIVATE LIMITED, *New Delhi*
PRENTICE-HALL OF JAPAN, INC., *Tokyo*
SIMON & SCHUSTER ASIA PTE. LTD., *Singapore*
EDITORA PRENTICE-HALL DO BRASIL, LTDA., *Rio de Janeiro*

For Tatiana
The Sweetest Sound

Contents

Preface

Audio Design is the first textbook on sound and sound recording to deal with the creative use of the audio track in film, television, theater and audiovisual communication. The expressive manipulation of sound in an effort to tell a story is the primary function of this relatively new craft. The text sees sound shaping as a distinct and integral element in the production process, and it develops a vocabulary to explain the unique storytelling functions of the imagery that sound creates for the audience.

This is a book for the audio enthusiast with the heart of the poet and it, indeed, aims at a poetics of sound production. Emphasis is placed on the relationship of sound (auditory material) to the basic elements of composition: light, color, movement, shape, volume; and to the language of film and video—the formal elements that comprise a narrative program.

Anyone interested in increasing the impact of the soundtrack on the audience will find in *Audio Design* the means by which a personal aural esthetic may be formed, challenged, and reinterpreted. Moreover, the text aims at a broader understanding by the reader of the unique narrative functions of sound—aural image/facts that communicate what the visual cannot.

Common to all the communication arts, the eye follows the ear. *Audio Design* demonstrates the significance of the perspective of the audience in planning and producing an effective aural experience, one which goes beyond the limits of the visual. However, the practitioner must also develop a thorough understanding of the mechanics of sound recording, the technical and financial limitations of that recording process, and the ways the audience may be influenced.

Since the coming of sound, the soundtrack has been generally neglected. *Audio Design* attempts to foster an appreciation of the boundless creative potential of audio. In so doing, it questions the nature of the narrative experience in the theater and in front of the home video system. The pro as well as the uninitiated should find something of value—both challenging and inspirational—bound up with the premise that sound can be and should be as important to the communication of ideas and emotions as the visual. Even in the Theatre of the Deaf, listening comes first, then movement, then drama.

The text is organized into two distinct sections that are separated by a chapter devoted to budget. Chapters 1–6 deal consecutively with all the basic design building blocks in relation to narrative (fiction) programs. Chapter 1 provides an introduction to language, structure, and the basic elements of sound and music composition. Chapter 2 provides organizational guidelines, with emphasis on film music. The emphasis in Chapter 3 is on the generation and modification of basic sound track elements: voice, music, and effects. The role of postproduction in creating and modifying tracks is covered in Chapter 4. Chapter 5 proposes a relationship between sound and color. Chapter 6 covers the use of documentary sound.

The budget section, Chapter 7, is then presented midway as a technical and creative landmark. Its ramifications are too important to wait until last and must be considered by the audio designer as early on as possible to make choices. Instructually, the midpoint in a course in sound design or production must deal with financial realities that govern essential directions and limitations in the process. All the options become creative choices.

The second section of the text presents instructional roads to take relative to the emphasis of the overall program. Armed with the basic inventory of design elements, the reader is now free to enter into a dialogue regarding the nature of the sound image/fact, the aural object, (Chapter 8) or to delve into the more practical aspects of improving TV audio (Chapter 9) and learning the process of two-track recording (Chapter 10). These chapters take into account the realities of TV production, which tend to offer less opportunity for planning and more for "repairing." Chapters 11 and 12 introduce new and rediscovered directions that have more impact on exhibition than on design, but that are no less critical for a complete understanding of the technical limits and possibilities of influencing the audience.

Chapter 13 attempts to bridge the gap between media and live performance. In detailing the process of sound design for the theater, the chapter implies that concepts previously explored are relevant to the theater.

The Appendix contains a structured database that should provide adequate technical, commercial, creative, and practical reference for further study.

Acknowledgments

The author thanks the following for their unselfish contributions to the text: Bob Harris and James Painten, Elfriede Fischinger and William Moritz, Manfred Klemme and Tanenbaum, Greg Landaker and Ken Anderson, Eric Kampmann, Alex Kogan, Tobey C. Moss, Barry Friedman, and certainly not the least, Richard Einhorn.

The following manufacturers provided technical data expanding the scope of the text: Sennheiser, Inc., Nagra, Inc., Crown Int'l., New England Digital, Litewave, Inc., TEAC/TASCAM, Fostex, Imax, Inc., Showscan, Inc., Dolby, Inc.

Without Susan's support, this text could not have been completed. Without Mark Dichter's insightful groundwork, this text could not have been realized.

Tony Zaza

THE STRUCTURAL USE OF SOUND

Creating images with sound is the fundamental craft of the audio designer. This section details how sound may be used more potently as a source of narrative and emotive content. Analysis of the sound track includes spatial, temporal, editorial, and rhythmic components, as well as the functions of music as they relate to the formal language of film. Context and contrast are seen as prime storytelling modes. A "sonogenics" of film is suggested, with consideration of the chief methodological aspects of sound design: accuracy, articulation, allusion, image, facts, and physical causation.

Figure 1–1 A form without feeling is a failure.

Basic Elements

Sound is being used as an integral **structure,** a formal element in and of itself, when it ceases to be merely support for an image and becomes narratively significant. Robert Bresson has said that a sound always evokes an image,[1] but, conversely, an image never evokes a sound. While this extreme position may not always obtain, his insight is, nevertheless, essential to an understanding of how sound may be used to create allusions, associations, and evocations of new realities that have a logic in the aural, circular world.

The ease with which a sound may be deciphered can vary as much as the ease with which an image can be read.[2] Falling rain can be deciphered as crowd applause. The suggestion and/or ultimate decoding is made either by the association with off-screen space or some event before or after the aural event. Basic analysis, then, must begin with listening for spaces, for tonal arrangements, for emotive implications. "Deafness forces an inability to sense one's own identity which has no parallel in blindness," said E. V. Cameron in his *Sound and the Cinema.* Good listening is not only a prerequisite for recording, it is basic to effective sound design that carries narrative meaning.

Learning to think sound requires overcoming of the strong visual bias of Western society. "The eye demolishes what it sees and rebuilds it according to the idea it has made of it: the painter's eye, according to his taste or his ideal beauty."[3] This sensitivity of the painter must be transferred to the aural realm.

Through observation, we know that sound can signify changes in time or space. If we further analyze these two basic coordinates and relate them to the goal of adding to the story line what cannot possibly be expressed by picture, we can list several aural ideas:

Auditory perspective. There is a difference between the way the human ear hears and the way a microphone records. Sound can imply shot size. What is the sound of a close-up?

Apparent distance. Depth of field can be defined as a function of the resonance or echo created through microphone placement vis-à-vis the position of the camera. The perspective of the audience or characters may be manipulated. What then is "natural" sound?

2

Ambient silence. The unique and unrepeatable sound, characteristic of a given space. The pattern of the microphone and the axis of placement will define the space.

Equal presence. The characteristic of the microphone added to the quality of a given space. It tends to change from shot to shot and must be preserved, augmented, or **masked.**[4]

Aural masking. Property of one sound that inhibits the separation or audibility of a proximate sound. Often occurs when sound elements are mixed. Unless each track or element has been rehearsed or auditioned, it is not likely the mixer will notice the loss.

Separation. Capacity of sound to be **focused**[5] via stereophonic techniques into discrete localized positions, on or off screen (above, below, left, right, front, rear, and in-between visual planes, seen and unseen.)

Compression. Exaggeration of duration by manipulation of level or intensity, noise suppression, or position on the screen (within the shot). Time abridgement may be either implied or physically obtained through editing and processing, but the effect is to change one's perception of the **flow** of time. (*see* Doppler effect).

What is natural sound? For the audio designer as well as the director, this is no simple issue. It is a function of the overall texture[6] of the narrative, the shot-to-shot relationships, the transitions between all sequences in time and space, and the budget.

To turn the exhibition space into a dream factory, the designer must forget the assumptions inherent in the way we perceive and start listening to sounds, not the source of sound. The aural world has no corners. In a free field, sound radiates freely in all directions. The brain separates sounds it wants from sounds it does not want through a very complex psychoacoustical process not fully understood by scientists. We can listen in on a conversation between two people at a crowded, noisy party, but trying to re-create that experience on the screen is quite another chore. The question of the "natural" is rhetorical. The designer must define naturalism only insofar as sound elements **produce the desired effect.** What does someone sound like who is 20 feet away in relation to someone 1 inch from the camera? The logic is created within the shot and has a logic only in relation to screen space and time, not in real space and time.

In real time, our ears adjust to changes in pressure and background-to-foreground changes in level, as well as the changes from room to room, based on size and other physical considerations. We have **learned** to perceive **room tone** (presence), and we tend to unconsciously adjust to slight variation in room character in the real world. In the theater, however, focus is select, and small discrepancies previously tolerated are now glaringly evident, distracting, and destructive of the screen reality.

Intellectually, we cannot accept the physical fraud of straight match continuity, which dictates that the editor or mixer balance room tone throughout the picture to disguise the transitions and maintain the **illusion of continuity.**

Likewise, the perspective of each shot is defined by its composition and is felt as correct if the resonant quality or echo characteristic has been matched to the visual. The apparent microphone position, however, may correspond to the position of the audience, the position of a spectator in the shot, seen or unseen (a ghost, for instance), or the director. Only the sound can help decode the puzzle of what appears to be an arbitrary selection and arrangement of shots.

The **ambient noise,** which is the low-frequency sound of a specific space recorded at normal listening level, is felt from scene to scene as a change of pressure in the theater if no effort has been made to defeat naturalism in favor of the smooth, continuous transition. Lack of noise, of silences (no data on track), produces a booming, hissing sensation, which makes the audience aware of the presence of speakers. So it is necessary to add noise to create a silence!

Sound has had difficulty being accepted in filmmaking as of equal importance with the image. Film began as a visual art with no dialogue or sound effects, although usually with musical accompaniment. Within that structure, Griffith, Eisenstein, Dreyer, and others evoked sound through camera movement and rhythm. So well did they do this that Stanley Brakhage was prompted to argue that the great silent filmmakers were much more inventive and creative in evolving audio associations than sound filmmakers. "The sound sense which visual images always evoke and which can become integral with the esthetic experience of the film under creative control, often makes actual sound superfluous."[7]

Robert Bresson, on the other hand, emphasized the importance of sound in comparison with the image. "A sound always evokes an image; an image never evokes a sound."[8] Between these two opposing views lies a myriad of dialectical possibilities inherent in the joining and contrast of sound with image. The filmmaker must compose his or her film with the knowledge that both the camera and microphone are nonselective in comparison with the human eye and ear, and that neither sound nor image can be considered as the more realistic element.

Siegfried Kracauer in *Theory of Film* outlined three categories of distinctions in the sound–image relationship: (1) Synchronism versus asynchronism distinguishes between sound that has a visually identifiable source and sound that does not. (2) Parallelism and counterpoint differentiate between sound that complements the image and sound that carries a different meaning. (3) Actual sound arises from an identifiable source within the narrative; commentative sound does not have a source within the narrative.[9]

Claudia Gorbman[10] dismissed the first two categories as confusing and not precise enough; the third, she expanded. A sound, she argued, may originate in one of three narrative levels: (1) The characters themselves may speak or sing or make noise. (2) Sound may originate outside the narrative structure, such as muscial themes or verbal commentary. (3) Sounds (or silence) may be imagined by characters but not actually be heard by their ears.

Furthermore, Gorbman noted, the concept of auditory space has several important aspects:

1. Auditory depth of field is the sensation of the apparent distance from microphone to sound source.[11]
   a. Sound presence can counterpoint a visual presence, such as when a visual long shot is combined with an audio close-up.
   b. Auditory presence can be exaggeratedly congruent with the visual image, as in Orson Welles's *Othello*, in which close-ups are aurally intimate and long shots have booming echoes.[12]
2. On-screen or off-screen sound refers to either perceived visual space on the screen or inferred space outside the bounds of the visual image. On-screen sound originates from an identifiable source within the visual field.
3. On-track and off-track sound refers to whether or not the sound is directly perceived by the ear or merely inferred, such as where people converse behind a closed window.
4. Auditory masking screens one sound by drowning it with another.
5. Sound focus selects particular sounds and renders them clear and sharp in a hubbub of voices or noises, much as the ear selects sounds.
6. Sound texture can be muffled, resonant, thin, and so on, depending on the cinematic space in which the sound occurs, such as an auditorium, a mountainous area, or a bedroom.[13]

Within these parameters of auditory space, the three sound elements of dialogue, music, and special effects (or natural sounds) are interrelated in a hierarchical way. Dialogue is usually predominant, but early filmmakers, and some present-day experimental filmmakers, sometimes inverted the hierarchy. For example, René Clair's first sound film used music as the dominant element. It is now coming to be accepted that silence may be considered a fourth component of the sound track. Some young filmmakers have made distinctions in the "colors" of silence: a complete dead space on the track, studio silence, silence in the country, room tone, and so on.

Sound may be used to evoke ideational associations. For example, sound may be thematic, metaphorical, punctuational, ironic, or ambiguous, or sound may even serve as a trustworthy or untrustworthy source of information.[14]

Because of the interrelationship of sound and image, the sound track without the corresponding images is not a particularly useful teaching tool. The quality of the recording or printing or playback may be judged from only the sound track, but its function in the film can only be fully appreciated when the two elements are combined.[15]

The Formal Language of Film and Video

The basic analysis of the script requires an understanding of the following terms of measurement:

Angle of view: The position of the camera in relation to the subject. May be high, low, or eye level. The camera corresponds to the audience's, character's, or director's viewpoint.

Angle subtended by the lens: Qualifies the perspective or field of view in terms of horizontal–vertical and the human form. May be wide, medium or telephoto, or extremely close-up (macro) in relation to the size of an average figure. A shot from head to toe of a man filling the screen corresponds to a full shot.

Framing: Qualifies the position the primary subject occupies in the rectangular screen image. May be high, low, left, or right; the limit of the frame implies off-screen space.

Elements of composition: *Balance*: Symmetry of shapes, colors, and actions within the frame.
Growth: Capacity of light, movement, form, or color to express volume, size, or space and time.

Units of length: *Frame*: 24 units per foot of film, 30 units per foot of videotape. The smallest unit perceptible on the screen.
Shot: Series of frames implying unity of action, time or space.
Sequence: Series of shots which may or may not imply spatial/temporal continuity, but which has some unifying common element of narrative logic.
Scene: A complete narrative act that can stand alone.

Gauge: Width of the film or tape: 8mm, 16mm, 35mm, 65mm, 70mm, super 8mm, super 16mm; $\frac{1}{2}$, $\frac{3}{4}$, 1, and 2 inch, quad, video 8mm.

Size of image through lens: Signifies the relationship between the frame as completely filled from top to bottom with the human form and increments of that **(full)** shot:
Extreme close-up **(XCU),** smaller than the head
Close-up **(CU),** smaller than the full face and neck
Medium **(MS),** face to stomach
Long shot **(LS),** multiple of full figure **(full shot)**

Narrative function of the shot: Exterior, interior, establishing, master, or reverse angle (reaction): defines the **location** and/or **importance** of the shot.
Point of view **(POV),** two shot, three shot, insert, or cutaway: defines the **position of the audience** or **position of the character(s).**

Aspect ratio: The ratio of screen length to screen width, the most common being 1 : 1.33, 1 : 1.85, and 1 : 2.00.

Program Analysis Terms

Although borrowed from the classical models of visual structure in film and video programs, the following terms may provide possible points of approach in the analysis of aural imagery:

Separation: Fragmentation of a sequence into alternating details.

Parallel action: Two or more layers of narrative occurring simultaneously in different fields.

Slow disclosure: Gradual revelation of details within a given shot or scene.

Familiar image: Repetitive image or fact whose significance alters and is altered by its new position in the sequence.

Movement: Motion in space and time forward, back, in parallel, or off screen.

Multiangularity: Multiple point source (stereo) perspective (subject, object, director, spectator).

Orchestration: Overall gestalt or arrangement of structural elements (music, effects, narration).

Mise-en-scène: What occurs within the frame.

The Blend of Theory and Practice

The Soviet theoretician and filmmaker V. I. Pudovkin (1893–1953) had great difficulty perceiving film as anything but the result of the creative combination of bits and pieces of expressive images. However, his views regarding sound as an element that should be rich in association and, again, should be creatively joined as bits and pieces into a unified whole provides a formal introduction to fundamental editing concepts for sound.

Pudovkin sees sound for film as counterpoint. There is a "rhythmic course of the objective world," and via sound counterpoint a "tempo and rhythm with which man observes this world." This is the underlying feature in his use of sound chiefly as a mode for the reactive–subjective emotion of the spectator and the duration (real or psychological) of this emotion. It is not uncommon in this system to have a sound element directly in opposition to what is being seen on the screen if and only if the sound presents the emotion the director intends the audience to feel or accept.

Pudovkin's methodology relied on a weaving of several layers of auditory material. In his *Diserter*, for instance, a vast outdoor lecture is handled thusly: speeches are heard; then auditory close-ups (higher level) of interruptions consisting of small emotive reactions from individuals, such as words, grunts, and noises that interrupt the speeches; then a mix of general crowd noise. The durations of these three elements are editorially controlled to evoke the desired emotional buildup.

In 1958, Stefan Kudelski introduced into the Euro-American market a high-quality, portable, reel-to-reel synchronous magnetic tape recorder, the NAGRA. By 1962, spurred by the necessities of newsreel cinematography in France, Andre Coutant introduced the Eclair NPR, the first portable, quick-loading, silent 16mm camera for one-person, hand-held field use. Filmmaking had moved out of the studio into the territory of location shooting.

These two developments have had a marked influence on the choice of subject matter, the way a program is put together, and the nature of the sound track. Mobile, portable sound and film systems revolutionized news gathering. Their effect on feature filmmaking was more gradual as a generation of directors and camera personnel brought their sensitivities and field techniques to bear on feature production. With the introduction of wireless microphones that were trouble free (circa 1975), feature production produced more scenes with more movement: very agile, often noisy outdoor moving shots, such as chase scenes through crowds and car chases, and balletic, pyrotechnic, and ballistic extravaganzas. Action movies have preoccupied Hollywood for the past 20 years, and their sound tracks have made full use of the new mobility by matching every action with a crescendo of live and stock effects unfortunately signifying nothing more than, in the words of Pudovkin, "a mechanical device enabling us to enhance the naturalness of the image." This slavish imitation of naturalism he saw as primitive. His idea was to use sound to explain content more **deeply** to the audience.

Sergei Eisenstein (1898–1947), however, sees sound, and particularly, music, as an "emphasizer" grounded in the visual, but presenting an "inner sounding" of personal images and inner movement. Often the score to him "suggested plastic visual solutions," representational elements that cannot be expressed in the visual. He likens the transparence and dynamism of music to poetry and painting. Citing as an example Disney's use of a peacock in *Birds of a Feather* (an early Silly Symphony) with the use of Offenbach's "Barcarolle," he confirms that the love theme in no way contradicts the image, but is rather a substitution for "pictured" lovers by a "characteristic trait of lovers" musically evoked by the ever-changing opalescence of approaches and retreats. This was for Eisenstein a prime example of how sound could extend and reconstruct precise emotional meanings.

With dialogue, Eisenstein asserts that **intonation** is the **movement of the voice** flowing from the same **movement of emotion** that must serve as a fundamental factor in outlining the whole image. He further asserts that the creation of the track must take into account the graphics and compositional elements within and between shots. "The art of plastic composition consists in leading the spectator's attention through the exact path and with the exact sequence prescribed by the author of the composition."

Sound then is an organizer of movement, as well as an intensifier, and Eisenstein goes into great detail in his analysis of a scene from *Alexander Nevsky* to demonstrate the solidity of the audiovisual bond.

Problems in Sound Analysis

The following are some of the problems encountered with sound.

- Sound is abstract, exists in time, and is difficult to pin down for scrutiny.
- Sound is multilayered and operates on several planes simultaneously, especially in symphonic structures mixed with dialogue, and is hard to separate.
- Listening spaces are limited due to poor acoustics. Playback systems are not nearly sensitive enough to provide full response and density of detail.
- There are few, if any, practical approaches to an initial mapping of the patterns of sound (gestält) as they flow against each other. The format of the mixers' cue sheet provides a useful guide. Each major element is given a separate vertical column for tracing in time. Read horizontally, the map gives some indication of how elements combine and interact, producing meaning. See Table 1–1.

TABLE 1–1   Sound Map of the Introduction to *Becky Sharp*, Showing the Pattern of "Emotional Musical Ideas"

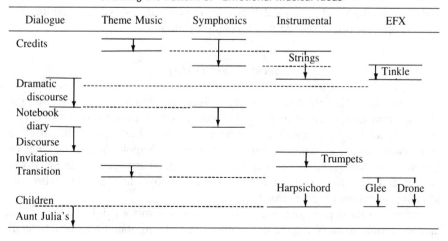

- Classifying terminology is limited:

Discrete atmospherics	Environmental
Unvocalized idiom	Nonverbal
Aural intrusion	Depth cue
Aural close-up	No background
Focus/density	Intensity

Definitions of the preceding terms of sound analysis are as follows:

Discrete atmospherics: The points of sound data that make up the entire texture of background-to-foreground noises that fill in the pictorial space and make it seem live, actual, real. These include the buzz of insects, wind gusts, rustling of leaves, and the like.

Unvocalized idioms: The complex guttural and nasal sounds made by humans and animals that are not part of speech, but which, nevertheless, convey presence, tone, or distance from the listener. These include snorts, sneezes, swallows, gurgles, and the like.

Aural intrusions: The range of sounds that provide depth cues or cues to the relative position of subjects that are either on screen or implied in off-screen space. These could be any natural or artificial effect, such as a train whistle or a door closing.

Aural close-up: All the clusters of sounds, including silence, that create or preserve the perspective of close-up. This might include breathing sounds and some unvocalized idioms. Background sounds are eliminated.

Focus/density: Class of sounds that reveal planes of action (density of detail) or that isolate an important subject (level of intensity) from a group of subjects and their backgrounds. Musical tones combined with nonverbal gestures, as well as effects, often provide this focusing of attention.

Becky Sharp (1935)

This dramatic (often seriocomic) melodrama (Figure 1–2) set in the age of Napoleon directs sonic and psychic energies into patterns of tension and relaxation to delay and amplify specific events; sound acts to create narrative anticipation (musical fanfare over the shadow of Napoleon and the map of Europe) and conflict (the whirls of wind and excited strings as both the storm of war and a warlike storm burst open the windows to the main ballroom, infecting merriment with menace).

For the most part, the film's soundtrack is a mix of lightly expressive, untroublesome melody fragments, often close to being inaudible, which detail

Figure 1–2   Almost all the musical interludes in *Becky Sharp* are *numbers*, that is, set pieces in which song or musical details express an aspect of Becky's changing character and fate. This form later becomes the convention for musical drama or comedy. Songs are like the German *singspiel*, which are emotive pieces of dialogue that are composed to be sung or canted. Miriam Hopkins (Becky) addresses Nigel Bruce and Pauline Gaton. Music has been lifted from its traditional "silent" role of support and elevated within the narrative, expressing emotional musical ideas. (Courtesy of the Museum of Modern Art Still Archive and Around-the-World Films, New York.)

a woman's emotions, punctuated with long segments with dialogue only. In the hectic "Call to Colors" sequence, voice becomes the punctuation for an elaborate series of atmospheric effects and nervous orchestration. (See Figure 1–3)

Exemplary of the film scoring techniques of 1930s Hollywood, *Becky Sharp* illustrates the classical principles of composition, blending, and arrangement.

- The technical apparatus of recording is never seen. For the most part, music emanates from on-screen sources: the harpsichord in the study, the ballroom orchestra, and so on.

- Dialogue is given primacy. When combined with music, music is underrecorded and mixed well below the level of voice. Often, the music is barely audible.

- As a signifier of emotion, music here sets all the specific moods of the *female* lead only. Both the mood of a space and the mood of the character (Becky Sharp) are echoed in the recurring theme (a love theme that becomes more diluted and then reconstructed toward a hopeful resolution).
- Music gives cues that establish landmarks (see Figure 1–3a) in the chapters of the story. Music often substitutes for voice, providing a melodic answer or reaction that is more emotive but less explicit than language (Becky's knowing glances via "tinkling sounds"). Pizzicato strings just prior to

(a) " Strand" Analysis from Becky Sharp (1935)

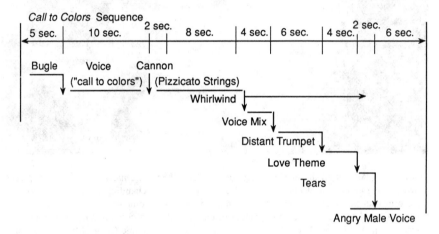

(b) *Shadow of Napoleon* Sequence

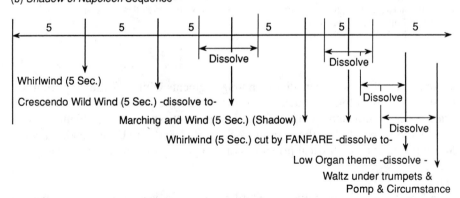

Figure 1–3 Strand analysis of sequences of *Becky Sharp* (1935) illustrates the multiple-tiered overlapping of the "Call to Colors" scene and the complex texture of musical and natural sounds creating the changing mood of the "Shadow of Napoleon" scene. The detail of the bugle motif shows metronomic design in the combining of drum beats and marching. The detail of a musical segue into the next scene follows a balanced pattern.

(c) Detail of Layering Technique

Bugle signals march to war as the party goes on

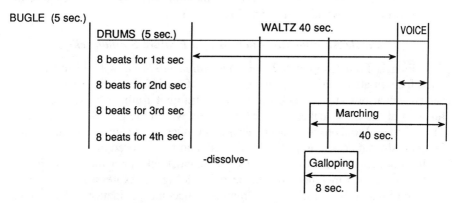

(d) Detail of Musical Segue

Scene moves from party ballroom/music hall

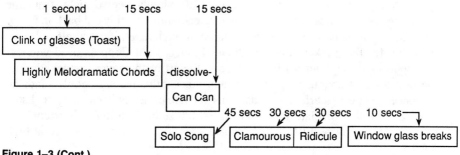

Figure 1–3 (Cont.)

(announcing) the moment of silence and whirling fantasy crescendo illustrating the onset of war. Music dispels uncertainty.

- Rhythmic continuity is ensured via the dreamlike power of music to lessen awareness of cuts and frames. All changes of setting in *Becky Sharp* are both announced and softened by music.
- Roy Webb's musical plan maintains a basic theme and variations; this formalism ensures emotional clarity and unity of expression.

Strand Analysis from Becky Sharp (1935)

The composition of the sound track is characterized by islands of complex sound layering punctuated by long segments of dialogue (up to 20 minutes at silent speed). Typically, the islands are cued by a vocal or musically percussive sound effect, which leads into a measured array (usually at 5 second intervals) of environmental effects mixed with orchestral phrases in which instruments are used to simulate atmospheric effects (the whirlwind is a complex mix of strings, wind, and woodwind). See Figure 1–3b–d .

Sample Approach to Analysis of a Feature Soundtrack

Francis Ford Coppola's *The Conversation* (1974) is notable in that the track focuses attention on the central theme of misinformation. Sound is perceived in various states, each providing a different truth. This self-reflexive function of the track makes the aural an object within the text of the narrative. The sound and tools used to decipher it form much of the action of the drama. Sound is slowed down, amplified, dissected, and recomposed in a mirror image of the production process of creating the sound track for a film. The drama starts to become a metaphor for unconscious desires as expressed by the half-realized truths of the aural images straining to become "evidence." The sound outside the investigator's self (Gene Hackman) merges with the sound (and sense) of the inner self, and it is perceived as discrete acoustic pixels, or space–time bits of information and feelings.

Surveillance expert Gene Hackman records a conversation. In the course of the film, successive layers of meaning are slowly peeled away from the recording, which takes on new significance each time it is played back in a new context. Exposing new levels of information through repetition is a self-reflexive metaphor for the work of the soundman. Francis Ford Coppola used wireless microphones throughout, further reflecting the art of the eavesdropper, that is, the director and character as cipher, and constantly making people (and the audience) aware of certain sounds, thus rechanneling their capacity to listen and listen well and relate to sound the way a soundman does. (Extremes of peaks to lows may be lost in some theaters and on video if not played at high level.)

Note: In an analysis of the visual, one can get away with poor projection, but with the aural image, entire tracks (and therefore levels of data and meaning) may go unheard due to the limited range or sensitivity of playback systems. Sound is more complex than imagined. A second listening often produces a revaluation of the first and often provides more detail. It is recommended that a given soundtrack be played and recorded on a microcassette or better-grade Sony or Marantz standard cassette recorded with an external cardioid microphone used from the spectator's position (measured as twice the width of the screen back from the center of the screen).

Analysis of Narrative, Spatial, Emotive, and Musical Content

The following describes some of the essential points to examine in the analysis of the role and meaning of sound in the completed program.

- **Narrative content.**
  1. Sound supports the space–time reality (of the director).
  2. Sound may imply a reality other than what is seen.
  3. The audience perspective is determined by sound focus.
  4. Audience attention is determined by sound masking.
  5. *Off-track* sound may be inferred by action and movement, color, and shape as perceived in the various planes within the picture (for example, a couple *seen* shouting behind a window in the rear of a set while quiet action occurs in the foreground).
- **Spatial content.**
  1. Screen space is defined by on-screen sound; the source is seen.
  2. Screen space is implied by off-screen sound; the source is unseen.
  3. Sound texture defines the characteristics of the space (muffled noises; thin rattles; loud, resonant steps).
- **Emotive content.**
  1. *Sounds not heard by characters.* Voice, music, and effects used to convey environment, rhythm, fantasy, dream states, or ghostly presence.
  2. *Sounds not heard by audience.* Sounds are inferred by the action or reaction of players (may have comedic or horrific responses).
     a. *Aural hallucination* of the character(s) used to punctuate actions and reactions or convey mental or physical movements not seen on screen, but operating in the spiritual domain.
     b. *Aural allusions* evoke imagery that must be understood by the audience as something a character perceives and, therefore, is understood in terms of what the audience already knows about the character. Or they evoke an image that the audience must interpret in terms of how the image further develops plot, character, or mood.
- **Musical (rhythmic) content.** Music may be used as metaphor, symbol, silence, rhythm/editorial pacer, atmosphere, reinforcer of "staged" realities, spatial definer, or for "inflecting the narrative with emotive values via cultural musical codes."[16] The structural use of music has included all the following:

  1. Melody that is used in place of natural environmental sounds as emulator and simulator of fictional or nonfictional notions of realism (a phonetic but not poetic contradiction).
  2. Musical phrases that replace speech or atmospheric dialogue and are used to define space, movement, or emphasis in the shot.
  3. Music that is used to pace and mask action, events, editorial transitions, and dramatic high or low points. This is both a physical process in which music acts as distracting "noise" and a **sonogenic** process in which melody displaces audience attention to cultural associations embedded in the musical scheme itself (for example, using regional pre-

recorded music rich in the idioms of the old South, interlacing with action and character narratively and implying a space–time structure).

4. Music that does not specifically refer to anything seen or implied in the shot but that acts asynchronously with the picture to impart meaning and emotion of its own. Melody acts idiomatically as a unique statement that carries new meaning with repetition or variation, or it acts commentatively to express additional aspects of the subject or film/video theme (musical thoughts).

5. "Any music will do something."[17]

Spatial Content

Every action takes place in an acoustic environment that has characteristics that are unique but repeatable. Localization and direction information that give the audience the sensation of space, volume, movement, and perspective are functions of microphone placement, microphone coloration, and recording level and audio processing. To a certain extent, filtering and equalization alone are sufficient to create the desired spatial effects, but only if the raw material is a close approximation of the final mixed sound.

Each shot has a size, composition, and perspective that implies a specific space (both within and outside the frame). There is also an apparent camera-to-subject distance that may or may not reflect the proposed aural distancing from the spectator. To define and preserve this set of spatial coordinates, care must be used in the analysis of what is *plausible* spatially in shots before and after the given image or fact. That is, the creation of an aural dimension for one shot ought to take into account the aural implications of what came before and what comes after. Although this is the province of the mixer, drastically contrasted aural proportions may not make it through the recording process into the exhibition space.

Emotional Content

There is such a thing as a "happy" cry as much as there is a "sullen" whisper, a "funny" car crash, and a "frightful" meow. When the audio designer assesses the ways in which the track may manipulate the audience emotionally, it is obvious that mere library prerecordings won't do in most instances where feelings count.

To accurately give emotive expression to the raw material of sound imagery, the designer may have to go as far back as Aristotle to become resensitized to poetic concepts. The designer must combine an interpretation of literary concepts with a sense memory of "felt" sounds and music (musical sensations), most of which may be wholly removed from visual association.

Certain frequencies, chords, combinations of tone, and resonance can, by themselves, produce feelings of sadness, fear, or joy (see Table 1–2). This

TABLE 1–2 Clichés of Program Music

	Interval	Emotion	Related Chord	Trait
C	Unison	Strength	Major	Passion
D	Whole tone	Rousing	Minor	Vitality
E	Major third	Calm	Minor	Logic
G	Fifth	Bright	Major	Enthusiasm
F	Fourth	Desolate	Major	Caution
A	Major sixth	Sad	Minor	Harmony
B	Major seventh	Piercing	Diminished	Receptive

psychosonic predisposition appears to operate essentially on an unlearned stimulus–reaction process operating free of any visual associations. This irrational, Dionysian[18] aspect of sound and music has a magical and potent, albeit involuntary, control of emotions. It could be possible to create an inventory of melodic and dissonant sounds for ''stock'' sensation. Even the voice, that most powerful of instruments, may be utilized to create sounds, or **phonemes**, that can evoke an endless array of private feelings.

Musical (Rhythmic) Content

Every natural event occurs with a pattern of fundamental movements or pulses that forms a rhythm or pacing. In some cases, for instance an automobile wreck, the duration of the components is **indefinite;** the time it takes for each phase of the accident to occur—tire screeching, impact, rumble, roll, glass shattering—may vary without any adverse effect on belief in the illusion created.

Some events, however, require perfect detail in order to suspend disbelief. A washing machine must be carefully timed with a stopwatch to determine each incremental event of the turning-on sequence, which seems to be identical for all makes of machines. Variance in this timing may create the sensation of another type of machine. A typical timing log of this simple sequence may look something like this:

000–003 seconds   Coins in
004–010 seconds   Water gushing
011–021 seconds   Machine whine
022–028 seconds   High-speed whine or rumble

Musical content may also refer to the overall structure of the program. The American musical is a case in point. The entire structure of the program is a musical map, a rhythmic series of musical numbers and silences. A discussion of the technique of producing the musical performance before the camera is important before we can assess the variety of styles that comprise the American musical idiom.

The lack of mobility of the early sound recording systems made it difficult to plan and execute complex musical numbers on the studio sound stages. Although these stages were fully soundproofed, there was too much room for error; singers and dancers had to be perfect, their movements strictly set to the movements and positions of camera and sound equipment, and this equipment had to function perfectly. Logistically, this led to the necessity of multiple **takes,** often just to get the best sound or picture recording. Even the systematic breakdown of master shot to medium and close-ups with cutaways did not lessen the chance for error.

The cost factors involved led to the adoption of setting the musical sequences to **playback.** That is, the performers essentially mimed their singing and dancing to a prerecorded sound track, which was played back in perfect electromechanical synchronization with the camera, since the recorder and camera were connected to the same AC line.

This allowed for even more complex compositions and scenes, since the director was freed from the worry of a bad sound take. In this strict **Hollywood studio technique,** as it came to be called, vocals, dialogue, and the full orchestral renditions were then recorded against the pacing of the original playback track as well as synchronized to the picture to achieve the best possible seamless and intricate musical experience. Filming-to-playback survives to this day, but the visual bias has moved from the studio back to the streets for more realistic, on-location musical events.

Two directorial methods currently dominate in the movement back into the "mean" streets: (1) the merging of documentary sound techniques to the narrative requirements of melodrama and comedy, and (2) the perfecting of the old Hollywood studio technique. In the naked jungle of the street, seamless, quiet sound often appears as an absurdity; the effort then is to preserve the live, vital quality of location sound using stereo two-track recording techniques for live numbers. Both the location tracks and the visuals are then used to orchestrate precisely a studio recording of the music with the time code holding everything in sync. An in-depth discussion of time code follows later in Chapter 10.

The American Musical Idiom

The theme song, as perfected by Judy Garland and Bing Crosby, operates in four primary modes:

1. It expresses an emotion (*A Star is Born*).
2. It is dialogue between characters (*Meet Me in St. Louis*; "Choo Choo Went the Trolley" is exposition to the group. *High Society*; "What a Swell Party This Is," Frank Sinatra to Bing Crosby).
3. It is a speech to the audience (*The Wizard of Oz*; "Somewhere Over the Rainbow").
4. It connects scenes (*Anchors Away, Hit the Deck*).

Some examples of styles of musical structure follow.

Seven Brides for Seven Brothers, 1954.   Michael Kidd's choreography and Stanley Donen's direction reinforce the narrative conventions of the Hollywood musical in which **song** replaces classical discourse and acts as **dialogue,** in the form of voice-over *Sprechstimme* (hybrid combo of sung & spoken words) narration, and **daydreaming,** in the form of thinking or emoting out loud, which functions as speech to the audience. Song also functions diegetically as performance arising out of the scene, for instance, the putting on of a show by children in the home for dinner guests as the natural encore for a song.

An American in Paris, 1951.   The musical idiom defines time, place, pace, and mood. Gene Kelly's entire motif is a story built around a theme and variations, a single essential melodic core sample with variations.

Love Me Tonight, 1932.   As early as 1932, Reuben Mamoulian demonstrated the multiple narrative versatility of one melodic line, "Isn't It Romantic," whose melodic theme shifts from scene to scene with changing tonalities that reflect characters' traits. His orchestral "Song of Paris" is composed of an ever more complex array of sound bites of the cityscape and is a stunning introductory overture in purely aural terms of the city awakening. Maurice Chevalier's rousing rendition of "Mimi" is a model for the effective cadencing of transitions in time and space and the fast-cut.

Invitation to the Dance, 1957.   Gene Kelly's experimental sequence, which merges live action and animation, has the dancers' knack for extremely seamless correlation between acoustic patterns and kinesthetic development in space. The film's expressionist set design (see Figure 1–4) leads into the dream scene.

Other Examples.   The musical remains one of the primary forms to study in an effort to discover patterns of emotion and story development experienced as melody and song. Other examples include Vincente Minelli's *Kismet* (originally released in a stereo format, 1955), King Vidor's 1929 *Halleujah*, the first sound picture with an all-black cast, the superb Technicolor production of Minelli's *The Pirate* (1948), the stereo version of *The Wizard of Oz* (1939) by Victor Fleming, and the archetype musical, *Singin' in the Rain*, the 1952 masterpiece of Gene Kelly and Stanley Donen, and *Something to Sing About* (1937) (see Figure 1–4).

The Structural Use of Music

Music in film and video represents a paradox of realism. Logically, there is only one basis in the narrative for the existence of music, that is, as the product of music sources seen (a radio, a brass band marching, an organ-grinder walking on Mulberry Street in New York), or implied by the visuals, such as a junior

Figure 1–4 *Something to Sing About* (1937) was a self-reflexive parody of musical formalism in which director Victor Schertzinger teamed Bill Frawley and James Cagney. It comments on the often failed attempts to tie together narrative with music, rather than allowing music to become part of the narrative.

prom sequence in the high school gym or action at an ice skating rink, where music is heard but its source is not necessarily seen.

But music performs many important structural tasks, which have been previously enumerated.[19] As a transition technique, music provides thematic, dramatic, rhythmic, and editorial continuity; that is, it softens and disguises changes. In contradistinction, music can also emphasize, call attention to, or clarify the same shifts in space, time, or point of view.

From the perspective of the composer or designer charged with the burden of creating an idiomatic expression in melody that makes sense vis-à-vis picture, music may function as an overall **theme,** that is, a distinctive harmonic progression that may be repeated (theme and variations) and evolve into songs, tunes, and instrumental melody, all carrying meaning that develops as new associations are formed when repeated.

A musical **motif** is, more or less, a phrase, fragment, tune, or chord that has taken on a **conditioned** denotation. It acts as an aural cliché through its redundant use in relation to a specific subject or mood (drums and horns for American Indians, bells and whistles for traffic, for example).

Claudia Gorbman points out that the linguistic origin of the musical motif denotes or is judged by the dramatic context in which it is utilized. She cites, however, the overused melodies of Richard Wagner, which are more **expressive** than **referential,** thus clouding the perception somewhat of melody as leitmotif or unique signature.

With the same logic, music, through redundancy, the conditioning of the cliché motif, and dependence on the culturally defined meaning of certain tunes, notes, and chords, for the most part gives very strong clues in support of the **desired** meaning of a sequence; music determines what we ought to perceive through atmospheric effects, shading, and expressive melody.

As with other classes of aural material, music tends to predispose the viewer or listener to accept a certain (directorial) viewpoint and it mediates borders between levels of narration, kinds of narrator, screen and psychological time, and points in space and time. Music enforces an interpretation of picture by acting like a poetic insert, an aural montage (*ancrage*)[20] of significance in relation to the story, but not categorically denoting narrative specifics.

Like color tinting in the early days of silent film, music overlays a tonal pallette by expressing mood, pace, and the feelings supported and reinforced by its rhythmic, textural, and harmonic qualities, which the visual is not capable of expressing. And the test is that the visual cannot be made to duplicate the sense of the sound.

The clichés of film music were codified by 1911 when the first **cue sheets** appeared; they were drawn from the elaborate inventories of stock effects that formed the popular musical lexicon of the day.[21] The cues marked entrances, exits, interludes, action, and climax in the classical dramaturgical sense making; as Gorbman supposes, ''words lose their necessity.'' Consider even the present-day use of musical images to denote women in flight, bandits on the prowl, or the shower stabbing in Alfred Hitchcock's *Psycho*.

Directors have turned to music as a replacement for speech, using tones, rhythms, and inflections to infect the audience with physical and dramatic depth by creating a spiritual dimension that is more difficult to obtain with the linearity of words, thus filling the tonal void obscured by the pecularities of performance.

It is at the spiritual level of narration that music performs its most severe and eloquent task, for no other element (lighting, effects, or acting) provides what Gorbman calls ''the fleshing out of the shadows and ghosts'' of the cinematic image—those shimmering, flickering, phantoms that resemble real people and real events but that lack vitality, three-dimensional immediacy, and **soul.**

Very nice, but how does music accomplish this? The answer lies in the psychology of music in general. See the bibliographical references and consider music's ''intoxicating'' effects, akin to the rhapsodic Dionysian ideal of Nietzsche.[22]

The Uses of Music

The most logical use of music is to support everything that is implied or suggested by the visual story. Although music is essentially a nonspecific, abstract language of mathematically coordinated feelings or **sense impressions,** musical thoughts seem to be easily comprehended in both denotation and connotation.

While sound has the power to evoke images, music seems to more directly bond the audience together and to the story. This bonding function is accomplished by rhythmically or in some cases arhythmically (dissonance) presenting data that describe (by binaural hearing) space, depth, movement, location, and duration. The impression is strong enough, when creatively applied, to overcome the explicit nature of the visual data, against which much performs its melodious signification of both a physical and emotional world.

Like any other sound, music functions either as the **actual** result of a seen or implied source within the narrative or as a comment on what is seen or implied on the screen. Music, however, operates on many levels, and this **auditory hierarchy,** which includes music, speech, and natural sounds, endows music with an extraordinary capacity to "inflect the narrative with emotive values via cultural musical codes."[23]

The cinematic musical code refers to film elements. Music can replace natural sound onomatopoetically. It can be used to eliminate the need for atmospheric or descriptive dialogue in certain scenes by being very precise or very nonexplicit.

Sound in general and music specifically have been shown to be an effective mask of action, events, noise, editing cuts, and **mistakes.** This purely utilitarian function, nevertheless, imparts a structural (directorial) perspective on how time and space ought to be organized in the particular story. Alan Resnais, for instance, employs sound overlays and masking techniques that impart a unique signature to the way he perceives the space–time continuum (see *Last Year at Marienbad* (1962), for instance). Here **silence** plays an important musical role in the way characters (unspeaking) are emphasized via musical pauses, and this musical silence is contrasted with the memory or dream state of no sound at all (Gorbman calls this nondiegetic silence[24]). That is, off-track silence theoretically differs from off-screen silence, supposing one could hear the difference!

Musical song with lyrics can function in several ways. Its sudden appearance on the track tends to freeze the action by focusing attention on the lyrics in a clean break with the reality on the screen. Formally, songs act like a Greek chorus by commenting on the visual, while often setting a narrative stage.

Luck is the residue of design and often, despite a lack of precision, music and breadth of orchestration and arrangement fleshes out film space, providing depth cues and describing physical volumes (all through the mix function). To

TABLE 1–3 Checklist of Functions of Music in Film and Video

Aural Expressions of Spatial Ideas	
Distance	Comparison of volumes
Position	Change in volume and intensity
Direction	Change in pitch or duration
Open field	Full tonal emphasis; diminished background
Closed field	Changes in reverberation
Articulation of Space	
Emotional	Connotation by inherent character
Symbolic	Connotation by familiar experience
Intellectual	Connotation by content of image
Functions of Musical Allusions	
Descriptive	Refers to what is seen (diegetic)
Decorative	Provides sonorous, sensual pleasure
Evocative	Creates an image
Provocative	Intensifies or enhances dramatic motive
Metaphorical	Referent unseen and nonverbal
Editorial	Provides continuity; imparts order by rhythmic development

a certain extent, music can influence the way the tempo of camera movement (movement of the frame) and movement within the frame are perceived by the audience (because of its beat).

In summary, a checklist of the functions of music in film is presented in Table 1–3.

Colorization

Each musical phrase is made up of notes and/or chords. Each note of the piano keyboard corresponds to a unique frequency that may be expressed in physical terms as cycles per second (or the movement in space back and forth of the waveform). Certain fundamental frequencies, in themselves, have the capacity to elicit specific emotive responses, which depend on the psycho-acoustics of the space and listener.

In F. Lanier Graham's *The Rainbow Book* (Random House, 1975), reference is made to the relationship of light, color, sound, and emotions. Pythagoras was the first to relate notes to colors, and the physicist Hermann von Helmholtz compared the colors of one electromagnetic octave to the notes of the diatonic scale:

G	Ultraviolet	C♯	Green
F	Violet	C	Yellow
E	Indigo blue	A♯	Orange-red
D♯	Cyanogen blue	G♯, A	Red
D	Greenish blue	G	Infrared

The range of frequencies present in the typical piano keyboard opens up a wide range of color–sound possibilities. For each wavelength there is a complimentary color waveform both of which can now be described electronically. See Figure 1–5.

In the near future, audiences will have an interactive role. From their seats, they will manipulate color, light and aural parameters via a digital Lumigraph whose keyboard would access one's emotional "colorization" of the movie/event. See Chapter 5.

The narrative levels of music are the following:

Realistic	Emanates from a visible source
Musical idea	Expressive of an unseen source
Melodic irony	Play on culturally conditioned denotations and connotations

C	4186.0091	D	1174.6591	G♯	415.3047	A♯	116.5409
B	3951.0665	C♯	1108.7305	G	391.9954	**A**	**110.0000**
A♯	3729.3101	C	1046.5022	F♯	369.9944	G♯	103.8261
A	**3520.0000**	**B**	**987.7666**	F	349.2282	G	97.9988
G♯	3322.4376	A♯	932.3275	E	329.6276	F♯	92.4986
G	3135.9635	**A**	**880.0000**	D♯	311.1270	F	87.3070
F♯	2959.9554	G♯	830.6094	D	293.6648	E	82.4069
F	2793.8259	G	783.9909	C♯	277.1826	D♯	77.7817
E	2637.0205	F♯	739.9888	C	261.6256 (middle C)	D	73.4162
D♯	2489.0159	F	698.4565	B	246.9416	C♯	69.2956
D	2349.3182	E	659.2551	A♯	233.0819	C	65.4064
C♯	2217.4611	D♯	622.2540	**A**	**220.0000**	B	61.7354
C	2093.0045	D	587.3295	G♯	207.6523	A♯	58.2704
B	1975.5332	C♯	554.3653	G	195.9977	**A**	**55.0000**
A♯	1864.6551	C	523.2511	F♯	184.9972	G♯	51.9130
A	**1760.0000**	**B**	**493.8833**	F	174.6141	G	48.9994
G♯	1661.2188	A♯	466.1638	E	164.8138	F♯	46.2493
G	1567.9818	**A**	**440.0000**	D♯	155.5635	F	43.6535
F♯	1479.9777	E	41.2034	D	146.8324	C	32.7032
F	1396.9129	D♯	38.8908	C♯	138.5913	B	30.8677
E	1318.5102	D	36.7081	C	130.8128	A♯	29.1352
D♯	1244.5079	C♯	34.6478	B	123.4708	**A**	**27.5000**

Figure 1–5 Cycles per second for each note of the piano keyboard. Certain notes stimulate emotive responses directly without the certification of a pictorial association. Now that you have found a new key, what are you going to play?

Musical time	Rhythm and beat affect perception of felt real time
Formal	Music defines the mood, pace, and place
Fusion with action	Music closely synched to movement and action (syncopation); some programs submit to the musical division of time (editing to music, or music video), not to a realistic use of time
Spatial	Orchestration defines the size of space, sense of depth (Doppler effect), and sense of volume (heavy bass often denotes a heavy object—or subject)

Narrative Functions of Sound

Through the faculty of hearing we become aware of unvisualized events, events happening only in the aural world; combined with sight, we then experience the deepest emotional engagement when synchronously recorded live.[25] The true faculty of the filmic experience is not merely seeing and hearing a film of a dying woman, for example, but rather experiencing it **by means** of film.

Sound operates on several levels in terms of its storytelling capacities. Characters may originate the sound. Sound may exist (as music or voice-over) outside the strict narrative logic of what is seen. Sound may operate as an abstract, imagined subjectively and creating **allusions** (associations or figures of speech). These figures may act as metaphor, punctuation, irony, ambiguity, or thematic entity.

Claudia Gorbman[26] has organized the functional classes of auditory material as follows:

Synchronism	Sound has a source that is visually identifiable
Asynchronism	Sound has no apparent source
Parallelism	Sound complements an image
Counterpoint	Sound has a meaning itself
Actual(ized)	Sound has a narrative source
Commentative	Sound has no story basis, but a directorial attitude

Literacy makes it possible for the audio designer or director to infer that people and space exist when not seen. This process of audiovisual closure is learned and **read** (usually but not necessarily left to right). The logically continuous flow of life on the screen is also experienced through inference from discrete and discontinuous frames and shots.

This is why the metaphorical image is as much a fact of reality on the screen as the representation of reality. Sound has a dominant role in revealing or discriminating between metaphor and fact. Conversely, sound without picture creates a formal ambiguity that is unresolved until linked to its own hallucinatory references.

Picture is inflexible. It is fixed in time, framed, and focused to a measurable degree; its **photogenics** comprise physical and measurable quantities: light, shade, color, texture, contour, and size. Sound is more flexible, more abstract; it seeks to escape everydayness, seeking ecstasy in a rapturous state of flux. Nietzsche in his *The Birth of Tragedy* states that art, rather than ethics, constitutes the essential metaphysical activity of humans. He cites Schiller, who confesses that as a composer he first experiences not images but **musical moods.** ''With me, emotion is at the beginning without clear and definite ideas; those ideas do not arise until later.'' Both were attempting to get at the core of the Dionysian spirit, the escape into the dream state that begins in reality.

Conversely, and more aligned with the visual, the Apollonian spirit moves from dream world to reality. The visual moves within itself and tries to clarify through detail. The aural forgets itself, obliterates its physical identity, and carries the listener off on a trip.

The visual bias of Western culture guarantees that the average person can operate a camera. Having viewed only a few photographs (or movies) imparts some basic sense of selection and arrangement. Cameramen arrive with a more critical eye and clever hand, but are, essentially, made. Soundmen are born.

The visual image has a boundary, a fixed reality subject to technical interpretations. Sound has no boundary, is an abstraction of reality, and is **invisible** in the human's primarily visual world. Sound cannot be fixed and held like a photo; it requires time to exist. Without time, there is no music.

Musicians, mixers, and audio designers rely on a unique apparatus to decipher the aural world and express aural ideas (Schiller's musical ideas). Ear and heart are the tools of passion and virtuosity. Only mathematics links the physical pallette of the cameraman with the imaginary inventory of tonalities of the sound designer. The aural person has keys. The cinematographer has fragments frozen in time.

Audio design is a road map with suggested directions to take; each is open to experimentation and development. Desire and intuition are helpful, and learning to listen well will smooth out the rough edges of creative sensitivity; but the audio designer is like a missionary with a mysterious calling, a vocation that asserts itself only after total immersion in the creative process of human communication.

How Sound Tells a Story

Through Context

As a part of the discourse surrounding an image, sound helps explain the meaning by describing circumstances that result in events or actions. Sound weaves together all the elements of spatial and temporal coherence within the shot and within the sequence. Sound is another tool to manipulate the audience; it focuses their attention emotionally by introducing culturally conditioned responses and physically by directing their eye line by rhythmically matching the dynamics of the visuals within, between, and outside the montage of image or facts.

Functional dialogue, music, and effects subordinate their forms to the context in which they are deployed. Sound acts as a **caption** by establishing a location (Latino salsa music), defining a historical period (Souza march), or setting a tone (dreadful beats of the shark movements in Steven Spielberg's Jaws).

Sound is used to **cover up** the technical process and the mistakes of live location recording that made it through the mix. Sound can make the image appear more magical, less a manufactured commodity. At the edit point, sound can smooth over the cut and make it invisible.

As a sonic and psychic bridge between sobriety and the unconscious, sound, and specifically music, intones a natural magic to the experience of the program by its abstract Dionysian nature, a kind of hypnotic attachment of the imagination of the audience.

By creating **auditory space** within and outside the frame, sound elicits psychic space, a "sonorous envelope,"[27] like the murmur of the mother's heart enveloping the infant afloat in the amniotic fluid of the womb. In the darkened space of the theater, the audience is removed from all other spatial context outside the controlled acoustic arena of the theater and the projected envelope of the screen. Sound removes barriers to belief.

Sound as energy has a presence apart from the visual interplay of light and dark on the screen, its hallucinatory resonance broken only by momentary flashes of visual energy. This is why popcorn noise is so annoying.

Through Contrast

The area between shots is as important as the assemblage. That is, the method of joining the editorial and narrative transitions can have a diversity of **adjacent parts** expressed in color, emotion, tone, and brightness. Music can create oppositions, resistances, and contrasts and can thereby show differences as well as create seamless continuity. As Gorbman has shown, any sound (music) will do something: create rhythm, atmosphere, space, spectator distance, or point-of-view, elicit colors, and so on. In the juxtaposition of dissimilar musical or aural elements, sound may reinforce or invert the meaning of the shot or scene and, perhaps, foster new ideas through repetition and the accumulated meanings that are produced, in spite of the cultural associations that it may have evoked and then contradicted.

Sonogenics

Elements that are eminently suitable esthetically for the representation of sound ideas comprise the sonogenics of the sound experience. The parameters include the following:

1. Interpretation of the needs of the story or subject in terms of **context** and **contrasts**
2. Analysis or creation of a **sonic script** that specifies: (See Tab. 2–2)
   a. Dominant key
   b. Discrete voices (timbre + tempo + volume + duration)
   c. Specific emotion (mood = tonality + coloration)
3. Synthesis through the **combining** and **shaping** of parts into whole phrases (parts include dialogue, music, and effects recorded live, sync, wild, naturally, or artifically):
   a. Monophonically
   b. Polyphonically
4. Levels of **narration:**
   a. Arising from a primary narrative, one narrator off camera.
   b. Through narrative intrusion, one narrator on camera.
   c. Narration by a third party (director, audience, Ghost and so on).
5. Levels of **music:**
   a. Realistic: Relating to a seen source
   b. Expressive: musical idea relating to an unseen source; musical irony playing on the denotation or connotation of the shot
   c. Time as felt through music
   d. Editorial pacing as felt through music
   e. Fusion with action: syncopation and the like; close synchronization (Eisenstein); coordination; orchestration (Fellini's matching of action to symphonic rhythms)
   f. Narrative submission to musical divisions of time, not real time
   g. Space defined by volume of music, depth cues,[28] clues
   h. Music as motivation of camera movement tempos

Accuracy

Details, minute imagefacts, are what comprise and empower the aural image to focus and manipulate the audience's attention. These details are drawn from experience as well as imagination, and they give the audience emotional clues to enable them to decode thematic content. The audio designer's power stems from the abstract expressiveness of clear, precise sounds, which perform as a kind of dramatic music while not being music per se.

Accuracy implies exactitude, that is, having no errors. In regard to the practical work of sound design, accuracy means being **faithful** to aural concept or emotion, rather than to the visual. Let the visual take care of itself! "The camera," critic Walter Kerr admonishes, "is the enemy of passion."

Unlike the picture, sound excludes certain distracting elements. The designer need only provide the most basic of auditory information to achieve the desired effect. The superfluous in the visual becomes ornamental busyness; with the aural, the unnecessary becomes a confusing nuisance.

Raw, unprocessed live sound recorded on location, according to Vlada Petric, provides a kind of "ontological authenticity."[29] A certain spontaneity and genuineness of the whole experience tends to be perceived, with all the natural details supposedly intact.

The eye has less toleration of deceit. The ear is much more accepting and flexible in what it decodes as natural. However, a paradox enters here. The ear is extremely critical of a sound the second time around. Having once heard a real Harley-Davidson motorbike engine rev up, the sense memory will not easily be deceived upon a second listening. During the broadcast of a "Chips" program, a late 1970s action/adventure television series, viewers called in and wrote letters protesting the use of "canned" engine noise for the Harleys. The fraud was glaringly recognizable to aficionados of the bike, and they persuaded the producers to use live recorded Harley engine sounds in future episodes. The Harley, after all, has a very unique sound, which sets it above the tide of the usual and mundane. But for those who had no previous **referential point,** the artifically produced sound was totally accepted as *real* and would have fixed in their sense memory something that was patently offensive to knowing bikers only!

The test, then, for the audio designer is to determine first, if there is any possible previous reference that could cause the intended sound to be misconstrued as something other than what it is intended to be or to convey. Accuracy dictates that the sound be faithful to that reference at the risk of failure—often ludicrous.

Unprocessed sync sound recorded location material is perceived as a kind of "noisy reality" only insofar as one has learned to read it as such. The sense of authenticity Petric alludes to is more a cultural trait than a perceptual bias.

Since it would be quite difficult for the audience to qualify and pinpoint a referential point for any outdoor environmental sound, almost anything will do, including the actual sound. However, the resonances are so rich in live location recordings that overall fidelity diminishes as level increases. Most playback systems cannot reproduce the fine grain of sound detail from free field sources, such as a meadow. Bo Widerberg's *Elvira Madigan* made use of a tapestry of high-level hiss, wind, and bee sounds, an open flowering field ambience that flooded the theater like a torrent of electrostatic cling noises. Mixed with the melodies of Mozart, audiences hardly complained about its self-asserting nature because they accepted the dramatic and subjective implications of the track, which reeked of romanticism. Newsreel footage of the same location with the identical ambience but with "factual" action, would, no doubt, come across as curiously inconsistent, a heightened reality that now draws too much attention to itself.

To be accurate here, the audio designer must pay strict attention to the implied emotive and rhythmic content of the shot before asserting a new reality on the track. **Leave something to the imagination of the audience.**

To ensure accuracy of detail, it is necessary to sample and analyze the components of the actual sound to be reproduced. In the case of the "Chips" team, trying to go with Honda sounds seemed more economical than making one recording of the Harleys, processing it, and reusing it for all successive shots. If the analysis was accurate, the artificially generated simulation should be believable.

Articulation

Articulation is the process of joining segments of sound into meaningful units. It is also a process of clarifying or making more distinct the meaningful parts of the sound track.

The designer must first **specify an experience** or feeling that must be evoked. Then **parameters must be chosen** from a wide range of **physical coordinates:** intensity, pitch, and resonance are the primary characteristics. (Tab. 2–2) Duration, repetition, and timbre are secondary characteristics. Each must be assigned a value in terms of prominence and in terms of emphasis. **Prominence** relates to and is a function of the position of the sound in the **pattern** of sound being constructed. **Emphasis** is a function of the sound data relationship to image and storytelling priorities.

Second, the designer should consider the real or apparent source of this sound (an electric fan or the Star Ship Enterprise's engine). The question to be asked is how the subject generates its sound. Although the answer may often be a figment of one's imagination, it becomes a necessary reference for the designer, who then has a skeletal outline upon which to drape the "bits and pieces" of auditory material necessary to create the desired effect.

How the real or imagined object generates the (proposed) sound defines the way the sound will be perceived in real space and time, as well as screen space and time. Either the sound will have a real-time reference (from real life) or it will be assigned a fictional reference. The reference should give clues to rhythmic structure. An engine could be, for instance, intermittant or metronomal.

In summary:

1. Specify an experience.
2. Choose physical parameters of sound.
3. Assign a value to each in terms of emphasis.
4. Assign a source as a design reference (aural object).
5. Determine the emotional content of the sound (as well as any visual content against which it will be positioned). Is it a happy engine?

Each sound has:

1. Objective truth (accurate rendition)
2. Emotional qualities (meaning)

A machine gun may be made to sound like an **instrument of death** or a less emphatic part of **mechanized warfare.** The accurate rendition, when reused, becomes a **stock** reality conditioning the audience to accept it as correct. Truth in drama seems irrelevant; only emotional truth matters.

Allusion

To allude means to refer to something indirectly. Visually, we are seldom told too little. Understatement does not seem to be popular with Hollywood directors. Pictorial detail leaving nothing to the imagination is the perfectionist response to the burden of narrative structure and possible failure.

The real world is a web of life, a rich tapestry that is difficult to record and agonizingly tedious to reconstruct. If we consider that each narrative line represents (or should) a **state of being** (ours, yours, the director's, the character's, the place, the object) and that it is either a **conscious** or **unconscious state,** we come closer to the central problem the audio designer must solve: what is being represented and how is it to be "felt" or preserved during theatre playback?

The designer must be aware of the limitations of the playback space and technology and the factors that contribute to effective exhibition. This will be examined in Chapter 12, but suffice it here to acknowledge that the audio designer should act the showman.

Assuming that we have maximized fidelity in the exhibition space, the designer must contend with the **poetic function** of sound allusion. This can be understood as the plastic manipulation of the audience through suggestion or implication. Creating allusions is a process of inventing aural metaphors that act independently of the visual component.

This is not an easy task in visually biased cultures. But the designer has two accomplices: **darkness** in the theater and psychological **closure** by the audience. This closure is a filling in of information not presented but alluded to in thought, word, deed, or noise. Omissions are as significant as additions and superimpositions. (Multitrack playback technologies open up the possibilities of layers of sound information acting over and beyond each other as perceived from multiple perspectives created in the dark of the theater.)

Acoustically (and metaphorically) sound inhabits a circular space. It has no center and no edge. When Margaret Mead showed African tribesmen an audiovisual documentary of people in motion speaking and then moving off the screen, the tribesmen ran up to the screen and looked behind it to find out where these "visions" had gone. In the circular, tribal culture, life moves radially in all directions, not impeded, framed, bent, absorbed or deflected; no fragmented Western literary-perceptual bias exists to condition the audience to accept unreal space or time. Thus, there must be a continuum of action, and those screened phantoms have not moved into an imaginary off screen space, but have been physically displaced in adherence to the strict logic of a culture that must now find an explanation that makes sense.

We are easier to fool. Allusions become representations of experience through the language of sound imagery. This language makes use of the same **figures of speech** as our Western narrative tradition:

Simile: Contrast of two elements explicitly compared (scream with a train whistle)

Metaphor: Suggest a comparison by application of an element to an object or concept that it does not denote (scream with cheers)

Irony: Contrast of opposites through the use of the least expected or anticipated form (scream with laughter)

Hyperbole: Obvious and intentional exaggeration (scream with phone ringing)

Personification: Embody living traits in abstract or nonliving entities (scream from a chair)

Metonymy: Substitution of one element for another to which it is related (scream with screeching well bucket)

Paradox: Seemingly contradictory sound used over an entity that in reality may express a possible truth (scream with typewriter keys)

Allegory: Representation of an abstract or spiritual image through concrete or material forms (scream in *The Shout*)[30]

Physical Causation

Psychokinetic stimulation is possible by flooding a theater with certain frequency sets. While this involves the spectator by **dictating** an emotion through physical discomfort, the overall effects must make sense in terms of the content of the shot. Hitchcock was quite fond of pumping low-frequency energy (below 400 Hz) from the track during scenes of impending trauma. Low frequencies tend to travel under the seats and are felt through the diaphragm, producing an uncomfortable sense of slight nausea (in sensitive people). The vibratory nature of this stimulus serves to prolong and enhance the nervousness created with fast cutting and movement on the screen.

This pressure wave has yet to be used in a way that would make the audience feel displaced in space, but experimentation with multichannel play-back and *Sensurround*[31] systems began in the early 1970s and have prepared the way for the audio designer to create anticipation, conflict, joy, surprise, and time-warps through the use of measurable, repeatable, and localized sound pressure manipulation.

Endnotes

1. Robert Bresson, *Notes on Cinematography*, Horizon Books, New York, 1966.

2. Noel Burch, *Theory of Film Practice*, Praeger, New York 1973 pp. 90–99.

3. Robert Bresson, *American Film* (Oct./Nov. 1983).

4. A frequency-based phenomenon whereby certain sounds may be made to dominate or diminish in relation to a complex array of sounds, as in a crowd scene in which one can pick out the voice of one character. This psychological reality has become an accepted physical reality in the storytelling lexicon of film and video.

5. This is aural depth of field created through layering of planes of sound back to front, left to right, and top to bottom in relation to visual planes seen or implied on the screen.

6. Texture refers to the state of being of characters who then define the kinds of narrative levels the story plays upon: dream, fantasy, realism, naturalism, expressionism, and so on. Average program sound levels give a sense of the reality or unreality of a scene.

7. Stanley Brakhage, "The Silent Sound Sense," *Film Culture*, (Summer 1960), pp. 65–67.

8. Noel Burch, "On the Structural Use of Sound," in *Theory of Film Practice*, Praeger, New York, 1973, pp. 90–101.

9. Claudia Gorbman, "Clair's Sound Hierarchy and the Creation of Auditory Space," *Film Studies Annual*, Purdue University, West Lafayette, Ind., 1976, pp. 113–123.

10. ———, "Teaching the Soundtrack," *Quarterly Review of Film Studies*, (Nov. 1976), pp. 446–452.

11. Gorbman, "Teaching the Soundtrack," pp. 448–452.

12. Burch, *Theory of Film Practice*, pp. 89–101.

13. Gorbman, "Teaching the Soundtrack," pp. 446–452.

14. Gorbman, "Teaching the Soundtrack," pp. 446–452.

15. Gorbman, "Teaching the Soundtrack," pp. 446–452.

16. Claudia Gorbman, *Unheard Melodies*, Indiana University Press, Indianapolis, 1987, pp. 13–17. Gorbman traces the modes that have conditioned audiences to "read" the denotation and connotation of certain melodies that have become clichés.

17. Gorbman, *Unheard Melodies*, pp. 63–69. This reflects the logical supposition that music creates an immediate and direct response by-passing cognitive faculties and appealing to emotional centers.

18. Friedrich Nietzsche, *The Birth of Tragedy and the Geneology of Morals*, Doubleday, Garden City, New York, 1956. Outlines two basic philosophical attitudes, the Apollonian (cognitive) and the Dionysian (emotive), in seeking the roots of artistic expression. The Apollonian lives in a dream world, but has the ability to see shades of difference between dream and reality. The Dionysiac seeks to escape everydayness through the rapturous ecstasy of dance and ritual, and the grape (alcohol).

19. Gorbman, *Unheard Melodies*, pp. 59–72.

20. Gorbman, *Unheard Melodies*, pp. 32. The term was first proposed by Roland Barthes to mean "anchoring the image more firmly in meaning" (see *Image, Music, Text*, Roland Baithes, Hill & Wang, N.Y. 1986).

21. Gorbman, in *Unheard Melodies,* pp. 85, cites Erno Rapee's 1924 lexicon, *Motion Picture Moods for Pianists and Organists: A Rapid Reference Collection of Selected Pieces.*

22. Nietzsche, *"The Birth of Tragedy,"* pp. 19–36.

23. Gorbman, *Unheard Melodies,* pp. 63–69.

24. Gorbman, *Unheard Melodies,* pp. 63–69.

25. Vlada Petric, "Toward a Theory of the Sync Sound Film" unpublished paper, 1980.

26. Gorbman, *Unheard Melodies,* Chapter 3.

27. Frederick Leboyer, *Birth without Violence,* Knopf, New York, 1975, pp. 11.

28. Depth cues define planes in a shot, for instance, a scene in which a window reveals frontally another room with a glass door through which action or a conversation is occurring. Sound can be used to reinforce the sense of depth as it diminishes or increases, as doors or windows open and close, or as the camera moves in or back to reveal or conceal planes of action.

29. Petric, p. 12 "Ontological" refers to the factual reality of an object. That is, the documentary can be understood as a cultural artifact, a thing in and of itself whose very existence is proof of its authenticity.

30. **The Shout,** by Jerzy Skolimowski. The audience waits the length of the movie for the dramatic climax, punctuated by the sonic inundation of an all-enveloping high-level shout— a narrative "gimmick" of ear-piercing intensity that performs a symbolic function.

31. Czerwinski, "Sensurround Sound," *American Cinematographer* (June 1976), pp. 577–581. Discusses the technology and applications of multichannel, low-frequency playback via specialized speaker systems.

References

BRAKHAGE, STANLEY, "The Silent Sound Sense," *Film Culture* (Summer 1960), pp. 65–67.

FLUDD, ROBERT, *De Musica Mundana,* in *De Fluctibus,* 1617–1629.

GOETHE, JOHANN VON, *Color Theory,* ed. Charles Eastlake, from *Farbenlehre* (1840), Dover, New York, 1971.

KENNEDY, RUTH, "Sound as an Element of Film," unpublished paper for Cinema 09 (LACC-1980).

SAVAGE, GOLDA, "Coppola's Electronic Cinema Process," *Millimeter* (Oct. 1981), pp. 53–71.

SOUND SHAPING

We examine the building blocks of
sound design and a technique,
articulation, which is the formation of
acoustic ideas. The process begins
with script breakdown and then
moves to considerations of tempo,
tone, volume, off-screen space, and
psychological distance. The electronic
cinema process and techniques of
synthesis and sequencing are
covered.

Figure 2–1   Sound either manipulates conditioned reflexes or stimulates thought.

Introduction

Audio designer, sound design, and sound shaping are relatively new craft designations that anticipate the assignment of total responsibility for creation of the film, television, or audiovisual sound track to a single craftsperson. By implication, this responsibility includes the imaginative utilization of sound to communicate information and emotions that the visual cannot or should not.

The audio designer is a person who creates meaning, narratively or metaphorically, through sound imagery. This notion assumes a directorial acceptance of sound as more than mere support for the visual, and it recognizes the rich storytelling possibilities, as well as the manipulative power of sound in the theater and in the privacy of one's mind.

Aural experiences are generally as intense as they are primal. From most accounts, the visual bias appears to be a learned response to the environment,[1] the complex process of search and focus having both cultural and physical parameters. Hearing, by contrast, appears to be more directly linked to survival instinct.[2] The ear is never turned off. Even in our sleep data are being perceived, the organism seemingly on silent vigil, monitoring every wave for signals of danger. It is not very evident how we learn to associate a sound with its source.[3] Nevertheless, a sound always seems to evoke an image or, better yet, an image/fact in the mind.

The first and most logical process for the audio designer, then, is to separate a sound from its origin, attach it to an image to create a new audiovisual unit. This new unity is closer to the Soviet cinema ideal and more Hegelian; in fact, it is attained from equal but separate components that enlighten each other and indicate more than they would be able to denote or connote alone. It is an associative combination of allusions, a reality with a logic of its own. Its force can convince us of the physical reality of an event we know never really happened.

What was in the past only a mechanic of sound recording is now, rightfully, a design problem to be solved; somehow, the designer must find a symmetry of technique and expression. First, by considering the entire narrative flow of the story, second, through an understanding of the limitations of the medium, and, finally, through the imaginative orchestration and manipulation of the technology of sound recording, the designer can create a sound track that adds something of significance to the audiovisual experience.

Ideally, the audio designer should begin the work of planning by analyzing the master script before the commencing of principal photography. The most basic approach would be to determine the overall thesis or theme of the narrative or story line. It would be helpful to classify or describe this basic theme in terms of emotional content, narrative content, and environmental content.

Since, in most cases, the designer would be called in after the production has been shot or recorded, the script may be used as a guide in making notes concerning the nature of each shot and/or sequence in a preliminary screening of an assemblage or rough edit.

Francis Ford Coppola had pioneered a technique of preplanning that took the customary pencil sketch storyboarding of the original story one step further. An **animatic** video[4] storyboarding of *Hammet* combined videotaped pencil sketches of shots with videotaped location setups that gave a semblance of the look of the finished film. This valuable aid would be an ideal reference for the planning and creation of sound tracks while the actual production is being shot.

Another option would be a basic script breakdown.

Script Breakdown

To budget accurately and prepare the many parts and processes for a film or video production, it is necessary to perform a script breakdown and/or production board. This is simply the shot-by-shot, scene-by-scene analysis of the finished show, laid out graphically using cardboard strips and organized by a design formula that might include at least the following:

1. Grouping of shots according to **day** or **night**
2. Grouping of shots according to **appearance of characters**
3. Grouping of shots according to **location**
4. Separation of shots according to **sync sound** or **silent (MOS)**[5]

The process allows for the compression of time and money. The audio design component of this breakdown is often neglected, but logic dictates that the production of sound for the project would be a much more creative and efficient endeavor if a separate abstract of **sound element** requirements are made.

The coordinates of the design problem are the prerogative of the individual; however, once a basic shot listing and/or script breakdown has been made, the second logical step would be to determine the nature or classification of each sound element in each shot or series of shots. The basic sound track elements are given in Table 2–1. Each element in column 1 can be obtained from any source in column 3 and can be used for any number of modes, including those yet to be invented.

Sound elements are often classified according to the way they are physically used in a given track as follows:

TABLE 2–1 Basic Sound Track Elements

Material	Mode	Source
Voice	Dialogue	Live recording
	Narration	Studio recording
	Voice-over	Library Prerecorded
Music	Spatial	Machine synthesized
	Temporal	
Effects	Artificial	
	Natural	

- **Synchronized:** Sound has been recorded **in sync** at the same time with image using one of several methods, including:
  a. Direct sound-on-film in which audio is recorded on a magnetic or optically sensitive portion of the film medium or directly onto the audio area of videotape (single system)
  b. Audio is recorded on a separate magnetic tape on a machine running synchronously with a camera (double system)
- **Post synchronized:** Sound is recorded after visuals, usually in the studio under controlled conditions using one of two techniques:
  a. *Automatic dialogue replacement* (ADR): Actors physically "lip-sync" voice to images they watch of themselves or others. The recording is made on a magnetic tape recorder running synchronously with the projector.
  b. *Looping*: Actors record their own voice after listening via earphones to a rhythm and mood track (usually the location track, which is noisy) without the necessity of a screening. Cue marking aids in this trial-and-error method.
  Both of these methods require rehearsal and coaching. The idea is to control pitch, intonation, pronunciation, inflection, and the subjective aspects of performance: anger, rage, joy, fear, and the like. All that is necessary is for the director to specify an emotion or emotional state. The narrator is also free to work on the overall theme of the piece. Although the technical limitations may be controlled, some actors are unable to recreate the requisite emotional accuracy and intensity in the clinical, detached environment of the studio.
- A final option would be to take a sampling of the required voice and use automated, computer-assisted digital synthesizers to create simulated voice tracks. The process involves the use of a video image playback reference and keyboard control in a complex series of samplings and comparisons.

*We infer the identity of others from what we **hear** them say; verbal expression is our most flexible tool for informing others of our mental and physical states. From E. V. Cameron, **Sound and the Cinema***

Building the Track

As a point of reference to begin creating the elements or bits and pieces that go into making the sound track, several questions should be asked:

1. What do we want the audience to **hear** at this moment?
2. What do we want them to **feel** and at what point?
3. What **size** space are we denoting?
4. Is the space a **natural, staged,** or **artificial** location, real or imagined (state of mind)?
5. What does the audience expect in terms of **mood**?
6. What are the **color** and **shape** of elements within the frame?
7. In relation to shots coming before and after this shot, what are we trying to **preserve, imply,** or **invent?**
8. In relation to a specific sound needed, for instance, a car crash, what **individual elements** are needed to create the total effect or concept of "car crash"?

Methodology.   Separate every concept into its components. This analysis of the **details of experience** is the single most critical and significant faculty that the audio designer may develop. For example, the details of a car crash (in order of event) might include horn, braking, skid, impact, glass shatter, second impact or recoil, hub cap roll, perhaps a cry, and the specifics of the vehicles in question.

Timing and pacing are a function of the nature of the shot and the desired emotional content. The audio designer must determine the nature and extent of the dramatics (or is it meant to be funny?). The selection and arrangement of the details will dictate the **intensity** of the experience, but they will not necessarily determine audience reaction. (See Figure 2–2)

Required data.   An inventory or basic program for assembling the components of a sound would include all of the following:

Shot specifications	Delineate environment
Emotions	Specify reactions
Space/time	Describe limits
State of being	Indicate real or imaginary
Form	Color and rhythm
Audience	Expectation and interpretation

Example: **Empire of the Sun,** *1987*

Using the sample format, the shot description for *Empire of the Sun* is as follows.

- *Shot*: Long shot
- *Emotion*: Sense of loss, chaos
- *Space/time*: Street scene, crowd, evacuation of Shanghai as Japanese invade
- *State of Being*: Childlike excitement and anxiety
- *Form*: Static frame but much activity within frame
- *Audience expectation*: Some kind of confrontation

What sound is needed? Steven Spielberg's solution was live sync-sound street noises mixed with relatively calm melody, which echoes courage and determination. The aural focus was neither on the troops or on the child. More of the interlude builds toward an understanding of the "bloodless" nature of the takeover and a reality that has not been heightened.

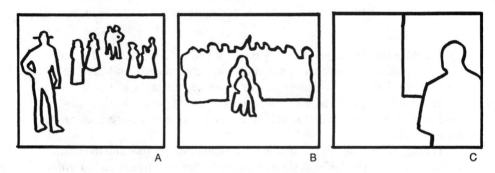

A   B   C

Figure 2–2   Regardless of the context of the image, the director or audio designer must choose an aural focal point which makes sense emotionally and narratively. In shot A, the composition presents easily discernable planes so intensity determines attention point. In shot B, the only clue which separates and gives a sense of isolation is the aural fact of lack of crowd noise. This sound texture creates a plane which only exists in the listener's mind. Shot C presents a mirror image composition—two distinct planes—but the ambiguous emotional perspective is one most directors solve unsuccessfully.

Functions of Auditory Material

Music and other auditory effects functions to achieve the following:

- Support the narrative with musically enculturated codes
- Support realistic textures of time, space, pacing, and movement
- Distract from and conceal noise
- Provide a "magical" link to the psyche; security
- Novelty (economics), a merchandising tool

- Combat the limits of television
- Fulfill the need for **melodrama** and theatricality (Wurlitzer)

Musical cliches were codified by 1924 in printed music lexicons listing stock melodies; see Erno Rapee's *Motion Picture Moods for Pianists and Organists: A Rapid Reference Collection of Selected Pieces Adapted to Fifty-Two Moods and Situations*.

Part of the romance of theatricality emerged from the modes of reproduction in the theater. Even well into the sound era, the Mighty Wurlitzer (see Figure 2–3) held center stage as part and parcel of the movie-going experience. Every performance was unique and the range of sonorous tonality the organ could produce has not been equalled.

The Psychic Payoff

Romantic tonality from Richard Wagner to Richard Strauss constitutes the core music lexicon of popular communication arts production including film, TV and theater. The psychic payoff for the reliance upon this class of music as a means of dramatic development includes all of the following:

- The audience is less awake; more susceptible to suggestion.
- The threshold of belief is lowered and uncertainty is dispelled.
- The audience is trapped within a sonorous envelope while taking a melodic bath.
- The audience is conditioned to accept the rhythm of events in terms of a musical division of time.
- Cultural codes denoted by themes and songs convey socio-political positions not necessarily informed by either plot or dialogue.
- Three-dimensional sonic space is created for the audience.

Organizing a Sound Map

One possible approach to constructing an overall plan for the design of a sound track is to use basic musical structures as guides. This method presumes that visual media communicate more effectively when conveyed via a rhythmic structure. And a cursory analysis of programs and movies the reader favors will reveal a well-organized pattern of ''objects'' and ''events'' that seem to flow with energy, yet effortlessly, like concise hard-hitting newspaper editorials, lean and lively with a definitive verbi-visi-voco point of view.

After a careful preview of the visual material and assessment of editorial movement, one may take two fundamental approaches toward a **sound mapping** of the narrative:

Figure 2–3 The Computer Musical Instrument is the rebirth of the Mighty Wurlitzer in spirit, but not in substance. (Courtesy of B'hend and Kaufman Archives/Wurlitzer Co. Collection.)

Melodic pattern. This form provides a basic linear organization, a series of tones, a row of notes, managed according to pitch and interval. Each kind of track (voice, music, effects) would be mapped individually in a one-to-one relationship to the story line and the visuals. The mix function will create aural–emotive–narrative bridges later in the process.

Chordal pattern. A less conventional form, this pattern is a vertical integration; it is nonlinear and more complex. The object is to preconceive the track in harmonic segments of voice, music, and effects set up with and against each other vertically.

Sound mapping requires a certain aural imagination to create a sonic tapestry. An easy way to "visualize" this sonic tapestry is to conceive of each element of auditory material as a "voice." At any point in the narrative, voices may be inserted vertically and horizontally: horizontally as a kind of monologue (homophonic), and vertically as a dialogue (polyphonic), a conversation, as it were, of interwoven voices in the manner of a Bach fugue.

The elements that may be varied according to the dictates of aural ideas were the following:

- Pitch (articulation)
- Intensity (volume)
- Timbre (tonality)
- Repetition (imitation)
- Acceleration (movement)
- Meter (rhythm)
- Attack–delay (envelope)
- Duration (interval)

A blank worksheet for the designer working on program sequence is shown in Table 2–2.

Content dictates theme. Theme is translated into picture and sound. If there is a rationale for the notion of the auteur director, then it is, at least, substantiated by the fact that specific programs have been translated in a way unique to a specific director and this translation has parameters that tend to repeat in other works by the same director. Directorial approach (see Figures 2–4, 2–5, and 2–6) is as evident in the use of sound as it is in pictorial patterns. Some of the more notable examples include the following:

- *The Magnificent Ambersons* (1942): Orson Welles orchestrated a "crescendo of voices," overlapping conversations and natural speech patterns in an auditory montage technique in which a highly stylized vertical organization of voices comes off as highly naturalistic.

JOB #_____ TITLE _____

CAMERA _____

DATE _____ SET _____

		DURA-TION			HAR-MONICS			EXPRES-SION			KEY			TIMBRE		
		Time out	Hold	Time in	Stereo	Mono	Poly	Color	Reverb	Tempo	Effect	Voice	Instrument	Tone	Overtone	Volume
SCENE	TAKE															

- The score Welles used in *Citizen Kane* (1941) was very functional, providing accents, transitions, and narrative binding of events. It conveys the spasmodically sensory pleasure and fear of a vivid dream.

Sound eliminates synthetic acting. It requires the writer to modify the poetic power of the stage play in favor of taut and vivid idiomatic prose. The naturalistic film/video media easily disintegrates character solely based in dialogue; yet, paradoxically, it fortifies acting as an art combining face, voice, mannerism, and temperament, rather than performance built up (editorially) from bits and pieces.

Figure 2–4 The problem of background-foreground is an age-old issue of movement in time and space (without actual displacement). In A, two strong front-rear planes are spacially and aurally close. In B, the shift from background to foreground is more severe but the sound need not echo physical reality. C presents a front-rear relationship (the chase) which is in flux. Properly approached, these are two-microphone set-ups designed to provide the designer with bi-polar data.

Figure 2–5 *This Sporting Life* (1963). Reality is a noisy, resonant slice of life whose idiomatic expressions for Lindsay Anderson include the roar of the unforgiving crowd, the clangorous din of the party, and the shouts of infidelity, all of which support the illusion of the present tense.

Elements of Sound Shaping

The elements of sound consist of the following:

- **Pitch:** The *perceived* frequency of a sound. Relative pitch is subjective and is a function of amplitude and duration. The rate of vibrations has a relationship to emotional states.

  Pitch bend: To change the frequency of a note while it is being played (common with guitars, string bass, and synthesizers)

  Pitch shift: To use a shifter to change the timing of program material through a slight correction to frequency; can also be accomplished through time compression and editing

- **Timbre:** The characteristic quality of a sound, independent of pitch and loudness, from which its source or manner of production can be inferred. It depends on the relative strengths of the components of different frequencies (mix of fundamental and harmonics; reflections), which are determined by resonance (tone).

Figure 2–6 The past and the future present identical aural ambiguity. No one knows what the past and future sound like. However, this does not imply that anything "plugged-in" would be believable. Strict observation and recording of the individual components of live sound form the basis for creating a world which never existed, but which presents to the senses the density of detail that speaks of reality. Sound can convert a hotel room into a spaceship. Shots A and B present elaborate set designs which are little more than Romanesque bathrooms without the signifying truth of auditory authority.

- **Resonance:** The prolongation of sound by reflection and reverberation; an abnormally large vibration is produced in response to an external stimulus, and occurs when the frequency of the stimulus is the same or near the original frequency of the system (harmonics).
- **Harmonics:** Integer multiples of the fundamental frequency, the partials or overtones of the first harmonic; they form an arithmetic progression.

  Harmonic tone: Tone produced by suppressing the first harmonic and bringing into prominence the overtone.

- **Amplitude:** Intensity of a sound measured in terms of the height of the waveform. It can be thought of as sound pressure level rated in decibels.
- **Meter:** Duration and arrangement of sounds measured in beats per unit of time; patterns of equal values.
  Rhythm: Patterns of regular or irregular recurring pulses, movements, or tones caused by the occurrence of strong or weak melodic and harmonic beats; distribution and combination of all sound elements.
- **Tone:** A musical sound of definite pitch composed of simple harmonics.
  Value: A quality of color with reference to degree of reflection or absorption of light; tint or shade. The distinctive quality by which colors *differ* from each other in addition to *chroma*; tint or shade = prevailing effect = *greenish*.
- **Chroma:** Purity of a color (freedom from white or gray); intensity.

Tempo, Tone, and Volume

In **sound shaping,** the designer must always imagine what a given sound represents.

Off-screen Space

What is seen on the screen corresponds to a fixed point of view. The frame cuts off real space, which can be made evident to the audience through the use of sounds inserted over the shot; these sounds have no direct relation to the visual, but refer to events previously seen or events or things yet to develop. A third possibility is the denotation of an entity or thing, character, or action occurring simultaneously with the action visualized or occurring at a different time and in a different locale. This sound, then, superimposes another plane of storytelling.

In *Ramparts of Clay* (1971), director Jean-Louis Bertucelli makes extensive use of natural environmental sounds occurring off screen, which imply musical and emotional movement just outside the view of things. Director Mark Reichert in his *Union City* justifies a whole range of emotional states through the fragmentation of little noises in and around the unusually quiet and claustrophobic period set, thus evoking the peculiarly vacant and sardonically truthful recollection of everydayness of the 1950s. Since the sound alludes to events or things just near the boundary of vision, there is no longer a need to show them. This economy of space/time also tends to involve and engage the viewer more completely, since he/or she must "fill in" the unseen.

Volume

Every spatial condition has a physical and emotional presence we can call **volume.** The size of this presence again is limited by the frame and shot size.

What cannot be suggested visually can be communicated with the selective use of sound. A large space has long reverberation times. A small space tends to have a greater rate of reflective sound and therefore has a higher hiss level or noise level, regardless of the quality of the surfaces (up to a point). A padded cell may suggest flat tonal silence, but there is absolutely no reason why, for dramatic or poetic reasons, it could not be made to sound like a resonant canyon (for instance, of despair). Whatever the emotional coordinate or despite the lack of such a coordinate, the designer has the responsibility to create a living space with emotional parameters.

Psychological Distance

Robert Altman has consistently attempted to defeat the limits of the playback space, which have conditioned the spectator to expect a linear point of view. He understands that sound emanating from a single source works against three-dimensionality in character and in screen space. *Nashville* (1975) and *Popeye* (1980) were as close as movies have come to having no acoustic center. Sound emanates from multiple sources and often simultaneously. The effect in the traditional screening room is chaos or cancellation. Most of the complex track is simply not heard. *Popeye* was meant to exist wholly in the primitive, tribal and childlike world of circularity and semantic confusion, a land in which the sound of words, not language, gives rise to emotional focus.

Much of Robin Williams mumblings are meant to distance us, and we are only invited back into some kind of intimacy when words become clear. It is an interesting dialectic between cartoon abstraction and realistic, multisensory expression, but it requires a theater with circular playback front to back.

If we cannot decode the intended distance or direction of attention from what is heard (in *Popeye*), we are left with no front to back texture, no foreground and background interplay, just the flat cartoon perspective where everything has equal weight and importance. This may not be what the director intends. Sound, then, can be used to distance the viewer from certain realities or from specific characters through incongruous environmental sounds, masked dialogue, or the suppression of vowel sounds in favor of consonants—through audio processing.

Tempo

Editorial arrangements of shots and their duration create tempo. Tempo may support movement within the frame, active or passive gestures, and the perception of lines, shapes, and contour. Functional sound effects, natural or artificial, along with musical fragments can take the narrative position of synchronous sound and dialogue. One example of this rhythmic use of sound elements occurs in René Clair's *Le Million*.[6]

More recently, the Hudlin brothers used the soul of rap music to propel the emotional development of their characters in *House Party* (1990).

Sound becomes a time scale against which we "feel" the editing rhythm, the integration of music and effects and images in what Noel Burch refers to as "audioplastics," which are exemplary modes in which synchronous elements can function as rhythmic punctuation and focus attention on details of emotional content. For example, the rasping sound of a turning rusted wheel in the desert against the rustle of the wind in *Ramparts of Clay* is a recurring aural image connoting sorrow and the slowly changing attitudes of certain characters.

Real-life sounds can be serialized into patterns of indeterminate pitch and then organized into overall decoupage or musical scheme. Much of Frank Serafine's audio design for Walt Disney's *Tron* (1982) accomplishes this musicality of the tonal arrangement of machine sounds. Like *Star Trek II* 1982 and *Star Trek III* 1984, the track suspends disbelief in a totally alien actuality, a world of unknowable sounds not recognizable through previous experience but, nevertheless, drawn from the designers' inventory of real experiences and then reorchestrated.

Tone

The play of light and dark, the qualities of light, the kinds of light sources and their connotations allude to tonality. As a symbolic representation of moods or emotions, sound can have a powerful effect on the viewer. Music is the shortcut, but it is possible to create or embellish a psychological state or state of being through the careful punctuation of voice with vocal and atmospheric effects. When the parallel is drawn to color and the narrative function of color, the options are unlimited.

If we coordinate all the preliminary elements, we can arrive at a schematic or program inventory that looks somewhat like a keyboard array of design combinations (see Figure 2–7). Once programmed, any coordinate can be made to orchestrate with any other in more and more dramatic arrays.

Orchestration

Orchestration is the arrangement, management, and organization of sound materials to achieve a desired effect. The early cinema theorists (Eisenstein, Dovzenko, and Konzintsev) postulated three basic elements in a logical succession: **musical chorus, chorus of bits and pieces** (of sound material), and **poetic commentary** (recitation and monologue), all extending the contextual meaning of the visual.

Seigfried Kracauer[7] further extended the classification of audio material as:

1. Synchronic: in parallel to storytelling
2. Asychronic: in counterpoint to storytelling

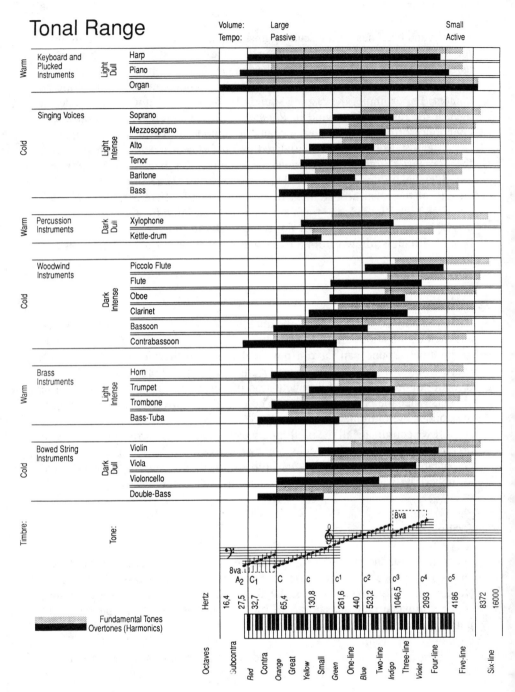

Figure 2–7 Each octave has a characteristic set of tonal parameters: timbre, tone, volume, tempo, color. The spectrum moves from hot, low-frequency reds to cool, high-frequency blue-violets.

50

Hollywood studio technique of the 1930s postulated a strict adherence to continuity, insisting on the use of sound in synchronous unity with picture as a support function, not the Russian emphasis on sound as reinforcement and self-expressive entity.

Orchestration involves the careful combination of classes of sound material:

Live location recordings
Prerecorded natural sounds
Prerecorded artificial (synthetic) sounds
Reformatted sound from other media

The methodology of orchestration is either acoustic or digital in nature. In this discussion we shall examine the digital mode.

Raw acoustic or electronic sound is fed into the digital system (Synclaver, Korg SI MIDI, or the like) and quantized, that is, converted from acoustical energy into a numerical representation of concrete points of amplitude of the given wave (something like slicing a salami infinitely thin). The number of slices depends on the sampling rate of the system. A fast scan rate is 16 bits at 3 seconds, 44.1 kilohertz. A slow scan would be 8 bits at 3 seconds, 5 kilohertz.

What we obtain is a waveform represented by numbers. This wave may now be reshaped by modifying the amplitude, timbre, and modulation of each frequency in the given spectrum. The process is sometimes called **line bending** or **curve fitting** because the visual display of the waveform can be physically modified by a keyboard or cursor (mouse).

A typical workstation performs two main functions:

1. Creates and stores constantly varying **tempo maps.**
2. Generates and stores mutes and cue points for each song or element. These cues are used for:
   a. Punch-ins
   b. Autolocating
   c. Rehearsal loops (in play or record mode)
      This function allows for add/merge and erase/replace.

From this basic database, several other functions are possible:

Note and event editing: The interval may be divided into an infinite number of segments within a single frame, allowing extreme precision.

Filtering: Memory allows for exact repeatability of filter positions and layered effects.

Quantizing: The waveform becomes a noise-free idealized version of reality.

Table 2–3 Flow Chart for the Audio Design Process

Source	Separation	Detailing	Referencing	Context
Origin ↔	Raw sound and natural acoustics / Acoustics ↔	List components / Nonidentifiable ↔	Scheme / Structure / Texture / Nonreferential ↔	Perspective / Point of view →

Apparent Source	Fidelity	Processing	Theme and Variations
Emotive source ↔	Clarity / Accuracy / Truth / Felt object–subject ↔	Editing →	

Synchronization	Rehearsal	Cooperation on the Set
Select a production Pkg. / Microphone survey / Mounting equipment / Acoustic treatment ↔	Voice / Analysis / Noise checks / Spatial audition ↔	Silence

Transposing: A piano whistles, a flute rumbles.

Transforming: Changing pitch-bend data into **aftertouch.**

The first step in orchestration is to identify the class of auditory material and its source; log and label it on paper.

Step two is to break down a pure tone or simple sound into its harmonic components.

The third step is to add performance controls through the use of processing systems or computer-assisted synthesis.

1. Synthesis (additive): Specify all harmonics. Specify change over time.

2. Sequencing: a. Select a pattern of arrangement.

                 b. Select processing modes: reverb, chorus, delay, filter, compress, and so on.

                 c. Edit by splitting and layering:
                    1. Splitting: disconnect a chain of tones
                    2. Combine a chain of tones

                 d. Simultaneous recording

                 e. Simultaneous sync to:
                    1. SMPTE/MIDI time code
                    2. MIDI clock
                    3. MIDI song position

                 f. Rechannelize any part of a track to MIDI channel.

Summary

A flow chart *for* the audio design process is given in Table 2–3.

Endnotes

1. Sound either manipulates conditioned reflexes or stimulates thought.

2. Roman Jakobson, "Verbal Communication," *Scientific American*, (Sept. 1972). Properties of the verbal code; and Charles D. Hockett, "The Origin of Speech," *Scientific American*, (Sept. 1960).

3. Georg von Bekeśy, "The Ear," *Scientific American* (Aug. 1957), pp. 2–11; and M. Rosenzweig, "Auditory Localization," *Scientific American* (Oct. 1961), pp. 2–11.

4. Richard Patterson, "Coppola's Electronic Cinema System," *American Cinematographer*, (Aug. 1982), pp. 777–781. The objective of the system is to increase efficiency. *Hammett* was 75% rewritten and then shot in 21 days for $2 million, while the other 25% cost $6 million! The Electronic Cinema Process was developed at the Zoetrope Studio facility in Hollywood to control every aspect of the production of Francis Ford Coppola's *One from the Heart*. From the standpoint of sound design, this process enabled one person to assume the responsibility from the preproduction stage on, for the total design and development of a sound track. The finished project

was remarkable more for its synthetic look than for any apparent inventive aural patterns. But the process served to set the standard for optimizing the editorial content of the sound track by providing many opportunities for planning, audition, rehearsal, and recomposing. An analysis of Coppola's production technique is as follows:

1. **Previsualization of script:** The script is programmed into a word processor, allowing constant rearrangement and revision.

2. **Electronic storyboard:** Preliminary sketches are recorded as a series of still frame compositions with a rough audio track onto $\frac{3}{4}$-inch video and stored on videodisc for recall and rearrangement.

3. **Rough edit:** Readings of the dialogue are set against the still frame selections and Polaroids of actors in rehearsal of scenes are inserted in the important sequences. The rough edit results in a master composed of sketches, still photos, and some location videotaping of rehearsed scenes. Scenes are rewritten, sets changed, and sequences redesigned after study of the rough cut.

4. **Technical rehearsal:** A run-through of the entire film allows the crew to iron out any technical problems. Technical rehearsals are taped, including complex moving shots to evaluate how they would cut.

5. **Principal photography:** After actors have studied their taped segments and modifications are made to the rough assemblage, actual photography commences with all cameras outfitted with video assist for instant replay of each shot, which is matched in the control room to the rough edit. Only good takes are selected.

6. **Video special effects:** As scenes are shot and re-edits made, transitions are planned and rehearsed via the video assist so that many effects can be done in-camera, reviewed, and checked against the rough tape edit for continuity.

7. **Video transfers:** The 35mm dailys are transferred to $\frac{1}{2}$-inch Sony Beta videocassettes with SMPTE time code for instant replay and rough sound mix. Original negative is stored.

8. **Editing:** Editing is done on film with flatbeds and Moviola while Coppola performs his own edit on $\frac{1}{2}$-inch video playing with editorial content. Video becomes a scratch pad.

9. **Sound:** Sound premix is done with a videotape fine edit, with tracks transferred to a multitrack recorder. Music, atmosphere, and background effects had previously been piped in (occasionally) to the set as a reference for actors during shooting. Identical processed tracks have been cut into a master sound edit in preparation for the mix.

10. **Conforming:** Final edits are listed on a computer printout with time code, which is then transposed to frame numbers as the original negative is matched to the final videotape and film edit masters.

5. From the German, *mit ohne sonde* (without sound).

6. Lucy Fischer, "René Clair, *Le Million*, and the Coming of Sound," *Cinema Journal* (Spring 1977), pp. 34–49.

7. Siegfried Kracauer, *Caligari to Hitler: A Psychological History of the German Cinema*, Princeton University Press, Princeton, N.J., 1966.

References

Bobrow, Andrew C., "The Art of the Soundman," *Filmmaker's Newsletter* (May 1974), pp. 24–28.

De Palma, Brian, "The Making of the Conversation," *Filmmaker's Newsletter* (May 1974), pp. 30–34.

Rossi, Nick, *The Realm of Music*, Crescendo, New York, 1974, 161 pp.

Sharff, Stefan, *The Elements of Cinema, Toward a Theory of Cinematic Impact*, Columbia University Press, New York 1982, 187 pp.

Sharples, Win, Jr., "The Aesthetics of Film Sound," *Filmmaker's Newsletter* (Mar. 1975), pp. 27–32.

Sturhahn, Larry, "The Art of the Sound Editor," *Filmmaker's Newsletter* (Dec. 1974), pp. 22–25.

3

RECORDING VOICE, MUSIC, AND EFFECTS

Methods of recording the basic auditory material required for building tracks involve natural and synthetic approaches. Music recording, music scoring, and the illustrated anatomy of a film score exemplify how sound may alter one's perception of filmic space and time. An examination of voice, with techniques for evaluation and improvement, is covered. The basic elements may contrast, support, extend, compress, and poetically comment on the visualized narrative. The creative role of computer-assisted systems is examined, with particular emphasis on the creation of special and natural effects. Considerations of prerecorded library sources are discussed, and a model for an audio design lab is presented.

Figure 3–1 The Manhattan Center scoring stage with its domed ceiling (M-1), control room with automated console (M-2), detail of the SSL console digital computer (M-3). Every acoustic space has a center of minimum distortion that maximizes recording efficiency.

Voice Recording

Vocal material for film, video, and audiovisual production may be dialogue, voice-over, or narration. In addition, the human voice may be used like an instrument to create unique sounds. The first responsibility of the audio designer is to record a signal that is of sufficient technical clarity to transfer to an editing medium without degradation.

Fidelity is the second consideration. As we have seen, the choice of microphone, its placement, the room acoustics, and the speed of recording can adversely influence the rendition of the harmonic details that give a voice its unique character.

Intelligibility matters more for entertainment media, which must be "clear" in the theater or over the airwaves. Although intelligibility of voice is a function of frequency response, many other factors (masking, speaker placement, poor transfer) may ruin the emphasis and intonation parameters of a given dialogue recording. Furthermore, the elements against which the vocal track may be mixed will determine clarity overall.

The English language does not lend itself to ease of rehearsal and recording, especially in dubbing or rerecording sessions. For one thing, it is less melodious than European romance languages. For another, the syntax of English is filled with seemingly illogical forms, as well as words that sound the same but have different meanings, words that change meaning with pronunciation, words rich in low-frequency energy and deficient in high-frequency edge.

Recording and Generation Modes

Voice may be created in several ways:

- Synchronously: Live, location miking with a sync-sound recording system using time-code or pilotone references.
- Wild: Using a sync recorder in the studio or on location without camera present. Slates and/or time codes maintain cue or edit points of reference. For noncritical nonsync use, almost any system that runs at a consistent speed (the slower, the better the fidelity for voice) may be used.
- Postsynchronously: Using standard or high-speed interlock recorders and reproducers in the studio, a timed recording of dubbed lines is made in

sync with the cued-up picture (automatic dialogue replacement). Without picture, but with closed 20-foot loops of continually running magnetic film, the process is called **looping**. Apparent sync is achieved through trial and error of the performer trying to match dialogue to lip movement on the screen or to the rhythm and timing of a *cue track*.

- Synthetically: Digitally composed vocal tracks generated from a sampling of voice parts.

The Technique of Improving Voice

In a trial in Riverhead, New York, Criminal Court, prosecutors relied on a "voice lineup," a recording of the defendant in a serial rape case and other speakers, as the chief means to identify the accused rapist. The victim appeared able to make positive identification without doubt based on the complex subtleties of the human voice and the way it renders sound in specific situations. The case gave vivid evidence that the ear is extremely sensitive to even the low-definition characteristics, as long as there is a no distracting background. The rapist, evidently, made the effort to speak softly and clearly in a very quiet space; the woman's bedroom.

Teaching a Stone to Talk

- The moral of the story is to **listen** to the **pecularities** of voice recitation through a public address system in the studio. Have the speaker demonstrate the formative aspects of the vocalization process: plosive, fricative, vowel, trill. These formants are unique for the person.
- Using enunciation exercises, explore the speaker's capacity for vocal manipulation through control of breathing.
- Practice modifying and redistributing energy patterns and frequency range by passing the voice signal through equalization networks and reverb channels, and allow the speaker to listen. Separate and emphasize low-, mid-, and high-frequency sounds while maintaining average speaking levels.
- Examine the synthetic modes of modifying voice: Vocorder, Synclavier, Moog, and other synthesizers that can compress time, alter speed, and eliminate background.
- Ask the speaker to visualize the real and psychological space of both the character and the audience via videotape replay rehearsals.
- Setup improvisatory voice recording to picture. Run interlock after preparing a log for timing. Playback should indicate to the speaker how the process affects the voice.
- Discuss the basic tone or mood of scenes and make an inventory of desired effects and emotions.

Narration Recording

A narrator is always given the opportunity to view the entire program to make notes, even if the director or designer intends to coach shot by shot or line by line. Questions to ask yourself are:

- What are we trying to obtain?
  a. Dramatic presence
  b. Intelligibility
  c. A live, rhythmic pacing that appears natural
- Will this track be combined with music and effects or stand alone?
  a. Mixed with music and effects at one-third level above music
  b. Sound effects interspersed at balanced levels
  c. Faded up and down over sync dialogue and music interludes
  d. Inserted as off-camera commentary without background or spatial reality, requiring more emphasis, greater variety in intonation
- What are the recording techniques?
  a. Soundproof booth with an omnidirectional microphone
  b. Simulated normal-sized room with drapes and furniture
  c. Screening room with seats and projection
  d. Real location with timing clock
- Which microphones are best suited?
  a. Standard ribbon cardioid at 2 feet should provide ample clarity for most applications where fidelity is primary.
  b. Lavalier omni would lend intimacy (enclosed drama).
  c. Directional microphones tend to render a more crisp vocal recording with greater intelligibility.
- Other considerations?
  a. A $3\frac{3}{4}$-inch per second recording speed provides more acoustic energy but less fidelity than $7\frac{1}{2}$ ips.
  b. Microphone should be placed to de-emphasize the physical mechanical deficiencies of a specific voice.
    - place a cardioid off-axis to decrease vocal sibilance.
    - hang omni close to throat to accentuate bass.
    - suspend a ribbon omni above nose level for boosting weak sub-glottal pressure.

Effect of Distance in Recording Voice

At a short distance from the speaker, most microphones are within the **hall radius,** recording only direct sounds. When the distance is increased (while varying the gain in volume accordingly to maintain the same level), the ratio between direct and reflected sound increases until reverberation prevails and intelligibility becomes limited; this is recording outside the hall radius.[1]

Approaching the hall radius, the voice apparently gains in liveliness and presence, while the room information breaks up the original sterility of the direct signal at short distances. The characteristic of the microphone affects this ratio. Omnidirectional microphones affect the proportion the least. The ratio can be varied as one pleases by careful selection and placement of directional microphones. When the distance is increased, spatial effects occur. When close positions are used, intimate but "dead" presence is achieved. Somehow the talented recordist must find a happy midpoint through trial and error. For directional microphones at close distances, low-frequency pads must be used to nullify the usual low-frequency boost common to these mikes.

Evaluating Narration

Determining the quality of a speaker's voice is based on the observation of all the following:

- Pitch
- Flexibility
- Articulation
- Pronunciation
- Tempo
- Force
- Phrasing
- Emphasis

The suitability of the script depends on all the following:

- Vocabulary: words must be simple
- Diction: sound must echo sense of words
- Structure of sentences: designed to be spoken, not read!
- Idioms: expressions common to a region must still obey English forms
- Inflection: indicate how a performer should intone or emphasize by underlining syllables and the like; give directions
- Colloquialisms: avoid slang unless understood universally or unless coining a new expression that fits the character

One approach to evaluation is to record a series of vocal exercises by an actor or actress, analyze deficiencies as they appear during playback and make suggestions for change. It is important for the performer to listen to this test recording over headsets and from a speaker system. A typical exercise series follows in Table 3–1.

TABLE 3-1 Vocal Exercises

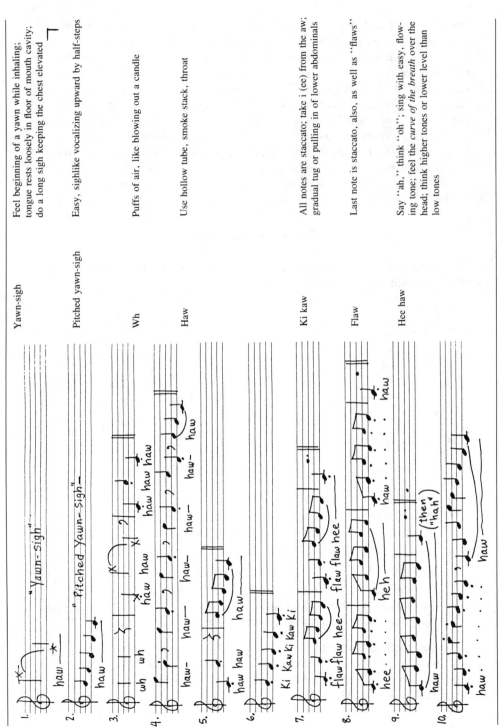

Syllable	Instruction
Yawn-sigh	Feel beginning of a yawn while inhaling; tongue rests loosely in floor of mouth cavity; do a long sigh keeping the chest elevated
Pitched yawn-sigh	Easy, sighlike vocalizing upward by half-steps
Wh	Puffs of air, like blowing out a candle
Haw	Use hollow tube, smoke stack, throat
Ki kaw	All notes are staccato; take i (ee) from the aw; gradual tug or pulling in of lower abdominals
Flaw	Last note is staccato, also, as well as "flaws"
Hee haw	Say "ah," think "oh"; sing with easy, flowing tone; feel the *curve of the breath* over the head; think higher tones or lower level than low tones

Helping the Actors

Controlling actors is the province of the director. However, there are some things the audio designer may spot and pass along to the director to correct.

1. The speaker's chest cavity must be constantly filled up with air or levels will suffer appreciably. Asking the actor to "speak up" won't help as much as asking to "deep breathe" and fill the lungs.
2. Deep, slow, diaphragmatic breathing will lessen nervousness.
3. Avoid long discussions between actors during breaks. Long, animated conversations will tire the voice.
4. A timing log (Table 3–2) is very helpful to aid in the pacing and intonation of narration.

Laugh Tracks

Critics of the laugh track say that the audience is being manipulated. However, a sense of shareable values, of community is reflected in the use of the laugh track. Not so much an effect, but functioning more like a Greek chorus of voices, the laugh track is constructed of overlaid singular laughs and group laughter separated onto multiple channels and remixed to the desired

TABLE 3–2 Timing Log for Voice-over Narration

00:00	Among the BILLIONS of beings created after the
	first BIG BANG, ... the primordial bomb,
	one took many FORMS, TRAVELING through the creation
00:15	of the starmaker.
00:20	Each . . being existed in TWO places . . . . . . simultaneously
	in ORDINARY space–time . . . and in a CONNECTION to hyperspace,
	a CONNECTION . . . to . . consciousness-without-an-object,
00:35	a CONNECTION to the STARMAKER.
00:40	Its contained MEMORIES were only . . of how to make TRANSITIONS
	and retain memories of its INDIVIDUALITY.
	In each form, . . . it was permitted to develop NEW memories
00:60	based upon its experience.
	As knowledge of its SELF developed . . . . . each being
	was endowed with a DOUBLE consciousness,
	a consciousness of itself and a
01:15	consciousness of its CONNECTION.

Legend: Each line is a spoken unit. Capitalized words are given emphasis. Dots (. . .) are pause beats. Times at the edge are the points the narrator must reach; that is, the speaker must recite lines within the exact time allotted. Time is broken down in terms of natural and editorial pauses, as well as dramatic pauses. The length of each line is determined by the point at which the speaker is meant to pause or breathe.

complexity. Live recorded laughter operates best, as synthesized laughter tends to sound like rain when broadcast.

One of the oldest names in the business, Carroll Pratt, has created laugh tracks for more than 40 years using a machine that operates something like an organ. A foot pedal controls the length of laughs; ten horizontal keys and four vertical keys are hooked into a tape loop of prerecorded laughs which run from a man's low warm chuckle to a woman's innuendo laugh to a child's full-belly laugh. Coughs, chatter, whistles, oohs, and ahs fill in the background texture, which can be "composed" or played on the spot to cues.

Early shows like "I Love Lucy" were recorded in front of live audiences. The live laugh track had to be embellished, enhanced, made smoother. By the mid-1960s, live audiences were virtually eliminated and "canned" laughter was required to be editorially laid in. After 1971, more and more shows went back to live audience ambience ("All in the Family"). According to Pratt, early laugh tracks were louder, more consistent, and therefore less "sincere." Because different cultural traditions are expressed in current sitcoms, the business of composing the laugh track is a far more subtle and changing craft. The demographics of the audience (real or intended) must be taken into account vis-à-vis the proportion of women and ethnics and the like.

Like any other sound element, the laugh track insertion and drop-out must be perfectly timed, and this seems more a matter of intuition than technical virtuosity. Too soon, and the track begs the question; too late, and it kills audience confidence. Too loud, pretentious; too soft, perhaps, a snicker.

Modifying Voice Tracks

Simple level adjustment, in itself, is sufficient to produce some startling perspective and transitions. So it is quite possible to use the vocalist on the Foley Stage as a generator of special effects.

In his Whitney Gallery of American Art installation, artist Richard Artschwager used a recorded tape of a choral of voices to simulate the sound of an elevator going up and down. One enters a room that looks strangely like an elevator interior. The chamber is virtually anechoic, although the surfaces are all hard and smooth. When a button is pressed, the voices "go on," and the sensation of movement is astonishing.

Using a parametric equalizer, the audio designer may reshape the pattern of vocal information into a new pattern. With a time compressor, the duration and continuity of vocal puffs may be reconstituted into something that more approximates a nonliving thing. With an echo chamber or digital delay black box, the designer can further disguise the vocalization by adding volume, intensity, perspective and scale.

Changing the resonant nature of voice, that is, altering its rate of decay, can provide an allusion to water, metal, oil, neon gas, ice, or any other material, which could obviously never have a live recorded sound provided for it. What, for instance, would be the tone of a melody sung through a block of glass or ice?

Processing voice to define a change in its movement through various media or spaces (phone booth, cave, underwater, and so on) is a prime function of audio design since it involves both conceptual and technical decisions. The following coordinates must be known:

1. Rate of decay in a given medium
2. Position of the audience
3. Mood of the sequence
4. Is this natural or abstract?

It is also possible to create music from voice. The human voice has great dynamic range and is sonically flexible; it is capable of great subtleties in tone, rhythm, intensity, and pitch.

Composer Karlheinz Stockhausen, a serial musician, has experimented in the use of purely vocal music. About his orchestration of voices for his *Der Stimmung*, he wrote for the album jacket:[2]

> *After the music had been committed to paper, I chose the name Stimmung which has several meanings:* **Pure tuning,** *in which vocalists sing the 2nd, 3rd, 4th, 5th, 7th, and 9th overtones of a low B fundamental, readjusting whenever they become impure (tuning is assisted by a softly reproduced perfect overtone mixture on tape); a vocalists's* **Tuning-up,** *which occurs* **during** *the performance every time he introduces a new* **sound model** *into the context; the* **attuning of rhythm:** *dynamic and timbre during the integration of a Magic Name, freely called into the context; and not the least, the German word* **Stimmung** (= *mood) involves the notion of atmosphere, of aura, of the* **soul's harmony** *(for example, one talks about "good Stimmung" or bad Stimmung meaning the more or less sympathetic vibration between men, and between man and his surroundings); and in* **Stimmung** *lies "Stimme" (voice)!*

> *Over several months the singers learned a completely new vocal technique: the vocal notes must be sung rather quietly, with specific* **overtones** *(indicated by a series of numbers from 2 to 24, and a series of vowels drawn from the phonetic alphabet) as dominant as possible; without vibrato; resonating only in the forehead and the outer cranial cavities; with long, gentle, even breaths. If necessary, each voice should be amplified by a microphone and loudspeaker so as to make all the nuances of each singer audible. Each singer has 8 or 9 "models" and 11 Magic Names which—following the formal scheme—he can bring freely into play according to the context, and to which the others react with "transformations," "varied deviations," "beats," and "Identity." Nothing is to be conducted. In a given voice-combination the lead is always taken by the "model singer," and he relinquishes the lead to another singer when he senses that the right moment has come. Once a Magic Name has been "called" by a singer, it is repeated*

*periodically in the tempo, and with approximately the same articulation **as the model** until renewed **identity** is achieved, and is thus integrated into the prevalent model. The lip and mouth positions of the model are retained as far as possible, so that the name is more or less transformed. The reaction to a Magic Name makes a **change in mood,** occasioned by the character and meaning of the name, clearly perceptible.*

Certainly STIMMUNG is meditative music. Time is suspended. One listens to the inner self of the sound, the inner self of the harmonic spectrum, the inner self of the vowel, THE INNER SELF. Subtlest fluctuations, scarcely a ripple, ALL THE SENSES alert and calm. In the beauty of the sensual shines the beauty of the eternal. [*translated by Richard Toop*]

Humanizing Harmonies

Other examples of tonal compositions that make use of the human voice include the following:

Atlas Eclipticalis (John Cage)
Four Illustrations (Giacinto Scelsi)
The Marriage of Heaven and Hell (Burton Goldstein)
Pure Land (Dusan Bogdanovic)
100- -1011 (Arthur Jarvinen)
Wild Woman with Steak Knives (Diamanda Galas)
Compositions for Film (Phil Niblock)

In these works, either voice is simulated by atonal music or voice is transformed into atonal melody. The elements to be recorded to build each sonic unit (whether it be voice, music, or effects) are identical and equally important:

- Environmental ambience
- Specific "natural" details
- Specific "artificial" details
- Direction cues, localization cues

Analysis of the German Hörspiel

For the last 40 years the most innovative work in recorded radio drama has been produced in West Germany, where it is called *Hörspiel*—literally, to hear (*hören*) + to act or play (*spielen*), which, as noted by the Austrian writer Ernst Jandl, is a "double imperative."

Hörspiel unfolds with a compelling, surrealistic, almost liturgical quality.

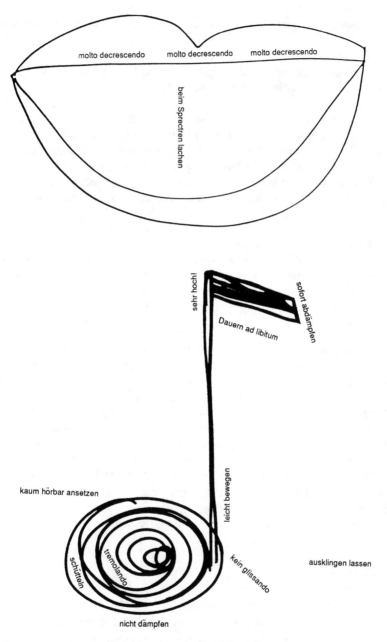

Figure 3–2   Kagel's diagrams for a radio drama format.

This is achieved primarily through a function of audio design that considers the drama as neither a narrative based in the literary nor a performance based in the realistic theater. Rather it is understood as a ''text/sound composition'' in which poets, composers, and performance artists collaborate in text/sound creation.

The recurring elements found in *Hörspiel* include natural sounds recorded live on location, music, vocalizations, "readings," intonations, which express the emotional **results** of previous sounds heard, and speech, breath, and song constructions.

According to Mauricio Kagel, an early practitioner/composer, *Hörspiel* is an acoustic genre divorced from the literary or musical, but utilizing dramatic elements only expressible in the aural milieu. One of his diagrams for the experimental use of voices in radio drama is shown in Figure 3–2.

Radio, made up wholly and solely of sound, concentrates attention on language as a spoken medium in which the voice is an instrument in the creation of meaning.[3]

> *Word is first revealed as sound, as expression, embedded in a world of expressive natural sounds which, so to speak, constitute the scenery . . . elemental force lies in the sound, which affects everyone more directly than the meaning of the word. The pure sound in the word is the mother-earth from which the spoken work of art must never break loose, even when it disappears into the far heights of word-meaning.*[4]

Bertolt Brecht (Figure 3–3) was one of the first to recognize this power, this return to the essence of "oral traditions" in which aural sense is made without the "passage through the frozen medium of print." His early 1930s "earplay," *The Trial of Lucullus*, is a study in the art of the disembodied voice. "Robinsonate" (1985), (Figure 3–4) by Gotz Naleppa, is representative of the new age of radio art, a textured weave of natural **soundscapes** with solo and ensemble vocal and instrumental **responses.** Soundscapes are neither music nor backgrounds for action. "It **is** the sound it makes . . . ,"[5] a genre made of sound, realized in a studio, and approaching the condition of music. *Hörspiel* provides an **acoustic equivalent** to poetry **concréte** by using the pallette of postmodernist expressionism, and its techniques are ideally suited to the work of the audio designer composing for film and video.

Recording Music

Music may be first **composed** and then set to picture cues.

Music may be **scored** first and then composed to picture cues.

Music may be **synthesized** spontaneously to picture, frame by frame.

Music may be drawn from library prerecorded inventories and **edited** to picture.

The most direct approach to creating the music track is to first have a **spotting** session. With script in hand, the audio designer and/or composer views

Figure 3–3 Bertold Brecht used the human voice as an instrument of metaphor.

MONTAG, 4.2.'85 17.00 UHR
HÖRSPIEL IM RIAS-STUDIO 10
ROBINSONATE

Ein Insel-
klangspiel
in 15 Sätzen
von
TRANSIT
COMMUNI-
CATION
nach einer
Idee von
Götz Naleppa
Produktion:
WDR
Köln

Robinsonate
= eine
Robinsonade
in Klängen
75 Minuten
Sound-Poesie
ein Klang-
spiel aus
Musik und
Sprache, Atem,
Gesang und
Naturklängen
aus oberitalie-
nischer Land-
schaft –
15 Variationen
über Grundsitu-
ationen aus
Defoes "Robin-
son Crusoe":
Angst und Ein-
samkeit, Reli-
gion und
fremde Kultur,
Agression und
Begegnung mit
der Natur.

Eintritt frei

Figure 3–4 "Robinsonate" poster. Radio drama forces the listener into the role of accomplice.

the entire program and makes notes with the director regarding points where music is needed. These points are described in terms of start and stop time code numbers. With this inventory in hand, the audio designer must determine the basic classes of musical materials, which are:

- **Source music:** music that emanates from things in the shot, like a radio or a dance hall band
- **Narrative music:** music that has no visible source, but that furthers the storytelling independently of picture
- **Textural music:** music that supports action or states of being seen on the screen
- **Atmospheric music:** music that neither supports nor extends the meaning of the picture, but rather acts as a tonal background that establishes the:
  a. Basic "key" for the film/video program (for example, rock compilation)
  b. Basic rhythm
  c. Space/time continuum

Recording Technique for Musical Instruments

Each instrument must "live." Each tone, each nuance of the **performer** must be preserved. Music must breathe. To control or shape the sound of groups of instruments, the audio designer must separate them into tonal and resonant sections of similar classes of instruments (Figure 3–5), including the human voice, and record and process them as discrete elements to be mixed together.

A position must be found that will eliminate:

- Excessive presence
- Excessive reverberation
- Low-frequency boost at short distances with directional microphones

An angle of incidence must be found that will take into consideration:

- Radiation characteristic of each instrument
- Acoustics of the room
- Absolute distance between microphone and instrument as a function of what happens on the screen

The following basics must be taken into consideration:

1. The characteristic of the microphone determines the ratio of direct to reverberation signals.

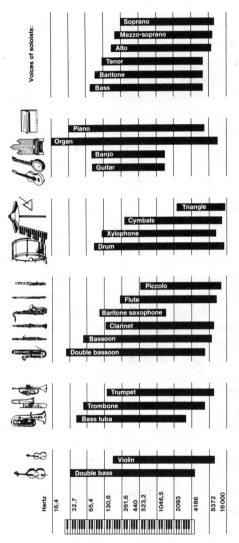

Figure 3-5 The family of musical instruments. Propagation of sound is different for each member of the family.

2. Omnidirectional microphones at any point record the ratio of direct to reverberation signals occurring there independent of their orientation in space.

3. Standard directional microphones favor direct signals transducing the same mixture of direct and reverberation signals at a distance 1.5 times that of the omni, or superdirectional microphones, and twice that (3) for the same mixture.

4. The ratio may be altered depending on the choice of room microphone, distance, and level. At close range (10 to 20 centimeters), an omni microphone should be used or a cardioid with a low-frequency attenuator.

5. The recordist must determine what should dominate.

6. The sound spectrum of an instrument consists of a fundamental tone and harmonic overtones; overtones determine the sound color (timbre) of an instrument. Therefore, loss or attenuation of overtones must be avoided.

The most significant portion of these characteristic overtones or "voices" is in the range from 1000 to 4000 hertz. Human hearing has the ability to perceive the spatial structures of sound impressions. The space and direction characteristics, as well as the intensity ratios of direct and reverberation signals, support and certify each other.

To obtain truthful reproduction of a sound event, multiple microphones must be utilized, especially for fidelity in terms of position and acoustics. Ideally, in a controlled sound studio, each instrument could be miked close up (see Figure 3–6), fed into a mixer console, equalized on the spot, and filtered. What is required is:

- Optimum balance between voices
- Balance between direct and reverberation signals
- Optimim presence of voices and instruments as discrete items

The music recording industry has developed a multitude of recording techniques. The following is a sampling of the most efficient methods for producing tracks for film or television applications:

- Single microphone technique
- Stereo microphone technique
- Three-point technique
- Multiple microphone setups

Whoever wishes to make music recordings must have a thorough knowledge of microphones, as well as a basic understanding of acoustics. The radiation

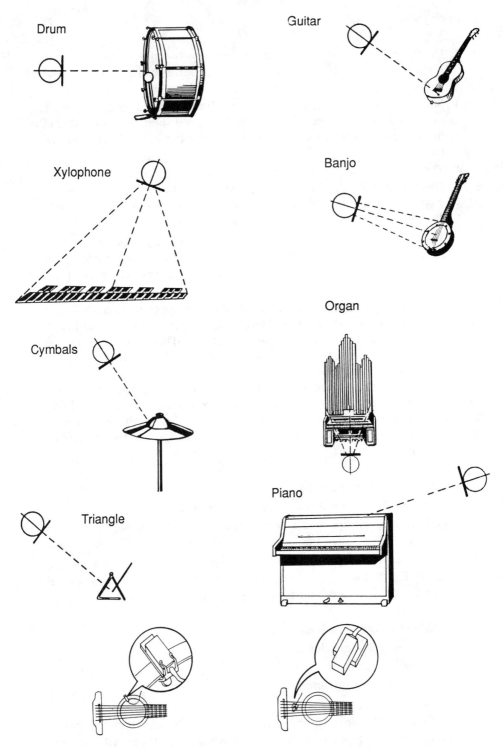

Figure 3–6 Suggested placement for a typical cardioid microphone in proper relationship to the sound propagating cavity.

Trombone

Clarinet

Trumpet

Saxophone

Double bassoon

Flute

Bassoon

Piccolo

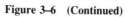

Figure 3–6 (Continued)

properties of each instrument must also be visualized. They can be characterized as follows according to groups:

Woodwind: An air column is vibrated by blowing techniques and key arrangement. Favorable placement should de-emphasize excessive blowing and breathing and "beaming" of the performer.

Brass wind: The mouthpiece gives the characteristic. Pitch is obtained by lengthening the pipe or overblowing the fundamental tone. Instruments with bell shapes radiate very directionally the high frequencies.

Polyphonic wind: Organ and harmonica. Bellow and foot pedal noises must be dampened or eliminated. The pipe organ has the widest tonal range of all instruments. The pipeworks are the essential points of recording interest; placement is from above.

Bowed string: A resonant case and strings have at low frequencies a figure 8 radiation. The F-shaped holes are used for microphone positioning on axis.

Plucked string: Position mike toward the sound "hold" at the lower half of the board. In the case of the harp, the microphone is placed at the player's back over the shoulder due to problems of wide tonal range and sound volume.

Keyboard: Room affects quality more than other instruments. Set the microphone from above toward the strings of the two-line octave; use directional or pressure zone microphone (PZM), as very few rooms are suitable for full-range reverberation.

Percussion: Sound pressure level (SPL) causes problems of overload. Set microphone (PZM)™ close and obliquely.

Electronic and loudspeaker: Place mike to eliminate ac hum, while taking advantage of the directional traits of some speakers.

Three-point Recording System

The Nakamichi Company advanced a theory of recording triangulation, using a pair of similar mikes in combination with a dissimilar point source microphone that is usually more directional to achieve a curious sense of depth and to maintain sonic fidelity. Good binaural recording makes a poor stereo recording; the brain is forced to fill in the details.

A blend or proximate microphone is used in combination with a spaced pair of wide-coverage microphones. The blend mike may be omni- or unidirectional; the coverage mikes are cardioid or supercardioid.

Depending on the instrument and the space, a carefully triangulated combination of slightly overlapping patterns tends to yield very faithful spatial renditions.

Use the omnidirectional pair to lessen the sonotrim proximity effect with percussion. Use superomni mini mikes (Tram, etc) for smoother, high-frequency response within 4 feet of the source. Where proximity effect (bass boost) is desirable, use the unidirectional microphone in front of the spaced pair, instead of in its normal rear position. The hypercardioid is very useful in overcoming long reverberations in large halls and churches.

When recording a solo performance, the blend microphone picks up the primary radiation; the stereo pair positioned at least 6 feet above and 3 feet apart captures the harmonics.

When recording a vocalist with musical accompaniment, the blend microphone (usually dynamic) covers the vocalist. The level of instrumental music should be 45% to 50% down from the vocals. If a blend mike is placed too high above, the rendition will be monaural; if the stereo pair is too high, the sound will be muddy. None of the microphones should ever be parallel or perpendicular to each other.

When recording larger groups, the stereo pair becomes the primary frontal pickup, while the blend directional mike is placed to the rear, which will aid in the suppression of background noise. Symmetry is not a factor. Achieving the proper blend is a matter of careful listening. With PZM microphones, the correct position must be obtained by walking the mike through, finding the position where the sound is best to the ear, and dropping the PZM there. The spacing between instruments and the surface reflectivity of the space determine the maximum placement distance for the three-point system. Some suggested setups are shown in Figure 3–7.

Music Scoring

D. W. Griffith used musicians to inspire his actors to passion on the set. The earliest piano scores were written for the films of George Melies. The music was used to mimic the action on the screen. By 1930, Max Steiner had begun to tailor music to specific dramatic situations. He converted Richard Wagner's invention, the leitmotif (leading motive), in a canonical array of filmic music clichés (themes identifying a specific character, situation, or emotion).

Full integration of symphonic textures with the sights and sounds of action/ adventure sequences is nowhere better illustrated than in the pioneering work of composer/conductor Erich Korngold for director Michael Curtiz's *Captain Blood* (1935) staring Errol Flynn in his first featured role.

The monothematic score utilizes a single musical theme to designate a particular overriding emotion, such as Lara's theme in *Dr. Zhivago* and the shark theme in *Jaws*.

The film score can speed up or slow down the action on the screen. The kinetic function of music can often control the attention span of the typical television viewer.

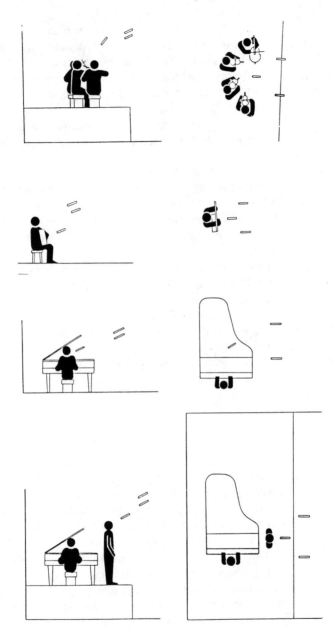

Figure 3–7   The Nakamichi three-point system of alternating matched pairs with "blend" microphones seen in possible recording solutions.

With Dimitri Tiomkin's title song for *High Noon* (1951), the success of the song itself led to the merchandising, as well as the narrative, importance to the work of lyricists and composers. The pop tune that could be exploited via record distribution often made more money than the movie for which it was written.

Music is the art that begins where words and images leave off—which is what makes it so effective in films. Sonic vibrations set part of the body in motion and touch the listener in an almost purely visceral manner. Music can stimulate the greatest possible range of moods, shades, and fantasies.   Elmer Bernstein[6]

From the beginning of the sound era, audio was considered a novelty. Film music existed as accompaniment from the earliest days of the silent cinema. The literature of film music indicates that the choices of music were from standard repertoire and the well-known symphonic and operatic classics.

Any number of fine composers emerged from the traditions of the music hall and Broadway to make a mark in film music, among others, Erich Korngold, Alfred Newman, Max Steiner, Bernard Herrmann, Hugo Friedhofer, Alex North, Franz Waxman, and Earle Hagen.

Pop, jazz, and New Age composers from the music industry found their way into film music by the mid 1960s. One of the earliest artists was Paul McCartney (*The Family Way*, 1966). And with the Stewart Copeland score for the 1983 *Rumble Fish* (Francis Ford Coppola), a new trend in populist film scoring began.

Marketing and merchandizing people saw the sound track as another source of revenue. Moreover, many scores were composed or assembled from popular hits (or became popular hits) to match the interests of the film's target audience. *Dirty Dancing* (Vestron) and *La Bamba* (Columbia) are startling examples of the symbiotic relationship of film music to theatrical movies.

Scoring for film and television has now become an integral creative element in the production process, and the job of the audio designer is to make certain that the score is more than mere support.

The creation of film music is achieved through a complex process that culminates with one of several recording session options:

Full orchestral session
Chamber music session
Small instrumental or vocal group session
Synthesizer additive process session

Many steps must be completed before the following process commences (for instance, legal clearances, prescoring, preparation of a sample "temp" track to give some basic idea of the flow and structure of probable styles of music to be used, and so on). Then a composer/designer begins the **reel** work; here are the steps:

1. **Spotting session:** The film in its rough edit is viewed and, if available, a script is reviewed and an inventory of the areas where music is needed is made. This might involve an editor, director, and producer. (See Table 3–4.)

2. **Music editor:** Dialogue timings and action timings are supplied by the music editor to the composer. Picture events are translated to music paper (bar breakdowns); "click" tracks are made (pacing references), and the music tracks already recorded are prepared for the mix.

3. **Composer:** He or she must somehow find a **key** or a **voice** that expresses the film's dramatic concept. The music editor's cue sheet is used to time and pace the score to be composed.

4. **Orchestrator:** Translates the composer's music into orchestral form.

5. **Copyist:** Copies out by hand the individual instrument parts from the orchestral score and creates sheet music for the recording session.

6. **Contractor:** Assembles union musicians for the scoring and recording sessions. Books the scoring stage, handles all contracts, and assists the composer during recording.

7. **Recording:** Session players, projectionist, director, and other music and production personnel with a vested interest in the quality of the music score attend the session.

8. **Dubbing preparation:** Music editor builds reels of recorded music (the live recorded score, library materials, and songs), and marks and leaders them for the mix session.

9. **Rerecording:** The dubbing or mix session in which all music elements are combined and blended into a master as one of three masters (dialogue, music, and effects). Music generally is mixed "around" dialogue, which takes the principal position of import. A **cue sheet** maps the position and timing of each musical element. Copies of the cue sheet are sent to performing rights agencies like the American Society of Composers, Authors, and Publishers (ASCAP) so that the composer can obtain royalties.

10. **Processing:** The master is transferred to a 1-inch videotape or transferred to an optical negative for component printing of release prints. If the release format calls for something special (six-track magnetic, stereo Dolby optical, and so on), other stages occur.

11. **Marketing:** Uses soundtrack for trailers, commercials, and other promotional materials.

12. **Preview:** Test screening to determine if any changes are necessary. If problems occur, editor provides new timings and/or scenes to the composer for rescoring.

13. **Rescoring:** Score is partly redone if scene changes occur or completely redone if it does not work well in test screenings.

A **song score,** one that is essentially a compilation of pop tunes, orchestral atmosphere, and background melody, may be assigned to a supervisor, who would be responsible for all selection and management functions (rights, budget, scheduling, and spotting).

What can the director do for the composer?

- Help find strong melodic hooks or keys that make sense narratively and emotionally.
- Determine which is more appropriate in a given instance, acoustic or electronic melody.
- Define the limits of the release format (Dolby spectral recording, stereo TV, super VHS, 70mm six-track magnetic, and so on).
- Help avoid ''wall-paper soundtracks,'' which do not add anything to the drama.

The director and composer must decide if the opening theme sets the tone for the entire film or acts as a preview of more complex development. They

Figure 3–8 In Rene Clair's *Le Million* (1931), all dialogue is sung, subverting the illusion of realistic sound while exploring ways in which harmony can express emotions and denying the illusion of synchronous sound. Editing conforms to the rhythmic musical structure of light comedy and is in conjunction with Clair's use of rhythmic speech. A Brandon Films release.

must avoid overuse of music. Research into the relevant idiom for period films will help. They must go over script carefully, as ideas are often triggered by a phrase or line in the script.

But with a director like Rene Clair (Figures 3–8 and 3–9), music replaces dialogue while fulfilling the function of dialogue.

Several steps comprise the process of music composition and editing; they tend to work hand in hand. After the spotting session, a music breakdown sheet is prepared by the editor for the composer. (See Table 3–3.)

The sample timing sheet (Table 3–4) herewith illustrated is also prepared by the editor to give precise verbal descriptions of the narrative that will link up to the music cues. The cues are the actual melodic fragments that comprise the score and are measured mathematically with great precision to fit into desired intervals.

It may be necessary to catch scene cuts or important actions on specified beats. If the designer/composer knows the approximate **tempo** appropriate to the cue, a **variable click track** must be prepared to calculate the precise beats without drawing attention to tempo variations. The computations for making a variable click track require that each interval between the click numbers be computed individually in frames rather than seconds. Then the actual track is prepared. The computation scale looks something like Table 3–5; the number

Figure 3–9 *A Nous la Liberte* (1931), the third of Clair's early aural triptych, which includes *Sous les Toits de Paris* (1930), continues his poetic use of sound to contradict image, while devising ''off-track sound''—the sound inferred by the content of the image but that is not heard on the soundtrack—thus creating off-track auditory space. A Joseph Burstyn release.

TABLE 3–3 Sample Music Breakdown (Spotting Breakdown)

Cue Number and Cue Duration	Description	Footage/Frame Start
1M11 (1:22.4)	Main Title information	30 + 0
1M12 (0:28.2)	On cut as Joe enters room	210 + 10
1M13 (1:48.1)	On cut of Susan's reaction SEGUE on cut to window	445 + 3

standing alone (actual tempo) is the calculator readout, and the decimal fractions in the second lines represent eighths in decimal notation.

The Click Track

In music editing, the second is divided into 192 parts. This amounts to eighths of a frame. The interval between 24/0 and 24/1 is $\frac{1}{192}$ or one-eighth of a frame. This interval is called a **click.**

A 12-frame clock (or 12-frame beat) is the elapsed time during every 12 frames of running time, after which a sharp click is produced on a timed click audio track, which is used by the composer, conductor, and orchestra to time music to picture. At 24 frames per second, a 12-frame click (12/0) is a series of clicks at $\frac{1}{2}$-second intervals. A 24-frame click (24/0) is a series of clicks at 1-second intervals. The running time of any number of frames does not change. In one minute, 1440 16mm or 35mm frames pass the projector gate.

The decimal equivalent of eighths are as follows:

$$1/8 = 0.125$$
$$2/8 = 0.250$$
$$3/8 = 0.375$$
$$4/8 = 0.500$$
$$5/8 = 0.625$$
$$6/8 = 0.750$$
$$7/8 = 0.875$$

TABLE 3–4 Sample Timing Sheet (Telling the Story of Each Cue)

Seconds + Tenths of Second	Description (dialogue underlined)
0:50.2	Cut back to Susan as she says: "Don't you ever knock?"
0:56.6	Facial reaction is a grimace.
0:58.0	Door slams and gust of wind enters window.
1:08.8	Joe responds as she looks up: "I'm too tall."

TABLE 3–5 Computations for Making a Variable Click Track*

Click Number	Intervals to Next Click	Timing	Footage	Frames to Next Click	Actual Tempo	How to Correct	Adjusted Tempo
1	30	0:00	000	624	20.800 20.750 × 30 = 622.500	Must gain 12 eighths	18 clicks @ 20/6 12 clicks @ 20/7
31	41	0:26	39 + 0	866	21.121951 21.125 × 41 = 866.125	Must lose 1 eighth	40 clicks @ 21/1 1 click @ 21/0
72	21	1:02.1	93 + 2	427	20.333333 20.375 × 21 = 427.875	Must lose 7 eighths	14 clicks @ 20/3 7 clicks @ 20/2
93	8	1:19.9	119 + 13	164	20.500	As is	8 clicks @ 20/4
101	53	1:26.7	130 + 1	1116	21.056603 21.000 × 53 = 1113	Must gain 24 eighths	29 clicks @ 21/0 24 clicks @ 21/1
154		2:13.2	199 + 13				

* Reprinted from Milton Lustig's *Music Editing*, Hastings House.

If you wanted to correctly express 12 plus seven-tenths (12/7), the decimal version would be 12.875 (not 12.7).

In practice, **click loops** are meticulously prepared by hand by actually recording and cutting up magnetic film strands for each click interval, for instance, from 7/0 to 24/0 at intervals of typically every other eighth: 7/0, 7/2, 7/4, and so on. The process is covered in detail in Milton Lustig's *Music Editing for Motion Pictures* (Hastings House, New York, 1980, pp. 46–49).

The click track is used to aid the composer in preparing a score that exactly matches important segments of the narrative. It is also used to help cue musicians during the actual scoring session. A music recording session log (Table 3–6) is prepared by the editor or composer. After the final score is approved and edited in (laydown in video), a music continuity log (Table 3–7) is prepared by the editor or composer, which lists all selections, original or acquired. In the event that changes are made before release, these logs become a valuable tool in recomposing and editing the music tracks.

A **bar chart** provides a graphic representation of the action of a scene in terms of musical notation on music paper (See Figure 3–10). The sample page by Carroll Knudson (Table 3–8) allows the editor or composer to find the beat number of an action in any tempo. With the tempo, the timing sheet, and the click track guide, one may define actions and cues in terms of beats. A moviola can be used instead of a timing log.

Often the music written by a composer is prepared in a simplified form called a **sketch** which is used by the orchestrator to prepare an orchestra chart (Table 3–9), which lists compositions according to the density of orchestration. The copyist also makes use of the sketch to draft individual instrumental music sheets. We see, therefore, that the entire process in music production is integrated by a precise system of measurement and logging, a kind of creative accounting.

Anatomy of a Film Music Score

Richard Einhorn has composed original music for features, documentaries, short subjects, and television commercials, and has produced more than 30 classical albums for CBS. *Dead of Winter*, directed by Arthur Penn for MGM and starring Mary Steenburgen, serves as an illustration of his approach to composing for narrative using a traditionalist's sensitivity with modernist technologies.

The process begins with a viewing of a rough cut of the film with dialogue only, in a search for literary or filmic elements that may lead to musical ideas. In this case, character and Einhorn's interpretation of emotional states of being provide the source for musical ideas. The story line suggested a theme of innocence. Assessing the **pattern** of events, he designed a simple line of musical development from innocence through fear and concluding in irony.

From Einhorn's perspective, one well versed in musical traditions, the basic theme (and variations) requires a style (in musical terms, a musical idiom

TABLE 3-6 The First Sheet of a Log for the Music Recording Session or Scoring Session

The Bad News Bears in Breaking Training   *Music Recording Stage "M" June 25th 1977*

Title	Cue No.	Start	Click Tempo	Warning Clicks	Timing	Record With	Playback With
Main Title	M11	11 + 0	8/0	8	1:41	Picture–Digital	Picture–Track
Mr. Manning	M12	240 + 15	11/1	4	0:25	Picture–Digital	Picture–Track
Kelly's Bike, Part I	M13	530 + 4	8/0	8	0:32	Picture–Digital	Picture–Track
Kelly's Bike, Part II	M13A	577 + 14	8/0	8	1:10	Picture–Digital	Picture–Track
Lupus, Part I	M14A	679 + 5	25/6	5	0:51	Picture–Digital	Picture–Track
Lupus, Part II	M14B	759 + 4	19/3	4	0:28	Picture–Digital	Picture–Track
They're Off	M21	553 + 5	8/3	8	0:53	Picture–Digital	Picture–Track
Kelly's Reverie	M31	503 + 0	None	None	0:55	Picture only	Picture–Track
Smoke Signals	M41	162 + 11	10/6	8	0:38	Picture–Digital	Picture–Track
Indian Victory	M42	548 + 10	14/0	4	1:18	Picture–Digital	Picture–Track
A Cruddy Pitcher	M43	668 + 6	None	None	0:36	Picture only	Picture–Track
The Dome	M51	9 + 0	None	None	1:08	Picture only	Picture–Track
Vacancy	M52	294 + 0	18/0	4	0:55	Picture–Digital	Picture–Track
Kelly's Dad	M53	588 + 0	None	None	0:56	Picture only	Picture–Track
The Practice, Part I	M61	289 + 0	Special 13/7	4	1:02	Pic.–Optical Clix	Picture–Track
The Practice, Part II	M62	352 + 0	Special 12/4	4	0:20	Pic.–Optical Clix	Picture–Track
The Champs	M63	511 + 4	None	None	0:58	Picture only	Picture–Track
The Hilton	M71	207 + 8	16/3	6	0:15	Picture only	Picture–Track

The log often presupposes the use of a digital metronome in the studio to coordinate events.

TABLE 3–7 The First Page of a Music Continuity

Title *The Voyage Of The Damned* Prod. by *Transcontinental Films Prod. Ltd.* Date *Aug. 18, 1976*

Cue No.	Title Of Composition	Timing	Instr.	Bgd.	Vocal	Visual	Composer	Publisher
1M1	Main Title Part 1	1:05	×	×			Lalo Schifrin	
1M2	Main Title Part 2	1:24	×	×			Lalo Schifrin	
1M3	Artists Life	3:05	×	×			Johann Strauss	Public Domain
2M1	The House Painter March	1:50	×			×	Lalo Schifrin	
2M2	Deutschland Uber Alles	1:30	×			×	Joseph Haydn	Public Domain
2M3	Tales of the Vienna Woods	0:56	×			×	Johann Strauss	Public Domain
2M4	I've Lost My Heart in Budapest	0:48	×			×	Erdelyi Mihaly	Francis Day & Hunter
3M1	Society Rhumba	1:13	×			×	Lalo Schifrin	
3M2	I Can't Give You Anything	1:30	×			×	Jimmy McHugh	Lawrence Wright
3M3	Lovers and Children	2:22	×	×			Lalo Schifrin	
4M1	Hotel Nacional	2:14	×			×	Lalo Schifrin	
5M1	Perfidia	3:00	×			×	Alberto Dominguez	Southern Pub. Co.
5M2	What's Past is Past	1:31	×	×			Lalo Schifrin	
6M1	Siboney	1:27	×			×	Ernesto Lecuona	Francis Day & Hunter
6M2	An Affirmation of Love	1:11	×	×			Lalo Schifrin	
6M3	Peanut Vendor Song	2:30	×			×	Moises Simons	Lawrence Wright
7M1	Moonlight Serenade	3:37	×			×	Glenn Miller	Big Three Music
7M2	Blue Moon	1:10	×			×	Richard Rodgers	Robbins Music Co.
8M1	Frenesi	0:44	×			×	Alberto Dominguez	Southern Music Co.
8M2	Vienna Dreams	1:37			×	×	Rudolf Sieczynski	Chappell Music
8M3	Dining Room Conga	0:47	×			×	Lalo Schifrin	
8M4	Denise	1:43	×	×			Lalo Schifrin	

Milton Lustig

This is a form in which information concerning musical property is recorded for report to the company's legal department.

TABLE 3–8 A Page from the Click Track Book, *Project Tempo*, by Carroll Knudson

The Tempo Is 14.375 Frames Per Beat (14–3)				Metronome—100.18					Page No. 68
Click No.	0	1	2	3	4	5	6	7	8	9

Click No.	0	1	2	3	4	5	6	7	8	9
0	.00	.00	.60	1.20	1.80	2.40	3.00	3.60	4.20	4.80
10	5.40	5.99	6.59	7.19	7.79	8.39	8.99	9.59	10.19	10.79
20	11.39	11.98	12.58	13.18	13.78	14.38	14.98	15.58	16.18	16.78
30	17.37	17.97	18.57	19.17	19.77	20.37	20.97	21.57	22.17	22.77
40	23.36	23.96	24.56	25.16	25.76	26.36	26.96	27.56	28.16	28.75
50	29.35	29.95	30.55	31.15	31.75	32.35	32.95	33.55	34.15	34.74
60	35.34	35.94	36.54	37.14	37.74	38.34	38.94	39.54	40.14	40.73
70	41.33	41.93	42.53	43.13	43.73	44.33	44.93	45.53	46.12	46.72
80	47.32	47.92	48.52	49.12	49.72	50.32	50.92	51.52	52.11	52.71
90	53.31	53.91	54.51	55.11	55.71	56.31	56.91	57.50	58.10	58.70
100	0/ 59.30	0/ 59.90	1/ .50	1/ 1.10	1/ 1.70	1/ 2.30	1/ 2.90	1/ 3.49	1/ 4.09	1/ 4.69
110	1/ 5.29	1/ 5.89	1/ 6.49	1/ 7.09	1/ 7.69	1/ 8.29	1/ 8.89	1/ 9.48	1/ 10.08	1/ 10.68
120	1/ 11.28	1/ 11.88	1/ 12.48	1/ 13.08	1/ 13.68	1/ 14.28	1/ 14.87	1/ 15.47	1/ 16.07	1/ 16.67
130	1/ 17.27	1/ 17.87	1/ 18.47	1/ 19.07	1/ 19.67	1/ 20.27	1/ 20.86	1/ 21.46	1/ 22.06	1/ 22.66
140	1/ 23.26	1/ 23.86	1/ 24.46	1/ 25.06	1/ 25.66	1/ 26.25	1/ 26.85	1/ 27.45	1/ 28.05	1/ 28.65
150	1/ 29.25	1/ 29.85	1/ 30.45	1/ 31.05	1/ 31.65	1/ 32.24	1/ 32.84	1/ 33.44	1/ 34.04	1/ 34.64
160	1/ 35.24	1/ 35.84	1/ 36.44	1/ 37.04	1/ 37.64	1/ 38.23	1/ 38.83	1/ 39.43	1/ 40.03	1/ 40.63
170	1/ 41.23	1/ 41.83	1/ 42.43	1/ 43.03	1/ 43.62	1/ 44.22	1/ 44.82	1/ 45.42	1/ 46.02	1/ 46.62
180	1/ 47.22	1/ 47.82	1/ 48.42	1/ 49.02	1/ 49.61	1/ 50.21	1/ 50.81	1/ 51.41	1/ 52.01	1/ 52.61
190	1/ 53.21	1/ 53.81	1/ 54.41	1/ 55.00	1/ 55.60	1/ 56.20	1/ 56.80	1/ 57.40	1/ 58.00	1/ 58.60
200	1/ 59.20	1/ 59.80	2/ .40	2/ .99	2/ 1.59	2/ 2.19	2/ 2.79	2/ 3.39	2/ 3.99	2/ 4.59
210	2/ 5.19	2/ 5.79	2/ 6.39	2/ 6.98	2/ 7.58	2/ 8.16	2/ 8.78	2/ 9.38	2/ 9.98	2/ 10.58
220	2/ 11.18	2/ 11.78	2/ 12.37	2/ 12.97	2/ 13.57	2/ 14.17	2/ 14.77	2/ 15.37	2/ 15.97	2/ 16.57
230	2/ 17.17	2/ 17.77	2/ 18.36	2/ 18.96	2/ 19.56	2/ 20.16	2/ 20.76	2/ 21.36	2/ 21.96	2/ 22.56
240	2/ 23.16	2/ 23.75	2/ 24.35	2/ 24.95	2/ 25.55	2/ 26.15	2/ 26.75	2/ 27.35	2/ 27.95	2/ 28.55
250	2/ 29.15	2/ 29.74	2/ 30.34	2/ 30.94	2/ 31.54	2/ 32.14	2/ 32.74	2/ 33.34	2/ 33.94	2/ 34.54
260	2/ 35.14	2/ 35.73	2/ 36.33	2/ 36.93	2/ 37.53	2/ 38.13	2/ 38.73	2/ 39.33	2/ 39.93	2/ 40.53
270	2/ 41.12	2/ 41.72	2/ 42.32	2/ 42.92	2/ 43.52	2/ 44.12	2/ 44.72	2/ 45.32	2/ 45.92	2/ 46.52
280	2/ 47.11	2/ 47.71	2/ 48.31	2/ 48.91	2/ 49.51	2/ 50.11	2/ 50.71	2/ 51.31	2/ 51.91	2/ 52.50

290	2/ 53.10	2/ 53.70	2/ 54.30	2/ 54.90	2/ 55.50	2/ 56.10	2/ 56.70	2/ 57.30	2/ 57.90	2/ 58.49	
300	2/ 59.09	2/ 59.69	3/ .29	3/ .89	3/ 1.49	3/ 2.09	3/ 2.69	3/ 3.29	3/ 3.89	3/ 4.48	
310	3/ 5.08	3/ 5.68	3/ 6.28	3/ 6.88	3/ 7.48	3/ 8.08	3/ 8.68	3/ 9.28	3/ 9.87	3/ 10.47	
320	3/ 11.07	3/ 11.67	3/ 12.27	3/ 12.87	3/ 13.47	3/ 14.07	3/ 14.67	3/ 15.27	3/ 15.86	3/ 16.46	
330	3/ 17.06	3/ 17.66	3/ 18.26	3/ 18.86	3/ 19.46	3/ 20.06	3/ 20.66	3/ 21.25	3/ 21.85	3/ 22.45	
340	3/ 23.05	3/ 23.65	3/ 24.25	3/ 24.85	3/ 25.45	3/ 26.05	3/ 26.65	3/ 27.24	3/ 27.84	3/ 28.44	
350	3/ 29.04	3/ 29.64	3/ 30.24	3/ 30.84	3/ 31.44	3/ 32.04	3/ 32.64	3/ 33.23	3/ 33.83	3/ 34.43	
360	3/ 35.03	3/ 35.63	3/ 36.23	3/ 36.83	3/ 37.43	3/ 38.03	3/ 38.62	3/ 39.22	3/ 39.82	3/ 40.42	
370	3/ 41.02	3/ 41.62	3/ 42.22	3/ 42.82	3/ 43.42	3/ 44.02	3/ 44.61	3/ 45.21	3/ 45.81	3/ 46.41	
380	3/ 47.01	3/ 47.61	3/ 48.21	3/ 48.81	3/ 49.41	3/ 50.00	3/ 50.60	3/ 51.20	3/ 51.80	3/ 52.40	
390	3/ 53.00	3/ 53.60	3/ 54.20	3/ 54.80	3/ 55.40	3/ 55.99	3/ 56.59	3/ 57.19	3/ 57.79	3/ 58.39	
400	3/ 58.99	3/ 59.59	4/ .19	4/ .79	4/ 1.39	4/ 1.98	4/ 2.58	4/ 3.18	4/ 3.78	4/ 4.38	
410	4/ 4.98	4/ 5.58	4/ 6.18	4/ 6.78	4/ 7.37	4/ 7.97	4/ 8.57	4/ 9.17	4/ 9.77	4/ 10.37	
420	4/ 10.97	4/ 11.57	4/ 12.17	4/ 12.77	4/ 13.36	4/ 13.96	4/ 14.56	4/ 15.16	4/ 15.76	4/ 16.36	
430	4/ 16.96	4/ 17.56	4/ 18.16	4/ 18.75	4/ 19.35	4/ 19.95	4/ 20.55	4/ 21.15	4/ 21.75	4/ 22.35	
440	4/ 22.95	4/ 23.55	4/ 24.15	4/ 24.74	4/ 25.34	4/ 25.94	4/ 26.54	4/ 27.14	4/ 27.74	4/ 28.34	
450	4/ 28.94	4/ 29.54	4/ 30.14	4/ 30.73	4/ 31.33	4/ 31.93	4/ 32.53	4/ 33.13	4/ 33.73	4/ 34.33	
460	4/ 34.93	4/ 35.53	4/ 36.12	4/ 36.72	4/ 37.32	4/ 37.92	4/ 38.52	4/ 39.12	4/ 39.72	4/ 40.32	
470	4/ 40.92	4/ 41.52	4/ 42.11	4/ 42.71	4/ 43.31	4/ 43.91	4/ 44.51	4/ 45.11	4/ 45.71	4/ 46.31	
480	4/ 46.91	4/ 47.50	4/ 48.10	4/ 48.70	4/ 49.30	4/ 49.90	4/ 50.50	4/ 51.10	4/ 51.70	4/ 52.30	
490	4/ 52.90	4/ 53.49	4/ 54.09	4/ 54.69	4/ 55.29	4/ 55.89	4/ 56.49	4/ 57.09	4/ 57.69	4/ 58.29	
500	4/ 58.89	4/ 59.48	5/ .08	5/ .68	5/ 1.28	5/ 1.88	5/ 2.48	5/ 3.08	5/ 3.68	5/ 4.28	
510	5/ 4.87	5/ 5.47	5/ 6.07	5/ 6.67	5/ 7.27	5/ 7.87	5/ 8.47	5/ 9.07	5/ 9.67	5/ 10.27	
520	5/ 10.86	5/ 11.46	5/ 12.06	5/ 12.66	5/ 13.26	5/ 13.86	5/ 14.46	5/ 15.06	5/ 15.66	5/ 16.25	
530	5/ 16.85	5/ 17.45	5/ 18.05	5/ 18.65	5/ 19.25	5/ 19.85	5/ 20.45	5/ 21.05	5/ 21.65	5/ 22.24	
540	5/ 22.84	5/ 23.44	5/ 24.04	5/ 24.64	5/ 25.24	5/ 25.84	5/ 26.44	5/ 27.04	5/ 27.64	5/ 28.23	
550	5/ 28.83	5/ 29.43	5/ 30.03	5/ 30.63	5/ 31.23	5/ 31.83	5/ 32.43	5/ 33.03	5/ 33.62	5/ 34.22	
560	5/ 34.82	5/ 35.42	5/ 36.02	5/ 36.62	5/ 37.22	5/ 37.82	5/ 38.42	5/ 39.02	5/ 39.61	5/ 40.21	
570	5/ 40.81	5/ 41.41	5/ 42.01	5/ 42.61	5/ 43.21	5/ 43.81	5/ 44.41	5/ 45.00	5/ 45.60	5/ 46.20	
580	5/ 46.80	5/ 47.40	5/ 48.00	5/ 48.60	5/ 49.20	5/ 49.80	5/ 50.40	5/ 50.99	5/ 51.59	5/ 52.19	
590	5/ 52.79	5/ 53.39	5/ 53.99	5/ 54.59	5/ 55.19	5/ 55.79	5/ 56.39	5/ 56.98	5/ 57.58	5/ 58.18	

Without Carroll Knudson's Click Track Book, one would be working endlessly with a pocket calculator or counting clicks from tracks on a moviola, the kind of work that drives editors to drink.

TABLE 3-9 Orchestra Chart

Production: Heaven Can Wait   5/10/78   No.   9:30 A.M.

Scorer: Dave Grusin   Conductor: Dave Grusin   Studio "M": Dave Grusin

Sequence	Composition	Timing	Composer	Arranger	Violin	Viola	Cello	Bass	Flute	Oboe	Clarinet	Sax	Bassoon	Horns	Trumpets	Trombones	Tuba	Harp	Piano	Drums	Guitar	Soprano Sax	Total
103/201A	Heaven Walk	1:56	Dave Grusin	Dave Grusin	12	6	4	2	2	1	2		1	3	1		1	1	2	2	1	1	42
205	Walk to House	:29	Dave Grusin	Dave Grusin	12	6	4	2	2	1	2		1	3	1		1	1	2	2	1	1	42
501	Meeting of the Bored	:15	Dave Grusin	Dave Grusin	12	6	4	2	2	1	2		1	3	1		1	1	2	2	1	1	42
502	To the Meeting	:15	Dave Grusin	Dave Grusin	12	6	4	2	2	1	2		1	3	1		1	1	2	2		1	40
906	Last Walk	:52	Dave Grusin	Dave Grusin	12	6	4	2	2	1	2		1	3	1		1	1	2	2	1	1	42
901	Garden Walk	1:44	Dave Grusin	Richard Hazard	12	6	4	2	2	1	2		1	3	1		1	1	2	2	1	1	42
1202	End Titles	2:25	Dave Grusin	Dave Grusin	12	6	4	2	2	1	2		1	3	1		1	1	2	2	1	1	42
401A	Dinner at Eight	:47	Dave Grusin	Richard Hazard	12	6	4	2	2	1	2		1	3	1			1		1			35
801	Training Montage	1:41	Dave Grusin	Richard Hazard	12	6	4	2	2	1	2		1	3	1			1	1	1		1	38
904	Goodbye	1:38	Dave Grusin	Richard Hazard	12	6	4	2	2	1	2		1	3			1	1	1	1			37
1005	Stadium Transition	:41	Dave Grusin	Dave Grusin	12	6	4	2	2	1	2		1	3	1				2	1	1		38
1102	Goodbye Mr. Jordan	:40	Dave Grusin	Dave Grusin	12	6	4	2	2	1	2		1	1	1				1		1		34
902	Marry Me	:29	Dave Grusin	Richard Hazard	12	6	4	2	2	1	2		1					1	1		1		32
903	Bad News	:30	Dave Grusin	Richard Hazard		6	4	2	2	1	2		1	3					1		1		22

Note that the left column does not have the cue numbers in consecutive numerical sequence.

that mirrors the emotive or dramatic theme of the film and the "best intentions" of the director). Again deduced from characterization (Katie played by Steenburgen, the heroine), Einhorn defined the idiom of New Age music as "exactly right" in conveying the kind of mindless naiveté that leads to the simple solutions to life's problems (problems unknowingly complex) and proceeded to improvise a childlike, simple, New Age melodic line.

The third compositional stage was to find a suitable structure for the chosen style. Inverting the traditional consonant interval, Einhorn chose to use Bartok's musical form of the most dissonant interval (the so-called "devil in music" interval from C to F♯) to reflect the devilish characters to be encountered.

Katie's Theme begins in one tonality, a rather "pretty" theme, as Einhorn evaluates it; moves to a new, darker tonality; and returns via an ironical musical twist. This is the fourth stage of transposing the basic line to fulfill the narrative requirements of the entire film.

A design diagram of the musical flow would look like this:

Key of G	C♯	Key of G
New Age theme: warmth, innocence, trust	Tritonal: cold, evil, fearful	Ironic warmth of the aftermath

Compositionally, the centerpiece of the film is an extended blizzard, and director Penn orchestrates these scenes to convey a rather choking sense of being trapped. The musical equivalent for Einhorn is a section in which two notes are held for over 4 minutes: The sequence begins inside the house; G is sounded, rises, and is held until a "screaming" C♯ is sounded at the point outside when Roddy's foot enters the frame as Katie collapses from the fatigue of trying to escape; C♯ is held and becomes the **primary pitch** (a turning point musically) for the film.

To further enhance the musical tension between warm and cold, Einhorn asked the sound editor to tune some of the critical effects (for instance, the wind) to tonal samples of G. A harmonizer was used to reprocess live and canned effects to the G sample provided. A rough tape of the basic thematic movement was auditioned for director Penn and approved. The simple musical idea, again, was the play of tension between warm and cold developing toward the very cold.

The following sequence for creating the finished score then occurred:

1. A music cue sheet was prepared after spotting or timing the entire film to determine (by committee: composer, director, editor) the sections requiring music.
2. Other effects were sent out for tuning to obtain a true sense of what fit into the composition.

3. A shot-by-shot breakdown was provided by the editor for the composer, based on a viewing of the final "locked" edit of the picture.

4. Via piano, the musical theme and variations were performed, modified, studied, and finalized on a scratch tape recording.

5. The acceptable parts were transcribed to paper.

6. The themes were again performed on Einhorn's customized MIDI studio keyboard setup, which utilizes 10 keyboards, an IBM PC, and the audio design software program TEXTURE, which allows the composer to "sculpt" the waveform. These rough pieces were then sent to another (more accomplished "pianist") for refining.

7. The director now had the luxury of listening to the "textured" score and giving the go-ahead with a strong sense of what the finished score would sound like. Einhorn considers this accessibility brought about by new technologies to have great impact on the quality of compositions, since it avoids the often unpleasant surprises wrought from decades of looking at sheet music and months undergoing "the shock of the real" in the scoring studio recording session.

8. Ten synthesizers were used to simulate primary orchestral parts directly composed to video visuals of picture, in sync via SMPTE time code. The track was transferred to 35mm magnetic film and an interlock screening was provided for the director.

9. The composition was transcribed for live instrumental parts. Musical ideas were fine tuned. A **condensed score** for musicians was printed from the computer. The orchestrator then "blew up" the condensed score, yielding scoring session parts.

10. The final scoring session was booked; the finest musicians were hired to obtain top **performances,** avoiding the necessity to edit scores for ideal performances (editing between takes), which is costly, time consuming, and ultimately self-defeating. The synthesizers were integral to the recording session as other instruments (especially strings) must be tuned to them. Three channels on a multitrack recorder were allocated to the synthesizers for overdubbing with the live recording.

The overall directorial concept regarding music was to use it sparingly and only to further deepen really frightening themes, rather than acting as a "sonic Band-Aid." Einhorn sums up this radical change in the tradition of film music composition by recalling that prior to 1960 most music acted as "wall-to-wall" accompaniment. Directors more sensitive to the need for silence have opted for islands of sound mostly linked musically. Einhorn's design guideline was to always conceive of the film in terms of "best intentions," never losing sight of John Cage's admonition that it is not the music but the silence in between (see Table 3–10) that is most important.

TABLE 3–10

NEUMATIC SYMBOLS

Tempo	Accelerando	↗	↗	**Duration**	Beats	••••
	Ritardando	↦	↘		Bars	‖
Timbre	Harmonic	○		**Coloration**	Saturated	●
	Dissonant	▽			Diffuse	◐
Volume	Crescendo	>		**Mood**	Simple	♪
	Diminuendo	<			Chordal	♫
Tonality	Monophonic	~		**Orchestration**	Digital	⊓⊔⊓
	Polyphonic	≈			Acoustic	⋀⋀⋀
Silence	Ambiance	⨎				
	Quiet	Q				

Classical Forms				These medieval symbols were designed to indicate motion from one pitch to another as if signified by the motion of the hand.
Punctum	~ ⌣	▪	♪	
Virga	╱╱	╕	♫	
Podatus	⌣✓	⊐	♪	
Clivis	⌒	⌐	♫	
Scandicus	⸴╱	⌐	♬	
Climacus	╱⸴	⌐⸴	♬	
Torculus	⌣⌒	⌐⸴	♬	
Porrectus	⋀	∿	♬	

Neumatic Legend for Musical Analysis (TABLE 3–10)

- This is a short-hand notation to describe the musico/emotive development of the sound track of a given film or television program.
- The medieval symbols are designed to indicate motion from pitch to pitch, as if signified by the motion of a "conductor's" hand. (See Figure 3–10.)
- The bar graph shows the progressing of intensity and pitch for each interval in the sequence. The plan appears to be symmetrical, becoming sonically

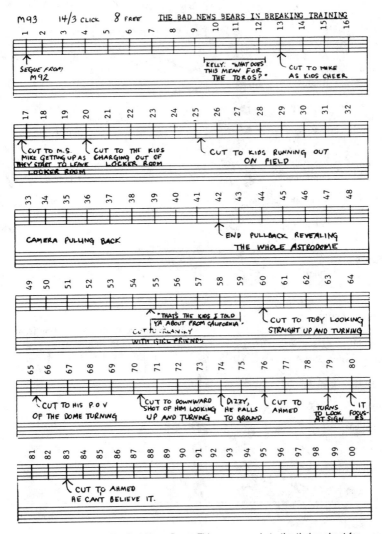

A Bar Chart: *The Bad News Bears*. This corresponds to the timing sheet for the same cues.

Figure 3–10 A bar chart. Alternative form, marker 4/4 time. (Courtesy of Eric Campmann, Hastings House.)

hyperactive as the number of cuts per unit of time increases. (See Figure 3–10.)

- The neumatic code signifies changes from shot to shot in this concluding sequence of the film in terms of tone, tempo, timbre and intensity. Can you detect the musical irony? (See Figure 3–11, 3–12.)

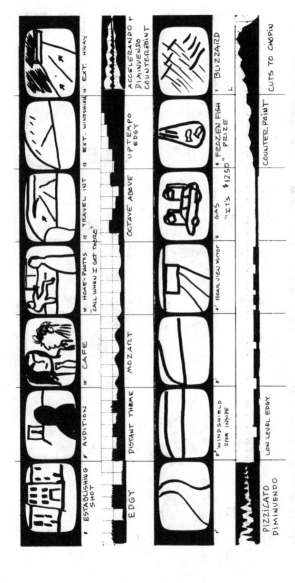

Figure 3–11 Shot analysis from *Dead of Winter*. Waveform grid indicates changes in intensity and tempo per unit of picture. (MGM)

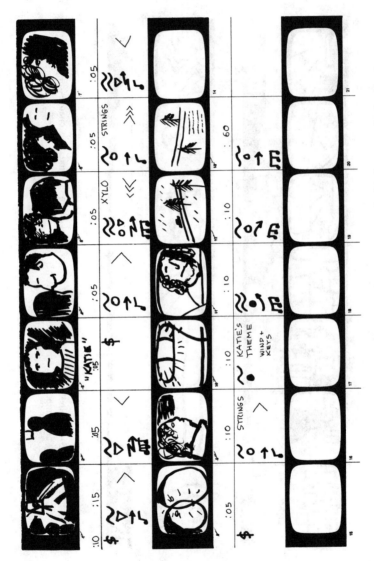

Figure 3–12 Shot breakdown from *Dead of Winter* annotated with the neumatic shorthand.

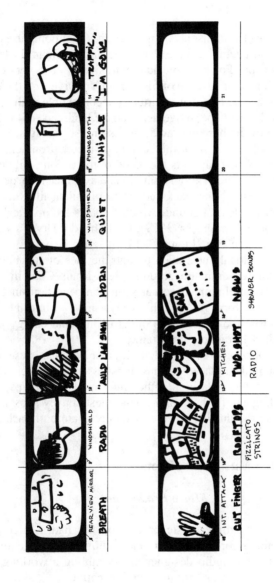

Figure 3-13 Opening sequence from *Dead of Winter* with sound effects indicated.

- Pointillist use of sound effects is suggested in this schematic display of the introductory sequence, which is essentially quiet with a growing interjection of "sound bites." Each sound denotes physical or emotive spatial orientations. (See Figure 3–13.)

Dead of Winter (1987) displays a more or less traditional use of music as emotional coding and cueing. Unlike Penn, Ingmar Bergman disdains the use of music for any reason. For him, music is intrusive; it does not belong in the naturalistic psychological landscape of his films. Carl Dryer, on the other hand, conceived of a pictorial texture that is virtually incompatible with sound of any kind. Composition, light, shape, movement and the landscape of the face should convey the essence of the human drama, the essence of being.

For Dryer, rhythm is born of the action and the environment of the film; drama creates a rhythm that supports the mood of the action while it influences the audience's state of mind. He only saw music as a means of deepening the audience's frame of mind. The tracks added to his silent films have little resemblance to Dreyer's ideal of sound, which displays the mystical.

In *The Passion of Joan of Arc* (1929), Carl Theodor Dryer's stark, austere exploration of social injustice [Figure 3–14(a)] relies heavily on musical accompaniment for emotional cues, even though the face of star Falconetti embraced nearly all known dramatic gestures. Jean-Louis Comolli, the French theorist, states that silent film music acts as sonic compensation since the silence of intertitles acted as a form of "psychic censorship," while introducing the spoken word would be too concrete an outlet of libidinal energy. Music as a caption serves to dispel dramatic uncertainty.

In *Cries and Whispers* (1972), director Ingmar Bergman's use of fractional (minute) bits of sound data placed at transitions lessens awareness of the frame and cuts, and draws the viewer into the illusion of a sonic/psychic bridge coercively demanding careful listening. Sound must convey substance or spirit without jeopardizing the integrity of the meditative nature of each shot.

Computer-Assisted Music and Effects

Music Production

The world of electronic music production has had a direct impact on postproduction methods for film, video, and audiovisual production. The fundamental attitude for the audio designer in assembling a working music and effects system is to **improvise, adapt,** and **overcome!**

The typical generation/editing system is a keyboard synthesizer system that takes the sounds it generates or samples and transfers them via MIDI (Musical Instrument Digital Interface) coding (translating) into a form that can be acted on by an interlocked computer/editor. With the addition of SMPTE

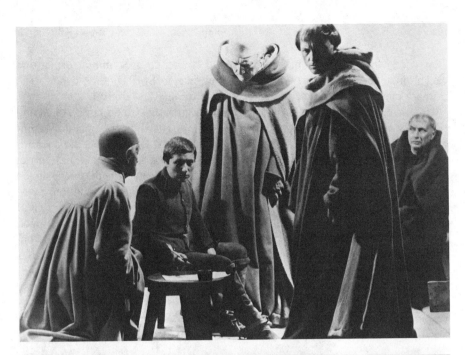

Figure 3–14(a) Shot from *The Passion of Joan d'Arc* (1929). **(b)** Jean Vigo's *Zero for Conduct*, breaking all the rules. Jaubert's score is anthropomorphic. Strings play a trainlike female motif, music decelerates with a shot of a train, and there is no way to tell it is slowing down without the musical hint. Later a battery of natural locomotive sounds parrots the rhythm of the boys' speech. Everyday sounds have a rhythm and a life.

Time Code, the data may be processed and converted back into a format that can be matched to film or videotape, which is also SMPTE time coded. The primary classes of automated synthesizer are **analog** and **digital.**

A video projector replaces the film projector, and a computer stores and prints out an editing/compositional log (events list), while the operator (composer/sound designer) is free to compose and edit. Instantaneously, the operator is able to generate a sound, embellish it, and position it into a minutely exact place within each frame. The sound may be rerecorded, reassigned, or redesigned to be used again and again in many new combinations and permutations.

The creative act is closer to a "reinterpretation" and modification of expressive modes. The possible modes are not limited to those programmed into the software of each keyboard/computer tandem (see Figure 3–15), but remain infinitely open to invention and discovery. The choices are so numerous that the distraction amounts to a clever paradox of economy: high speed takes more time. The ease with which a sound may be manipulated makes it more difficult to arrive at final decisions!

Music Synthesizers for Scoring

Electronic composing to picture has become possible due to the introduction of Musical Instrument Digital Interface (MIDI), a world-wide standard that allows musical instruments to interface with computers.

Figure 3–15 The Synclavier (digital) synthesizer allows direct composition of tracks in real time when utilizing a MIDI/SMPTE time code interface with a videotape recorder. A complete digital studio system is now standard.

Sequencing, the digital storage of music data on a disc, allows for replay, note by note of multiple instruments and voices via the synthesizer, the modern "player piano."

The new generation of synthesizer (see Figure 3–16) also provides hard-copy printouts of scores (transcription), mapping out of film cues, sound editing, sampling sound editing, and library functions. Some software allows for the automatic sync-up of sound track to film frame speed.

Computer-Based Music

Although the technology is rapidly providing new options and a vast array of design parameters, the audio designer must remember that the invention of engaging sounds is more significant than the hardware that produces them.

Accordingly, the creation of computer-assisted and digitally generated music and effects is limited by the cost involved (worker-hours) in the trial-and-error methodology of composition. Systems with higher memory capacity (which allows for storage and replay of longer track elements) and higher sampling rates (which improve sound clarity) are necessary for film and television work. Processing speed frees more time for creative manipulation and more choices in a given amount of time.

The Computer Music Instrument by Fairlight typifies the new generation of keyboard-controlled, electronic, digitally based musical instruments. It provides the designer with three compositional programs:

- Non-real-time Music Composition Language
- Real-time Multitrack Sequencer
- Real-time Composer

The real-time Multitrack Sequencer records performances from CMI's six-octave dynamic keyboard, together with all the expressive nuances from either the keys or the six real-time controllers.

Total storage capacity is in excess of 50,000 notes, offering no limit to the number of tracks that may be laid down or overdubbed. After recording, each track may be patched to any of the CMI's voice channels for reorchestrating, even while the music is replaying.

The non-real time Music Composition Language allows the non-piano-playing composer/designer complete access through the CMI typewriter keyboard. The MCL's powerful editing ability allows the designer to locate and alter any part of a composition quickly and easily. An error-detection program identifies false notation.

The real-time Composer allows high-speed development of complex phrases. All **pitch, timing,** and **dynamic** information is recorded and displayed, while an automatic **quantizing** facility corrects playing inaccuracies. Editing may be performed "live" or through the typewriter keyboard.

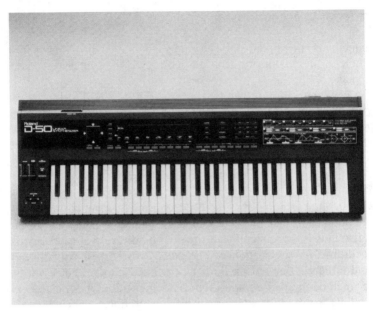

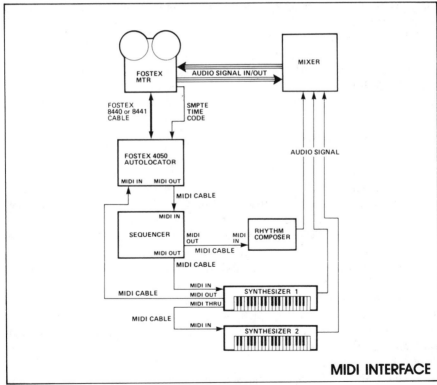

MIDI INTERFACE

Figure 3–16(a) The Roland synthesizer keyboard, one of a generation of components that may interface with studio gear. **(b)** The MIDI interface. A typical link to a multitrack recorder may be used to lock many systems in coded sync. Precise repeatability, infinite track modification, and efficient storage characterize the power of digital-based music and effects generation.

The CMI system also acts as an eight-output multitrack recorder, which can then be looped for **indefinite sustain.**

Through **digitizing,** a voltage form of signal is processed through an analog-to-digital converter into numerical form. Analyzed and displayed on a CRT screen, its sound parameters are defined and then modified on the screen visually by means of a light pen (cursor). Cross-fading is possible by keyboard control.

Computer Musical Instrument Data

1. **Composer: Pitch, velocity,** and **duration** are automatically recorded and quantized to desired interval resolution to correct playing inaccuracies.
   - Each measure is a **pattern.**
   - Each pattern may contain 48 notes for each of 8 lines.
   - 225 Patterns may be **assembled** and **repeated.**
   - Any 8 patterns may be grouped to form 26 sections.
   - Sections may be commanded to play from within sections.
   - Time signatures are possible for each pattern.
   - Pattern map and comments are provided.
   - **Bar counter** keeps track of **location** in a composition (cues).
   - Notes are displayed on a screen and may be edited with a light pen. They may be played, programmed, edited, and corrected.
2. **Keyboard Sequencer:** The system employs a 50,000-note memory, touch sensitivity, fader recall, foot pedal movements, eight-instrument overdub, and playback at manually conducted tempo without pitch variation.
3. Music Composition Language:
   - Allows programming of the entire composition.
   - Composition = sequence of **notes, pitch,** and **expression.**
   - Sequences are called into play by **part files** (instrument choices).
   - Part files are orchestrated by a **piece file.**

The Mamoulian Stew.   Purely synthetic sound originated with the narrative work of Reuben Mamoulian, exemplified in *Dr Jekyll and Mr. Hyde,* 1932 (Figure 3–17). Exaggerated heartbeats, reverberating gongs played backward, expressionistic bells, and experimental use of direct optical sound recording using the Fischinger system of painting the track edge with light photographed to create frequency patterns producing sounds upon playback all added up to a highly creative aural mix not previously integrated into conventional narrative drama.

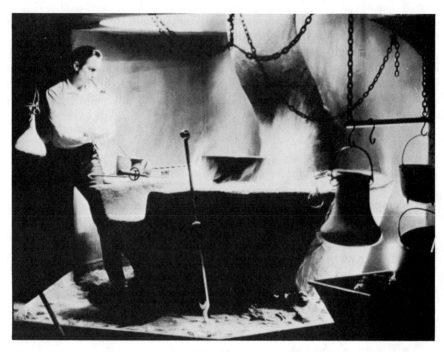

Figure 3–17   *Dr. Jekyll and Mr. Hyde* (1932), way ahead of its time in aural manipulation techniques.

Effects Recording

Brief History

In the days of the silent movies, "effects" were created through musical accompaniment and were a direct function of the spontaneous creativity of the piano player or the masters of the mighty Wurlitzer!

The creation of effects by electronic methods dates back to the late nineteenth century. The **Telharmonium** designed by Thaddeus Cahill created **tonal colors** through additive synthesis. Huge dynamos produced fundamental and overtone signals, which were manipulated and modified.

In the 1930s, the Hammond organ represented a new class of electromechanical musical instruments using the newly invented vacuum tube. By the 1940s, a more sophisticated tool, the **Melochord,** made use of new frequency modulation techniques and user control of attack and decay envelopes.

RCA's Mark 1 synthesizer, introduced in 1955 by Harry Olsen, used a preprogrammed punched tape; digitally controlled filters, pitch, and waveshape; frequency and amplitude modulation effects; and random noise generation.

Recording Sound Effects

Sound effects are sounds that correspond to real objects and real events or they represent imagined or implied objects, events, or spaces. Effects are **special** if they must be re-created in the studio or **natural** if they have been recorded on location. (See Figure 3–18.)

Effects play an important role in setting mood, localizing focus of action, creating off-screen space, and involving the imaginative faculties of the audience in the narrative.

In *The Origin of Consciousness in the Breakdown of the Bicameral Mind*, Julian Jaynes expresses the fundamental design spirit for the audio recordist:

> *Sound is a very special modality. We cannot handle it. We cannot push it away. We cannot turn our backs to it. We can close our eyes, hold our noses, withdraw from touch, refuse to taste. We cannot close our ears, though we can partly muffle them. Sound is the least controllable of all sense modalities, and it is this that is the medium of that most intricate of all evolutionary achievements, language. . . . To hear is actually a kind of obedience.*

Sense memory allows the viewer to accept the sound of closing doors, raging streams, and church bells as natural since they are identifiable and verifiable. In terms of creating these sounds, all that is important is that the

Figure 3–18   Named after an early sound effects artist, the Foley stage is a room with many differing surfaces and objects used to create and simulate natural or artificial sounds.

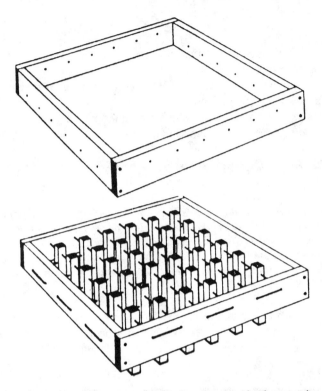

Figure 3–19 Marching blocks, handmade of wood, are used to simulate a variety of marching sounds.

sound evoke the correct image, the appropriate illusion, or a similar allusion. (See Figure 3–19.)

Methods for Creating New Sounds from Old

Assume that your working inventory of sound effects is live recorded acoustic events like doors closing, air-conditioner motors, auto ignitions, and the wind. These elements should be either separated with at least one minute of spacing between takes to allow for various playback processes or they should be separated and discretely placed on individual reels or dispatched to separate channels in a mixer console.

The following basic processes can then be used:

- The playback transport may be retarded or sped up to a different rate. For instance, applause played back at a higher rate, let's say, from $7\frac{1}{2}$ to 15 inches per second (ips), will sound like rain. Conversely, the same sound recorded at 15 ips and played back at, let's say, $3\frac{3}{4}$ ips may sound like some sort of repetitive machine noise. It takes a combination of thought and trial and error—piety and mirth.

- The second method is to selectively filter and/or equalize entire bands within the element until a new effect is created. Time compression and reverberation (echo chamber) processing will also significantly alter the quality of the aural image.
- The third basic route is to physically edit out minute portions of the sound or identifying segments, thereby creating a new composite relinked or played as a fragment building block to which other sounds will be added.

A bell sound must sound like a bell. The object used to generate that sound, however, may not necessarily be a bell since every bell has a characteristic timbre. The job of the designer is to create a very specific bell or the general concept of "bellness."

Often the actual location sound of a bell does not match the shot of the bell, but it is a valuable reference for reprocessing the sound into an exact sound that fits the image on the screen. However, you might discover that a wine glass may produce a better bell tone than the bell.

Furthermore, there are directorial considerations: the dramatic nature of the shot may require a **somber** bell, an **angry** bell, or a **cheerful** bell. These emotional concerns make the recording process much more than a simple technical chore and make it less desirable to rely on library canned sounds. The limitations of the real bell, the microphone placement, the background, and the kind of microphone all may render the original location sound useless, albeit real!

Effects are defined by the response they are intended to evoke. In ascertaining the role of each element, the signal must be separated from its background since it will ultimately be remixed back into a multiple of other sound layers. For example, recording the opening of a bus door on location will yield traffic noise, mechanical noise, passenger noise, wind noise, and, maybe, a usable door (air burst) noise. However, the overall noise level may render the take useless. In this case, both the door noise and the traffic ambience are needed. Each will be created separately in the studio. (See Figure 3–20.)

Reconstruction of any natural sound requires a breakdown of the steps in which the source creates the sound. With the seemingly simple bus door opening, there is more than meets the eye. The event involves the following sequence:

Bus braking
Door latch opening
Air pressure release
Door creaking

Figure 3–20   Instruments of the scoring stage may be used as effects generators.

The traffic ambience is, of course, intermittent, with any other noises thrown in to define the **location** (near a river, subway, factory, or airport?) and the **time of day.**

Perspective may also be a relevant element. From what position is this effect heard (inside, outside, from a moving car)? Various objects and instruments (including the human voice) may be used to create each element needed. They are then combined into a continuous effect edited to the picture.

To summarize, the steps in creating effects are the following:

1. Breakdown of source elements
2. Separation of background
3. Define perspective
4. Determine localization
5. Establish time of day
6. Define emotional content or mood
7. Level in relation to other sound layers in the shot

Listening determines the correct order of the sound-generating components of the source. Each element is recorded at full modulation. Allow the mixer/editor function to orchestrate the changes in gain per point in time. Each element must be distinctly audible prior to the final combining. Length should allow for slight overlapping.

Noncorresponding sounds.   Some effects have no source in reality to act as an audition reference. Therefore, use your imagination or use the closest reference in generic terms. An example is the Starship Enterprise engine room; no one knows what this sound is. It is a "should sound like" situation. Logic says to start with a general understanding of motor sounds; however, this is a post-nuclear-age system. What clues can be found in script or on screen? For one thing, **speed;** the ship is capable of incredible speed. No moving parts? That is likely, since this is the distant future. In any event, the audience must be made to be an "obedient" listener to our design concept.

We can deduce with some certainty the following parameters, which form the basis for our hypothetical source:

- The system is electronic.
- The system is relatively quiet.
- All "motor" concepts denote some form of cyclic movement.
- A pulse form is more likely in terms of rhythm.

So we have a quite mellow, electronic-sounding cyclic system of some sort. Enter pure illusion making. In a craft spoiled by technique, learn to make creative judgments. Anything from an Osterizer blender run at a low speed and then processed (forever) to a synthesizer-generated tonal work should get the job done. Then hope for some "mix magic" to solidify belief.

The aural component.   Some trial and error is associated with both the source-correspondence and non-source-correspondence effects. The third realm of sound effects is creating the aural component of **states of being** or **state of mind.** The easy way out is to use music! What is the sound of a psychotic killer in deep quiet thought? Is there an emotional component inside the capsule as the astronauts descend to Earth? Music is the poor mind's way out of a creative predicament (see Recording Music section and Claudia Gorbman's notions on the role of music in *Unheard Melodies*, cited in the Chapter 1 references).

We do not always go through real life events with an ongoing musical background that provides a culturally referenced "communal" understanding of the emotional content of the shot. Why do we accept the convention?

In the case of creating sound to fit a state of being we must **specify an emotion** and then orchestrate a series of (for want of a better term) **tonal colors** that create real physical reactions in the audience. These sounds may be melodic, dissonant, fragmented "points" (as in Japanese Kabuki), or a series of multilayered sounds acting polyphonically on several planes. It will boil down to a *kind* of music, while not conforming to any known style. However, utilizing a keyboard instrument in the simulation of a musical form may aid in the composing of this **sonic assemblage** of notes, noises, phrases, and extrasensory esoterica.

In summary:

- Specify the emotion.
- Measure the duration.
- Orchestrate bits and pieces into an assemblage.

Techniques for Recording Effects

The following methods are used for recording effects:

1. Live location recording using stereo to separate background from individual source effects.
2. Studio recording (Foley). Record directly to picture interlocked to 16mm or 35mm magnetic (sprocket) recorders. Incorporates high-speed projection for trial-and-error work. The Foley stage employs multiple surfaces, objects, and real people (Foley Artists), creating noises in sync to picture. They try to mimic the rhythm and meter of screen events while the mixer later augments the shape of the signal to fit the limitations of multitrack playback.
3. Automated Computer Controlled Editing Sound System (ACCESS), which provides a memory bank of sounds that can be called up and assembled against a time-coded video image of picture.
4. Synclavier and other computer-assisted keyboard instruments, which can be used to compose on-the-spot tracks made up of melody and nonreferential sounds to time-coded (MIDI/SMPTE) video image.
5. Noninterlock studio recording, using objects and noisemakers in the classic tradition of effects recording (see list of classic methods) (Table 3–11).

TABLE 3–11 Review of Recording Effects

Effects Are	Effects Represent
Natural, when source is seen	Objects
Special, when source is implied	Movements in the air
Structural, when not corresponding	Emotional states of being
to visual narrative (editorial)	Thought processes
	Movements in time
	Physical contact of things
	Implied space
	Unreal entities

TABLE 3–12 Audio Processing Components for an Audio Design Lab

Types of Units	Design Function
Dip filters	Alter pitch
Digital delay	Shape space
Parametric equalizer	Change contour/volume/mass
Time squeezer	Augment duration
Vocal synthesizer	Unique noises
Phaser	Focus harmonics
Flanger	Change perspective/position

6. Library of prerecorded effects. Pull them, cut them, lay them in. Go home. You don't have a conscience with this one.

7. Reprocess a stock live or canned sound in your audio design lab using all the fun gear you have leased and bake a sonic pie.

A digital effects system like ACCESS (described in detail herewith) can either process a sample library signal that is fed into the system, which then modifies it as if playing an instrument and recording a new sound, or it can generate a new sound from its keyboard input. Memory allows for constant reprocessing of the signal, while simultaneously editing it to fit into the appropriate sequence. An infinite number of editorial cuts are possible in the digital domain, and the signal may be time compressed or expanded at will.

As with the basic components of an audio design lab, each system has a job best suited for it, as shown in Table 3–12.

Stratagem for Creating Unique Narrative Effects

A possible stratagem for creating narrative effects is outlined next:

Conceptual issue:	What is the core sound, the key, for the program?
Answer:	Sound of a special **new** world.
Responsibility:	Create sound elements that have **clarity, fidelity, and noise reduction.**
Methodology:	• Build noisemakers, machines, and objects that generate unique sound signatures.
	• Compose on a synthesizer.
	• Select library elements to reprocess.
	• Record live source material, use natural acoustics.
	• Unique sound will have a nonrepeatable texture.

Technique: 1. Change speed of playback recorder and rerecord; speed up or slow down to alter a natural sound and make it become something new (**wave shifting**).

2. Make an **inventory** of elements needed.

3. Determine the aural perspective, the *liminal* clarity. The emotional content of a sound is conveyed through the behavior in the space in which it operates.

4. Determine *points of origin*.

5. Change the "realities" of visual/aural associations:
Objective truth—Accuracy
Emotional truth—Affectation
Dramatic truth—Character's mindset
Contextual truth—Spatial behavior

Analytical Approach to Sound Effects Creation

Sound elements like those of Star Wars generally can be made believable when they are composed of familiar but unrecognizable fragments drawn from the events shown in Table 3–13.

The process by which sounds are manufactured is a process of deduction:

Concept: Coffee blender   **Components:**   Heavy, made of metal
           Giant door   Rumbles, crunches, squeaks

The designer must think through, step by step, the bits and pieces that make up the **concept.** If the object does not exist in reality (like the Starship Enterprise's engines), the concept of motor/engine must be redefined within certain limits that, at the very least, give some aural clues as to what the audience is meant to decode.

Serafine's Method

Frank Serafine was an early pioneer of the audio design movement, a one-man sound and music production talent who combined processed natural sound with electronic sound. In a 1983 interview he stated his method:

First, I listen to tape libraries. Then I go out and record sounds. I bring them back and listen to them, process them and study the science or amplitude in which the sound works. Motorcycles, for instance, have a Doppler effect. You learn these things after a certain time. . . . Suction, for example, is a backwards impact sound.[8]

TABLE 3–13 Comparison of Acoustic
(Live) and Processed Events

Acoustic Events	Synthetic Events
(Organic)	(Electronic)
Insects Motors Water	Wookie grunts Laser swords Droid's voices

Some Examples

Aside from the purely intuitive sense one must have to think through the nature of the effect and how to generate it, chance (with theme and variations) can also play a part in how an effect is created. Some examples will serve to illustrate options.

Apocalypse Now, 1980

What is the dominant sound here? For instance, in the attack on the village, I decided it was the helicopters. Take that concept aside for a moment. Now, what's the next most constant sound? Well, that's the munitions: off-stage and on-stage gunfire. What's next? Maybe "The Ride of the Valkyries." Then the Foley effects (such as footsteps and other studio-recorded sounds).

Within each of those dominant themes—say the helicopters—there are variations; the drone helicopter sound that fills the air like a hive of bees—a constant yet shifting veil of sound; the Huey attack ships' chop-chop-chop sound; then the Loaches with a more insect-like "nnnnyyowww" sound. In the munitions, there is the Russian munitions—Ak 47s and all that stuff; M-16s mortar whizzes and crumps—a whole series of subtexts. Walter Murch[9]

Seventh Sign (Tri-Star), 1988. Hollywood's first hailstorm. Real hail sounds had never been recorded (or at least saved) before. Sounds of ice chunks hitting the same surfaces that appear in the scene were sampled. Hundreds of layers of these samples were built up on a multitrack and "performed" while the sound designer looked at pictures.

All the President's Men, 1976. A train wreck effect was created from a car interior. The crew goes to a railroad switching station; they load a Nagra into a car and sit waiting for a train to approach; they jump out as the train hits the car; the Nagra keeps rolling, and great train wreck sounds are saved.

The Bear, 1989. *The Bear* (Figure 3–21) featured a sound track composed entirely of synthesized sounds emulating natural exterior sounds of the wilderness and the bears and other animals that inhabit it. Thousands of bits of

A wounded male kodiak bear and an orphaned cub struggle for survival in "THE BEAR," an emotional story of love and adventure. Jean-Jacques Annaud directed the film from a screenplay by Gerard Brach. Price Entertainment presents a Claude Berri Production of a Jean-Jacques Annaud Film.

Figure 3–21   Jean-Jacques Annaud's *The Bear* (1989). Dialogue intrudes on the solemnity of nature. (© 1989, Renn Productions. All rights reserved.)

aural information were sampled and stored in a Fairlight, the overall sound design orchestrated by Laurent Quaglio. Hundreds of live recorded sounds of bear and cougar roars, cub snoring, owl hooting, dog barking, cricket chirping, and faraway waterfalls are woven into the synthetic soup that will become the track. A catalog is made of bear vocal expressions: growls, rattles, yawns, purrs, roars, moans. They are integrated into tracks since bears cannot do ADR.

Sound loops.   The basic recorded effect, for example, a wind chime, is cut into a 9-foot continuous loop and played back on a sync record/playback machine in the studio. Through interlock recording, the sound is recorded over and over, end to end until the desired duration of repetition is achieved.

Some Sources for Special Effects Generation

The following are some suggestions for creating special effects:

Bells: Brass bowls, vases, and pipe sections can become chimes, old brake drums when struck with a mallet yield fire gongs or fight bells; when struck with padded mallet, church bells. Metal plates can be suspended by wires; the larger the plate the lower the tone.

Brook: Gently blow through a straw into a glass of water.

Creaking floor: Twist an old, dry desk drawer.

Doors: Place mike near latch; avoid rush of air as door closes.

Elevator: Any speed-controlled motor (sewing machine).

Elevator door: Roll a roller skate along a short plank. Let it strike a metal plate (for closing).

Falling body: Simulate with arms and -elbows dropping onto a table simultaneously; then let forearms drop together.

Fire: Crumple cellophane slowly or vigorously; playback slowly.

Fist blows: Hit a large, wet rubber or cellulose sponge.

Footsteps in snow: Fill chamois bag with cornstarch. Knead bag in foot rhythm. Twist and pinch for sleigh-ride sound.

Hoof beats: Alternately strike half-coconuts against various substances.

Marching feet: String 36 block pegs into a square frame and let one side hit a table top before the other to simulate steps.

Railroad locomotive: Rub a stiff brush over coarse sandpaper glued to the top of a resonating box.

Rain: Sand or salt sprinkled into paper held above microphone. Rice simulates hailstorm.

Shot: Slap a leather or plastic pillow or a cardboard box with a wooden dowel or yardstick. Keep mike from air blast.

Surf: Roll BB shot around the inside of an oval hat box.

Telephone: Talk into a glass tumbler.

Walking in mud: Make walking sounds with hands on soggy newspaper.

Wind sounds: Blow gently across mike or try Mole Richardson's Wind-howler, a device that creates moaning wind, hurricane wind, desert wind, mountain wind, and winter wind through a series of 15 valves and resonators, which may be combined and varied as a continuous fanned air pressure blows across them.

One advantage of producing live sounds is that they can be cued directly to projected image, recorded, played back, and auditioned in the studio/theater. Many sounds can be made in a straightforward manner, like crumpling newspaper. Others require approximation since no direct sound can be manufactured and recorded. Looping allows for the repetition of a sound.

Problems Posed By Location Recording

Some problems encountered in location recording include:

- There are very, very few quiet locations on Earth.
- Effects require the elimination of background.

- Natural events are seldom controllable or repeatable.
- Real-time recordings seldom convey the exact illusion or allusion.
- Raw sounds always need to be refined and processed.

General Tips for Effects Recording

Here are some useful tips to consider when recording effects:

- Directional microphones tend to give better results due to isolation characteristics.
- Room tone or environmental ambience is critical to record for proper blending in the mix.
- Never filter or equalize on location. Record at high levels to obtain well-defined image/facts.
- Always make at least two takes even if the first seems good enough.
- Altering recording speed can provide startling approximations to desired effects.

Computerized Foley Stage Recording

The process of recording sound effects synchronized directly to projected image in the studio is called *Foley* recording in honor of the man who was first to do so. Working from a sound log listing the required sounds, the Foley artists (often directorial types) walk, jump, run, clack pots and pans, and use wire screening, aluminum foil, glass, wood, cloth, toys, or anything else they can find in more or less perfect time to screened events. High-speed (rock-n-roll) projection allows for fast forward and backup to audition and evaluate each take until exact marks are hit and the desired effect achieved.

Library Recordings

Prerecorded materials (voice, music, and effects) may be obtained from a variety of sources. Most are fee-based and also require limited rights payments. Some are in the public domain and may be obtained for the cost of the medium on which they are distributed.

For the audio designer, library canned sound may be an expedient way to solve problems. However, auditioning the materials is time consuming and ultimately self-defeating, since titles often do not give a fair estimate of usability. A listing may say "diesel powered engine," but upon listening, one discovers that it is not quite what was expected for any number of technical and creative reasons. The option is to buy it and reprocess it (more time and money) or check another source. This can become unwieldy.

In addition, the fact that the material is prerecorded indicates that this is second-generation information with concomitant noise, which will be transfered yet again to an editing medium. Digital recordings provide a clear septic sound, often devoid of background. However, this does not always solve the problem of generation noise, as some programs might require the vintage sound of old radios, appliances, audiences, guns, and the like that give a sense of the period by virtue of their very inaudibility and raspiness!

Hazard Checklist for Library Materials

Consider the following disadvantages of library materials:

1. You must pay usage and performance fees.
2. Length may not fit the shot, entailing editing costs.
3. Quality may be poor.
4. Audition time is costly.
5. Second-generation signal has noise.
6. The recording may not be **exactly** what you want.

How to Buy Usage Rights from a Library

When applying for clearance contracts, the following information is needed by the library:

- Name and catalog number of selection
- Number of "needle drops" or cuts to be used in the program
- Name of your production
- Total length of the production
- Contract name
- Legal owner of the program
- Type of film or video format for release
- Classification as to commercial, theatrical, educational and/or if broadcast: local, national, public access, and so on

Copyright Protection

Sound recordings are copyrightable. The law in effect is the copyright law as modified in 1976, but check with the U.S. Copyright Office as the law is under constant redefinition.

Music Rights (for Pop and Classical Records)

Music rights include the following requirements:

1. Prior *written* permission is required from:
   a. Music copyright owner (publisher)
   b. Record company that issued the recording
2. You must request *synchronization licenses* from the copyright owner *prior* to usage; this will grant you permission to use their music in timed relationship with your program.
3. Performance rights grant the producer, station, or user the right to perform the music on the air, but synchronization rights are not included in this agreement. ASCAP and BMI govern performance rights.
4. Dubbing rights are obtained from the record company or library; these allow you to use the *actual* recording produced by the record company. If a vocal or instrumental artist is *featured*, it is also necessary to obtain the permission of the artist. The musicians must also be notified and paid according to the regulations of their union (AFM). Because it is time consuming to "clear" the music, many producers turn to *clearance services* to negotiate for packages of original music or libraries.

Not all recordings are protected by copyright. For music, certain **arrangements** are protected. Selected **lyrics** are protected. Some protection is valid only in country of origin. As of this writing, there is still no universal copyright agreement that all nations accept.

Tape, cassette, cartridge, record, compact disc, videodisc, microcassette, and videocassettes with sound material are the primary distribution media for copyright materials.

The bearer of the copyright is due compensation for use. Care must be taken when producers select **public-domain** materials as a copyright search may be necessary to avoid any claims after the fact. Don't always trust the seller. Old original recordings may be recognizable, and it is amazing how infringement problems can arise when big budget productions are involved.

Musician's Union

It may be more practical to hire a new group to perform in a live recording. Once rights have been secured (arrangement, lyrics, performance, and publishing rights), a recording session may be booked at a studio. The average booking is a 3-hour rehearsal and a 3-hour recording session in one day.

The American Federation of Musicians sets the **union scale** for the recording sessions. Consult the music section in Chapter 7.

Note: Often when an original recording is purchased, the performers in the original session may have a claim to compensation if one or any are recognizable; for instance, Charlie Bird is likely to be recognized in a jazz ensemble recording.

The **related costs** for a live recording include:

- Studio rental
- Composer/arranger
- Tape and transfer
- Conductor
- Copyists
- Sidebars

The **design functions** of the recording session include:

Scoring: choosing music bits to fit the picture

Cutting: elimination and/or measurement of takes

Cueing: creating a written plan or log

Laying-in: actual building of music track from fragments, phrases, and melodic lines

Public-domain Music

In the United States, a musical work secures copyright protection for 50 years past the composer's lifetime. A work in the public domain does not require synchronization license. However, caution must be exercised since a later version, a new arrangement, or the addition of new lyrics may have placed the public-domain selection back into copyright.

The original version of a public-domain work may be used royalty free.

The **National Archives** has a sound recording unit that started collecting recordings in 1934. There are more than 50,000 selections dating from the turn of the century to present, all in the public domain. The bulk is of speeches, interviews, news broadcasts, and news commentaries. Fullest coverage is of the eras of World I and World War II, including some musical and entertainment materials.

An index of voices includes such personages as Ezra Pound, Tokyo Rose, and Franklin Delano Roosevelt. A subject index sample shows "Fibber McGee and Molly," Edward R. Morrow's "I Can Hear It Now," and every oral argument before the Supreme Court since 1955.

The **Library of Congress, Recorded Sound Section, Music Division** produces tape recordings of a variety of musical and spoken works. Selected special collections include: folk songs (150,000), Hispanic literature, and recorded poetry and literature.

Original Music

The composer usually works for a creative fee and may receive residuals. However, in addition to payment for the original recording, the music arranger, orchestrator, conductor, contractor, copyist, and musicians always receive residuals within 13 weeks after a television program's initial airing cycle.

Musical Arrangements of Popular Songs

You decide that a pop song is exactly right for your film. You will purchase the synchronization license from the music publisher (often through the Harry Fox Agency, New York). This fixed fee license will state that the use is instrumental and/or vocal. It will list the geographical areas of (air) use, and it will limit the term of years that the license will be in effect.

The music must be arranged and recorded, and a contract filed with the AFM for the recording session. The same payments, conditions, and residuals apply as if this was an original music recording.

Music Libraries

Libraries provide cleared versions of all types of classical and pop music. The fee is a one-time payment for indefinite use in conjunction with one project. If the same music is used for a revision or new version, it must be reported to the library. A small additional fee is due to satisfy the copyright.

ASCAP

The American Society of Composers, Authors, and Publishers is open to membership from anyone who has had a musical work commercially recorded or whose sheet music has been published and made available through retail outlets.

The society negotiates its usage rights fees with users who are often represented by national associations. The fees are nondiscriminatory between users who are similarly situated, and any user who considers the fee quoted unreasonable may ask a federal judge to determine the fee. The fees vary widely among different kinds of users. A local radio station will pay a lower rate than a television network. A tavern pays a lot less than a Las Vegas hotel. Under a blanket license, users may pay only a single license fee for the right to use **any and all** of the member's musical works. They do not have to account separately or pay for each work performed.

ASCAP uses a random sampling technique to arrive at an average census of music usage throughout the country because it is not feasible to count the millions of musical performances in the United States. The sample is stratified and disproportionate. Samples are stratified by media (local radio, local TV), by type of community (rural, metro), by geographic locale (Mid-Atlantic, New England), and by size of the annual license previously set ($1000; $10,000; $20,000, and so on).

Feature works that cannot be identified through the usual process of taping sample broadcasts are given to "solfeggists"—music specialists who file works alphabetically according to the do–re–mi scale.

BMI, New York

Broadcast Music International is another principal licensing agency that forms package agreements with the television networks and with individual stations for the use of copyrighted music. These contracts are usually for a period of one year, are renewable, and are priced at a flat fee which is negotiated according to the size of the station or network and is computed as a function of ad revenue as well as probable usage.

Sources for Further Study

The **ASCAP Film Scoring Workshop** is given annually by invitation only after a preliminary audition of a composer's previous work. Making use of the Fox scoring facilities, the eight-week session culminates with an orchestral scoring/ recording session. Contact ASCAP, 1 Lincoln Plaza, New York, NY 10023 (212-595-3050).

Microphone and test equipment manufacturer **Bruel and Kjaer** hosts seminars in the science of acoustics and measurement, as well as specialized engineering seminars in audio processing. For further information, they may be reached at 185 Forest Street, Marlborough, MA 01752.

The **Visual Music Alliances** sponsors seminars and meetings regarding the multifaceted aspects of synthesized music and sound, interactive videodisc technology, and related "hypermedia" events. For information contact them at 8435 Geyser Avenue, Northridge, CA 91324 (818-885-7316).

The **Academy of Motion Picture Arts and Sciences** has devoted an annual program to film music with guest speakers (who run most of the Hollywood seminars) Elmer Bernstein, John Cacavas, Dan Carlin, Bill Conti, James Horner, Harry Lojewski, Arthur B. Rubinstein, and Nyle Steiner. Contact Academy Foundation, 8949 Wilshire Blvd., Beverly Hills, CA 90211 (213-278-8990).

For hi-fi enthusiasts, the top-notch agency for helpful hints is the **Audiophile Systems Ltd.** group at 6842 Hawthorn Park Drive, Indianapolis, IN 46220 (317-849-7103).

The **Film Composer's Lab** at Sundance Institute, a yearly event held in Provo, Utah, teams noted composers with new talent. Students compose music scenes from motion picture footage using state of the art recording facilities at no charge. The finished scores are performed by a live orchestra. The business and legal aspects of the music recording process are also discussed. Sundance Institute also fosters a film music preservation program in which the film industry's musical heritage is recorded and played during regional film music concerts. Contact Sundance Film Music Lab, 19 Exchange Pl., Salt Lake City, Utah, 84111 (801-328-3457).

Endnotes

1. The *hall radius* defines the sphere of maximum aural influence on the microphone.

2. *Der Stimmung* is a Deutsche Gramaphone recording.

3. Everett C. Frost, "Why Sound Art Works and the German Hörspiel," *Drama Review* (Winter 1987), p. 109.

4. Rudolph Arnheim, *Radio: An Art of Sound*, (1936). Reprinted by Da Capo, New York, 1972.

5. Frost.

6. Elmer Bernstein, "On Film Music," *Journal of the University Film Association* (Fall 1976), p. 4.

7. Penn's film carefully balances interior and exterior sequences, but is essentially a "closet" drama of suspense from the perspective of Katie.

8. George Sanger, "Sounds for the Eye," *Millimeter* (May 1983), p. 103.

9. Frank Paine, "Sound Design: Interview with Walter Murch," *Journal of the University Film Association* (Fall 1981), p. 15.

References

BERLINER, OLIVER, "The Bark Heard Round the World," *db* (Dec. 1977), pp. 35–37.

"Edison's Parisian Triumph," *db* (Dec. 1977); reprint of the Oct. 12, 1889 issue of *Scientific American*.

HARVEY, F. K. "Momentos of Early Photographic Sound Recording," *SMPTE Journal* (Mar. 1982), pp. 237–244.

KRANTZ, HAZEL, "Eldridge R. Johnson, Builder of the Talking Machines," *db* (Dec. 1977), pp. 28–31.

LINDSAY, HAROLD, "Magnetic Recording," Parts I and II, *db* (Dec. 1977, Jan. 1978).

REEVES, H. E., "Development of Stereo Magnetic Recording," Parts I and II, *SMPTE Journal* (Oct. 1982, Nov. 1982), pp. 947–953 and 1087–1090.

THIELE, HEINZ, "On the Origin of High Frequency Bias for Magnetic Audio Recording," *SMPTE Journal* (July 1983), pp. 752–754.

ZIDE, LARRY, "Making of the Ampex ATR-100," *db* (Dec. 1976), pp. 32–35.

POSTPRODUCTION: QUELL, QUENCH, SQUELCH

Editorial functions of sound are expressed. A consideration of premix concepts and the design functions of the mix are outlined. The dialectic of aural materials and strategies, including separation, analogies, event simulation, and virtual space, are discussed. A sound map illustrates the sound construction of a segment of Francis Ford Coppola's *Tucker*.

Figure 4–1 *King Kong* (1933), RKO, produced by David O. Selznick, directed by Merian C. Cooper, music by Max Steiner. One of the early triumphs of the sound film, it made use of every known aural effect and displayed aural "pointillism," a carefully orchestrated melodic line composed by Steiner and, for the first time, mixed by layering of effects and dialogue on a prototype multichannel audio console.

The rationale for postproduction has moved from a process of correction and repair to a process of elaboration and embellishment. Prior to 1975, nearly 80% of feature film sound had to be postsynchronized utilizing looping and automatic dialogue replacement. Production tracks were simply too noisy, and complex scenes could not be miked adequately with conventional means. Furthermore, sound had not achieved status as a merchandising element (sound track album). Dubbing stages were booked up sometimes over a year in advance. Budgets ran over, release dates were held up, and talent inconvenienced.

The turn to the use of good production tracks and the concentration on the more creative functions of postproduction were due primarily to several technological advances:

1. Improved wireless microphones that opened up location recording for more spontaneity and authenticity (it's moot whether content demanded new technologies or new gear dictated new directorial approaches)
2. Shotgun microphones provided isolation and range
3. Dolby noise reduction cleaned up the input–output chain
4. Stereo recording provided clear separation of background and foreground

Other factors that had a positive effect on sound recording production practice included the refusal of some stars to go back into the studio to dub voice on the grounds of the artistic limitations of the process (Robert Blake in "Baretta"); the upgrading of theatrical exhibition and home video playback; the advent of digital (echoless, color-free spatial) recording and synthesized sound; automated video editing and mixing systems with source material drawn from disk and floppy disc; sound designing in conjunction with the **music video** revolution; and direct-to-disk tapeless studios with LEDE (live end, dead end) acoustics.

Postproduction Processes in Audio Design

Strategies

The concepts presented herewith are drawn from the Russian tradition as espoused by Pudovkin, Eisenstein, Kuleshov, and Dovshenko, the poets of the early cinema. British director/editor Karel Reicz and French theorist Nöel Burch have also exerted a great influence on the basic tenents of audio design. The reader is urged to go back to the original texts by these structural pioneers as listed in the bibliography.

For the audio designer, certain basic editing fundamentals can become the occasion for greater manipulation of multitrack sound elements. Each script has an implied auditory space–time continuum, which can be understood as fundamental to the theme of the program and the attitude of the director or writer. The multitrack tapestry that is woven should reflect an understanding of the following:

- Any change in angle or scale (matching shots from the same angle but closer or farther away) generally establishes spatial continuity between shots.
- Any shift in screen position necessarily corresponds to a shift in real space.
- The transition between shots may occur anywhere.
- The essential unfolding in time and space (decoupage) is the breakdown of the narrative into bits and pieces, shots, scenes, and sequences.
- **Time abridgement** (temporal ellipsis), the **gap** or **omission** of time between shots may be implied by images and sound acting at the cut. The types of temporal ellipsis are:
  - Perceptible and measurable—sense of real time.
  - Indefinite—no clue to time elapsed.
  - Continuous temporal: auditory action joined to a discontinuous temporal–visual action—action is fragmented, sound is not.
  - Two distinct spaces—cut end to end.
  - Two distinct times—implied or felt.
  - Reversal (flashback or flashforward): measurable distinct change.
  - Indefinite time reversal—no clue to time removed.
- Temporal continuity may be preserved or established by the track alone: For example, a shot of a speaker with a shot of the listener as the dialogue of the speaker continues over the shot of the listener without a break, a straight match cut. Other matching options include:
  - Eyeline—direction of eye contact.
  - Speed of movement within frame—action in shot.
  - Camera movement (speed of movement of frame)—pace from shot to shot.
  - Props and position of actors in the shot
  - Axis: crossing plane created by the position of the camera whose view corresponds to the viewpoint of director, audience, or a character
- Any camera movement converts nonscreen space (offscreen) into screen space. This space is defined by planes at left, right, top, bottom, foreground, and background.

- Each composition has a scale best suited to it (relationship of the subject to the whole, the **relative importance of things**).
- "Editing is the creative force of filmic reality" (Pudvokin). Transitions, the passage from one shot to another (one subject to another), have a physical and emotional reality. The basic physical links in strict Hollywood tradition are straight match cuts designed to create seamless continuity. The more invisible the visual and sound transition, the better, more fully realized is the illusion of unbroken space–time. There is a Western (Hemi) social-political rationale to accept this studio aesthetic, a knowledge of the basic cuts serves as a point of reference.

  - **Cross-cutting:** links events happening in the same or different locations at the same or different times, effecting the belief that action occurs in parallel. A sound laid over this transition could supply yet another level or plane of action occurring simultaneously.

  - **Cut on action:** connects a moving frame or movement within the frame with a shot of similarly paced movement. The visual gap is diminished by forcing the eye to follow movement.

  - **Form cut:** matching of shapes or contours from end frame of first shot to first frame of the second shot. The effect of this symmetry of design is to disguise the spatial leap. The aural link would be a rhythm and meter match.

  - **Hidden cut:** an action cut that utilizes a fast movement within the frame or a blurring to disguise or obscure the change to a new locale. A very fast in-frame wipe, let's say, affected by the suit jacket of a character crossing in front of the action and obscuring the view until the cut.

  - **Jump cut:** abrupt leap in time or space to jar the viewer into closing the action. Tends to make one very aware of the medium, while forcing the focus of attention on the fixed elements of the composition or perspective.

  - **Dynamic cut:** creates meaning through the association of two images that have no functional relationship, but that when presented side by side or one after the other blend into a metaphor. An example would be a shot of an army officer followed by a crowing rooster; one implication is that the officer is "cocky," egocentric, and so on.

  - **Crossing the axis:** severe time and space reversal created by the joining of the frontal view of a space or object cut to the reverse or back view. This may correspond to a change in audience position.

  - **Cutaway:** a shot is joined to a detail (insert) or section of the whole in the next shot, which will then link up with the master shot or to a totally new space. Often used as a hidden cut, it is better used in series to explore the details of a room, by preselecting audience focus of attention to only those elements the director deems of import.

Virtual Space

Off-screen space is revealed and/or converted to screen space by any one of the following methods of classic stagecraft:

- **Character entries or exits:** imply progress to next shot or return from previous shot, from an unseen space.
- **Empty frame:** sound indicates what is happening or what exists outside the frame and just at the edge.
- **Brushing past camera:** the frontal plane of space at the edge of the screen is revealed.
- **Actor looks off screen:** sightline implies a subject in an unseen space in a specific direction.
- **Camera movement:** the motion of the frame from its fixed position within the shot, instantly creates or reveals proximate space as if the viewer is turning or moving.
- **Partial framing:** a compositional imbalance that cuts off part of the picture, implying that there is obviously more off screen. For instance, we seldom see ceilings but are always made to accept the fact that it is there from the perspective of a given shot. The frameline becomes a window on the world, and the window suddenly makes itself apparent by limiting your world view (unless you are tribal).
- **Auditory allusion:** unseen object, presence, or location is suggested through hearing the sound it makes. It is unnecessary to see a fast-moving train passing by when we can more effectively convey that sense through creative juxtaposition of its sound (with Doppler effect) over a simultaneously occurring action. These allusions are often stronger than the impact of the visual it replaces, because the allusion forces the imagination to take flight.

Editorial Use of Sound

The classical formula is to use sound as accompaniment to the picture by the selection and arrangement of aural elements in constant dependence on the image in order to:

- Reinforce the connotation of each shot
- Support the denotation of each shot
- Eembellish our sense of reality
- Synchronize dialogue, noise, music, and aural effects to the screened image

The nontraditional formula insists that a sound evokes imagery and supplies meaning in and of itself, despite the content of the visual. The microphone becomes a creative instrument, not a passive device. The audio designer ought to establish allusions rather than create associations with images, by detaching a sound from its origin and stimulating the aural imagination through the powers of suggestion inherent in off-screen space.

Sound Parameters

Sound parameters have a **form** and a **function.**

Auditory material: May be live or synchronous or recomposed—applies to real world.

Recomposed sound: May be used over improvised shots—processed.

Live sound: Often used over staged shots—unprocessed.

Equal presence: Sometimes works against the aural, seamless transition creating attention to the visual—background only logically different shot to shot.

Apparent microphone distance: A function of anticipated echo—each sound suggests a distance.

Doppler effect: Conditions a response to a direction or trajectory of action.

Acoustic shadow: May mask the illusion of continuity.

Transformations: Create a tapestry of tonal music and natural sounds.

Separation: Creates specific positions in space corresponding not so much to stereo perspectives as to points of interest in the field.

Superimpositions: Weave natural and artificial sounds over and under each other.

Presence: Background noise may imply a certain emotional state; silence may do likewise.

Dissonance: Focuses attention on a spatial or emotional image/fact—self-reflexive sound.

The Doppler Effect

When a listener is in motion toward a stationary source of sound, the pitch (frequency) of the sound is higher than when he or she is at rest. If the listener is in motion away from the static source, he or she hears a lower pitch than when at rest. Similar results occur when the source is in motion toward or away from the stationary listener. The pitch of a train whistle is higher when the train is approaching the hearer than when it has passed.

When the listener is in motion toward the source, he or she receives more waves in each unit of time than when at rest. When the source is in motion, the effect is a **shortening** of the wavelength. When the source moves away, the wavelength is greater, so the observer hears a decreased frequency.

> *AXIOM: The motion of the source through the medium shortens or lengthens the wave transmitted through the medium.*

Acoustic shadow.   An acoustic shadow is a region of reduced sound pressure caused by an obstacle in the path of travel of a sound wave. The reduction in sound intensity is governed by the wavelength and the size of the obstacle.

Transformation.   This is the treatment of sound or changes in sound quality, pitch, or duration, by any continuous or discontinuous process that may be used to convert the **content** of a sound into any other sound form.

Superimposition.   This is the recording of a second signal on a tape without passing the previous recording through the erase head field. The high-frequency bias on the new recording reduces the volume of the earlier recording but does not disguise it, except for certain frequencies that become masked by those residing close by in the spectrum.

Separation.   Separation is the degree to which each of several microphones discriminates in favor of the sources being recorded. Separation allows individual control of source perspective and spatial orientation.

Image/Facts

If sound design is the process of creating sound textures and sound elements that convey emotion and meaning, those sounds do not necessarily have to be tied to real events in the program; but they may have a relation to the **formal** image/facts that comprise narrative flow.

Image/facts are joined together in two primary ways: (1) as a series of fragments (montage) whose selection and arrangement provide meaning by association, or (2) as a series of fragments in time (decoupage) whose sequence gives rise to **spatiotemporal continuity.**

Both visual and aural materials may be linked by the identical **transitions.** These transitions between elements or shots can be listed under two general directorial attitudes as given in Table 4–1.

Pudovkin was right, editing **is** the force of filmic reality. This notion is everywhere apparent during the audio editing process. The bits and pieces of each aural fact and the way they are selected and arranged create both recognizable and original associations with image. To cite some examples of aural ingenuity, the following may be considered:

- Familiar, identifiable noises may be joined within an unfamiliar context. Use of "punch and crunch" sounds for Ninja combat was made up of cheese grating and wet pillow noises. Bergman's *Cries and Whispers* alters level of voice making the whisper a metaphorical device. (See Figure 4–2)

- Two unrelated, realistic sounds may be combined to produce an unrealistic effect. *Legend, Willow, Cries and Whispers*, and *Raggedy Man* all employ atmospheric sounds created from raw kitchen utensil soundbites. (See Figure 4–4)

- An unfunny obvious sound may be edited into a funny unexpected sound. For instance the beeping of robots and androids in *Star Wars*, Roadrunner cartoons and *TRON* vehicles; punching and photo flash in *After Dark, My Sweet*. (See Figure 4–3)

- The incongruous placement of sound introduces fantasy into realistic settings. *Legend, Willow, Cries and Whispers*, and *Raggedy Man* all employ atmospheric sounds created from raw kitchen utensil soundbites. (See Figure 4–4)

- The force of editing can convince us of a reality, a physical reality of an event we know never really happened. For instance, the pounding of *Raging Bull* fight scenes; the Kazoo in *La Jetee* heard over the operating table; the wind in *E.T.* as a bicycle floats in space. (See Figure 4–5)

- Synthetic, shaped sounds may be wed to naturally occurring ambience to produce the simulation of actuality. Engine sound from *Star Wars*, the wings and craws of *The Birds*, both tapestries of many details of real and synthetic sounds. (See Figure 4–5)

- Library and prerecorded sounds may be linked to dialogue to create vocal resonance. *Darkman, Harry and the Hendersons*, and *Dick Tracy* employ characterizations with synthesized vocalization. (See Figure 4–6)

- A combination of sounds may indicate more than each separate sound image would denote or connote alone. Drones, chimes, wind and rumble in every scene of *Rumble Fish* mesh into a music of effects reflecting psychological space. (See Figure 4–7)

- A sound may be used to **extend** the contextual meaning of the image through an aural "figure of speech." *Altered States*; $8\frac{1}{2}$; and *Last year at Marienbad* use silence to focus primal sounds into reflections of states of mind. (See Figure 4–8)

Event Simulation

Strictly speaking, concepts of realism in the cinema and television practicum are limited to (1) emulation, the effort to equal or excel beyond the structure of the real world, and (2) simulation, the effort to create the effect or appearance of the real world. The differences between dramatic realism and

TABLE 4–1 Classes of Transitions

Straight Match Cut	Space–Time Elepsis
Through:	Of:
Eyeline match	Screen space
Screen direction	Off-screen space
Camera angle	Aural allusions
Screen movement	Reversals
Movement within frame	Definite time
Perspective	Indefinite time
Fade, dissolve	Silence
Superimposition	Separation

AXIOM: The transition between shots may occur anywhere.

documentary (newsreel) realism, in practice, tend to be a matter of emphasis and degree of aural or sonogenic relationships that are heightened or diminished through color, contrast, movement, setting, and directorial attitude (point of view).

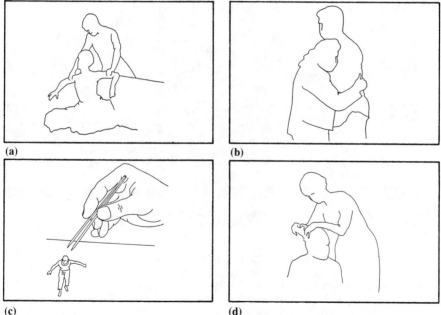

(a)

(b)

(c)

(d)

Figure 4–2 Vertical integration of auditory material is quite rare. In these compositions, sound must preserve **(a)** "hard-to-get detachment"; **(b)** emotions which cannot be adequately "dubbed"; **(c)** an incomprehensible reality; **(d)** intimacy of the bath. In each situation, there is an upper and lower case involved—dominating and recessive sound sources that must be recorded in separation and given equal presence, while maintaining individual integrity. We have not yet learned how to creatively deal with this top-bottom structure.

Fresh from the sewer, TEENAGE MUTANT NINJA TURTLES, Renaissance Turtles named Leonardo, Donatello, Michaelangelo and Raphael, heroes on a half shell, who are fighting for truth, justice and a larger slice of pizza.

Figure 4–3 *Teenage Mutant Ninja Turtles.* "Toons" provide the ideal setting for auditory invention. *Inverted counterpoint*, for instance, is the use of sounds wholly out of their natural context and inserted for humorously unexpected effects. The designer can make a world that does not exist sound plausible while creating ironic twists. (With permission of IVE, Inc., Mirage Productions and Surge Licensing.)

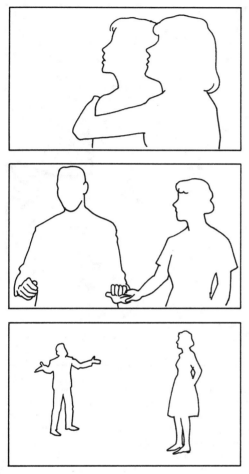

Figure 4–4 The two-shot is the fundamental narrative building block. Proxmity between subjects differs widely as per the possibilities in **(a)**, **(b)** and **(c)**. The nature of the emotional link is solely a function of the qualities of aural information including language. **(a)** Background sound without music would provide clues to the emotive content of the profiled two shot characters. Mood options must be specific. **(b)** Moment of reaching out requires aural focus on details of the felt experience. Music can be the short cut but there are better ways to create sentiment. **(c)** Felt distance conveyable via voice as much as through ambiance or background texture can be felt as "warm or cold."

Traditionally, the least likely component of the sound continuum, music, has been used to almost subliminally support the emotional integrity of the visuals. For a thorough exploration of the reasons for this contradiction, see Claudia Gorbman's *Unheard Melodies*, Indiana University Press, 1987. The cinematographer selects a set of coordinates from her or his visual inventory to depict or simulate reality: camera-to-subject distance, size of shot, angle of view, sharpness of focus, camera or subject movement, and so on (but it must be understood that the picture is only a representation of the real).

The audio designer has a more varied pallette and the luxury of mathematical proportion and synthesis. This sonogenic inventory has both emotive and narrative functions, depending on the director's concept of realism (or naturalism). The design parameters for the simulation of real events would look something like Table 4–2 (see p. 137).

Figure 4–5   The combining of different kinds of voices, principally male and female, presents technical problems for the mixer since different settings are necessary for each voice. In the three-shot, there is the further complexity of close-miking to insure clarity. Notice that very few program sequences dare to convey the reality of people talking over each other. It is virtually a myth that any three speakers consistently follow a linear rather than a polyphonic pattern of dialogue. This is why speech in film and TV is seldom rhythmic and musical. Steeped in theatrical convention each voice has its due despite the implications of the composition. A shot whose reality would be impossible to control and render aurally because of chaotically high noise levels and aural masking is rendered plausible through the selective layering of real and "unnatural" sounds.

The documentary tradition.   With the heritage of John Grierson and the documentary tradition, we are cautioned that "sound must help to fulfill the mute" and "music must create the mood of theme." In this sense, the track seems particularly relegated to a support function when depicting or simulating reality unless one is willing to contemplate the way in which live, location recorded sync sound can affect our perception of the "real" event.

Vlada Petric calls the sensation "ontological authenticity."[1] Petric refers to the holistic experience of the sync sound continuum as if it embodied some sort of pure cinema/video, an unpolluted space–time continuum with self-cer-

Figure 4–6 *Blackmail* (1929). Diegetic music has both a decorative and performance aspect. It can provide a real-time reference of period and setting while forcing the audience to become a passive witness. In the hands of a master, this music provides a rhythmic framework for editorial pacing while fulfilling the narrative obligation to provide cues and clues to plot, a favorite Hitchcock technique. This is the first use of auditory POV (subjective sound). Annie Ondra and Cyril Richard prepare for the worst.

tifying integrity. There is, in fact, a certain background/foreground relationship in the documentary that we have learned to accept and recognize as denoting a certain "version" of recorded reality. This simulation experience is based on the acceptance of the single-system film/video camera/microphone package as the eye/ear apparatus of the inquiring interlocutor, whose task it is to "document" the real.

We assume the position of the documentary cameraman and are required to suppress any attempt to **interpret** what is chosen to be recorded. Live sync sound lends the primary sense of spontaneity and authenticity, the felt immediacy of the event as if it were not selected, focused, composed, and cut. In fact, there are too many details left out, with sound instantaneously separated from its origin and from the entire fabric of life as it is lived by the viewer. There is, nevertheless, something akin to truth in the unprocessed, live recording of

Figure 4–7   The sound track is used to bridge the gap, the interval between mystical moments of truth and the absurdities of real space/time. Music resorts to trancelike melody orchestrated to lift the spirits and suspend disbelief. It works on the plane of imaginative experience: (**a**) shows a foreground/background relationship; (**b**) forces the male-female bridge which must be aurally balanced and (**c**) sets up the focus and identity of individual voices in a left-right symmetry or hierarchy. Often picture composition provides the suggestion of aural perspective.

events in **documentary style,** but for the audio designer, the key issues are more strenuous than for the theatrical fiction program, which allows for poetic license in the utilization of sound.

The issues in the utilization of live, unprocessed sync sound materials offer a wealth of paradoxical methodology:

- The psychoacoustic limitations of the theater directly affect the perception of "ontological authenticity" since the subtleties and nuance of location production tracks are often masked by the level of exhibition noise. Moreover, television greatly limits the dynamic range, with only stereo broadcasting offering some possibility of preserving realistic textures. Everything sounds like drama on television, especially the news.

- Postproduction audio shaping allows for the enhancing of the aural experience in that sound may be made to feel more alive and real. How is it possible to capture extemporaneously in the field (with only intuition at work) more "kinesthetic"[2] appeal and "truth" than can be designed into the track to ensure clarity?

- Observation leads to new relationships of sound to picture; but can states of being, the conscious and the unconscious, be conveyed through direct reportage?

- Pointing a lens or choosing a focal length "subjectifies" all objects in the chosen path. The camera is the enemy of passion. Detachment is not possible. What is the felt difference between:

  - A close-up of a face taken with a telephoto lens in combination with highly directional sound imaging?

  - A close-up of a face taken with a wide-angle lens close to the subject with an omnidirectional microphone used in tight to the subject?

Figure 4–8 $8\frac{1}{2}$ (1963). Auditory choices are defined by what is implied as much as by what is seen within the play of light and dark; fantasy and filmic reel-ality are either enforced, obscured, or extended by a *lack* of aural distinction. Sound makes the dream state highly specific and, therefore, rational. Fellini created a cadence of acoustic shadows, half-sonorous, half-mute, conveying the movement of the mind in time. Music added irony.

TABLE 4–2 Composer's Grid

Orchestration	Primary	Secondary
Length of a tone Tap of beats Pattern of rhythm	Duration	Transitions Movement
Accent Timbre Tempo	Articulation	Perspective Aural focus
Pitch Amplitude Meter	Volume	Shot angle Shot size
Ornamentals Repetitions Tonality	Movement	Shape Contrast

Phonogenically and photogenically, the shots are as dissimilar as painted portraits by Giotto and Warhol. Meaning and truth are forever immersed in the pecularities of the recording apparatus. With video, the mosaic of sight and sound is less problematic because it is a medium hostile to detail.

Even with the best reception and a picture conforming to the recommended standards of High Definition Television, the best one can hope for is approximately half the resolution of a screened 35mm print in a very dark theater.

Even with the best stereo sound reproduction system linked to the home television, the best one could hope for is a range limited by the current FCC standard transmission range between 100 and 8000 Hertz. Expensive audio processing gear will mask the deficiencies. Some home audio systems can cost over $112,000.00, but they are still limited by the clarity of the signal as actually appearing at the TV receiver over the air or via cable. Fiber optic linkages will improve the frequency range but the promise has yet to be made.

Editing and Sound Shaping

Sound shaping is the orchestrating of bits and pieces of aural information (note, phrase, word, syllable, noise) into a new expression that can stand by itself or create a new audiovisual metaphor when attached to a picture. Functionally, the process is a composing of individual sounds that have been separated from their origin, analyzed, and then reconstructed (physically and in duration) into image/facts, that is, atmosphere, emotion, presence, poetry.

Razor's Edge to Digital Domain

The process of editing sound has evolved from a tedium of manually cutting finite strips of tape or film (fragments of sound limited to the unit of a frame), trimming, rearranging or discarding, and/or splicing back together to a highly intuitive and mathematical process of automated synthesis, which occurs completely within the digital domain.

The functions previously assigned to audio processing and its numerous "black-box" systems have been engineered into the basic programs of sound synthesizers and the related composer-oriented systems developed in the music industry. Postproduction, nevertheless, still serves as the final cleansing and embellishing stage prior to final transfer to the release format.

Each electronic music/effects system has a unique **tone color** that is a function of the system's principle of operation.

Fairlight CMI. This system operates on the waveform manipulation principle, which is based on the assumption that natural sounds and those occurring nonelectronically have characteristics that are far more complex than is possible to resynthesize. And it is not desirable to exactly re-create existing sounds. The nature of the sounds themselves become a fundamental part of the music (event-oriented composition).

Natural sounds are simply sampled or synthesized with the computer and screen system. Modifications are made to existing sounds, which may include **editing** and **blending** with other sounds. **Sonic realism** and **imaging shaping** are two chief goals with effects, while unique timbre and clarity are of prime import for music.

MU sync.   In this system, a flatbed editor with a computer and CRT gives visual representation of the frames of film, with action and music cues over the frame. Moving a cursor to a frame moves the film to that point. Programming in a tempo marks the frames on which beats or downbeats appear. A third screen shows the conducting display, visualizing the exact placement of each beat and number of beats remaining in that measure. The computer will fix tempos to coincide with important visual events and will perform **accelerandos** and **ritardandos** between sections of different tempos. When the MU Sync controls a synthesizer playback, the result is a frame-accurate programmable electronic orchestra. The length and speed of the piece may be changed at any point.

Virtual instrument.   This system takes a raw note and samples, trims, loops, filters, and transposes it in order to enhance **brightness, transient definition,** and **clarity;** the primary traits of any instrument. (See Figure 4–9)

Premix Concepts

Whatever the subject matter, it must be reflected, to a certain extent, in the overall aural thematic of the program. While the process of inventing an overall sound plan requires imagination as well as technical competence, the strictly narrative force of sound must be specified in a way that makes sense of all the other relationships: sound to color, voice, mood, motion (real and implied), the editing function, photogenics, volume, form, contour, and space–time.

What the audio designer should attempt is to draw comparisons between the **emotionally evocative** and the **purely rational** elements or functions of composition. Sound imagery creates a dialectic between **dramatic** and **epic** forms of narrative. Answers are needed to basic questions:

1. What is the basis of the plot?
2. What formulates conflict?
3. What is the character of the setting?
4. What is the role of props?

The choices available are not exhausted by those listed in Table 4–3; however, the aural image created by the designer should be molded or refined to fit into some of these structures.

Some examples of premix concepts follow:

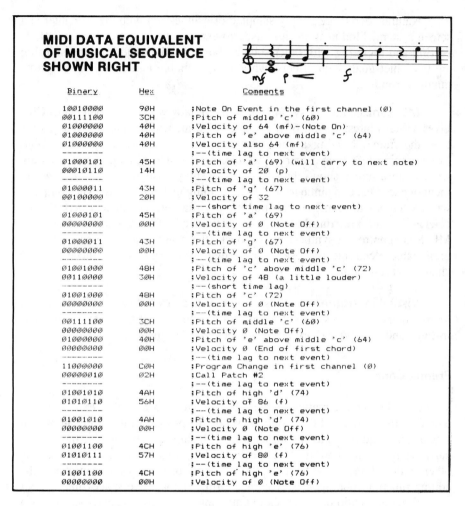

Figure 4-9   MIDI data equivalent of musical sequence.

1. **Dialogue as texture:** In *Quest for Fire*, A complete language is invented for the apeish characters of early humans, who communicate by a primal phonetic guttural set of sounds. The plan is to orchestrate the grunts and groans into a kind of emotional tapestry that can be understood by anyone. Speech origination becomes an aural leitmotif.

2. **Effects as metaphor:** Pounding in *Raging Bull* and *Altered States*, which is repetitive throughout these movies, becomes a psychic resonance expressing inner pain, breaking apart, and spiritual dissolution. The pounding is a choreographed simile for a soul at war with great forces of destruction. Robert De Niro as Jake LaMotta, prizefighter, pounds the bag in the early days of his development, pounds the pavement, pounds his brother's face,

TABLE 4-3 Forms of Narrative

Dramatic	Epic
Involves the spectator	Makes the spectator an observer
Lets him feel something	Forces him to make decisions
Spectator is emerged in something	He is faced with something
Suggestive	Argumentative
Feelings are conserved	Forced to reach cognition
Spectator is in the middle of the action	Spectator is outside the action
Excitement as to climax	Excitement as to progress
One scene leads into the next	Each scene stands alone
Linear progress	Irregular progress
Evolutionary reluctance	Jumps
Humans as an unchanging species	Humans as process
Ideas determine life	Life determines ideas
Feelings	Rational thinking

From Bertolt Brecht, *Schriften zum Theater*.

pounds the bodies of his opponents, and succumbs to the pounding of his own painful life. In Robert Altman's *Altered States'* climactic scene, William Hurt is transfigured through a pounding space–time continuum, a kind of incantation of beats that are mystical and physical at the same time.

3. **Music as state of being:** In *Mephisto* and *Lili Marlene*, melody is a mirror reflection of inner states, a revelation of changes in time, mood, and the nature of the performance space (mise-en-scène). Both films augment theme and variations of basic orchestral pieces. Time is felt as a function of changes in orchestration. The quality of the musical performance echoes the state of world politics. We are always in the position of the audience we see on screen, never a passive spectator in our own theater. The music tracks echo the propaganda whose narrative exposition they support.

The mixer/designer is anticipating or defining what the public thinks the experience of the filmic world (the world as screened) will be. The responsibility is primarily to:

- Preserve location dialogue through repair and enhancement to avoid the need for ADR (which tends to ruin performance and emotional content)
- Eliminate the irrational, irrelevant sounds
- Shade the aural range by adding emphasis, focus, or defocus to indicate importance or perspective
- Intensify perception by connecting "little lies" of sound information that add up to a truth

From Eisenstein, we have a secondary array of mix functions, including:

- Syncopation: the precise marriage of visual movement to aural motion, rhythm, and meter
- Purely acoustic distortion: modification of a sound to create a new visual association or to create a nonrepeatable, nonrepresentational sound (noise)
- Contradictory volumes: contrast of loudness and softness
- Sound structure: the equivalent of a musical **glissando** and **crescendo**
- Creation of a leitmotif and the subsequent distortion of the leitmotif (see *The General Line*, Figure 7–3)
- Abrupt leaps in aural continuity
- Deformation of an element (saw) into its allusion (sobbing); fanfare into laughter.
- Create a meaningful pause. Let silence speak.
- Intensification of auditory material until it is unidentifiable.
- Condense the rhythm of aural time; work with "snatches of sound," producing **staccato** pacing.

Audio Design Components of the Mix

The following are the chief functions of the multitrack mix listed in order of importance and the order in which they should be accomplished.

Compression. The dynamic range of the master finished track is well beyond the range and greater than the capacity of the playback chain. To compensate for anticipated losses, the entire program level is dropped uniformly below a maximum level standardized as the Academy cutoff. Both high frequencies and extremely low frequencies are diminished, creating a more reproducible dynamic range in the theater.

Balance. Levels differ greatly from sequence to sequence and shot to shot, in spite of the care taken in location recording. Dialogue is first equalized to gain clarity and fidelity; noise is eliminated and a level sought that ensures intelligibility. Other tracks are balanced in tone, level, and predominance **against** the primary voice tracks. This balance tries to avoid distraction, while maintaining a continuity of amplitudes throughout the show.

Enhancement. Some sounds must be made to "sound" better. Some must have a mood assigned to them. Still others must be brought more closely faithful to the source they represent. Some must dominate, last longer, become clearer. Filtering, time compression, equalization, reverberation, synthesization, flanging, phasing, and other processes fulfill these needs.

Layering. The final master is a blending of many discrete elements: voice, music, natural effects, artificial synthesized sounds, sound loops, cassette inserts, and disc inserts; the mixer must blend these multiple arrays over, under, beside, and around each other by selectively fading up and down as the perceptual presence of each discrete element becomes necessary for the narrative to continue or to be embellished. Masking is another technique that uses certain frequencies to disguise others. Cross-fading is yet another system of careful manual adjustments to levels and tonality, instantaneously changing as tracks play.

Positioning. Perspective of events in time and space from the screen is a function of apparent acoustic distance, as well as some more subtle parameters. Amplitude adjustment seems to give hints as to apparent position in space, size of subject, and direction and movement in time and space. Likewise, frequency discrimination to a certain extent also provides data about where things are. The illusion of the apparent sound source can be created by manipulation of pitch and amplitude.

Transitions. Sometimes a world changes in a flash. What occurs between cuts is significant. There are many breaks in a given show. They must be hidden, embellished, exaggerated, or matched to maintain continuity as defined by the director or the flow of the narrative. The transition between shots may occur anywhere. In straight match continuity, the transition must be invisible, inaudible, and unperceptible. For instance, if one wishes to denote some abridgement of time or space, perhaps the transition must be made more noticeable. If all action takes place in the same location, sound must match regardless of subject to camera position, and regardless of size of shot or quality of movement. This is in keeping again with the Hollywood notion of straight match spatial–temporal continuity; all events flow without any apparent breaks, even though time is compressed and there are great leaps in perspective and position. This does not take into account any narrative or psychological associations one may wish to construct.

Addition. Only during the multitrack interlock mix can the director, editor, or audio designer determine if all the elements are sufficient to create the necessary experience. It is not unusual to find holes in this fine tapestry, spaces however minute but noticeable, where there is no sound, where noise lingers still, where an element's effect is incorrect, inaccurate, out of place. New elements must be added and carefully blended in. There can be silence, but lack of even a noise or room tone track will reproduce as distracting speaker hum in the theater.

Noise reduction. Finally, noise makes dialogue difficult to hear. Intelligibility suffers. It can be diminished, mashed, or psychoacoustically covered up by using an array of techniques at the end of the mix. Dolby and DBS, as well as Kintek and other new systems, code noise and then decode it "away." The process is accomplished better during the transfer to the final release format, which may be 16mm optical or striped magnetic prints, 35mm optical or stereo optical, 35mm six-track magnetic or four-track magnetic, or 70mm six-track magnetic. Noise reduction is essentially a masking technique by which noise components become more difficult to hear in relation to peak program levels in the theater.

The mix presents yet another chance to make creative choices, since all the necessary information to create nuances of sound imagery is here present on a channel by channel log. Total control is possible, as is programmable repetition. Combinations and permutations, last minute alterations, are made by comparison of discrete and combined tracks. Finances dictate. When time runs out, time runs out!

A cost comparison may serve to illuminate some points here regarding creative options. Cost-effective methods have been introduced into the post-production chain to accommodate the touchy director and uncooperative talent. Several principal performers refuse to dub. Robert Blake, for instance, believed so strongly in his location performance that he would not contract for dubbing time on any "Baretta" show. The show exhibited a strong reactive performance in relation to the street environment in which the show developed. In this case it was up to the mixer to achieve clarity and intelligibility with the live and noisy location track. A handful of top mixers monopolize the craft. Their sensitivity acquired from years of dealing with seemingly insurmountable quality problems cannot be taught; it must be felt.

The craft of the mixer begins and ends with a thorough understanding of the playback chain—its limitations and potential for manipulating the captive audience. The mixer knows that much of what is achieved by blending, matching, equalizing, correcting, embellishing, and so on, can be lost because of deficiencies of exhibition. The technology of the theater has changed little in 50 years. Given decent equipment, the average theater owner lacks competence in acoustics, maintenance of projectors, position of speakers, matching of amplifiers, and hearing!

The playback level alone matters intensely in the theater. A film like *Raggedy Man* becomes a metaphorical land of enchantment when experienced at low levels. Its air of suspense and mystery is heightened. What is unheard compels the imagination to fill in with doubt and anticipation. The texture becomes quite unrealistic, a quiet fable in which attention focuses on little nuances of the actors craft—gesture, facial movements, eyeline clues, and the like. The same experience at high program levels in the same theater provides a harshly realistic tale of terror in which all actions are telegraphed by interior noise and discordant effects. Every discourse seems separated from the background in what appears to be a poorly mixed simplistic track. It is perhaps a case in which poor exhibition yields an insincere performance. Regardless of how **content may be influenced by the program level,** the meaning must be decoded by a careful viewer. We are still faced with the situation of the silent-movie days in which spontaneous accompaniment by the organist or pianist provides, as does today's theater owner, only the simulation of the emotional environment the director intended.

Dialectic of Materials in Sound Mixing

Like the editor, the sound mixer works with several classes of auditory materials, each with its own characteristics, which are often "felt" more than they are "heard":

High-definition digital audio master from a disk

Low-definition third- or fourth-generation canned sounds

Recomposed studio recordings with no background

Live, on-location production tracks

Computer-generated or processed sounds from disk

Second- or third-generation sounds from tape cartridge

Second- or third-generation sounds from $\frac{1}{4}$-inch tape

Audio transferred from video tape, home movies (8mm), archival records, old magnetic film, 16mm, 17.5mm, 35mm

This is a pallette of second-generation sound at best. All elements will ultimately be transferred to 35mm magnetic film and put up onto dubbers in the machine room, or be individually transferred to a multitrack recorder (soon, to hybrid systems incorporating video and digital technologies; see the video section).

The design problem for the mixer is to design **if and when** the nature of each type of source material should be allowed to assert itself. For instance, in what situations would the sound of an old radio show or music be preserved and when should it be remixed to current standards? More a directorial decision, this choice (rhetorical for our purpose) has a powerful effect on the narrative structure and meaning.

Separation

Simply stated, separation is the mixing process of combining dissimilar aural image/facts, creating a new sensation and/or meaning for the composite sound. When set against picture, yet another new composite sensation or meaning is possible.

The kinds of categories this composite may fall into include but are not limited to all the following:

- Spatial (localization, perspective)
- Metaphorical (poetic, abstract)
- Psychological (emotional, moody)
- Temporal (time elipsis)
- Physical (volume, color, shape, and so on)
- Kinetic (movement, displacement)

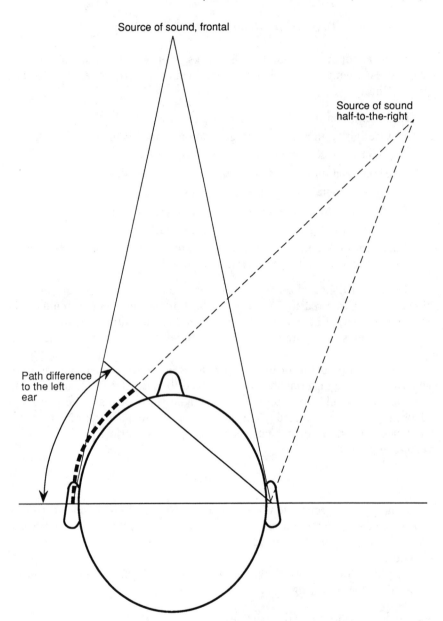

Figure 4–10(a) Path difference and shadowing are important factors enabling spatial discrimination.

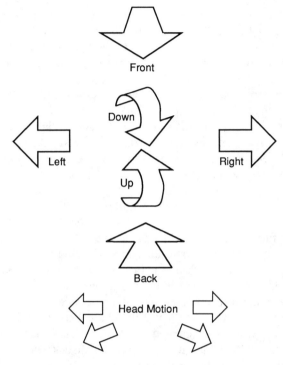

Figure 4–10 Cont. (b) Binaural hearing experiments reveal that localization is more than a right–left phenomenon. The total spatial orientation of the organism looks something like this.

The methods of combining aural materials include but are not limited to all the following:

- Omission of specific details of each sound
- Reprocessing of each sound
- Level, equalization, and reverberation changes of specific aural intervals, for instance, between syllables or effects patterns or tones

The sense memory inventory the mixer/designer may refer to includes:

- Culturally conditioned audience responses to particular sounds (baby's cry)
- Physically conditioned responses from low-frequency resonance (nausea), high-frequency pitch effects (ache), high-amplitude pressure (general discomfort), silence (imbalanced pressure of inner ear), and the like
- Conventions of spatial hearing: path difference and shadowing factors giving strong clues to perspective and spatial positioning (screen, off screen); use of the Doppler effect (see Figures 4–10(**a**) and 4–10(**b**))

- Referential conditioning, as in reversing or subsuming what the audience expects or anticipates hearing immediately after the previous shot or sequence: sudden silence after a blow to the face (instead of a shout); water or taxi horn after hearing desert winds, to cite an extreme case.

These are tools that can either manipulate or confuse the listener unless woven into a shaped pattern (a good gestalt) that makes sense either emotionally, narratively, or poetically. In this sense, all the sound elements may be treated as music whose rhythm, meter, tonality, timbre, and emphasis may be constantly recomposed "orchestral" phrases that serve an emotional, narrative, or editorial purpose.

Aural Analogies

The mix function provides the chance to create a correspondence in some respects between otherwise unlike elements of sound-to-sound and sound-to-picture. The power of audio design is that it enables a logical **inference** based on the assumption that, if two things are known to be alike (a clock and a metronome) in some respects, then they must be alike in other respects!

Eisenstein, Hitchcock, and Mizoguchi have explored this area with some success, and their work is punctuated with various discordant attempts to **quell** a visual bias and **quench** an aural passion. Hitchcock knew of the power of silences as much as he understood the necessity of packing the "edge" of the cinematic frame with aural imagery. Like an old-fashioned matriach, he demonstrated that the heart could be reached via the stomach (low frequencies pumped into the theater during tense scenes in *Vertigo* created a sense of nausea and discomfort for some viewers).

Eisenstein converted the shot of the Imperial Globe in *Ivan the Terrible* into a resonating icon of mellifluous power with low bass notes that concurrently ring of menace.

The early silent masters appear to have had more of a sensitivity to the power of sound. In fact, very few, if any, silent movies were exhibited without some sort of sound accompaniment. The movies were hand-projected with the pacing (speed of projection) determined either through the craft of the projectionist or by a premeasured cue sheet that gave instructions to the technician. This melodic and sometimes dissonant orchestration of the drama and pacing is a kind of **personal choreography** (movement in time) that now resides with the craft of the mixer.

Through the same recomposing of musical/sound textures, the mixer may, more or less, "hand-project" a dramatic pacing and emotive intensity, focus, or detachment that was possible in the intrepretative, albeit spontaneous, sound accompaniment of the silents.

With the coming of sound, production takes a strange turn toward a strict illusion of space–time continuity, which tends to render the track inaudible to preserve the illusion. With meticulous attention, all elements are blended to **conceal** rather than expand or extend the cinematic experience. This paradox explains the low ebb of narrativity in most Hollywood **product,** which emphasizes **surface textures** above conceptual depth. Movies, after all, are entertainment! To be perfect, however, is to be less of a dramatist.

Visually, every shot can have a validity in and of itself, a single image/fact—an artifact of sorts, a sign that is also defined by what precedes and follows it. There is absolutely no reason why sonogenic image/facts should not stand alone in much the same way as signs, signifiers or artifacts with plastic potential.

The mix can make us involved in much more than the specific content of the shot. There can be an extended experience with referents outside the literal visual. There is an active/passive, conscious/unconscious, kinesthetic/passionate reality just like real life. Strangely, filmic approaches to realism serve a mimetic function; simulating, but hardly reflecting, the densities of reality (both physical and spiritual); and have particular difficulty dealing with the spiritual.

Sound Map of *Tucker*

The **sound map** (Figure 4–11) is a graphic representation of the flow of sound elements (dialogue, music, and effects) in a feature film. It is simplified to conform to a version of a sound mixer's log sheet. However, unlike the mixing log, the sound map is based on the perceived positions of auditory material, which are based on its interaction with image and the theater acoustics. The flow chart is meant to give a sense of the movement and pattern of the sound design relative to landmarks, major scenes, expository dialogue that reflects themes, and the general flow of the narrative.

TABLE 4–4   Legend

Dissolves	≈
Fades up	<
Fades down	>
Increases in intensity	∧
Decreases in intensity	∨
Severe cut	⧸

Tucker was directed by Francis Ford Coppola, the sound designer was Richard Beggs, and the music was composed and arranged by Joe Jackson, with additional music by Carmine Coppola. Tucker's sound track has a driving, bittersweet jazzy flow, interrupted often by silences that introduce tempo transitions from upbeat to downbeat. Music plays a strong role thematically, moving from contemplative, planning scenes reflected in keyboard and bass tones to action scenes in which ideas take shape in the form of the Tucker automobile. "Tiger Rag" and variations serve to promote this dominant theme of pragmatic optimism.

FIGURE 4-11 SOUND MAP of "TUCKER" (1988), Paramount

Landmarks	Narration	Theme Music	Instrumentals	Effects	Expository Dialogue	Silence
Newsreel	Mock ad →					→
Homestead		Bee-bop →	Honky-tonk →		Family →	
			Piano solo		"Intimacy" →	
			Sad keys		"Heart strings"	→
Armored Car		"Tiger		Car		
Test		Rag" →		Noise		
Chase		→				
Ice Cream	→		Dreamy		"plans"	
Homestead			upbeat →			

Location			
Factory	Big Beat drums	low drone	"Men at work"
Conference Room	Bass solo		
	Alto sax w/ bass beats		"Negligence"
		Rubber stamps	
Fed Bureau Office			
Split-field			
Telephone			Foreground/ background conversation
Kitchen	Bass + keys		
Uncle Abe's			
Check Junkyard	Upbeat tune	Rumble	"Work ethic"
Bennington's	Flute/strings	Blowtorch	
Plymouth Office	Bass + strings		
Senator	pizzicato		
Homestead	Gentle keys		

151

FIGURE 4–11 (Continued)

Landmarks	Narration	Theme Music	Instrumentals	Effects	Expository Dialogue	Silence
Quiet Boardroom	Radio jingle					
		Sinister				
Howard Hughes			Chords/chimes			
Test Track						
			Jazzy + xylophone		"Build a better	
			+ sax riffs		mousetrap"	
Homestead	Voice over		Dreamy bass + crickets			
	"Drew Pearson"		Sax			
			Solo piano blues			
Factory						
	"Tiger Rag"					
Chase	Crescendo			To police		
			Bass chords		"Horse sense"	
Courtroom						
Factory			Horns			
Courtroom			Bass chords			

152

Celebration	Box car jazz		Xylophone riff		Rousing toast	
Newsreel	Voice over	Brass band	Symphonics		Tucker's announcement	
		"Girls" interlude w/ trumpets				
					Personal triumph	
Conclusion: um-pah-pah waltz refrain, "Let the Rest of the World Go by"						
Publicity Tour	Jingle		Symphonic			
			"game show" atmospherics			
	Cool samba		Jazzy			
	Cold Lindy finale					

Sound Map of *Tucker* (1988), Paramount, directed by Francis Ford Coppola. The map is read like a mixer's cue sheet—horizontally to determine layering and vertically to assess transitions and continuity. Size of arrows indicates increase or decrease of intensity of sound element. Any sequence has an inherent rhythm unique unto itself. The role of the audio designer is to elaborate upon what is given and extend what cannot be visualized, in musico-acoustic terms. The breakdown of a shot can be orchestrated into unique patterns. An entire film can and should be designed with this ideal of rhythmic balance. *Tucker* provides an example of a rhythmic structure evident in each sequence and conforming to the whole.

Endnotes

1. Vlada Petric. "Toward a Theory of the Sync Sound Film," unpublished paper, 1980.
2. Petric.

References

BALAZS, BELA, "The Spirit of Film," as quoted in *Theory of Film*, edited and translated by Edith Bone, Dover, New York, 1970, 197 p.

HLYNKA, DENIS, "Eisenstein, Prokofiev, and the Visual Literacy Movement," unpublished research paper, University of Manitoba, 1977.

LEWIS, JOHN R., "J. T. Tykociner: A Forgotten Figure in the Development of Sound," *Journal of the University Film Associates* (Summer 1981), pp. 33–39.

MARCORELLES, LOUIS, *Living Cinema*, Praeger, New York, 1973.

MORITZ, WILLIAM, "The Films of Oskar Fischinger," *Film Culture* Nos. 58, 59, and 60 (1974), pp. 37–188.

NICHOLS, BILL, "Documentary Theory and Practice," *Screen* (Winter 1976/77), pp. 34–48.

PAINE, FRANK, "Sound Design–Walter Murch," *Journal of the University Film Associates* (Fall 1981), pp. 15–20.

ROGOFF, ROSALIND, "Edison's Dream: A Brief History of the Kinetophone," *Cinema Journal* (1976), pp. 58–68.

ROSENBAUM, JONATHAN, "Sound Thinking," *Film Comment* (Sept. 1978), pp. 38–40.

SPARSHOTT, F. E., "Vision and Dream in the Cinema," *Philosophical Exchange* (Summer 1971).

WEIS, ELIZABETH, "The Sound of One Wing Flapping," *Film comment* (Sept. 1978), pp. 42–48.

COLOR

5

A program for the color of sound is
suggested with formal references from
antiquity, which relate color to shape,
frequency, and emotions. The work of
Oskar Fischinger is examined in
relation to sound, color, and
movement.

Figure 5–1 Vasily Kandinsky's *Three Sounds*, 1926. (Courtesy the Solomon R. Guggenheim
Museum, New York. Photo by Robert E. Mates.)

Introduction

Sound is light moving at a slower speed. The energy is more like a pulse or electron cloud but is studied as a waveform. Your body is another electromagnetic cloud moving at a still slower speed. The cumulative average vibratory nature of each body can be measured, and we can arrive at a specific wavelength or series of wavelengths that make up the harmonious whole person. A particular sound wave may be resonant or not in relation to our body and, thus, we can account for our likes and dislikes in sound and music.[1]

The physicists of antiquity arranged matter into a hierarchy of waveform values, and it is no accident that our modern notion of good and bad "vibes" traces its meaning back to alchemy and natural magic. We have added very little to our understanding of sound since the early inquiries of Pythagoras. We are only recently learning to harness sound waves as a form of healing energy and therapy. It is not within the scope of this text to discuss the psychophysiological aspects of sound, but the audio designer, nevertheless, needs an understanding of the ways sound may affect the audience. The rationale for relating sound to color, light, and movement is based on the belief that there is a continuum of all vibrating matter, an atomistic viewpoint that sees each form as a part of the primary force, a force that has a design, even when it appears random and chaotic.

Since the birth of spectroscopy, most of what we know of the universe and nature has been revealed through color analysis. Wavelengths of all radiation producing visible light are functions of the distances between the atom's shells (electronic orbits) down to shell 2; 3 to 2 = red, 4 to 2 = blue, 5 to 2 = violet (second overtone), and so on in the spectroscopic array.

Even humans can be understood as a "living" vibratory mass with a fundamental resonant character made up of all its vibrating atomic parts. On that elemental subatomic level, there is harmony and sound pulses.

Pythagoras would have been pleased to know that his basic musical ratios reflect a common periodic pattern in nature. Physicist Hermann von Helmholtz compared the relation of the visible light occupying one octave in the long keyboard of the electromagnetic spectrum to color and musical notes:[2]

G	Ultraviolet
F, F♯	Violet

E	Indigo blue
D ♯	Cyanogen blue
D	Greenish blue
C ♯	Green
C	Yellow
A ♯	Orange-red
A, G ♯	Red
G	Infrared

Color of Music Forerunners

Some highlights in the use of color and sound follow:

- In 1915, at Carnegie Hall, Alexander Scriabin, composer, mystic, and color-composer gave a performance of *Prometheus, Le Poeme du Feu* designed for colored light shows using Rimington's color organ (clavier á lumieres).
- In 1720, Louis Bertrand Castel, a Jesuit, devised a *clavessin oculaire* using prisms and translucent tapes and natural daylight through a window.
- In 1943, Leopold Stokowski's adaptation of Bach's "Toccata and Fugue in D minor" was initially conceptualized by Oskar Fischinger as a free association of colors, forms, and music.
- 1000 years before, the Hindu ragas embraced each note as a color and a feeling (mode, rhythm, intonation, and character phrases); each association becomes a color mood in time for playing.

We cannot see the mixed tones of a color, but we can hear the mixed tones of a sound. The relationship of light and sound waves has long been an area of experimentation for artists.

> *The sound of colours is so definite that it would be hard to find anyone who would express bright yellow with bass notes, or a dark lake in the treble; Wassily Kandinsky,* Art of Spiritual harmony.

Shortly after the turn of the century, American painting was seized with a new passion, perhaps born in the European "Blauer Reiter" movement, but undoubtedly bred in the States. The movement opposed the realist tendencies brought on by the advent of new camera technologies. In substance, it dictated that color and its essence, light, were the formal basis for truthful painterly expression. Morgan Russell was a chief innovator and Stanton Macdonald-Wright its theorist; its foster parents were Sondra and Robert Delaunay of Paris.

From 1910 until its dissolution during the war, **synchronism** preoccupied

American and European thought with its concern for the spiritual and rhythmic expressiveness of color and form. Early pioneers in film adopted the esthetic. Fischinger in Germany and Eisenstein in Russia began innovative experimentation with color and sound.

By 1919, a full-blown "school" had been established de facto, principally through the teaching of Macdonald-Wright and the earlier work of Tudor-Hart, who structured an entire array of tonal modalities relating the 12 chromatic intervals of a color spectrum fathered by Chevreul and the 12-note octave range of traditional musical notation. He stated that **pitch** relates to **luminosity, tone** relates to **hue,** and **intensity** relates to **saturation.** From this fundamental palette, the painter of light might fashion a "synchronism" of color rhythms. In reference to the theories of Macdonald-Wright and Russell, one might sacrifice the fact in figurative painting and allied arts and keep the music (See Figure 5–2).

Color becomes the subject, its reasonating relationships with pictorial space, the object. Light is conceived as projection and depth, and its mandate became the construction of a kinetic light machine. Fanciful or otherwise, the movement found a brief but lively flourish in the work of many filmmakers who began creating a kind of emotional chart of light/emotions, painting directly on film with elemental components of light, shape, color, all of which implied movements in relation to a strict musical code but exhibited without sound.

The camera ceased to be the **kino** eye and quickly became the brush with which to express a vigorously constructed emotional statement. For whatever reasons, despite the grand edifice of Kandinski's *Art of Spiritual Harmony*, the seminal manifesto of synchronism, the interest in the narrative potential of color and sound disappeared, not to be considered again for 50 years.

Of the various commercial color theories, that of Rood, who conceived of a color wheel whose triads of hue at 120 degrees to each other provide for the audio designer a model of harmony, and that of Maratta documented in the *Scientific American*, Supplement 68, November 1909, survive (see Figure 5–3).

The first attempt at a holistic theory of color was formulated by Goethe, who related his study of optics to the perception of values from vibration theory in music (see Figure 5–4). He arrived at a conjunction of values and masses

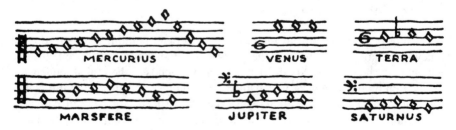

Figure 5–2 Frequency relationships: Music of the Planets. (From *The Rainbow Book*, F. L. Graham, ed., Shambhala Publications, Boston, 1979.)

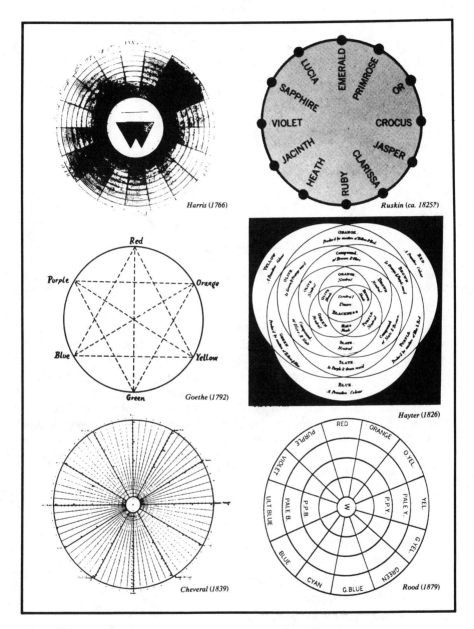

Figure 5–3   Classic color systems. (From *The Rainbow Book*, F. L. Graham, ed., Shambhala Publications, Boston, 1979.)

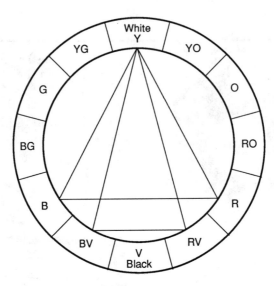

Figure 5–4 Goethe's color wheel. (From *The Rainbow Book*, F. L. Graham, ed., Shambhala Publications, Boston, 1979.)

and shapes. An order of harmonics between color and elemental musical notes based on wavelength can be expressed on a revised electromagnetic scale as a reference for the designer. Relationships may be programmed between sound and color (considered as frequencies that can be arranged in a musical hierarchy of lesser and greater orders to achieve an explicit emotional response).

Ten functional contrasts emerge from a melding of color theory and musicology. These pairings provide examples for possible audio design programs that could utilize MIDI gear in relation to (for instance) the color pixels of the video monitor, which, linked to video animation components, allows painting with light and sound directly on tape.

Examples

Tonal harmonies versus color complementaries
Rhythm versus pitch
Amplitude versus duration
Light sources versus sound sources
Shape versus amplitude
Light and dark versus movement
Depth versus frequency
Off-screen space versus hue
Orchestral mood versus chroma (color intensity)
Projection/recession versus tonal arrangement

Program for the Color of Sound

A preliminary structuring of sound–color vibratory relationships requires discrimination between light and pigment. A color may be:

Cold   = degree of white or black
Warm   = degree of white or black
Light   = brilliance, tonal gradation, resonance
Dark   = brilliance, tonal gradation, resonance
Dull   = quality, chroma (purity versus mixed hues)
Intense = quality, chroma

The emotionally expressive power of color cannot be overestimated. The control factors are based on the subjectively conditioned color perceptions born of nature and culture. Color esthetics may be evaluated from three positions:

1. Impression (visually)
2. Expression (emotionally)
3. Construction (symbolically)

How we perceive the effect of color depends on several factors:

- Presence or absence of other colors in the field
- Choice and juxtaposition of hues in a field
- Size and orientation of color fields (shape, contour, blurs)
- Fundamental contrasts present (pure hue versus mixtures)

Each viewer has subjective color modalities that can be focused through the juxtaposition of sound (see Table 5–1). For the composer the fundamental contrasts are:

- Contrast of hue: modulations of wavelength
- Light and dark: modulations of shading
- Cold/warm: degree of retinal stimulation in contrast to other colors
- Complementary contrast: for each hue the sum of all others is the complementary
- Simultaneous contrast: complementary generated in the eye if not present
- Contrast of saturation: pure intense color versus dull, diluted color
- Contrast of extension: harmony relative to size of field of each hue

TABLE 5-1 Cycles of Experience

Color	Properties of color	Interval	Properties of Interval (Helmholtz)	Properties of Interval (Hindu)	Related Chord	Related Planet	Properties of Planet	Signs Ruled By Planet	Planet (Alternate)
Red	Birth, beginning, heat, heart, primal matter, violent change	Unison Do (C)	Strong, firm	Home, tonic, primal sound from which all sounds derive	Major	Mars	Passion, desire, energy, initiative, violent change, war	Aries Scorpio	Mars
Orange	Power, glory, radiant energy, sun, the kiss of life	Whole tone Re (D)	Rousing, hopeful	Assertive, forceful, brilliant	Minor	Sun "Apollo"	Life, vitality, illumination, will, leadership	Leo	Venus
Yellow	Intellect, joy, sensation, brightness	Major third Mi (E)	Steady, calm	Pleasing, calm, contented	Minor	Mercury "Winged Messenger"	Intelligence, logic, mental activity, communication, speed	Gemini Virgo	Mercury
Green	Growth, youth, healing, vegetation	Fifth So (G)	Grand, bright	Active, brilliant	Major	Jupiter "Jovial"	Enthusiasm, good fortune, optimism, spontaneity	Sagittarius Pisces	Jupiter
Blue	Spirit, sky, heaven, prayer, psychic	Fourth Fa (F)	Awe-inspiring, desolate	Sadness, yearning	Major	Saturn "Satan"	Limitation, caution, crystallization, time (chronos)	Aquarius Capricorn	Saturn
Indigo	Intuition, seeking, sorrow, beauty, spirituality	Major sixth La (A)	Sad, weeping	Soft, calm tender	Minor	Venus	Beauty, harmony, love, the arts	Libra Taurus	Uranus
Violet	Transition, death, separation, yearning, advanced spirituality	Major seventh Ti (B)	Piercing, sensitive, leading	Soft, voluptuous, sensual	Diminished	Moon "Diana"	Instinct, feeling, subconscious, receptivity	Cancer	Neptune

Goethe determined a relative weighted value for each color in terms of how much of each is required to achieve balance or harmony in a given space. Goethe's values are as follows:

Yellow	Orange	Red	Violet	Blue	Green
9	8	6	3	4	6

The proportionalities for complementary pairs are as follows:

Yellow : Violet		Orange : Blue		Red : Green	
9	3	8	4	6	6

Harmonic areas yield static, quiet effects. When the harmonious proportions are used, contrast is neutralized.

Color harmony and variations: Discover the strongest effects by correct choice of antithesis (color chords may be formed of two, three, four, or more tones)

Dyads: Any two tones symmetrical with respect to the center of a color sphere spectrum can be combined (tint of red plus shade of green).

Triads: If the positions of three hues in the circle can form an equilateral triangle, those hues form a harmonious triad (yellow plus red plus blue).

Tetrads: Two pairs of complementaries whose connecting diameters are perpendicular to each other form a square, rectangle, or trapezoid and can be combined (yellow-violet, red-orange, blue-green).

Hexads: Three pairs of complementary colors inscribe a hexagon in the circle. There are two such hexads in the 12-hue circle (yellow, violet, orange, blue, green, red).

Johannes Itten and others believed that each color has a shape best suited to it. This is as rational as the notion that each shot has a sonic perspective best suited for it as well as a most suitable focal length (perspective) (See Figure 5–5).

Fundamental Shapes in Relation to Hue

Color theorist Johannes Itten prescribed the spatial effects of colors:

A pure color advances relative to a duller one of equal brilliance. But if dark/ light or cold/warm contrast is also present, the depth relationship shifts accordingly.

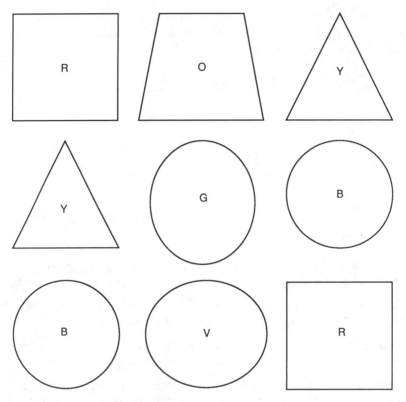

Figure 5–5 Itten, while teaching at the Bauhaus, developed a program relating color to shape. Every contour has a color best suited to its shape and volume.

The background is as essential to depth perception as the applied color. Extension is another factor. When a large red area bears a small yellow patch, red acts as background and yellow advances; as yellow is extended, it reaches a point where it dominates and becomes a background.

- Any light tone on a black ground will advance.
- A warm tone of equal brilliance will advance while cold tones retreat.
- Dark tones on white advance.
- Location affects apparent depth (position of color in field.)

Luminous and Merry: Oskar Fischinger and Synchronism

Pioneer artist and animator Oskar Fischinger was a central figure in the marriage of American synchronist painting, with its emphasis on color and contour, and the early cinema, with its emphasis on manipulation of light, time, and movement. He provided the foundation for some of the most sophisticated sequences

TABLE 5–2 Music of the Spheres

Red	Do	Mars
Orange	Re	Sun
Yellow	Mi	Mercury
Green	Fa	Saturn
Blue	Sol	Jupiter
Indigo	La	Venus
Violet	Ti	Moon

Edgar Cayce related colors, notes, and planets as shown in this table.

Color	Note	Sign
Red	C	Aries
Red-orange	C$\sharp$	Taurus
Orange	D	Gemini
Yellow-orange	E$\flat$	Cancer
Yellow	E	Leo
Yellow-green	F	Virgo
Green	F$\sharp$	Libra
Blue-green	G	Scorpio
Sky blue	A$\flat$	Sagittarius
Dark blue	A	Capricorn
Indigo	B$\flat$	Aquarius
Violet	B	Pisces

in Disney's *Fantasia* and continued to experiment with the abstract dialectic of sound and color in his films. (An analysis of some of his more important works relevant to the audio designer are presented in the next section.)

Between the great World Wars, there occurred first in Russia with the work of painter Wassily Kandinsky and filmmaker Sergei Eisenstein and then in Germany with the work of Oskar Fischinger (see Figure 5–6) a flourishing of the spiritual and substantative foundations of audio design. The interruption of World War II laid the movement to rest, but only temporarily; it was rediscovered 50 years later by a new generation of artists seeking a new idiom for emerging technologies and to avoid rampant commercialism devoid of creative boundaries.

Visual music and audio design have revived interest in the relationships of light, color, and sound. Every person with a PC can become an instant composer of sound and graphics (see Figure 5–7); this modern *sonogenic* is but an updating of the formative idea of the color (sound) organ first introduced by Laszlo and others at the turn of the century.

Wassily Kandinsky had written about the formal relationships among light,

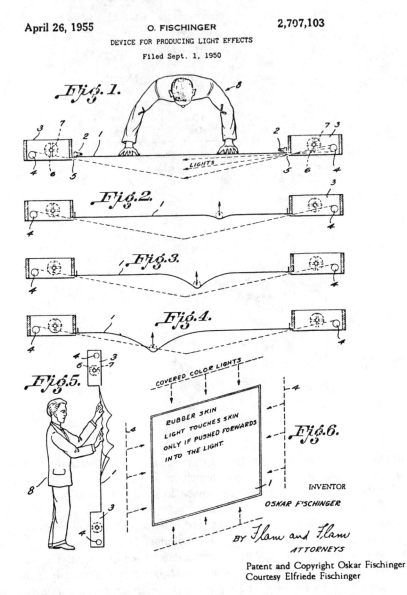

Figure 5–6 The Lumigraph. Fischinger had related physical movement to light and color.
First using neon light sources and then incandescent, the lumigraph was the forerunner of all
light shows, and suggests the kinetic relationship of sound, color, and movement.

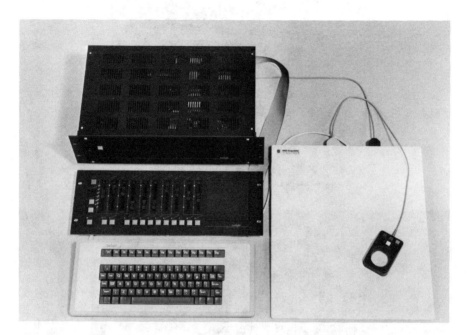

Figure 5–7 The Fairlight CVI. A digital "light organ" that marries electronic light and color to sound through the programmability of the computer.

color, and music. In his 1923 treatise, *Point and Line to Plane*, he begins to illustrate how music may be translated into points. These "tonal" points formed the basis of a new abstract expressionist codification, a painterly time code, as it were, that could be encoded in the experience of the viewer back into music while viewing the canvas. Kandinsky's oil on canvas, *Several Circles* (1926), is a virtual freeze frame of color/shape equivalents of sound mirroring precisely the early motion studies and films of Oscar Fischinger, specifically *Kreise* (*Circles*) (1933) (See Figures 5–8 (a), (b), (c))

Kandinsky's system of "sounds" invoked the power of angles and lines to convey movement and tonality. Color provided the textural timbre, the musicality as it were, of his compositions. And, indeed, in his *Three Sounds* (1926), **geometric elements,** patterns, and color give rise to a lively association of sight to sound.

As a teacher at the Bauhaus, his ideas were taken one step further by his students, notably Heinrich Bormann, whose *Tonal Color and Music Evaluation* (see Figure 5–9) (1930) illustrates a systematized approach to organizing a pallette of sound and color. (see Table 5–3)

Although the earliest public exhibition of the abstract relationships between sound and image on film was made by Walter Ruttmann in 1921, it was Oskar

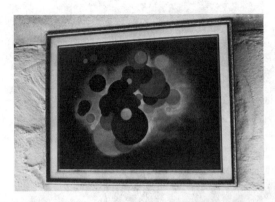

Figure 5–8(a)   Fischinger's *Optical Poetry* (1941), oil on paper. (Courtesy of the Tobey C. Moss Gallery, Los Angeles. Photo by John Thomson, Los Angeles.) **(b)** Vassily Kandinsky, *Several Circles* (1926). (Courtesy the Solomon R. Guggenheim Museum, New York. Photo by Robert E. Mates.) **(c)** Fischinger's *Circles* (1933). (Courtesy Elfriede Fischinger and William Moritz.)

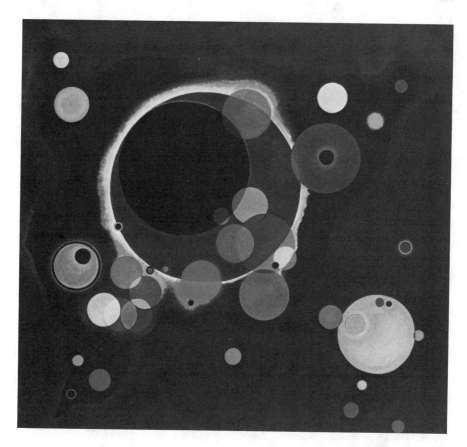

Fischinger who seized the fire and lit the way for further development of a true aural mise-en-scène, a formal logic and technique sustained for a period extending from 1923 to his death in 1967.

Fischinger's pioneering efforts in the synthesis of light, color, shape, sound, and movement were marked by a preoccupation with changing moods, a "flow of emotion," an intensity, style, and flourish of ideas that provided sensory experiences created by the process of the action (of filmmaking). For audio designers, his early works set the standard for **passion** and **virtuosity.**

The Wizard of Friedrichstrasse

Perhaps Fischinger's most significant discovery, one that was the outcome of his study of Far Eastern religions and philosophy, was that all objects contain an inherent sound. This elemental understanding of the relationship of matter to energy, of the electromagnetic spectrum and the relationships among light, sound, and color is at the center of his work and his life.

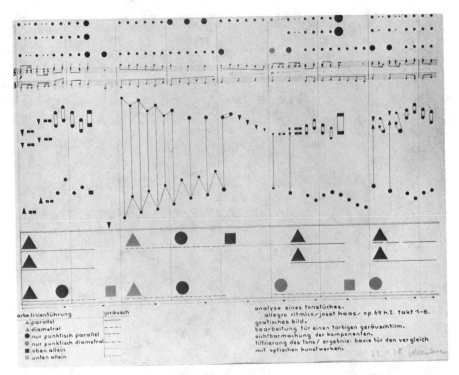

Figure 5–9 Heinrich Bormann's "Tonal Color and Music Evaluation" (1930), a Bauhaus exercise in the relationships of music, color, form, and tonal intensity. The gray dots are deep yellow; the darker triangles are blue; the darker circles are red. This colored "sound film" is a response to eight measures of a piece of music by Josef Hass. (Courtesy of Barry Friedman Gallery, New York.)

His early experiments included the photographing of objects directly onto a film sound track in order that shape "could be released to speak"—the contour of light and dark produces sound waves from the optical negative.

His influence will be felt more now that technologies are accessible even to the nonmusical to create a wealth of complex and rich tonal shaping. While Hollywood struggled to make sound a viable commodity in the marketplace, fostered by industrial giants (RCA, ATT) and ushered into a shotgun marriage with a new generation of stars who could speak, Fischinger was busy inventing a vast technical vocabulary, interpreting tonal colors and synthesizing sonic patterns.

He had set the young John Cage to work on *An Optical Poem* (1937, bought by MGM) to find musical resources in natural sounds, chance noises, and silence. He had distilled from the ideals of Plato and Einstein, and Tibetan painters and Hopi shamen, the magical and "absolute landscape of geometric color (energy) fields, organic auroras and mathematical trajectories."

He had created the physical experience of space travel and bodily trans-

TABLE 5–3 Frequency Relationship (in cps)

Frequency ($\times 10^{12}$)	Color	Frequency Down 40 Octaves	Frequency (chromatic)	Note
430	Very dark red	391.3	392	G
440	Dark red	400.4		
450	Dark red	409.5		
460	Darkish red	418.6		
470	Red	427.7	415	G♯
480	Red-orange	436.8		
490	Orangish red	445.9		
500	Reddish orange	455.0	440	A
510	Light orange	464.1		
520	Yellow	473.2		
530	Greenish yellow	482.3	466	A♯
540	Yellow green	491.4		
550	Yellow green	500.5		
560	Light green	509.6	494	B
570	Green	518.7		
580	Green	527.8		
590	Green	536.9		
600	Bluish green	546.0	523	C
610	Blue green	555.1		
620	Sky blue	564.1		
630	Bluish indigo	573.2	553	C♯
640	Indigo	582.3		
650	Indigo	591.4		
660	Indigo	600.5	587	D
670	Indigo violet	609.6		
680	Indigo violet	618.7		
690	Light violet	627.8		
700	Violet	636.9	622	D♯
710	Violet	646.0		
720	Dark violet	655.1		
730	Dark violet	664.2	659	E
740	Dark violet	673.3		
750	Very dark violet	682.4		
			698	F

From *The Rainbow Book*, F. Graham Lanier ed., Shambhala Publications, Boston, 1979.

migration on film decades before the ''trip'' became a hallucinatory by-product of the American psycho/sexual cultural revolution of the 1960s.

In works like *Study #7* (1930), the expression of ''fluent kinethesia'' provided physical filmic proof of the Russian ideals extolled by Ziga Vertov and Lev Kuleshov. ''Pulsating, urgent rhythms of fast czardas melody are represented visually by sharp, razor thin blades that seem to penetrate a deep space.''[3] (See Figure 5–10(a)).

Prefiguring the New Age composers and synthesized music, he demon-

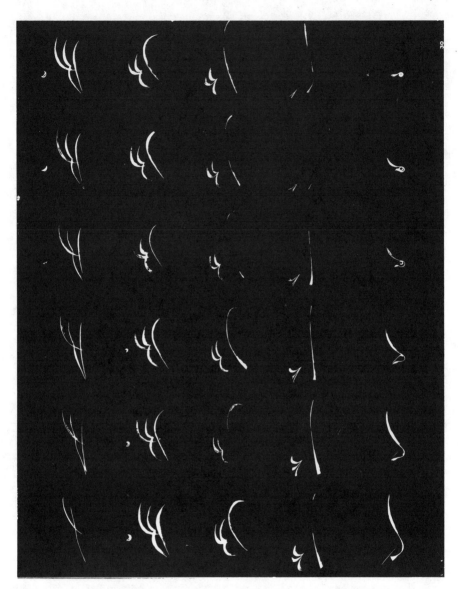

Figure 5–10(a)   Fischinger's *Study #7* (1930). (Frame study courtesy of Elfriede Fischinger and William Moritz.) Fischinger merged musical cadence with the expressive coordinates of light, color, contour, and movement, an internalized coordination of sight and sound that goes far beyond the mere setting of visuals to music. The body of his work demonstrates the indispensability of each—each element interacting to create a truly "extended" experience. (With kind permission of Elfriede Fischinger and the Fischinger Archive, Hollywood. Photos by William Moritz.)

Figure 5–10(b)   Refrain from "The Venusberg Ballet of Richard Wagner's *Tannhauser.*

strated that music made possible the application of acoustic laws to optical expression on film—new motions and rhythms sprang out of the music into the film. Study #7, visually similar to the early work of Leopold Sauvage, exhibits in time "smooth, languorous chords of slow gypsy violins (which) seem to nestle against the flat surface of the screen, curling in sinuous *Art Nouveau* tendrils and soft diamond-shaped enclosures."

With *Allegretto* (1936), commissioned by Paramount, Fischinger distilled symphonic (jazz) textures into precise visual equivalents, accomplished through his first attempt at multilayered cel animation (5 layers, 100 cels per second), in which forms and colors (California pastels) suggest and define melody, harmony, and tonal colors of instruments, setting the parameters for the audiovisual idiom that was to influence the outcome of his initial developmental work on the "Toccata and Fugue" section of Disney's *Fantasia* (1939).

Fischinger demonstrated to Disney how the visual equivalent of the weaving of several themes (Bach's D minor fugue) could be accomplished, but the sophistication was deemed too inaccessible to the Disney "family audience." But Fischinger's impact was obvious in the final version (after he left the studio in frustration) of the moving patterns and wave action sequence of *Fantasia*. His ideas of rhythmic design, of patterns and tones arranged in counterpoint, delicate, exquisite relationships between planes and plastic movement, profoundly affected the work esthetic of a generation of postwar talents (John Whitney, Harry Smith, Jordan Belson).

Fischinger's first color film *Kreise* (1933) was also a pioneer effort in Europe to standardize a new color process, the three-strip **Gasparcolor** system: vibrantly colored circles moving in synchronization to Wagner's *Tannhauser.*

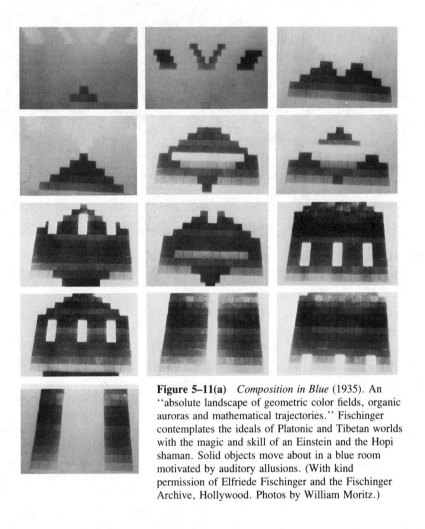

Figure 5–11(a) *Composition in Blue* (1935). An "absolute landscape of geometric color fields, organic auroras and mathematical trajectories." Fischinger contemplates the ideals of Platonic and Tibetan worlds with the magic and skill of an Einstein and the Hopi shaman. Solid objects move about in a blue room motivated by auditory allusions. (With kind permission of Elfriede Fischinger and the Fischinger Archive, Hollywood. Photos by William Moritz.)

Figure 5–11(b) Refrain from "Huldigung's March" from *Sigurd Jorsalfar* by Edvard Grieg.

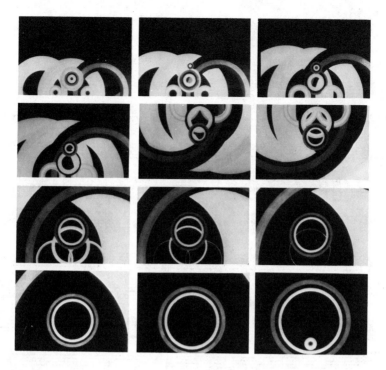

Figure 5–12(a) *Kreise* (*Circles*), 1933. Fischinger produced the first color-on-film movie in Europe using the Gasparcolor YCM three-color separation black and white negative process. The sequence clearly relates the movement and contrasts of color to the frequencies and intensity of the "auditory abstract space—time art: music." (Courtesy of Elfriede Fischinger and William Moritz.)

Figure 5–12b Sample cadence from Johannes Brahm's *Hungarian Dance No. 5*. Sensuous gypsy violins, smooth and langorous, play against the soft but solid shapes that "seem to nestle against the flat surface of the screen curling in sinuous Art Nouveau tendrils. . . ." Fischinger here explores the relationships of sound to images and movement in deep (dark) space. Thousands of black and white charcoal drawings were used.

Figure 5–13 Overture fragment from Otto Nicolai's *The Merry Wives of Windsor*. The symphonic structures of the ''Merry Wives of Windsor Overture'' serve to propel the startlingly swift flow of mosaic squares across a field. It is a study of color, movement, and mood. Beyond the comic facade lies a serious contemplation upon the yin–yang polarity principle.

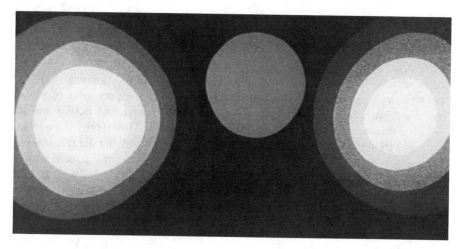

Figure 5–14 *Radio Dynamics* (1943). A silent film invoking sound. The film has the structure of yoga, a series of exercises for the eyes; mystic rhythms, the eye follows sound. Changing colors, sizes, and speed create kinesthetic allusion to the theory of relativity. A meditation on synthetic sound and the rhythms and pulsations that create and are caused by light and sound. (With kind permission of Elfriede Fischinger and the Fischinger Archive, Hollywood. Photos by William Moritz.)

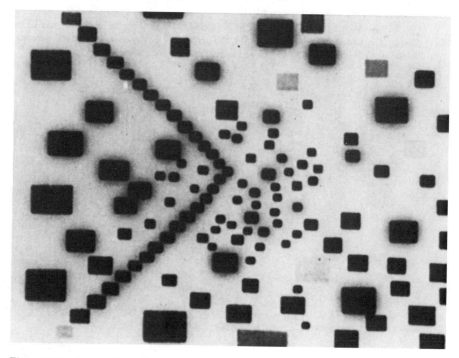

Figure 5–15 *Stereo Film* (1952). Three-dimensional pictures in parallel, eye-information panels, different colored brushstrokes; rectangles appear one by one, fill the frame, hang in space; one series forms a perfect V-shaped alignment with the point at a great distance and the arms coming forward in perfect perspective up to quite close to the viewer.

Black and white images were tinted with filters during the printing process; the second half uses painted poster colors on white paper photographed by the three-color separation process. Fischinger's passion for the philosophical basis of color theory again asserted itself in his association of the principles of **yin** to the color **blue** and **emotion (passive),** and **yang** to **red** and **active** and all possible themes and variations therein (See Figures 5–11(a)–(c)).

In Fischinger's work there is a marked affinity for drawing the relationship between movement, light, color, and the frequency patterns of the melodic line (see Table 5–3). More than the first "visual music," Fischinger's significant contributions were the first to demonstrate that sound could markedly affect the perception of abstract imagery presented in two planes, but transformed into a three-dimensional experience in time (See Figures 5–12(a),(b) through 5–15).

Endnotes

1. Particle physics defines all matter as a form of electron cloud, resonating about an averaged midpoint, with a positive or negative valence; thus the notion of "good vibes."

2. Evans and Valens, "Harmony and Harmonies" in *The Rainbow Book*, F. Graham Lanier (ed.), Shambhala Publications, Boston, p. 113.

3. William Moritz, "The Private World of Oskar Fischinger," notes for the Pioneer Laser Disc Album, The Visual Pathfinders Series. Fischinger's work is shown as the natural outcome of a lifelong devotion to utilitarian design and a Buddhist-inspired world view.

DOCUMENTARY SOUND

Nonfiction film and video have
unique structures utilizing raw,
unprocessed sound as well as
traditional track construction. Voice
tracks in cinema verité are referenced,
as is an example of mock
documentary and the simulation of
reality. Theories of the sound film and
a list of films for study are
appendixed. Stereo two-track
recording technique is outlined.

Figure 6–1 *Battle of Algiers* (1965). Acoustic waves. All distinction between the "aural object" as recorded and the "acoustic shadow" as created is down-faded. Director Pontecorvo opts for the ideological truth of the event, not the newsreel sound bite, but something similar, a kind of aural biopsy that hopes to reveal the emotional meaning of the whole pattern of events.

Nonfiction Use of Sound

Acoustic environment, the acoustic landscape in which we live, the speech of things, and the intimate whisperings of nature; all that has speech beyond human speech, and speaks to us with the vast conversational power of life and incessantly influences and directs our thought and emotions, from the muttering of the sea to the din of a great city, from the roar of machinery to the gentle patter of autumn rain on the windowpane. The meaning of a floorboard cracking in a deserted room, a bullet whistling past our ear, the death-watch beetle ticking in old furniture and the forest spring tinkling over the stone. Sensitive lyrical poets could always hear these significant sounds of life and describe them in words. It is for the sound film to let them speak to us more directly from the screen. . . . Bela Balazs in "The Spirit of Film," as quoted in **Theory of Film,** *Edith Bone (ed.) Dover, New York, 1970, p. 197.*

The effort to record **reality** is as fraudulent as the effort to create reality. The image on the screen has a life of itself. Is it real or is it . . . Memorex?

Sound in the documentary tradition has always been taken for granted. The work of the documentarian has always been to define what is to be documented and then to define what is to be communicated. Sound was never an emotive issue. When notions of objectivity are discussed, the journalist mentality tends to accept reportage as truth, the camera as an objective recording device, and the sound it captures as a passive concomitant. Voice-over and narration rule the aural world of nonfiction film and video. There has been the pretense of actuality, but no esthetic of documentary sound.

Simply pointing the camera lens involves a series of choices. This choice obviates the possibility of objectivity. Focus, composition, and light further taint the "object" of record.

The two elements that make any media experience read as document (nonfiction) are authenticity and sponteneity. Raw, synchronously recorded sound (dialogue and/or background) conveys process, the spontaneous freezing of life; but it is only a semblance of reality because it requires the sense memory of the viewer to **verify** the look and sound of real life.

In an effort to enhance the sense of spontaneity, producers tend to process the raw sound, taking poetic license to add narration and often musical elements to clarify. This naturalist approach is not meant to be an embellishment, but rather a clean-up job to make the track easier to hear. However, carried to the extreme, must PBS-dubbed BBC nature shows sound like solemn eulogies?

If clarity is the only issue, the process of selection and arrangement so integral to the documentary message is of little import. **Truth** seems to imply **accuracy.** Eliminating distractions may be an aid to clarity and ultimately to accuracy, but it is nevertheless tampering with image/facts. Furthermore, in editing the duration of shots, any option other than real-time events presents a serious burden to the notion and goal of authenticity. A rational approach is normally taken, a middle ground between a personalized history and clinical record.

The temptation to heighten reality, to editorialize diminishes the validity of most nonfiction work, relegating it to fact-based fiction. Better to concentrate on the drama of the subject than the posture of journalism.

Basic Technique

Always use a very directional microphone. Isolate the most important sound and try a live mix in the field that augments the naturally occurring emotions of the moment. Background sound is very critical to felt spontaneity. When possible, use a stereo recording system with background on one track and principal data on the other track (see Figure 6–2).

The following discussion is a simplified technique for recording documentary in a two-track format as recommended by Manfred Klemme (formerly of Nagra Magnetic).

Figure 6–2 Cassette recorders can be made to run synchronously with the addition of a crystal oscillator pack. The Sony Pro Walkman can be "piggybacked" with most cameras.

Stereo Two-Track Field Recording

Two-track provides greater flexibility on location while offering extra information for the postproduction process. Let track 1 be the upper track or L and let track 2 be the lower track or R.

Dialogue and ambience

Production dialogue mix
Time code signal
Background ambience

The dialogue mix is recorded on track 1 but has some of the background data mixed in (see Figure 6–3). Track 2 (using a different microphone) has background noise only. This becomes a master production track. Singles or close-ups are shot in such a way as to exclude the background.

Two dialogue tracks

Actor A
Time code
Actor B

Each actor is given a separate track (Figure 6–4) by using separate microphones (wireless, for instance). When the visual is a close-up of actor A, track 1 carries the usual close-up sound of actor A; track 2 carries the close-up sound of actor B. On actor B's close-up, the recording will remain as in Figure 6–4, actor A on 1 and actor B on 2.

The following elements are then available to the postproduction process:

- Sync sound of the background sound recorded with the master
- Sync dialogue of the master
- Sync dialogue of each actor's close-up
- "Wild lines" recorded off camera at the time of shooting the preceding items

This may reduce the amount of dialogue replacement necessary.

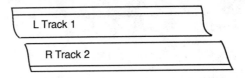

Figure 6–3 Dialogue and ambience tracks.

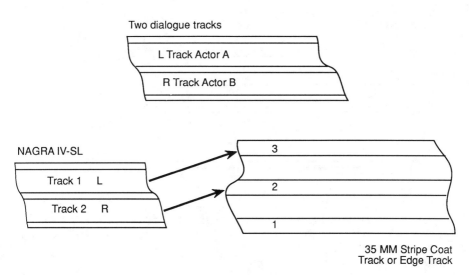

Figure 6–4   Two dialogue tracks.

Techniques with Two recorders (Stereo and Mono)

We can provide actor A with his own track (1), actor B with her own track (2), and the sync ambience/effects with its own track (M) (see Figure 6–5). With wireless microphones it is not uncommon to encounter radio-frequency interference, clothing noise, and drop-outs. Since these noise elements often come on only one microphone (usually from the actor who is not talking), this technique provides backup data.

Intereference does not manage to coincide with dialogue in the two-track system, unlike mono. Clips from an ambience or room tone track may be used to fill in the gaps of noise on the stereo production track.

Postproduction

Typical transfer is from two-track ¼-inch to three-track (see Figure 6–6) 35mm stripe or full-coat magnetic film on a sprocketed master. "R" track 2 transfers to track 2 on the three stripe. Tracks 2 and 3 of the three-stripe contain unmodified standard transfers. Track 1 (three stripe) is recorded as **transfer mix.**

If fully modulated tracks 1 and 2 from the Nagra IV-SL are mixed equally and transferred, the result will be an unacceptable 35mm track 1 due to imbalances. The production mixer should order special mix ratios, for instance track 1 at 0 dB and track 2 at -6dB, or eliminate the ambience on the edge completely. An option is to prepare a precise log with instructions to drop out the sections on each track that have noise and instructions to reduce the level in certain sections of ambience.

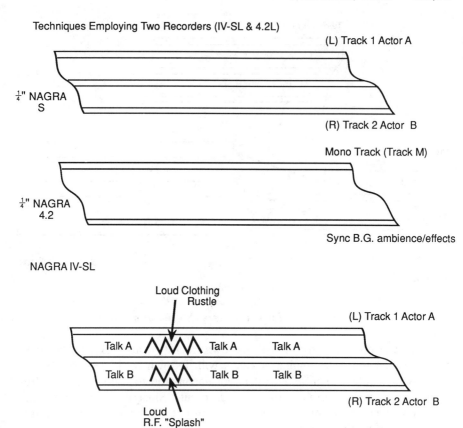

Figure 6–5   Dual-track recording; Nagra IV-SL track.

Structure of the Sound Documentary

The documentary is an argument. Either its perspective is a window on the world or a reflection of the surfaces of reality. It generates meaning by the "succession of choices and the continuous selection of pertinent features,"[1] in an effort to project reality and possess truth. Whether as reportage or reflection, documentary provides a formal organization (patterns of sound/image relationships that specify somewhat different places or attitudes for the viewer). The viewer is addressed by:

> characters (social actors in social role playing), or
>
> narrator (who represents the point of view of the director or producer.

For the sound designer, the modes of address provide a clue to content and its appropriate relation to the kinds of auditory material:

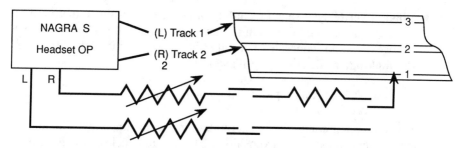

This can be made up to sit under the NAGRA-S

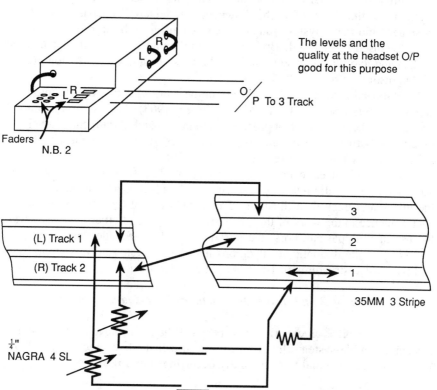

Figure 6–6 Postproduction use; track mix is on a three-stripe magnetic tape.

- Sync sound (narration) provides a "voice of authority"
- Nonsync sound (narration) acts as a "voice of God" or serves an illustrative role
- Sync sound (character) yields the "interview" and authenticity
- Nonsync sound (character) yields a sense of the "witness," less intimate and spontaneous but equally illustrative.

- **Cinema verité** sync-sound recording of characters results in the voice of a "social actor" and differs in presentation from all other modes in that "process" is not concealed but rather is integral to the feel of **truth in the making,** while still being illustrative.

Voice Tracks in Cinema Verité

Spatiotemporal continuity is intermittent in the documentary. The logical ordering of facts supports the exposition of the argument. Logic is not filmic but journalistic. Social actors begin as real people who contribute to the exposition. In the work of Richard Leacock and Don Pennebaker, Frederick Wiseman, and the Maysles brothers, the relationship of background to voice is never cleansed or clarified. Both camera and sound systems attempt intimate contact and avoid detachment. Audio is bothersome and exerts the low fidelity of "ambisonic"[2] real life.

A second formal strategy appears in the work of Emile de Antonio (*Milhouse, A White Comedy*, 1971; *Point of Order*, 1963). The use of a narrator is avoided and the overt sense of process is de-emphasized. Argument is developed by editing between the comments of characters. The viewer must make the effort to follow the line of reason.

The classical expository documentary of Pare Lorentz formalizes each sequence with narration, setting in place a block of factual argumentation, which the image and track then illustrate. This formal use of the narrator as well as shot sequence in the work of the "Newsreel Group" and others, moves toward the use of multiple narrators, the introduction of the female voice, and a rediscovery of the dramatic vocalizations first demonstrated in Movietone News and the classic structures of Basil Wright's *Night Mail.*[3]

States of Being in the Documentary Sync-sound Program

Sync-sound as an experience is special. Whether achieved through single-system or double-system film or video, the so-called "live" recorded track has the semblance of actuality or naturally occurring sound if and only if:

- The microphone is not very directional and has a flat response, especially for the range of speech (2 to 4kHz).
- The microphone is used on axis.
- The position of the microphone corresponds to the real or implied field of view of the **audience.**

If sync-sound conforms to this regime, then the details of sound as perceived in real life carry over to second-hand experience in the theater and in front of televisions which exhibits the following:

- The size of the window (field of view) of the spectator determines the **density of detail** absorbed and absorbable from the multilayered free-field sound source.
- The sound field is never discontinuous but rather, always "on," regardless of perspective.
- Changes in sound pressure level cause aural compensation by the hearing apparatus of the ear.
- SPL is a function of cumulative layering of nondirectional, naturally occurring sound waves, producing a homogeneous wall of sound in which nothing dominates.
- The introduction of extraneous sound into the window at a level above that of the sonorous wall, the threshold of environmental sound (6 to 9 decibels above), produces sensory **localization** (perspective, focus, on- and off-screen space).

Audio Animatronics

This is a technology in which acoustics is married to robotics resulting in the simulation of live action events with people and/or animals. Animatronics synchronizes audio with movement while duplicating apparently accurate sound localization and propagation parameters. The process involves precise duplication and repeatability of completely natural action. Careful observation of reality provides a basis for determining naturalistic rhythms and complex gestures of hand, eye, mouth, and so on, that form a pattern of sensory-motor coordinates.

Some of the basic parameters of interest to the sound design include:

- The ear detects subtle changes in sound pressure level and discriminates between what is perceived as **real** and what is understood as a **dream state** or altered consciousness. This altered state is called **aural-hypnotic projection** because the spectator projects him or her self into the seemingly less than real aural world and accepts its logic as the difference between pretending and being.
- Movement produces sound (sound waves). Within the aural window, movement corresponds to a displacement of the subject. Movement or motion of the aural window (through camera and microphone movement) corresponds to displacement of the spectator. Sound synced to movement reinforces the illusion of animated life.
- Music aids in the transport, transformation, or transposition of the spectator into the altered state. It is an aural-hypnotic suggestion that operates from one of three spheres of influence:
  - Enculturated cliché: Erik Satie's *Furniture Music*[4]
  - Conditioned reflex: "wallpaper music" whose meaning is derived from utility; to be heard, not **listened** to

- Referential: source music with a reference on the screen
- The synchronization and/or in-phase orchestration and arrangement of sound with electromechanical systems, including robotics, holographics, cinematographic projection, and any real-time event, result in the **polyphonic syncopation** of parts with the whole, creating timed aural patterns (good gestalts)[5] that are repeatable. This is good audio-animatronics.
- Changes in sound intensity as the camera moves through space suggest motor-sensory displacement. This encoded "sense of movement" is known as **kinesthesia.**
- The simultaneous perception of the auditory with the kinesthetic produces a **kinesthetic center,**[6] which produces in the spectator:
- Dynamic impact
- Visceral tension
- Bodily resonance
- Insight into subject
- A tertiary quality of sync-sound is **synesthesia,**[7] which is derived from the emotional responses through sensory-motor sensations and aural hypnotic suggestion. The results include:
- Possibility of astral projection
- Psychophysical identification
- Subjective emotional responses
- Aural intrusion: penetration into the film/video space as a function of movement (perceived) and sound value intensity (felt)
- Slow disclosure: spreading the limits of the frame-expanded view.

Satie once related that "furniture music creates a vibration; it has no other goal" [cited in Roger Shattuck, *The Banquet Years: The Origins of the Avant-Garde in France, 1885 to World War I*, rev. ed. (New York: Vintage, 1968), p. 169]. This notion of purely utilitarian sound prefigured by nearly 70 years the era of canned background music: Muzak—the industrial-grade aural experience.

Other Traits of the Sync-sound Program

Other traits to consider include the following.

Phono-photogenia.[8]   Physiognomic characters depend on facial expressions occurring together with speech. The voice of a "great man" (Cronkite) possesses a unique **physiophonic** (phonogenic voice is needed for fine interpretation, identification, security, drama, and so on). False vocalization (a bad dub or a poor voice recording of the recognizable Cronkite voice) creates a breakdown of narrative coherence.

Sonogenics.[9]   This is the capacity of sound to reveal the intrinsic nature or clarity of subject (truth). (Is the aural more truthful if it is not manipulated by the filmmaker/videographer?) Cinema verité postulates a slow disclosure and revelation of the subject/object by "knowing it" well (ego–object intercourse through observation, discovery, detachment). In the sync-sound documentary, one hopes for **insight.** Two approaches are provided by (1) (self-referential, allow process to be seen, intrusion of the filmmaker becomes an element), and (2) Frederick Wiseman (candid camera; long periods of watchful waiting for "personal moments" of human revelation; camera is invisible).

Aural montage.   This technique expresses meaning by the metaphorical juxtaposition of various perceptual elements (intellectual).

Aural decoupage.   The experience of sound is something greater than the interaction of sound and image/facts. This is a reality of a different order, a phenomenal fact[10] (psyche).

Ontological authenticity:[11]   This is credibility born of structural (cognitive elements) and perceptual (sequential elements) in the sync-sound film. **Sync sound** is kinesthetic, stimulating the auditory and sensory-motor centers of the brain. **Post-synched sound** is conceptual, supporting the concept of the event in the director's mind.

Natural perception is deep field; we hear sound from a full 360 degrees simultaneously and continuously, while only seeing a window from 50 degrees to a maximum of 120 degrees peripherally. The blending of multisource stimuli occurs involuntarily; however, the eye does not produce multiple exposures of the visual field. The mind selects significant details of sound according to cues of:

1. Loudness
2. Uniqueness
3. Meaning

The subject dictates a complex, subtle gestalt or pattern of sound from the entire sound field. The screen holds up a flat image, the ear perceives spatial three-dimensional sound; the mind seeks insight, the deep penetration into character and place (**synekinesthesia**).[12]

Sound colors our experience of **space, time, and motion.** The sync-sound field is one of unitary interaction, a tactile awareness of both the aural and visual, a new gestalt different than the post-synched program.

Sound/Image Relationships in the Documentary

Consider the following relationships:

- Sync sound linked to a character's image.
- Nonsync sound that provides an illustration, a "cutaway," or an interlude; clarifies a speaker's point.
- Nonsync sound that acts as counterpoint, subverts the integrity of the character, or becomes satire; iconoclastic diversion (Dusan Makavejev, Claude Jutra, Chris Marker).
- Nonsync sound that acts as an extension of a character's commentary through the use of metaphor: "likening prisoners to workers" in a politically motivated documentary by association of images and sound. Either narration or social actor provides:
  - Verbal statements linked to musical illustration.
  - Verbal statements linked to visual confirmation.
  - Verbal statements contradicted by image/facts.
  - Verbal statements that become ironic vis-à-vis association to an image.

Kon Ichikawa's *Tokyo Olympiad* (1965) weaves all three primary modes of address, utilizing live *verité* sound and going so far as to bury microphones in the running track to obtain auditory close-ups; eliminating background music; and maintaining synchronized sound without distortion (going down in pitch) throughout slow-motion sequences. The original score by avant-garde composer Toshiro Mayuzumi rejected Ichikawa's penchant for black humor set within the drama of the human dimension of the games.

> *I've tried to grasp the solemnity of the moment when man defies his limits and to express the solitude of the athlete who, in order to win, struggles against himself. I wished people to rediscover with astonishment that wonder which is a human being.*[13]

"Up-close and personal" sound in *Tokyo Olympiad* (Figure 6–7) reinterprets both the role of the filmmaker and the audience. Athletes become the "social actors"; their goal is to explain changes of consciousness and, as with all classical forms, changes in values and beliefs by a more personal involvement with the audience than could be provided by a narrator and narration, which tends to be didactic.

Ichikawa's extensive use of live sync sound follows no clear inherent necessity, but lack of location sync sound tends to present the argument on an abstract plane to which images operate on another abstract plane, appended rather than concretely linked to each other and the flow of the exposition.

Figure 6–7 *Tokyo Olympiad*, a document of raw sound of the unadulterated event, such as Greco-Roman wrestling seen here. (Courtesy of Michael Jeck, R5/S8 Distribution, Washington, D.C.)

Mock Documentary and the Simulation of Reality

Tanner 88

Tanner 88 (Figure 6–8) exhibits director Robert Altman's penchant for multilayered vocal lines. These dialogue textures flow over each other in a real-to-life tapestry of coherence (when the director wants us to hear something) and incoherence (when action or emotion must dominate). The suppressed background noise is symptomatic of television news documentary in which foreground events are the primary focus, and the otherwise noisy spontaneity of the live videotape format threatens at any point to overwhelm clarity.

What we are left with is a curious mix of soapy "naturalism," with the use of colloquial dialogue delivered matter of factly, often off-mike (a la Frederick Wiseman); intrusive little dittys sparingly punctuating scene or emotive changes; the sense of a "simulated" documentary, which tape tends to foster with its metallic, hard-edged contrast; emotional intimacy that comes with high melodrama rather than news; and *verité* editing of scenes like a series of family clips with discontinuous sound, immediacy, and quasi-authenticity spotted with some tricky self-reflexive pauses in which Tanner views a series of video portraits

UNCONVENTIONAL: Dark horse Jack Tanner (played by Michael Murphy) continues his quest for the Democratic presidential nomination in two new editions of **TANNER '88** debuting on HBO in May. Bottom, the candidate (at mike) joins a demonstration at the South African embassy in **MOONWALKER AND BOOKBAG**, debuting MONDAY, MAY 2 (10:00-10:30 p.m. ET), and confers with former contender Bruce Babbitt (top left) in **BAGELS WITH BRUCE,** debuting MONDAY, MAY 16 (10:00-10:30 p.m. ET). **HB⊕**

Figure 6–8 *Tanner 88.* Director Robert Altman's simulations of live TV is quasi reportage, personalized reality/drama for HBO. (Photos by Clif Lipson, courtesy of Dark Horse Productions, © 1988, Zenith Productions and HBO. All rights reserved.) As seen first on HBO.

(interviews) with his suggested cabinet appointees, including snippets of Ralph Nader (attorney general) and Studs Terkel (labor secretary), among others.

Tanner 88 utilizes an extension of Altman's wireless mike/multitrack recording technique in which every actor is given a perspective focus and is always "on" mike. But, unlike his filmic efforts, the result is neither layered drama nor "alive" broadcast news. Audio flexibility serves to question the truth of all news gathering, because it makes the viewer aware of gaps and silences that paradoxically interfere with the simulation of authenticity that network news strives for technically in their daily doses of "factoid" reportage.

As an event, *Tanner 88* sounds as real on television as anything else claiming validity as a "window on the world." Altman demonstrates the facility of the video/audio image in simulating "truth," yet he also demonstrates that we can no more determine the truth of a Tanner than we could assess the truth of a Dukakis or Bush or Jackson on television due to the way the medium tends to "overcook" the tone and timbre of character down into homogenized melodrama; television has even succeeded in fragmenting war into melodrama. The sound sense here echoes "news/diary"—personalized history in the making.

Angelo, My Love, 1983

Director Robert Duval's investigative drama (Figure 6–9) uses documentary sync-sound equipment and technique to capture the essence of the gypsy. It is fact-based, improvisational, and fluid, with a hand-held feel ready for elements coming together in front of the lens, while feeling one's way through the narrative. The whole is more than the sum of its parts. There is a tactile quality to the sync-sound recording—frenzied babble, witty off-screen interjections, the disembodied assemblage of dubbed noises, melodic patter overlay, and integration of music, dialogue and atmospherics.

Ideal of the "good gestalt": "Each part is where it is due to the demands of the whole, not owing to extraneous factors or constraints." From Kurt Koffka, *"Problems in the Psychology of Art"*

The Thin Blue Line, 1988

In this story of a cop killing in Dallas, investigative director Errol Morris's re-creations of the murder and events surrounding it have a stronger presence than the seemingly innocent "drifter" sentenced to death row (Randall Adams). With Phillip Glass's nocturnally evocative score, the documentary that is neither "newsy" nor fact-based fiction evokes a kind of existential unease in the audience as it reveals the texture of falsehood. Morris has turned the case into a kind of tabloid poetry, a meditation on uncertainty and the fascination of violence.[14]

Figure 6–9 *Angelo My Love*, directed by Robert Duvall, has the simulation of reality preserved by aural inconsistencies. (Distributed by New Yorker Films.)

Documentary sound has become a cliché of street noises and unprocessed dialogue. Truth is not in the facts of sound and image, but rather in the selection and arrangement and duration of each event. As Harold Rosenberg remarked in his *Act and the Actor*, University of Chicago Press (1986), "Every act involves a seepage of poetry into practical life."

Endnotes

1. Vlada Petric, "Toward a Theory of the Sync-Sound Film," unpublished paper (circa 1975).

2. *Ambisonic* refers to 360-degree sonic perspective in which innumerable sound sources mix in a free field.

3. *Night Mail* (1934) is unique for its vibrant use of sound with motion cutting (Basil Wright, director).

4. Lucy Fischer, "Rene Clair, Le Million, and the Coming of Sound," *Cinema Journal*, (Spring 1977), pp. 34–50.

5. Kurt Koffka, *Principles of Gestalt Psychology*, Harcourt Brace Jovanovich, New York, 1935.

6. Kurt Koffka, "Problems in the Psychology of Art," paper 1939, Bryn Mawr Symposium, Oriole Editions, New York, 1972.

7. Petric, "Toward a Theory. . ."

8. Alexander Sesonske, "Aesthetics of Film, or a Funny Thing Happened on the Way to the Movies," *Journal of Aesthetics and Art Criticism* (Fall 1974).

9. Petric, "Toward a Theory." *Sonogenics* is my term, but Petric refers to Bastian's "phenomenal fact" in coming to terms with cinema verité.

10. Henry Bastian, *The Brain as an Organ of Mind*, Appleton, New York, 1980, 543 p.

11. Vlada Petric, "Sight and Sound, Concept or Entity," *Filmmaker's Newsletter* (May 1973), pp. 27–31.

12. Petric.

13. Kon Ichikawa in press kit notes for *Tokyo Olympiad*, distributed by R5/S8, Washington, D.C.

14. Terrence Rafferty, "True Detective," *The New Yorker*, Sept. 5, 1988, p. 76.

References

ADAMSON, JOE, "Crabquacks," *Take One*, Take One Publications V6N2, Jan. 78, pp. 18–22. A case is made for the "flawless logic" behind every cartoon vocalization that followed the physical characteristics of the "toons."

ARMES, ROY, "Entendre, C'est Comprendre—In Defence of Sound Reproduction," *Screen* (Spring 1988), pp. 8–22.

LEVIN, LEAR, "Robert Altman's Innovative Sound Techniques," *American Cinematographer* (Apr. 1980). His use of multiple voices by wireless mikes and a multitrack recorder results in a kind of "stychomythia" or renewal of the Greek chorus, which functions both as commentary and texture.

MUNK, ERIKA, "Film Is Ego: Radio Is God—Richard Foreman and the Arts of Control," *Drama Review* (Winter 1987), pp. 143–148.

NICHOLS, BILL, "Documentary Theory and Practice," *Screen*, (Winter 1976), pp. 46–48. Narration or "address" falls into several modalities, direct or indirect, sync and nonsync, each with its own power to reposition the audience.

VINCENDEAU, GINETTE, "Hollywood Babel—The Multiple Language Version," *Screen* (Spring 1988), pp. 24–39.

7

BUDGET

Money determines what can and cannot be done. Armed with an inventory of techniques and technologies from previous chapters, the reader is guided through the complexities of a detailed sound budget, with emphasis on the pricing and selection of cost-effective processes. Time is money. Being able to estimate the time it takes to record 5 minutes of usable narration is as important as the actual recording. An analysis of the budget indicates areas where technical problems become strictly financial considerations. However, the budget presents options to the producer who must be able to anticipate problems and allocate funds accordingly. The budget vividly illustrates the need for careful preproduction planning, a stage in which too often creative options are lost because of little or no understanding of the sound recording process.

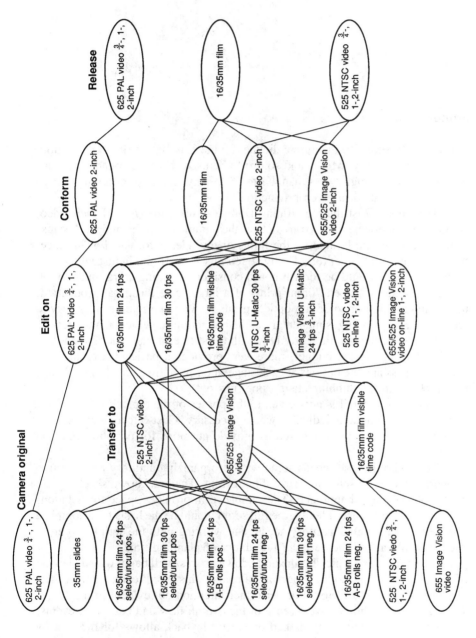

Figure 7-1 Budget (options).

Introduction

The budget, not creative invention, dictates for the most part the kinds of auditory material (live, library, MIDI, and so on) to be used, because sound represents only a portion (averaging less than 4% to 5% of any feature or program budget) of the overall costs of a given production.

The mode of distribution (70mm, Dolby 6-track, video disc, 1-inch video, 35mm standard optical, and so on) dictates the parameters of the budget, because technical choices are limited by the limits of the release format. For instance, there is no need to budget for a Dolby stereo mix for a 16mm industrial training film; likewise, it would be foolish not to consider allocating extra funds for 50 six-track magnetic striped 70mm prints of a large-scale theatrical production, in addition to 1500 or so 35mm optical prints for national release. It is easy to see that careful planning is mandatory at the budgeting stage, and many creative choices must be made quite early before the first line of dialogue is recorded.

Understanding the budget, moreover, provides a basic idea of the production process and the options at each stage in terms of time and dollars. When time runs out in the dubbing stage, time runs out!

Attention to detail is now given to the phases of the typical sound budget breakdown, with options indicated where necessary. Cost-effective choices are at every turn, and care is required to provide cushions for possible technical mistakes.

The audio designer needs some way of organizing auditory material into categories that make sense in terms of budgeting. The breakdown sheet (Figure 7–2) is one suggested approach. The sample form provides space for notations for one shot or sequence. Ideally, the full script would be the basis for a complete overview of anticipated auditory needs, and working with the script in preproduction would afford the designer the luxury of planning time.

However, most typically, the breakdown process will begin with a viewing of a first cut or final cut of the program. Of course, this avoids certain ambiguities of space, time, and directorial or performer intention not evident in the script. The first preview should give a sense of the overall flow and pattern of events. A more detailed viewing by flatbed or video playback allows for the shot by shot specification on individual breakdown sheets.

Some directors have a clear sense of what they want the track to be—how it is to interact with visuals, how elements are to work together. Eisenstein,

SCRIPT BREAKDOWN		PAGE NO.
PRODUCTION TITLE		
SET	SEQUENCE	LOCATION
PERIOD	SEASON	DAY NIGHT	TOTAL SCRIPT PAGES

CAST	BITS	SCENE NUMBERS & SYNOPSIS
	EXTRAS	
PROCESS - EFFECTS - CONSTRUCTION		
MUSIC - MISCELLANEOUS		
PROPS. - ACTION PROPS. - ANIMALS		

Figure 7–2 Breakdown of script elements.

more than 60 years ago, made up simple inventories of auditory material. His *The General Line* (1929) suggested a complex texture of sounds, which he listed in two major categories, **kinds** and **degree,** and his notes for use constitute one of the earliest of audio design logs (see Figure 7–3).

Explanation of Budget Detail

Table 7–1 provides daily equipment rental rates.

Phase I: Production

1. A one-week rental of a production package is normally charged at four times the daily rate. One month is billed at 20 days. Sales tax applies.
2. Budget for the use of the Nagra as a logging playback machine for creating transfer and edit lists. Since audition of location tapes during the transfer in the studio is costly ($75 per hour), an additional day rental for the Nagra while paying an assistant to listen and log is worthwhile (see Table 7–1).
3. The Fisher boom is recognized as the most flexible system available. It replaced the more cumbersome Mole Richardson Perambulator Boom.
4. Actually an editorial requirement, the transfer of dailies should provide a master of all takes to be "printed" and a duplicate for protection. How much time should it take to transfer 10,000 feet of $\frac{1}{4}$-inch tape? The minimum is real time $+ \frac{1}{2}$ hour adjustment time per reel (30 minutes at $7\frac{1}{2}$ ips). Transfer flat with no equalization. If there are great changes in level throughout, allow 30% more time for transfer with quality control.

TABLE 7–1

Basic Location Recording Package		
Nagra 4 (stereo time code)	$ 50.00/day	
Sennheiser MKH70 TU mike	20.00/day	
Tram TR 50 mini mike	10.00/day	
EV RE 15 hand-held dyn. mike	8.00/day	
Stereo mixer (Shure)	25.00/day	
Fishpole	8.00/day	
Windscreen/shockmounts	20.00/day	
Misc. cables/parts/batts.	25.00/day	
Total minimum	$166.00	
Crew	NABET	IATSE
Location mixer	$166.00	$344.00
Boom man	$140.00	$202.00
Cable man	$140.00	$130.00

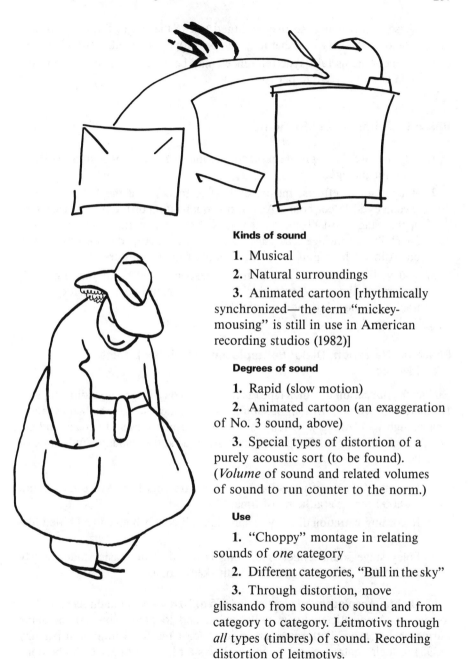

Kinds of sound

1. Musical

2. Natural surroundings

3. Animated cartoon [rhythmically synchronized—the term "mickey-mousing" is still in use in American recording studios (1982)]

Degrees of sound

1. Rapid (slow motion)

2. Animated cartoon (an exaggeration of No. 3 sound, above)

3. Special types of distortion of a purely acoustic sort (to be found). (*Volume* of sound and related volumes of sound to run counter to the norm.)

Use

1. "Choppy" montage in relating sounds of *one* category

2. Different categories, "Bull in the sky"

3. Through distortion, move glissando from sound to sound and from category to category. Leitmotivs through *all* types (timbres) of sound. Recording distortion of leitmotivs.

Figure 7–3   Eisenstein's Log of Auditory Materials for *The General Line*, a pastoral symphony. Sergei Eisenstein's Sound Design for *The General Line* (1929) consisted of three primary concerns: classification, degrees, and utilization. As in his line drawings, sound traces movement, not intellectualized, but, rather, primitive, religious, sensual.

These will become the master edited tracks that go to the mix, so they
should be the very best that they can be. Hope for cleanliness and clarity.

5. If sync systems fail, sync references may be added manually or via time
code at an hourly rate per roll.

Phase II: Editorial Requirements

1. Reprints are the duplicate protection copies of 16mm or 35mm magnetic
track for dialogue.
2. Budget sound effects, music, and ADR transfers at the flat studio rate
(averages $175 per hour). Again, no equalization or filtering is necessary
at this stage; just clean, quiet tracks. Source material may come from
$\frac{1}{4}$-inch tape, cartridge, cassette, disk, videotape, striped old prints, and so
on. Allow 1 hour plus for nontraditional format transfers.
3. Today, this means a transfer from kinescopes, old prints that are being
preserved, and single-system video to 35mm full-coat magnetic master
tracks. Studio labor rates are taxable.

Phase III: Narration, Dialogue Replacement, Foley Effects, and Music

Budget the **narration** to $\frac{1}{4}$-inch tape (as if recorded on a Nagra or studio Ampex).
Estimate is based on how long it should take a trained narrator to handle lines.
This is highly inflationary. Often the director must be present to coach and get
just the right intonation. Budget 10 lines per hour at the standard studio rate of
$175/hour.

1. Flat rate for cost of narration *talent*. A name celebrity voice may claim
$20,000 for several hours of time.
2. Recording narration directly to sprocket full coat is booked and billed like
ADR time.
3. Foley stage sound effects recording is billed at the basic studio hourly
rate. Allow 20 effects per hour with Foley artists.

Dialogue replacement is estimated at 5 to 10 lines per hour direct recording
to picture. Automatic dialogue replacement and looping may cost the same
during peak season. Performers are paid at least the SAG minimum per day
($395) or their contract price. Looping allows all lines of one actor to be done
at once. ADR is wasted if all actors whose lines must be dubbed are not present.
Costs can escalate greatly if more time must be booked due to crossed schedules
for talent. The production board breakdown (done in preproduction) groups
dialogue lines as a reference for each performer to avoid this problem. However,

it is safe to overbudget for time since rebooking may be impossible for talent going off to another picture.

The rate for **Foley sound effects** recording includes the talent of studio Foley artists. Experience here saves lots of time and aggravation. Foley requires a very precise list and cue sheet. Usually, an editor and director are present to approve the final result, avoiding the probability of tossing the effect later because its wrong.

The **music** budget requires studio time and talent payments. The quality of the scoring stage matters greatly in the overall acoustic coloration of the orchestral or symphonic effect. There are few workable spaces left for recording. The Manhattan Center Studio, for example, at $300/hour is well worth the expenditure for its characteristic sound.

Table 7–2 provides an outline for the various phases of music production.

TABLE 7–2   Music Production

A. Rights: Publishing (copyright)		
Synchronization		
Performance (pricing depends on the publisher, the composition to be used, and the method of use)		

B. Preparation (scoring)		
Picture Timing	$30.000	(hour rate)
Orchestration	$40.00	(page rate)
Arranger	$300–800	(flat contract fee)
Copyist	$60/day	(page rate) $1.30 +
Librarian	$583.00	(week rate)
Composer	$Negotiate 1000–10,000	(flat rate contract fee)

C. Facilities Rental	
Studio 7	$300 per day
Recording engineer Director Sound Consultant/Director	Package deal $1000–2000/day

D. Rehearsal	
Music supervisor (orchestra manager)	$125.00 per 3-hour session
Leader	$125 '' '' ''
Sidemen	$125 each (average, 10 men)

E. Recording	
Music supervisor	$175.00 (if doubling, paid 150%)
Recording musicians	$175.00 per 3-hour session

Arrangers prepare and adapt an already written composition for presentation in other than its original form. Arrangements include reharmonization, paraphrasing, and/or development of a composition so that it fully represents the melodic, harmonic, and rhythmic structure and requires no changes or additions.

Orchestrators score the various voices and/or instruments of an arrangement without changing or adding to the melodies, countermelodies, harmonies, and rhythms. They are paid an hourly rate.

Copyists provide a visual representation of parts to be performed by instruments and/or voice of a musical ensemble systematically placed on a series of staves, one above the other, in which none other than two identical instruments are combined on a single staff (full score). Also do condensed scores and sketches, vocal parts, and conductor parts. Page rates apply.

The **music supervisor** is usually a playing musician who doubles as a union representative, ensuring that regulations are followed. A supervisor is required for any group of 10 or more musicians.

Either a copyist, sound consultant, or music supervisor will prepare the music **cue sheets,** which are furnished to television stations for music clearance (ASCAP) and to the American Federation of Musicians. Information listed on the cue sheets includes air date, date and place of recording.

Table 7–3 provides average rates for a scoring session (TV).
Note: For a typical TV drama ($\frac{1}{2}$-hour series), the minimum scoring hours required for a 13-program series is 21 hours. Special rates have been adopted for public broadcasting (see sample rate sheet, Figure 7–4).

Phase IV: Rerecording (Mixing)

1. This phase is the heart of the budget, accounting for perhaps 50% of the total cost, and is a necessary expenditure. Most studios have a 9-hour minimum booking. Unused time is partially refunded. Never underbook. Mixing involves the use of a handful of very experienced mixers whose time is often booked well in advance (often one year plus). On the East Coast, studios go with one mixer; on the West Coast, a team of three is traditional, with specialized music and effects mixers working with a dialogue mixer with overall responsibility. Even with a computer-assisted board, it is difficult for one person to handle more than three tracks at a time. The mix may run from one week to months. Aside from the complexity and numbers of tracks, it would be a good idea to budget for at least two weeks (90 hours) for an average feature.

2. Quality control is a nice contingency fee to ensure monies to cover unforeseen problems. Allow 10% to 20% of total mix budget.

3. Premixing or preview run-throughs prior to the mix are an absolute necessity to avoid nasty surprises in the expensive mix session. Premixing

TABLE 7–3 Music Production, continued.

Musician's Minimum Rates	Recording	Nonrecording
3-Hour single session	$166.52	$101.03
6-Hour double session	333.04	181.86
Overtime/hr (8 A.M. to 12 P.M.)	13.85	8.40
Trailers, cartoons, shorts (flat)	$166.52	

Minimum Scoring Hours

For 13 $\frac{1}{2}$ hour shows	18 hours (documentary)
For 13 $\frac{1}{2}$ hour shows	21 hours (drama)
For 10 one-hour shows	33.85 hours (drama)
For drama pilot	10.15 hours

Miscellaneous

Cartage $6 per instrument
   On location $26.41 for travel time
   Meals   provided if session runs over 6 hours
Orchestra manager (contractor): required for 10 or more players
   and leader. He may be one of the musicians and is then paid at
   twice the minimum rate used for sideman.
Residuals: 50% of TV scale for musicians paid at time of exhibition.

Orchestrators

Page rates: 13 lines	$17.27
45 lines	36.20
Timing picture	27.66/hour

Copyists

Page rate minimum	$60.53 (3.39/page)
Piano with orchestra cues	9.18/page
Conductor parts (complete)	10.62

should be budgeted for one day's run-through of tracks in interlock for notes to be made and a precise mixing log created. Any problems can be noted, cleaned up, or cut out before the actual mix. This avoids wasted time due to mechanical and esthetic problems.

4. The master mix is transferred to a $\frac{1}{4}$- or $\frac{1}{2}$-inch protection copy. Budget 2 hours for the master three-track transfer to 35mm full coat and separate music/effects masters for foreign distribution.

   a. Dolby spectral recording or stereo shows: allow 10% increase to hourly mix rate.

   b. For TV programs, allow 1 hour for a playback check through a standard TV receiver speaker system.

Figure 7-4 Musician's union scale sheet (old rates).

MASTER SCALE LIST	INDEFINITE LIVE PERFORMANCE	TO JUNE 1st, 1982 LIVE T.V.	DECEMBER 1st, 1981 PHONO	MAY 1st, 1983 COMMERCIALS	TO JAN 15th, 1982 MOTION PICTURES T.V. FILMS
ORCHESTRATORS					
ORCHESTRATION—4 BAR PAGE 10 LINES OR LESS	9.60	14.19	11.96	11.44	NO MORE THAN 13 LINES 12.56
EACH ADDITIONAL LINE	.80	.55	.52	.60	20 LINES 16.14
VOCAL SCORING—4 BAR PAGE 4 VOICES OR LESS	9.00	6.19	4.87	5.03	25 LINES 18.06
EACH ADDITIONAL VOICE LINE	1.00	.55	.48	.46	30 LINES 20.05
SKETCHING—4 BAR PAGE—BY ORCHESTRATOR	8.60	8.60			35 LINES 22.03
—BY REHEARSAL PIANIST	5.80	7.11			40 LINES 23.97
—BY REHEARSAL DRUMMER	2.90	3.56			MORE THAN 40 LINES 25.95
HOURLY RATE	20.00	21.29	19.07	17.39	20.10
TAKE DOWN	TIME RATE	TIME RATE	TIME RATE	TIME RATE	TIME RATE
MINIMUM CALL (Orchestrators)	46.80	42.52		69.56	60.33
AFM — EPW	5 PER CENT	8 PER CENT	10 PER CENT	9 PER CENT	9 PER CENT
LOCAL 47 HEALTH AND WELFARE (or Motion Picture H. & W.)	5% OF FIRST $300.00	3.25 PER DAY/16.25 WK	2.60 ARR.—3.75 MIN.	4.00 PER SESSION FORM B MAX 7.80	WAGES - 10 OR ½ HRS. = 90¢ = MONEY / Aug. 1st 991 = MONEY

COPYISTS

PER PAGE — *DENOTES PRO-RATED PRICES @ Denotes Bar Numbers included in price	LIVE PERF. REG	DUPE	LIVE T.V. REG	DUPE	PHONO REG	DUPE	COMM. REG	DUPE	MP T.V. FILMS REG	DUPE
PARTS @ SINGLE LINE	2.40	4.80	2.81	5.62	2.26	4.52	2.10	4.37	2.85	5.70
TRANSPOSED	3.60	7.20	3.97	7.94	3.23	6.46	3.00	6.25	4.09	8.18
DIVISI — CHORDED	4.10	8.20	5.13	10.26	3.71	7.42	3.43	8.31	4.09	8.18
DIVISI — CHORDED TRANSPOSED	6.20	12.40	7.45	14.90	5.57	11.14	4.99	12.16	5.94	11.88
SINGLE LINE CUED (SYMPHONIE)	3.60	7.20	3.47	7.94					4.09	8.18
KEYBOARD @ HARP — ORGAN — GUITAR — PNO — ETC.	4.10	8.20	5.13	10.26	3.71	7.42	3.43	8.31	4.60	9.20
PLUS MELODY (VOCAL) CUE	5.10	10.20	6.29	12.58	4.74	9.48	4.32	9.49	6.66	13.32
PLUS ORCH CUES — SEPARATE STAVE	6.00	12.00			5.72	11.45			7.06	14.12
TWO STAVE WITH ORCH. CUES						11.45			7.53	15.06
CLASSICAL — CONCERT — ETC.			50% ADDITIONAL			12.25			7.53	15.06
NUMBERING BARS (INCLUDED IN THESE SCALES)			.49	.98	.29	.58	.31	.62	.39	.78
ADDING CHORD SYMBOLS SINGLE STAVE	1.00	2.00	1.19	2.38	1.10	2.20	.92	1.79	.77	1.54
MULTI-STAVE	.50	1.00	.62	1.24	.58	1.16	.45	.92	.77	1.54
ELECTRONIC SYMBOLS SINGLE STAVE	1.80	3.60	1.20	2.40	1.16	2.32	.94	1.88	1.02	2.40
MULTI-STAVE	.90	1.80	.66	1.32	.58	1.16	.54	1.08	.55	1.10
VOCAL @ CHOIR — 1 SET LYRICS		8.90		10.98		9.42		8.67	5.00	10.00
LEAD SHEET - 1 SET LYRICS		8.60		12.57		8.38		7.75	3.88	7.76
SONG COPY — 3 STAVE — 1 SET LYRICS		12.40	7.46	14.92			5.11	10.25	5.58	11.16
ADDITIONAL LYRICS — PER SET (FOREIGN PLUS 100%)	1.70	3.40	1.17	2.34		3.40	.92	1.79	1.00	2.00
SINGLE VOICE LINE WITH ONE SET OF LYRICS	4.10	8.20	5.13	10.26		3.23	2.99	6.85	1.19	2.38
MASTER RHYTHM @		12.00		14.00		11.24		10.30		13.17
CONDUCTOR PARTS @ SINGLE MELODY LINE — SINGLE STAFF				10.25						
LEAD LINE ONLY — W/WORDED CUES									4.60	9.20
LEAD LINE W/NOTATED INSTRUMENTAL CUES									5.91	11.82
* 8 STAVE		7.70		11.21		9.11		8.73		
& LYRICS		9.10		10.23		10.16				
* 9 STAVE		8.60		12.62		10.25		9.82		
& LYRICS		10.30		14.73		11.51		11.43		
* 10 STAVE		9.60		14.02		11.39		10.91		
& LYRICS		11.40		16.36		12.79		12.70		
* 12 STAVE		11.50		16.83		13.67		13.09		
& LYRICS		13.70		19.64		15.35		15.24		
HARMONICALLY COMPLETE FROM SKETCH		16.30								13.97
HARMONICALLY COMPLETE FROM SCORE		16.30		24.46						16.22
LIBRARIAN NON PLAYING	2 HR. MIN. 51.40		2 HR. MIN. 66.05						113.62	8 HRS.
PLAYING			2 HR. MIN. 20.26							
OVERTIME	PER HR. 19.20		PER HR. 22.07						10.66 @ ½ HR.	
PROOFREADING	20.00 HR — NO MIN.		18.51 HR. — 2 HR MIN.		13.58 HR — NO MIN.		12.94 HR.— NO MIN.		CALL FOR RATES	
SPECIAL ROUTINE (Transposition additional per part)	50% ADDITIONAL		50% ADDITIONAL		50% ADDITIONAL		50% ADDITIONAL		50% ADDITIONAL	
MINIMUM CALL (Copyists)	46.80		51.08				45.00		50.00	44.01
TIME RATE PER HOUR (Copyists)	15.60		12.77		9.82		9.78		9.46	
AFM — EPW	5 PER CENT		8 PER CENT		10 PER CENT		9 PER CENT		9 PER CENT	
HEALTH & WELFARE (Local 47 or Motion Picture)	2.00 ARR PER HR 5% OF 1ST $200.00		3.25 DAY/16.25 WK		3.75 EA. ORIG. SERV.		4.00 PER SESSION		WAGES - 6.30 = HRS. HRS. = 90¢ = MONEY	
STRAIGHT TIME	9 AM TO 6 PM MON. THRU SAT.		9 AM TO 6 PM MON. THRU SAT.		9 AM TO 6 PM MON. THRU FRI.		9 AM TO 6 PM MON. THRU SAT.		9 AM TO 6 PM MON THRU FRI / 6 PM to MIDNIGHT	
110 % PREMIUM TIME	6 PM to MIDNIGHT		6 PM to 9 AM		6 PM TO MIDNIGHT		6 PM TO MIDNIGHT SAT. 9 AM TO 6 PM		MIDNITE to 6 AM	
150% PREMIUM TIME	WORK IN EXCESS OF 8 HOURS IN ONE DAY ON A SINGLE JOB.		WORK ON SAME JOB AT ANY TIME FOLLOWING A CALL BACK LESS THAN 8 HOURS AFTER DISMISSAL DURING PREMIUM PAY HOURS.		WORK ON SAME JOB AT ANY TIME FOLLOWING A CALL BACK LESS THAN 8 HOURS AFTER DISMISSAL DURING PREMIUM PAY HOURS. "FOR WORK @ 8 PM SATURDAY"					
200 % PREMIUM TIME	MIDNIGHT 'TIL DISMISSED HOLIDAYS SUNDAY		NEW YEARS DAY — LINCOLN'S BIRTHDAY — WASHINGTON'S BIRTHDAY — MEMORIAL DAY — INDEPENDENCE DAY — LABOR DAY — THANKSGIVING — CHRISTMAS		FOR WORK FROM MIDNIGHT 'TIL DISMISSED				SAT — SUN LISTED HOLIDAYS EXCEPT — LINCOLN AND WASHINGTON BIRTHDAYS	

Rev. 6/81 MP MSL.101   SECOND EDITION

c. Premix may be used for balancing dialogue tracks, combining effects tracks, and cueing music tracks to picture.

d. Magnetic striping for six-track 70mm prints is an additional production cost averaging $20,000 per print.

e. Tax applies to mix hourly rates.

Average per Hour	
One mixer	$300
Two mixers	$450
Three mixers	$550
Premix	$300

Phase V: Optical Transfers

1. Transfer with quality control should be billed at a flat rate per show, specified positive or negative optical. Reel length for 16mm is 1200 feet, and for 35mm, 1000 feet. A 90-minute feature runs at 8100 feet times price per foot.

   a. 35/16 is for 16mm, which is slit down the middle, producing two 16mm negatives. This is done to make use of the flat field sharpness of image on double sprocket stock.

   b. 35/32 double sprocket produces one 16mm master.

2. Developing rates average 10 to 15 cents per foot. Developing should be done by the same studio or lab providing the exposure density standard to the optical transfer technician at the studio.

Phase VI: Raw Stock

1. One 7-inch reel of $\frac{1}{4}$-inch tape $= 600$ feet at $7\frac{1}{2}$ ips $= 28$ minutes
2. One 1200-foot roll (1000 inches, 35mm) full-coat magnetic film
   $= 10$ minutes (35mm)
   $= 28$ minutes (16mm)

$\frac{1}{4}$-Inch Stock Used for:
Location recording
Studio narration
Music recording
Special effects
Library sound
(Mix) Protection copy

Full Coat Used for:
Edit masters: Dialogue
Music
Effects
Duplicate copies
Master Mix
M&E master

a. Stock may be rented or purchased.

b. Stripe coat (edge coated only with oxide on three-track 35mm film) may be used as economy alternative to full coat.

c. It is wise to budget to keep all elements since you can never tell when changes may be made. Even after release, cuts may be required, necessitating going back to the original 35 mm full-coat dialogue, music, or effects tracks. In rerelease, this is especially costly to redo from scratch if old masters have been erased or discarded. Restoration efforts of many archival agencies have been greatly hindered due to loss or destruction of original tracks. However, studios tend not to store original materials for long periods of time, since storage space is lost real estate that isn't making money. The responsibility is the producer's to save and protect the masters. *Transfer to compact disk is advisable for archival safety.*

3. Optical negative stock is usually figured into the total lab charges for development.

4. White emulsion leader should be budgeted for editorial, printing, and storage use. Figure on ten (1000 feet) rolls for a given production.

5. Sales tax applies to all raw stock.

Phase VII: Contingency

There are several areas in which estimates may be well off the mark, given the time elapsed from budgeting to release; ADR time and MIX time are primary concerns. Add a 10% contingency fee based on the entire budget total to adjust for problems.

Table 7–4 provides a sample automated sound budget, taking in the considerations covered in phases I to VII. Software is by Movie Magic.

Appendix to Ryder Budget (Fig. 7–5)

A. Average Union Wage Rates for Sound Crew

NABET   **Minimum Daily Rate (8 hr), 1987**
                      (× 20% = 1990)

Production mixer	$168.00
Boom man	140.00
Cable man	140.00

TABLE 7–4 Movie Magic Sample Budget Printout   Page 42

Acct #	Description	Amount	Units	X	Rate	Subtotal	Total
760-00	POST PRODUCTION SOUND						
760-01	SOUND TRANSFERS						
	SOUND EFFECTS	50,000	FEET		0.03	1,500	
	DAILY REPRINTS	15,000	FEET		0.069	1,035	
	NARRATION & ADR	5,000	FEET		0.035	175	
	MUSIC	20,000	FEET		0.035	700	
	MISCELLANEOUS		ALLOW		2,000	2,000	5,410
760-02	OPTICAL SOUND TRANSFER						
	TRANSFER	11,000	FEET		0.22	2,420	
	DEV & PRINT OP NEG	11,000	FEET		0.05	550	
	OPTICAL STOCK	11,000	FEET		0.16	1,760	
	DOLBY	11	REELS		88	968	
	MAGNETIC TRANSFER		ALLOW		25,000	25,000	
	DELIVERY REQUIREMENTS						
	TELEVISION OP SND TRK		ALLOW		4,000	4,000	34,698
760-03	MAGNETIC FILM STOCK						
	NARR. & ADR TRANSFERS	5,000	FEET		0.04	200	
	SOUND EFX TRANSFERS	50,000	FEET		0.039	1,950	
	MUSIC TRANSFERS	20,000	FEET		0.07	1,400	
	DUBBING TRANSFERS-TEMP	25,000	FEET		0.069	1,725	
	MISC ALLOW. INCLD STOCK		ALLOW		10,000	10,000	
	SALES TAX	6.50%			15,275	993	16,268
760-04	ADR FACILITIES	36	HOURS		285	10,260	10,260
760-05	NARRATION FACILITIES						0
760-06	FOLEY STAGE	45	HOURS		285	12,825	12,825
760-07	SOUND EFX FACILITIES						0
760-08	MUSIC FACILITIES						0
760-09	DUBBING FACILITIES						0
	TEMP DUBS (3 MIXERS)	27	HOURS		560	15,120	
	PRE-DUB (2 MIXERS)	45	HOURS		490	22,050	
	DUBBING	90	HOURS		560	50,400	
	REDUBBING-PREVIEWS	9	HOURS		560	5,040	
	DELIVERY REQUIREMENTS						
	FOREIGN M&E	18	HRS		750	13,500	
	TELEVISION M&E	18	HRS		750	13,500	
	FICA	7.15%			84,210	6,021	
	FUI	0.80%			26,040	208	
	SUI	5.40%			26,040	1,406	
	TEAMSTERS	18%			27,000	4,860	
	WORKMAN'S COMP.	4.73%			92,610	4,380	136,485
760-10	OTHER RENTALS						0
760-25	OTHER PURCHASES						0
	DOLBY FEE		ALLOW		5,000	5,000	
	ENGINEERING FEE		ALLOW		2,500	2,500	7,500
						Total For 760-00	223,446

BUDGET BREAK-DOWN

PHASE 1 — PRODUCTION

A. Recording channel _____ dys/wks _____

B. ¼" tape Nagra sync playback _____ dys/wks _____

C. Studio microphone boom _____ dys/wks _____

*D. Transfer of dailies _____ feet _____

*E. Marking sync sound start
   on dailies _____ hours _____

   Miscellaneous items (PHASE 7) _____

PRODUCTION CREW (On producer's payroll)

Sound Mixer _____ dys/wks _____

Boom operator _____ dys/wks _____

Other _____ dys/wks _____

SUBTOTAL _____

PHASE 2 — EDITORIAL REQUIREMENTS

*A. Reprints of dailies _____ hours _____

*B. Transfer of sound effects _____ hours _____

*C. Transfer of music _____ hours _____

*D. Transfer of narration and
   dialogue replacement _____ hours _____

*E. Transfer from or to 16mm
   mag striped picture prints _____ hours _____

SUBTOTAL _____

PHASE 3 — NARRATION, DIALOGUE REPLACEMENT,
SOUND EFFECTS (Foley)

*A. Narration and sound effects

   1. to ¼" tape only _____ hours _____

   2. to ¼" tape with sprocket _____ hours _____

   3. to sprocket and picture (Foley) _____ hours _____

   4. to ¼" tape, sprocket
      and picture _____ hours _____

*B. Dialogue replacement

   1. Sound loops only (to ¼" tape) _____ hours _____

   2. Sync Check sound loops only _____ hours _____

   3. Sync Check with picture _____ hours _____

   4. Reverse-O-Matic (track only) _____ hours _____

   5. Reverse-O-Matic (w/Picture) _____ hours _____

SUBTOTAL _____

PHASE 4 — RERECORDING (mixing)

*A. Composite Rerecording (Tax applies to 50% of mixing
   charges)

   1☐ 2☐ 3☐ Mixers and crew _____ hours _____

*B. Quality control _____ hours _____

*C. Premixing (pre-dubbing) _____ hours _____

*D. Transfer of mixed 3 track to
   sync ½" tape protection _____ hours _____

   or Flat Rate per show _____

SUBTOTAL _____

PHASE 5 — OPTICAL TRANSFERS AND DEVELOPING

*A. Optical Negative Transfers

   1. to 35mm _____ feet _____

   2. to 35/32mm _____ feet _____

   3. to 35/16mm _____ feet _____

*B. Quality Control to Optical _____ hours _____

*C. Develop 35mm _____ feet _____

   Develop 35/32mm _____ feet _____

*D. Slitting 35/32mm _____ feet _____

SUBTOTAL _____

PHASE 6 — RAW STOCK REQUIREMENTS

°A. ¼" tape for original dailies
   5" reels ___ 7" ___ 10" _____ $ _____

   For scoring, narration, dialog replacement _____ $ _____
   600' ___ 1200' ___ 2500' _____ $ _____

*B. 35mm magnetic striped film for dailies
   transfers, reprints, looping, narration ___ feet $ _____

   For music transfers _____ feet $ _____

   For sound effects transfers _____ feet $ _____

*C. 16mm full-coat film as alternate for
   items A & B _____ feet $ _____

*D. 35mm full-coat magnetic film
   PURCHASES for 3-track dialogue
   replacement and mixing sessions _____ rolls $ _____

*E. 35mm full-coat magnetic film
   RENTAL as alternate for item D _____ rolls $ _____

*F. ½" tape for 3-track sync protection
   transfer of mixed original 3-track _____ rolls $ _____

*G. 150 mil SN tape _____ rolls $ _____

*H. 35mm optical negative sound stock
   for mixed track transfer _____ feet $ _____

*I. 35/32mm optical negative sound stock
   for 16mm optical sound tracks _____ feet $ _____
   35/16mm optical negative sound stock
   for Double Rank dual 16mm printing _____ feet $ _____

SUBTOTAL _____

*Sales tax applicable only where asterisk appears.

Subtotals Phase 1 _____

2 _____

3 _____

4 _____

5 _____

6 _____

Sales tax _____

Estimated Grand Total _____

With the exception of the production crew, in all cases
where labor charges are involved, employee fringe benefits
and payroll taxes are included in the price schedule.

Ryder Sound Services, Inc. maintains an extensive sound
effects library which is at the disposal of your sound editor
at no extra charge. Selection of sound effects by appointment only.

High speed transfers of sound effects and dialogue, cuts
costs.

Westrex negatives are supplied free of royalty charges.

All work performed is delivered promptly to your cutting
rooms at no extra charge.

Figure 7–5 Ryder Sound Picture Budget Detail Blank.

IATSE Local 695	Studio Minimum Day Rate (9 hr)
Mixer	$344.00
Music, production	299.00
Rerecording	299.00
Operations supervisor	231.00
Amplifier room operator	202.00
Tech test engineer	202.00
Service recorder	202.00
Recording machine operator	193.00
Dubbing machine operator	185.00
Mike boom operator	202.00
Utility sound technician	202.00
Add 22% fringe benefits	

Production Equipment Contingency Costs

Insurance (10% of rental budget)

Intercoms	$20/day
Raincover	$3/day
Location cart	$5/day
Bull horn	$6/day
Scoring clock	$25/day

Budget comparison for 10 minutes of sound effects by various methods:

Mode A. Live Recordings

1. Rental of recording package	$ 182.00
2. Labor, one recordist, one day	225.00
3. Raw stock, $\frac{1}{4}$-inch tape	25.00
4. Transfer to 35mm plus stock (1000 feet)	200.00
5. Effects editor: $100/hr, 2 days	1600.00
6. Edit room and equipment rental (film)	100.00
Average low budget estimate	$2332.00

Mode B. Foley Stage Recording

1. Effects recording to picture with one Foley artist, $200/hr	$ 600.00
2. Transfer, protection copy, and stock	250.00
3. Editor and room rental	1700.00
	$2550.00

Mode C. Library (Canned) Effects

1. Audition with supervisor and one day fee to $ 125.00
   editorial assistant   125.00
2. Transfer to full coat   250.00
3. Sound effects prelay to track on video cassette for
   automated edit   150.00
4. Access or computer edit, per hr   600.00
                                                        $1250.00

Mode D. Total Synthetic Generation/Editing

1. Audition, modify, store effects ($200/hr) $ 600.00
2. Edit to picture on VTR ($200/hr)   600.00
3. Computer layoff (1 hr)   100.00
4. Transfer with time code to master   250.00
5. Raw stock, $\frac{1}{4}$-inch master, video cassette, 35mm full   185.00
                                                        $1735.00

Mode E. Music scoring by Synthesizer

1. Sampling and sequencing ($40/hr) $ 400.00
2. Rights and releases for melodic phrases   400.00
3. Orchestration, resynthesis ($100/hr)   300.00
4. Time coding and edit to VTR ($100/hr)   100.00
5. Digital to analog transfer and stock ($400)   400.00
                                                        $1600.00

A feature with an average production budget of $5 million averages the following for sound (figures are based on the budget for Randal Kleiser's *Summer Lovers*, a typical low-budget feature of the 1980s).

1. Post production sound $124,360
2. Labor and studio mix   51,000
3. Premix   12,275
4. Looping   12,600
5. Final composite print cost   22,915
6. Rights to use the Pointer
   Sister's "Slow Hand" theme
   (however, this was never
   used except in trailer)   30,000
7. Composer and musicians   40,000
8. Location recording and crew   30,000

The recording equipment and crew used 50 days. SAG contracts allowed for three "free" days for talent to loop lines, but transportation and accommodations were paid.

The total allocation for sound was $250,000 or 2.5% of the total production budget, a disproportionately low sum considering the process involved.

Prices differ from coast to coast and are subject to seasonal changes. Some representative studios and guilds are listed. Contact them for updates.

Sound Recording Studios and Related Guilds

American Federation of Musicians
1501 Broadway
New York, N.Y. 10036
(212) 869-1330

National Association of Broadcast
   Engineers & Technicians
322 8th Avenue, 5th Floor
New York, NY 10001

International Sound Technicians
   Local 695 IATSE
11331 Venture Blvd
Studio City, CA. 91604
(818) 985-9204

Aquarius Transfermation
12 E. 46th St
New York, N.Y. 10017

Electro-Nova Productions
342 Madison Avenue
New York, NY 10017

Magno Sound & Video
729 7th Avenue
New York, NY 10019

Howard M. Schwartz Recording
420 Lexington Ave.
New York, NY 10017

TODD A-O Studios East
259 W. 54th St
New York, NY 10019

Motion Picture Studio Mechanics
   Local 52, IATSE
326 West 48th St
New York, NY 10036
(212) 399-0980

Broadcast TV Recording Engineers
6255 Sunset Blvd.
Hollywood, CA. 90028
(213) 851-5515

The Audio Department
119 W. 57th St
New York, N.Y. 10019

Sound One Corp.
1619 Broadway
New York, NY 10019

The Mix Place
663 Fifth Avenue
New York, NY 10036

Sync-Sound Inc
460 W. 56th St
New York, NY 10019

Studio Pass
596 Broadway
New York, NY 10012

THE AURAL OBJECT

Sound is matter. It occupies space. It
has a meaning in and of itself. This
section states a position to be further
developed.

t'ien
hsia
i
chia
THE LIMITS OF
MY *LANGUAGE*
MEAN THE LIMITS
OF MY WORLD

Figure 8–1   Calligraphic design: The limits of my language mean the limits of my world.
From the Chinese, t'ien hsia i chia.

An aural object is a sound that has an immediately recognizable denotation or connotation. It is a fact-based reality that functions like a sign or, better yet, a signal. The reference to which the spectator/listener links this sound may be visual or psychological (emotive/imaginative), but it is neither hallucination nor is it fantasy. The aural object is finite, measurable (in time and space), and memorable; that is, it reinforces itself with each repetition.

The aural object does not generally have a cultural link or a literary basis. Music presents the most clear and direct example of the experience of the aural object. Specific chords and combinations of chords produce very precise emotive responses, more a function of the physiological basis of perception than the psychological basis. The aural object should not be confused with musical allusions that stem from culture, media, or memory. The aural object is primal. The audio designer must learn how to tap into this primal mind-set.

Sound is a waveform. As a pulse-chord of energy, this waveform occupies space, is defined by its movement in terms of long or short intervals between pulses or vibrations. A waveform exhibits the characteristic of pressure. The magnitude of this pressure is inversely proportional to the square of the distance from its source. The source is independent of the effect of the sound it produces. Sound as an object dictates the spectator's response. Although it would be simple to consider music as the primary example of the psychological power of sound, not all sound is music. Noise and light are not music, but they are wave forms.

Sound behaves differently in every spatial context. Therefore, the aural object must be partially defined by its acoustic environment. However, it has been stated previously that the aural object can invoke a response that has not been "learned," that is not conditioned by environment, or that does not result from enculturation. The aborigine, isolated from all visual reference, manufactures a reference after hearing certain sounds. In the tribal world, sound occupies a much more central role in the perception of reality (see Julian Jayne's work on the nature of the bicameral mind).

More concretely, the aural object is a sound that produces an effect or reaction in the audience without the visual reference. We are suggesting that a purely emotive response is the meaning of the "object." Audience imagination is free to associate it with an image; however, this is simply a perceptual bias of Western civilization and as much a function of literacy as anything else.

If we can isolate the "object," we can create extremely powerful primal emotive responses. Observation reveals some examples:

- Low-pitched resonating frequencies around 20 to 50 hertz at certain levels produce a calming effect; raise the level, and the sensation is one of unrest. Discomfort comes at high levels and at higher resonating frequencies as they approach and pass the rhythm of one's heart beat.

- Again from nature, the resonating frequency of a buzzing bee is not generally perceived as a "comfortable" sound. Physiologically, it seems to register as a signal, a warning to action, and a kind of uneasiness sets in if the buzzing level rises.

- We need not understand anything about the source to immediately decipher the sign inherent in a roar. Both the Bantu and the beachboy will respond to the rattle of a snake in much the same way, and more so if their mutual contexts are switched.

In one way, then, of heightening the effect of the aural object on the spectator is to shift its acoustic referent (environment).

Any waveform not in harmony with the average resonant frequency of the body of the listener is bound to elicit discomfort. Hitchcock experimented with low-frequency stimulation to create discomfort in the theater. However, no one, as yet, has attempted to work with the potential of the full tonal pallette. The marriage of composer and Foley artists is necessary to bring about such a sensitivity.

The utilization of synthetic sound-generating systems opens up the possibility of fine-tuning the "object" by use of such programs as CHORUSTAT (see Figure 8–3) which display the waveform to be "adjusted" in such a way as to become graphic "objects" derived from the raw material of sound.

Leopold Survage, piano tuner and cubist painter, began a systematic exploration of waveform movement by relating it to his own painterly colorist patterns, which were to form the basis of a film entitled *Colored Rhythms* (see Figure 8–2). World War I brought the experiment to an end. Tonal compositions in light color and movement were also planned by Wassily Kandinsky, Arnold Schoenberg and others, but neither the technology nor the inspiration were at sufficient levels to develop any surviving examples of what would begin to be a vocabulary of the aural object.

But this understanding of sound as having certain inalienable qualities that could be expressed concretely in light, form, and color rhythms was revived momentarily by Walter Ruttmann, Oskar Fischinger, and others, only to be once again doomed by a world war.

The only commercial attempt to popularize aural concepts was Walt Disney's *Fantasia* (1940) (see Figures 8–4 (a), (b), (c)). As the first "concert" movie, it falls far short of what Survage had first envisioned a generation before; but, nevertheless, it has not been surpassed for sheer novelty of expression and technique. The psychological distancing, perhaps, is the feature of the film that most disappoints. Smooth and flawless, *Fantasia* certainly lifts the spirits but

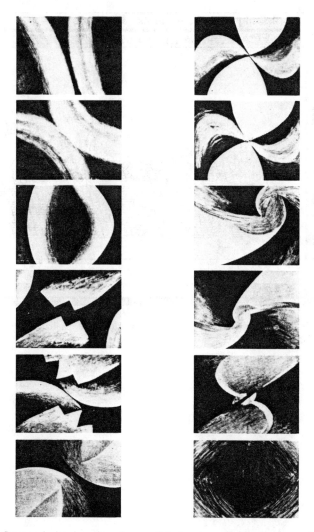

Figure 8–2   Survage insisted on the primacy of rhythm in assessing the power of the pictorial to compete with the aural. Cubism was an attempt to capture the vibratory nature of the universe.

has little dramatic substance. *Fantasia*'s overall aural effect will not be totally realized until it is properly exhibited. The Fantasound system, the color print quality, and the screen size have never been matched correctly. And the rerecording of the music with new orchestration and arrangement modifications served only to make one more aware of its commercial recording industry concerns.

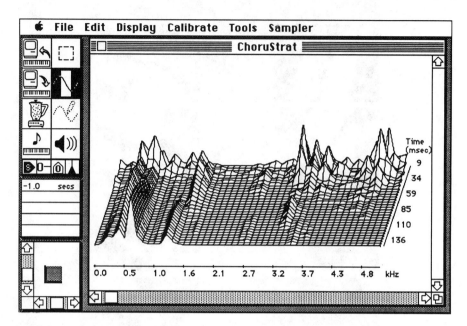

Figure 8–3 Chorustrat: DigiDesign's™ software program for the manipulation and modification of the waveform.

Figure 8–4 Frame abstracts from Walt Disney's *Fantasia*. The hologram would have been the ideal medium to explore the potential of the aural object. In the Fantasound process, separate instrumental sections were recorded on nine optical sound tracks and then mixed down to three discrete tracks combined with a complex control track onto a separate 35mm sound reel for an interlock presentation. The control track routed three channels (true stereo) to three speakers behind the screen and 96 surround speakers placed throughout the theater. Only 14 theaters could handle the system in 1942. The visionary Leopold Stokowski had experimented with the notion of a multichannel auditory perspective, which could be designed and composed directly to the image, foreshadowing by 70 years the intraframe creative precision accessible via MIDI interfaces.

Figure 8–4(a) Every action is a musical (aural) event.

Figure 8–4(b) Observations of the rhythm of nature provide a reference for the aural object.

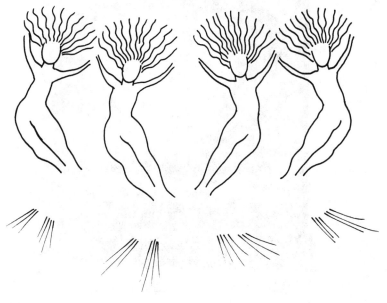

Figure 8–4(c) Patterns of movement yield design in motion, concrete poetry.

IMPROVING TV AUDIO

Television audio has always been a
stepchild to the limits of videotape.
This chapter outlines the conceptual
methods of overcoming the
limitations with a discussion of
audience, techniques of field
production, and the structures of
musicodramatics.

Figure 9–1 Magnet TV by Naim June Paik.

Introduction

Solving the problem of unappealing television audio requires an aesthetic approach, rather than a costly and logistically difficult upgrading of hardware. Whether the transmission of video and audio arrives by cable, fiber-optic phone line, external or internal antenna, satellite dish, and or shortwave/microwave systems, the principal problem remains one of creativity.

High-definition video, component home video systems, enhancement black boxes, simulcasting (with FM radio), and the luxuries of good external speaker placement and noise-reduction systems simply cannot makeup for dull, uninteresting tracks that add nothing to the television experience.

The nature of that experience has been well documented by Marshall McLuhan and others, and a practical understanding of its limits would help to foster an appreciation of its potential for seductive sonic treatment. If we eliminate the classic reasons for poor TV audio, that is, the producer does not care; there is no time or money for good location recording and postproduction; sound seems irrelevant to overall show appeal, marketing, and promotion (except for music videos); and television's formalist obsession with the face and the fast cut, we are left with one undeniable fact: the home arena has not been exploited properly.

There are fewer acoustic variables in the home showplace than there are in studios, theaters, and other venues. It would be valuable to discuss the elements of this space, albeit obvious, in order to come to terms with the options to mediocrity.

The average home viewing space is quiet. It has one window or door, which are potential sources of low-definition noise; however, the level is such that we can consider that background ambience is negligible. The television set or component system is usually positioned against a wall and rarely more than 20 feet from the viewer. Generally, we must consider that the sound is emanating from a single point source, and that source is usually more than 1 foot above the floor. This all suggests only one emotional mode: intimacy.

Intimacy is what video has over the theater. Television is a solitary experience, and it appears to require constant energizing by audio. It is no secret that the 15-second commerical spot often provides the most intense, memorable experience. Why? The TV commercial takes a pointillist approach: clear, clean, loud voice, clearly separated musical phrases or songs, isolated natural and artificial sound effects. Each auditory element is given its place in a linear progression, and there is very little attempt to orchestrate a complex array of sound textures. Silences are also given their due; silences allow sensory recoil, and this pause allows for greater retention as well as recognition. Because the ear also provides a closure apparatus that fills in the gaps, and because there is a physical point of sensory overload due to the high density of vibrations impinging on the hair cells of the organ of Corti, it would be better for producers of television shows (as well as station managers) to think in terms of the linear construction of radio drama. Radio understood the power of intimate communication. Television seems to forget that, despite the field of view of the TV image and what it implies, the aural envelope and acoustic dynamics of the home arena are "bite sized."

The great power of radio drama lay in the quality of voice. What is mediocre about television is the quality of voice and the quality of (density) dialogue. Writing and acting for television must improve. The meaning of a line is essentially provided by the actor or actress. One approach is to create "good gestalts," effective patterns of dialogue and narration that follow basic musical structures. And sound remains the chief source of meaning in television.

The connotative richness of spoken language should be emphasized in script writing and in performance. The choice of voice and its nuances of sound and rhythm—the virtuosity of a musical instrument—should be the chief factor after typage (physical typing).

The two primary forms of spoken language are monologue and dialogue in television. Acting reveals elements through voice and dialogue that the writer need not nor often cannot specify, nor provide by the image: speech can reveal class, regionalism occupation, age, attitudes, and the like. Producers have to discover the right balance of vocalization to referential music and impacting effects. Most on-air promotion spots distill the essence of a given program and achieve the appropriate balance for the subject matter; they embody exactly what most full-length programs lack.

What Every Program Needs

- Gripping aural introduction
- Memorable melody used inventively
- Vocal density and intensity
- Clearly defined "toon" effects
- Symmetrical, musically rhythmic pacing
- Compressed movement and space

Radio understood how speech patterns (internal, external, and direct) reflect qualities of character. Language is camouflage. The nuances of voice and delivery communicated who characters were, where they were, what they were doing, when they acted, and how they felt about what they were doing. Television rarely achieves this economy of aural association and drama. But TV audio is far more dense than the fragmented mosaic of the visual. HDTV will not greatly affect this gap. At its best, TV audio has a cartoon energy but lacks impact and definition, because it is not being mixed with a recognition of the intimate space in which it will operate. TV audio seems to be either too noisy or pointedly unimportant to the story.

The creative challenge is to express the nonverbal nonvisually. While precision sound tracks may supply narrative data through mood and rhythmic structure, they seldom express true aural objects. Aural objects cannot be reduced to the visual. **Thoughts, ideas, states of being,** and **mood rhythms** are aural objects.

The technical challenge for television audio is to increase narrative complexity without impairing clarity within the intimate aural envelope of the home arena. Because it is more difficult to find and deal with great voices and great dialogue, television programming has simplified itself to the level of action/ adventure; all clamor and movement to keep the viewer's attention kinesthetically. At the other end of the spectrum is the often tiresome and stodgy closet drama, which provides a quiet, balanced, albeit monotonous, talkathon, devoid of intensification.

Intensification is achieved through exceptional language, ''toon'' and radio ''tricks'' (aural illusions/allusions), and silences. Intensification is an outgrowth of the subtext of language, how words are intoned, delivered, and so on. The forms of narration in classical radio discourse are adaptable to television:

Subjective: Addressing the audience in first person

Continuous: Chronological description from the single point of view

Simultaneous: Expression of two or more events/actions/objects existing at the same time in different locations

Parallel: Expression of two or more themes or events that occur at different times (by comparison)

Elliptical: Aural movement back and forward in time; entering the spaces of the past while operating in the future

Curiously, television often uses the conventions of radio drama, resorting to musical clichés inserted over reaction shots in standard sitcoms and dramas to denote simplistic emotional states. The well-used laugh track is another convention overused due to lack of confidence in the material and the ability of talent to convey what is intended. At best, such tracks are aural distractions that grossly contradict the intimate nature of the aural envelope in the home. In contradistinction, the TV commercial is always personal and confidential, speaking to the one-and-only you, never to an ''audience.''

Addressing the Solitary Viewer

When the TV is turned on, the viewer is ready to listen. The rhythmic requirements of dialogue for television must take into account that the **choice** of words often determines **actions** or defines **emotions**.

1. **Internal dialogue:** Formally a cinematic soliloquy or interior monologue, it is private, subjective, and has a component that is unheard, requiring pauses (listening to self) to distinguish it from narration. What changes the meaning of words?
   - Juxtaposition with reaction shot of the listener
   - Juxtaposition with insert shot of object or event
   - Juxtaposition with environmental shots
   - Blend with music (echo, whisper, thunder, birds) and effects
   - Change in shot size; long shots and close-ups have different connotations
   - Change in vocal emphasis, intonation, inflection, or diction
   - Degree of density of performance; lack of or overdone articulation and gesture
2. **Narration:** can refer to on-screen or off-screen events. The narrator defines the geo-locus and time of the subject. Voice-over can overcome audiovisual discrepancies by masking mistakes.
   - Voice-over recaps the visual (Fox Movietone News)
   - First-person observer describes the unseen (*Night and Fog*)
   - Voice advances plot without being "witness" (*La Jetée*)
   - Voice entices participation of viewer by direct confrontation (may be seen looking out at you; a newscaster, for instance)
   - Organic voice that seems to be part of the event (*Battle of Algiers, Granton Trawler*)

Functions of Music in TV

1. **Program music:** Indispensable shortcut; the tone poem performs the function of creating emotional ambience without overstatement (at best) and without redundancy ("Avengers," "Hart to Hart").
2. **Theme music:** Provides specific emotional context for the narrative cues the audience may need; often a chord or musical brief or series of effects ("Twilight Zone" theme, "Peter Gunn," "Mission Impossible").
3. **Leitmotiv:** Nonliteral descriptive sounds that have entered into the musical iconography have a sign or a naming of parts (cliché of film music like "menacing" zither phrases). Used to identify event, idea, personage, or a "presence." Dramatic function is allusion; the reference leads the viewer to a specific recurring phenomenon; predictive; Pavlovian.

4. **Expressive synthesis:** Abstract sounds evoke feeling, create ''colors'';
   they describe the quality or condition of a thing or event, as in cartoon
   sounds that give the ''feeling of the bounce'' as a character tumbles.
   a. The **symbolic function** denotes nonliteral unseen (nondiegetic) image/
      facts or emotions, spatial orientation (siren before the forest fire); can
      form sonic bridges and transitions. In *Listen to Britain* (1942), visuals
      are extensions of the sound.
   b. The **onomatopoeaic function** denotes a sound, invented, or synthe-
      sized, that mirrors the sound to which it refers; the formation of words
      that have a sound imitating what they denote, for instance, *hiss, cuckoo.*
      The rhythms of dialogue and music re-create rhythms of the subject.
   c. The **contrapuntal function** denotes sounds or melodies that operate
      simultaneously, enriching each other; the sounds may be musical
      phrases played, words, spoken, or phrases sung. Orson Welles utilized
      vocal overlapping in *Citizen Kane* and *The Magnificent Ambersons*
      to mirror the patterns of everyday conversation in opposition to the
      clearly separated idioms of theatrical dialogue carried over from the
      stage to screen.
   d. The editorial function consists of conventions of rhythmic pacing that
      conform to the patterns of real movement. Musical form lends itself
      best to structures that denote or describe movement: A waltz is a three-
      meter movement that may parrot the skipping and sliding of children
      at play; a tango's quadruple meter may refer to yet another form of
      play (or work).

The musical values of language often conflict with the meanings of words.
The musicality of certain words enriches the sense of their own expression. In
television dialogue, specifically, the prosodic qualities of language should be
understood. Writing dialogue with an understanding of metrical form may serve
to enliven and enhance the density of the material, which the actor may then
mold and interpret, intone, and deliver. René Clair explored the different rhythmic ways in which work and play are performed.

Microphone as Voice and Instrument

Microphone placement and choice is dependent on four variables:

1. Pick-up pattern (isolation)
2. Room acoustic (limitations)
3. Presence/mood (desired)
4. Nature of vocals (emphasis, diction, pronunciation)

For example, you want to create (choose one from each set)

Large space   Dead space   Happy space   Rich/resonant space
Small space   Noisy space   Solemn space   Dry/sibilant space

In an *ideal* situation, accepting that the microphone is acting in linear fashion, we can make some general assumptions that may help to narrow the field in choosing the correct or most effective microphone for the given application.

1. The pattern of the microphone generally defines the size of the space, but placement can destroy the effect (off axis) or support it.
   - An omni placed in any size room will give a sense of the actual space at normal levels because it mixes a balance of background and foreground ambience with the principal signal (within its maximum area of sensitivity).
   - A directional system tends to create more intimacy due to isolation of the background; but when used in very large spaces, there is a point where it begins to act like an omni.
   - Multiple microphones should open up a space, but this is subject to pockets of sound and/or gaps as a function of placement. An omni placed near a boundary will act like a PZM system.
2. The size of the element and powering function (dynamic or condenser) determines how closely a given class of microphones acts like the ideal. Most omnidirectional systems provide a full sound, but the range of sensitivity differs greatly. A mini-mike will not pick up information beyond a 5-foot radius, while some studio omnis may be suspended from the ceiling to cover an entire room.

Most directional microphones specified as "cardioid" do not really tell you much about sonic limits. Their degree of isolation and range must be heard during use. Trial and error is the only way to build an inventory of sense memory so that the designer can qualify each mike according to performance in the field.

Table 9–1 provides a tonal comparison grid for four types of microphone. The pattern tends to approximate the shape of a given space.

The omnidirectional gives a full sound that includes all the background

TABLE 9–1 Tonal Comparison Grid

	Dynamic	Ribbon	RF Condenser	Electret
Omni	Cool	Warm	Cool	Hot
Bi	Cold	Cool	Warm	Warm
Uni	Warm	Warm	Hot	Hot
PZM	Cool	—	Warm	Warm

unless it is a "mini mike," whose receptive radius is approximately 5 feet. This limited range provides a quiet more intimate sound.

The unidirectional degree of isolation differs from microphone to microphone. The ratio of background to wanted signal is also determined by use on or off axis to the primary sound source. The aural image, therefore, may be tailored to suit needs by carefully listening to the effect of repositioning the directional microphone.

Bidirectional systems tend to perform well in a small space, giving adequate separation of background to foreground, but they must be placed centrally to avoid complete isolation of certain areas of the shot.

Pressure zone microphones provide full spatial fidelity (although this is not apparent from monitoring). Less reflected sound is transduced, but the system generally reconstructs the natural acoustics of a given room.

Microphone construction adds coloration to a given sound. These characteristics are generally perceived as imparting a certain mood or tone to a given sound in a given space.

Condenser	Tends to be **bright**
Electret	Tends to be **brassy**
Dynamic	Tends to impart **warmth**
Ribbon	Tends to convey resonance, **depth**

Fidelity to the sound source ought to be the primary value of a given microphone; however, many microphones are chosen for the way they modify or alter the pure tones from a source. The two parameters of fidelity are **vocal** and **spatial.**

Some examples of how microphones perform are:

Preserve	Dynamic omni (wireless) for news interview ("Latenight with David Letterman")
Improve	Electret cardioid for dialogue (soap opera "All My Children")
Augment	Stereo condenser shotgun for studio set piece ("Saturday Night Live")
Clarify	Condenser cardioid for location dialogue (TV Movie)
Dramatize	Ribbon unidirectional for vocals (Music/Variety)

The Structures of Musicodramatics

Any program can be understood as a series of scenes whose depicted or implied auditory spaces form a pattern. Sound structures do not necessarily have to follow this pattern; but as a design strategy, it would be easier, at first, to organize the basic building blocks (sound bites) into musically inspired structures.

These bites may be words, song, music, aural objects, and background. In the typical program, music may be linked to action, but it also may play a role in it. In police action dramas, such as "Hunter," for every action there could be a musical reaction.

Music can perform the function of background whose "redundant integrity" amounts to noisy, continuous levels or planes of punctuation.

Music can replace natural sound onomatopoetically as it mirrors both the sound and sense of objects and things.

Tonal music is continuous in time, with strict logical structures of rhythm, melody, and harmonic progress. Most program structures in film and video have seemingly been constructed with these notions intact. But there is no reason why a track cannot be composed atonally using the 12-tone aleatoric system, dissonant or otherwise, which characterizes the scores and tracks of, for instance, Japanese cinema and Kabuki Theater, with their emphasis on the significant moment.

Music provides keys to character and emotional truth, as expressed by musician and critic Michel Chion in Claudia Gorbman's *Unheard Melodies* (Indiana University Press, 1987); he ritualizes music's role in dramatic structure as threefold:

> **empathetic** [*giving hints or cues to the character's emotional state and their actions*]; **didactic counterpoint** *presenting an aural idea which must be interpreted* [*by audience*]; *and* **anempathetic**, *"evidencing the indifference (consequently) of the world as audience to the events foreclosed, in a massive transference often due to mere coincidence, the weight of a human destiny which it at once sums up and disdains. [from Michel Chion, Le Son au cinema (Paris: Cahiers du cinéma/Editions de l'étoile, 1985)].*

So we can see how music can "rub it in" as a concluding directorial viewpoint. But, in general, the choice and use of musical material should always conform to directorial attitude, although this is often not the case. The audio designer has the task to make it so. Nothing should be arbitrary.

Japanese classical music, used in Kenzo Mizoguchi's *The Crucified Lovers*, forms an organic and integral part of the overall formal texture. According to Noel Burch in his *Theory of Film Practice* (Praeger, N.Y. 1973), this is due to the extremely flexible, supple, "open" quality of this music, which is not subject to the tyranny of the bar line as Western music is and is not restricted to tonal structures. Atonal music is naturally more adaptable to the nonmeasurable rhythms of film and video action and editing. Our preoccupation with formal narrative structures seems pressured more by reliance on conventional music structures than with any storytelling necessity.

In his *Force of Evil*, Abraham Polonsky reverses and inverts this obsession with melodic precision by converting dialogue into musically organized sound—

alliterations, dissonant rhymes, rhythmical effects, "colors" of silence—which conform best to French director Michel Fano's ideal of "audioplastics," the conception and technical execution of the entire sound complex during shooting and editing as well. Preconceived sound structures can determine certain visual components and, as with Mizoguchi, visually identifiable on-screen sounds with distinct rhythms of their own synchronize naturally, not mathematically, with on-screen images and with images intimately associated with musical elements occurring off screen (nondiegetic).

Music as Technique Applied to Story, and Technique as Outgrowth of Story (see Figure 9–2)

1. Music is used to evoke an image. Chord alludes to a baby.
2. Music creates a resonant space. Tritone drone for machine room.
3. Music mirrors a character's emotions. Happy notes, distinct idioms, "stingers."
4. Music suggests inherent off-screen space.
5. Music becomes the structuring principle for dialogue, camera movement, movement within the shot, and editing (rhythmic or aleatoric) (see the work of Abraham Polonsky).
6. Music functions as punctuation. Kabuki Theater.
7. Music functions as special effect (piano chord for a slap).

Figure 9–2   The peacock was introduced to the public May 12, 1986, and is now the official symbol of NBC. (© 1986 National Broadcasting Co.)

8. Music functions as "accidental" nature. Chance sounds.

9. Music functions as anempathetic evidence of director's attitude. Ironic counterpoint.

10. Music functions as an "intimate reality," an aural object or third-person character in and of itself (out of a confrontation with the camera and reality, not necessarily from the perspective of a "spectator"). A musical presence.

11. Music faithfully observes the rules of continuity, providing scene transitions and thematic parallels, and smooths over discontinuities of space and time.

12. Music masks noise or action, allowing the audience to enter the dream state of film and video spectatorship.

Video Field Systems and Multitrack Magnetic Recording

The following sections are a basic introduction to problems in electronic news gathering (ENG) and electronic field production (EFP) and how to solve them. The discussion marries the basic mike and hardware applications previously considered in relation to video production. Intercom systems, noise reduction, and support gear are illustrated to provide a practical inventory of solutions. (See Figure 9–3)

The details of a representative 8- or 16-track table-top multitrack recorder are discussed with consideration of how the system can be used as a low-cost method of generating music, effects, and voice tracks and then combined into a simple mixdown and transferred to film or video.

ENG/EFP Audio

Reliability of performance is all that matters for the traditionalist newscameraman (team). Nothing is older than yesterday's news, and nothing is more of a burden than the responsibility of capturing the news as it happens (grab shots with sound bites). The team only gets one chance. Simplicity of operation and instantaneous recordability led to the total acceptance of video over film for news-gathering operations. (See Figure 9–4)

Even coaxial magazines were not fast or safe enough. Film presented the problem of processing time and limited-run recording capacity before reload. In addition, sound-on-film was no better or worse than sound-on-video. Although the cameras were more expensive and less rugged, videotape is much cheaper.

Conversion to stereo broadcasting created yet another field production problem. How to get clean, separated sound editable for same-day replay without sacrificing portability and ease of operation? How to obtain quiet tracks in anticipation of improved home receivers with stereo surround sound systems beyond the quality of average theatres?

Figure 9–3   Neumann MS system for field stereo recording. (Courtesy of NBC
TV Network.)

Clean sound at the source is mandated. The options are to use the single-
system sound recorded directly on video or to take along a van with a portable
multitrack recorder/mixer (See Figure 9–5).

Many ENG camera systems (Sony Betacam) have a directional electret
condenser shotgun-type microphone mounted directly above and to the right of
the taking lens and wired directly through camera circuitry to the recorder pack.
Its output is fed to the component recorder. The system affords only minor
adjustments to level and equalization. Essentially, it's a turn-on and shoot
operation. Systems like the Ikegami HL79 and later generations of chip cameras
offer a two-person option in which miking is done at the remote $\frac{3}{4}$- or 1-inch
recorder in a van (See Figure 9–6).

Since the microphone of the fixed Betacam cannot be quickly repositioned,
but rather follows the line of sight of the lens, the cameraman movement requires
traditional windscreen protection to decrease wind noise (See Figure 9–7).

Since the MS microphone pairing is the only system that is operable for

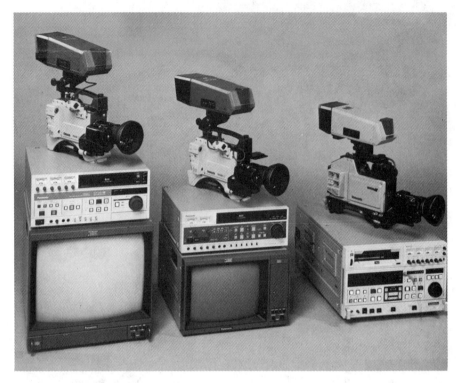

Figure 9–4   Double-system video requires a separate recorder/mixer unit and/or a Nagra IV TC machine. Mike: Sennheiser ME 80.

Figure 9–5   Component video has a piggyback recorder attached to the camera head. Audio is by direct connection. Here a foam screen is used over an electret short-range shotgun.

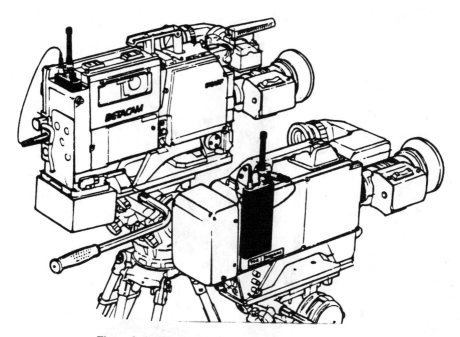

Figure 9–6   Wireless receivers piggybacked to Betacam.

live recording in stereo for location news, new swivel-mounted, double-element microphones are currently in use.

The alternative is the use of a soundman with fishpole. All the basic procedures obtain for the ENG crew. The pole need never be maneuvered more than 4 feet in any direction from its initial position within the shot. Movements should be discrete, nonvibratory, and level controlled through a portable shoulder-slung mixer (Shure FP31 or Audio Technica). The angle of incidence of the microphone element should always be at 45 degrees to the subject. Mechanical noise must be avoided. Get as close as possible without intruding on the camera–subject intimacy. (see Figure 9–8)

A more positive, trouble-free option is to piggyback wireless receivers at the rear of the camera and simply mount subjects with wireless transmitters or use the wireless fishpole. All the concerns of wireless placement must be mastered: antenna position, battery life, level adjustment, and secured mounting. (see Figures 9–9, 9–10)

Stereo Miking

There are obvious limitations to both possible approaches to stereo (two-track) recording: isolation of each source by individual wireless or conventional microphones versus miking of the sound field with a traditional MS double-element microphone to achieve "stereo" effect. Correct spatial separation and

Figure 9–7   Soundman ready for almost anything except dead batteries.

aural perspective will, nevertheless, have to be embellished in postproduction unless great care is taken in the field. Under the stressful conditions of live ENG, that is unlikely. (See Figure 9–11)

Current Audio Formats in Video

Longitudinal audio is a stationary audio signal recorded as discrete tracks by a fixed recording head. Tape speed and track width determine the limits of fidelity. In quad, consumer Beta, and some VHS machines, longitudinal audio is mono. Three-quarter inch, industrial high-end Beta, original Betacam, M-format, some VHS, and two of the tracks in Betacam SP and MII formats exhibit two-channel stereo. One-inch type B and type C video have three lon-

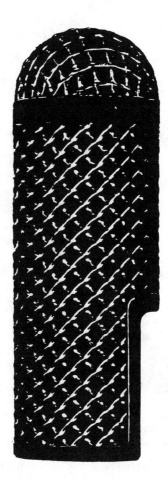

Figure 9–8 Betascreen from Litewave System, Inc.

gitudinal tracks. There are four longitudinal tracks in PAL/SECAM type B and C systems. Longitudinal audio recording is less prone to failure. Individual tracks may be recorded and edited apart from video.

Dolby type C noise reduction is now employed in the linear tracks of MII, Betacam SP, and U-matic SP. Type A Dolby inhabits the 1-inch world through outboard encoder/decoders or plug-in cards.

PCM digital audio provides greater fidelity and more channel capacity. Early systems were comprised of PCM adapters with the digital tracks being recorded on a $\frac{3}{4}$- or 1-inch machine. D-1 and D-2 hydrid digital formats feature four PCM digital audio channels plus a linear track for cue and a time code track. The Sony 1-inch format BVH-2800 series system has two PCM tracks, as well as conventional linear tracks. The current specifications for consumer Hi 8mm allow for AFM audio, linear audio, *and* PCM! The limit for Hi 8's PCM is the systems overall low sampling rate.

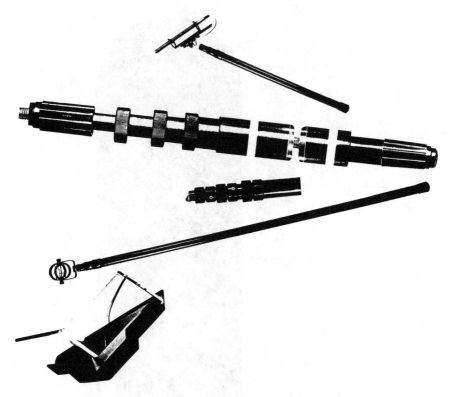

Figure 9–9 *Wireless fishpole* components: standard tubular fishpole,
shockmount for specific microphone; mounting board or clip attachment for
wireless transmitter may be placed at any point on the pole for proper balance
and user comfort. A PZM2.5 could be mounted without a suspension and wired
to the transmitter for full rejection of noise from behind.

Audio-frequency modulation (AFM) audio consists of two or more wide-
bandwidth audio channels free of mechanically induced errors; it was developed
for the Betamax consumer format. This system enables recording of audio within
video. The channels are multiplexed with the total FM signal and deposited on
the tape in the same manner as conventional video. This video recording isolates
audio from mechanical problems.

The VHS-HI FI technique (depth multiplex recording) uses a separate set
of video heads set at a severe azimuth offset angle to record the audio pair deep
in the tape's magnetic layer, with the standard heads depositing video over
audio. This process is employed in VHS and S-VHS formats. In VHS HI FI
or AFM, audio cannot be stripped off, edited, or mixed and laid back to tape
without disturbing video.

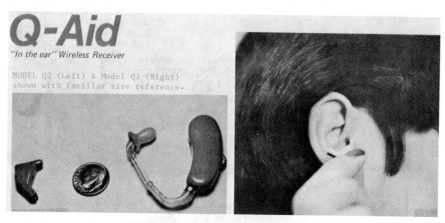

Figure 9–10 The Q Master receiver fits in the ear as a cueing device for soundmen, actors, and director. It can also allow a singer to vocalize to playback. Paging and intercom can be linked for private communication only to those wearing the Q-Aid or Q Master system. The system can be linked to a wireless microphone setup so that the soundman can monitor. For blue screen and chromakey work, audio can be fed from blue set to main set so that dialogue is possible between actors on separate sets. A wire induction loop that circles the stage or studio is connected to the output of a small audio amplifier, creating a magnetic field that is picked up by the receiver.

Field Options

Three-quarter-inch machines all have two linear audio tracks. Sony BVU decks have an additional address track for time code. SP decks have Dolby type C NR.

One-inch B and C decks have three standard audio channels. PAL and SECAM versions employ an additional EBU track.

In component video, Betacam and MII offer two linear tracks with optional noise reduction, with two AFM audio channels added to Betacam SP.

Four individual tracks may not be recorded, however, in camcorders or camera/recorder systems since they have only two inputs. Studio-grade SP decks allow for the breakdown of individual tracks, but AFM sound segments cannot be laid back to preexisting video.

MII has two linear tracks with selectable Dolby C and two AFM tracks with individual access to all tracks. The AFM and linear tracks are not paired.

Beta and ED-Beta systems have single linear audio tracks. ED-Beta pro decks and consumer decks offer two-channel Beta hi-fi (AFM technique), not separately accessible.

Older Beta SLO/SLP 300 systems have linear stereo by splitting the mono

Figure 9–11 Portable Shure ENG Mixer with Beyer DT-100 headsets (not to scale).

track, thus creating mono-compatible stereo, which is prone to phase cancellation when summed or played on mono decks.

VHS began with one linear track, grew to linear stereo, and then VHS HI FI, which cannot be split and laid back. Some VHS consumer machines have stereo VHS HI FI, but the linear audio is mono.

Hi 8mm machines have at least 1 AFM channel; some have a stereo PCM pair with the AFM track receiving a mono mix.

Shooting Film for Video Post

The following recommended practices are identified for shooting 16mm original negative with time code and ¼-inch Nagra with time code:

16mm Original Negative

- Label all cans correctly with frame rate used (24, 25, 29.97, 30 fps) and time code used (24, 25, 29.97 drop or nondrop, 30 drop or nondrop).
- If camera speed is 24 or 30 feet per second (fps), use 30 fps drop or nondrop time code; if camera speed is 29.97 fps, used 29.97 fps drop or nondrop time code.
- A 5-second **preroll** is required on the audio tape for **each take.**
- If using an electronic slate, make sure a clean, clear LED slate shot is seen in the camera viewfinder and always close the clapper for an audible backup slate. (see Figure 9–12)
- Make clear, legible sound reports.
- To avoid a 1% pitch shift when shooting music videos, always shoot at 29.97 fps and record audio time code at 29.97 fps, or shoot at 24 or 30 fps to audio playback where ¼-inch audio has been recorded at 29.97 fps and played back referenced to 30 fps.

NAGRA IV-S Time Code Operations

- Select one of the following recording standards:
  - 24 fps (American motion picture SMPTE)
  - 25 fps (European film/video EBU)
  - 30 fps (American film/video SMPTE)
  - 29.97 fps with drop frame
  - 29.97 fps without drop frame
  Selection is made via an internal switch on the time code circuit board.
- TC switch: When in TEST position, the signal at the output connector is not shifted (compensated for distance between time code and record head). This is pure time code used when Nagra is serving as the master clock.

- Mini keyboard: sets time code generator. Generator may be switched out of the circuit if required to work with external time code source. As long as there are batteries in the machine, the code will be preserved. Otherwise, a maximum of three days following the last time code or user bits modification is the life.
- Main switch and fast-forward switch control the record and playback functions of the time code circuit. In stop (main switch), the live memory RAM and the real-time circuit RTC are powered, keeping the clock running.
- Display: Keyboard entries provide the following:
  a. Time code display in hours, minutes, seconds, frames
  b. User data bits derived from internal or external source
  c. Time code status (24, 25 30 fps)
- Functions: Mini keyboard keys select direct, shifted, and numerical. Setting the internal clock with an external master clock is made through a connection to the exit time code right-side input, followed by pressing "Set from ext." To reset the time code to zero, press "Reset TC." "Set Disable" locks out a later time code or user data that might accidently be entered.
- To change a display digit:

  a. Press "Call TC" or "Call UB."
  b. Followed by the left arrow 1 or right arrow 2 to select the digit to change; it pulsates.
  c. Press up arrow 3 or down arrow 4 to increase or decrease digit value.
  d. "Inc UB" is used to change the last two digits of the user bits.

Using Time Code in the Reel World

Here are some helpful hints prepared by Manfred Klemme and Jim Tanenbaum from their time code seminar:

1. Many devices that use time code have an 8-digit display. Therefore, they can only show the time portion of the code or the user bits at one time. Often, "flag" information such as "Drop Frame" will be shown by the presence of a decimal point at a location marked on the unit's panel.
2. Drop Frame mode is dropping frame numbers, not actual frames of picture or sound.
3. Time code is recorded with **zero offset;** that is, the time code in the center track corresponding to a given point in the audio is directly in line with the location of that audio in the other two tracks (stereo). Since two heads cannot occupy the same point at the same time, there is a need to delay

the recording of the time code in the Nagra and also during playback; delay must occur before the code is ready by the sync head.

4. Unlike multitrack recorders, the Nagra does not have a crosstalk problem with audio and time code tracks.

5. There are some variants to the Nagra time code standard. Coherent Communications' time code generator records code on the FM track. AATON uses neopilotone sync with a burst of time code at the head and/or tail of the take. Fostex, Otari, Sony, Stellavox, Studer, and Tascam are compatible with the Nagra IVS-TC.

6. Most cameras expose the time code for each frame near the edge of the negative, outside the picture area. Some use numerals, while others use bar codes. There are two different formats for writing (exposing) the time code on film:

   a. **Continuous type C:** has 80 binary bits spaced uniformly along the film. There is no gap between codes.

   b. **Block type B:** adds extra bits as needed for its sync and timing, for a total of 112 bits per time code unit. There are gaps between codes. Gaps are filled with a fixed pattern of ones and zeros to avoid disturbance due to the gap. Splices can be made without loosing any code.

   The Arriflex time code system exposes a continuous bar code pattern type C on film during pull-down. The AATON time code exposes a checkerboard pattern of block type B code. Panavision has adopted a variation of this. Cameras without an internal generator can use an external source like a video monitor or electronic slate.

7. Many synchronizers do not "look" at the entire time code, just the frames and seconds. Shooting past midnight, the time code changes from 23:59:59:29 to 00:00:00:00, which reads as an error or triggers fast-forward (simulating the head of the roll). So, stop before midnight, wait, and then reslate with new date and roll number.

Some Uses of Time Code

1. Film-to-video transfer: Because video tape recorders take at least 3 seconds to get up to speed, each scene needs at least that amount of **preroll** (unusable sound and picture slack before transfer can take place). Without preroll, each take must be rolled back to a point 3 seconds into the previous take and then run up to speed. The Nagra T-Audio TC allows for direct transfer of audio to tape, saving one generation. In addition to the usual data, every slate should show camera frame rate, the time code standard used, and the frame offset.

2. Automated assembly in final edit: A computer controls a bank of dubbers and VTRs by a time-coded edit list log. For each cut, however, the system needs at least 10 seconds of roll-up to speed and sync lock.

3. Recording double-system sound at 24 or 25 fps to be edited and released on film: This requires a camera with code, a recorder with code, and an editor (flatbed) that can search magstripe dailies for code edit points.

4. Recording double system sound with the picture shot on film at 24 fps to be edited on videotape and released on film: The film negative is conformed to the edited videotape.

5. Recording double system sound with picture shot on videotape: The time code reference must come from the video tape recorder and the Nagra standard must match exactly. The audio transfer machine may search and locate sound on the $\frac{1}{4}$-inch production track through the time code and automatically sync-up and transfer audio to videotape. Time code generated by the audio recorder is either sent to one of the video recorder's **audio tracks** or entered as **user bits** in the video time code. Since audio time code is not synchronized to the video frame edge, it must pass through a regenerator controlled by the video master clock to match its timing to that of the user bits in the video time code. The sound is never perfectly aligned to the video picture with frame line accuracy. Apparent sync problems may be due to **acoustic delay.** Repeated loss of the video time code recorded on audio will cause defects in the transfer process. Recording **continuous** audio time code on audio tape allows for resolving and synching to videotape at some point where the audio time code was received and recorded on it, despite dropouts. (For additional references, consult Jim Tanenbaum's *The Production Mixer's Manual*, Sound Recording Services, Los Angeles, 1989.)

6. Recording double system sound with picture shot on film at 24 or 30 fps to be edited on videotape and released on videotape: Rank-Cinetel transfer systems run 24 fsp negative at 23.976 and 30 fps negative at 29.97 fps to 29.97 fps video (24 fps times the ratio of the TV sync frequency, 59.94 to 60, or 1% slower). Since sound should be recorded at 30 fps for video, in the transfer it will be slow by the same 1% and, therefore, in sync.
   a. Transfer method 1: Every fourth film frame is printed twice. In 1 second, 24 film frames become 30 video frames. The film's average speed is still 24 fps; audio recorded at 30 fps is then converted as above.
   b. Transfer method 2: Each video frame is made up of two fields. The first field consists of odd-numbered scan lines interlaced with the second field of even-numbered scan lines. At 30 fps, the **field rate** is 60 fps (fields per second.) In the **3.2 pulldown** transfer method, the first film frame is scanned by the first two video fields, the second film frame is scanned by the next three video fields, the third is scanned by the next two, the fourth by three fields, and so on. Half the frames will generate two video fields, and half will generate three. The average of 2.5 fields/frame times the 24 fps film rate = 60 fps, which is the requirement for 30-fps video.

The final result exhibits an undetectable lowering of pitch and slowing down of picture.

References

DI GIULIO, ED. "Developments in Motion Picture Camera Design & Technology," *SMPTE Journal* (Jul 1976) pp. 481–92.

———. "Report on the Status of Time Code for Films in the U.S.," *SMPTE Report* (Jul 1979).

"EBU Code for Synchronization Between Film Camera and Audio Tape Recorders," *Fact Specification—EBU Technical Paper* 3096E (May 1976).

ENGEBRETSON W. AND JOHN EARGLE. "Cinema Sound Reproduction Systems: Technical Advances and Systems Design Considerations," *SMPTE Journal* (Nov 1982) pp. 1046–57.

GLADDEN, QUINCY. "Electronic Time-Based Coding As Used in Film," unpublished paper for Cinema 09 (LACC, 1980).

KLEMME, MANFRED. "Notes On Using SMPTE Time Code," (Nagra Magnetic) 1987.

MALLION, B. "SMPTE Time Code Comes to Audio." *db* (Nov 1978) pp. 39–42.

$\frac{1}{4}$ *Inch Audio-to-Video Synching,* Illustrated Guide from Du Art Labs. 245 W. 55th Street, New York, N.Y. 10019.

ZARIN AND RIORDAN. "Practical Applications of SMPTE Time Code in Audio, Video, Film Post Production," *Recording Eng./Prod.* (Oct 1983) pp. 184–95.

Motion pictures—sound effects

"Hearing is not believing when sound designers . . . stick it in your ear" (includes glossary of sound designer jargon) by Frank Spotnitz il V15 *American Film* (Oct. 1989), p. 40(6).

"One hand clapping: digital audio is changing film sound; will audiences notice?" by Karen Wright V260 *Scientific American* (June 1989), p. 35(3).

"Joan Rowe: Foley mixer" by Michele Seipp il V33 *Los Angeles Magazine* (August 1988), p. 28(1).

"Audio alchemy" (Chace Productions Inc. converting sound tracks of old movies to stereo) by Gail Buchalter il V140 *Forbes* (Oct. 5, 1987), p. 188(1).

"Sound by Splet: Mosquito Coast's bugs, birds and burps" (moving-picture sound design) by Steven Gowin il V21 *Theatre Crafts* (Feb. 1987), p. 71(2).

Motion picture music—automation

"Automation drains musical gene pool: genius will have less chance to develop" by John Glasel V100 *Billboard Magazine* (Oct. 15 1988), p. 9(1).

Motion picture music—books

"The melody lingers on: the great songwriters and the movie musicals (book reviews)" by Roy Hemming A V326 *Variety* (Feb. 11, 1987), p. 92(1).

Motion picture music—criticism, interpretation, etc.

"The lyrical assassin at 5 A.M.; got a favorite movie theme? This man probably wrote it" (Ennio Morricone) by Jay Cocks il V129 *Time* (March 16, 1987), p. 83(1).

Motion picture music—history

Movie music: from King's Row and King Kong to Miami Vice, music from the movies and TV sounds better than ever on CD. (includes special section of CD reviews) by Steve Simels il V52 *Stereo Review* (April 1987), p. 59(1) 38J4173

Motion picture music—history and criticism

Music at the movies: turn it down! by Jon Pareles il V 93 *Mademoiselle* (October 1987), p. 96(3) 41B3321

Motion picture music—production and direction

'Singing Detective' soundtrack a fine collection of '30s tunes. V334 *Variety* (February 22, 1989), p. 354(1)

Recording "Ironweed"—with an audience. (Studio Log) (column) by Tommy Tedesco il V22 *Guitar Player* (November 1988), p. 126(1)

More on movie sound. (The High End) (column) by Ralph Hodges V53 *Stereo Review* (September 1988), p. 127(1) 46A3077

10

STEREO AND TWO-TRACK RECORDING

Basic examination is made of stereo recording techniques, with emphasis on separation of sound elements, accurate placement of sound elements, spatial orientation, and the division of voice from background. Classic stereo mike setups are illustrated, with a discussion of the advantages and disadvantages of each method. A brief overview is given of the features of the Nagra stereo and how to record as a two-track system on location as a technique for eliminating background noise. The reader is encouraged to develop a personal creative response to and understanding of stereo.

The movie industry introduced the general public to the experience of stereophonic sound first in the multichannel 1940 presentation of Warner's VitaSound for *Santa Fe Trail* and *Four Wives*. The war rendered the expensive three-dimensional sound system installation impractical, and it was not until Disney released *Fantasia* (1942) that any other effort was made to establish stereo sound as an integral part of the entertainment complex. Conductor Leopold Stokowski had experimented in 1926 at Bell Laboratories with "auditory perspective,"

Figure 10–1 Title stereo.

which required two or more telephone connections arranged in proper perspective to the sound source, to record what would become, for Rouben Mamoulian, a pioneering two-track sound process for *Applause* (1929).

Not until the 1954 release of *A Star Is Born* were audiences again inspired by the prospect of stereo through Judy Garland's stunning stereo numbers. Although a consumer market for high-fidelity stereo recordings arose, the film industry after the brief success of stereo as presented with the Cinerama process, made spot attempts to produce stereo pictures but, for the most part, released all their features in mono sound. With CinemaScope, four-track sound made sense in its embellishment of a process that was more accessible to the average theater owner. Fox especially made headway in refining stereo recording techniques, as well as playback technology. But little improvement was forthcoming until the six-track systems of the 1960s epics and musicals.

In 1975, Dolby Labs developed a four-channel process that introduced the element of directional sound between its front and surround channels. Using a refined bilateral, variable-area optical sound track, two optical tracks are mixed into a golden matrix from which the Dolby Surround Decoder extracts a left, right, center, and surround channel, with the addition of Dolby type B noise reduction and delay for the surround. (See Appendix for comprehensive list of Dolby releases.)

Stereo

In the fall of 1988, the CBS Television Network began transmitting all programming in stereo format, an expanded service "enhancing the viewer's enjoyment of our programming." As with color technology, the networks were not quite certain why they needed it, but they were convinced they could not compete favorably in the marketplace without it. What exactly is stereo and how is it achieved?

Born of the hi-fi industry, **stereophonicity** is a mode of audio playback that emphasizes the binaural nature of listening. Practitioners felt that, because we have two ears, audio information must arrive from at least two discrete directions, left and right, in accordance with the position of our ears. A third "centered" source was added as a reference to fortify the illusion that the ear actually differentiates left of center from right of center.

The notion is somewhat nonsensical. In fact, the aural world has no center. Sound emanates in a free field out in all directions. Furthermore, the entire human body acts as a sound receptor, with the ears aiding in **localizing** the sound source. The spatial orientation goes well beyond the simple notion of left, right, and center. And the perception of these positions (of sound-producing bodies in space) seems to be a function of **duration** and **intensity.** It is misleading to qualify the notion of stereo as fundamentally a two-channel system because we have two ears.

Tests have proved that monophonic recordings may be played back in such a way (manipulating intensity and duration) as to simulate the ideal of left, right, and center, with a strong sensation of separation.

Recording in stereo really means the recording of separate discrete aural sources whose dominant parts are quite arbitrary. It is no more affecting to hear a harp in the distance than one proximate to strings, woodwind, and vocalist; there is only a "preference" of aural positioning conditioned by some ideal of where it ought to be.

Try as we may to design the ideal "stereo" microphone system to capture this very ephemeral notion of separation, we are limited by the fact that the way a microphone records is not similar to the way the ear hears.

The issue of how to create "true" stereo perspective (whatever that is!) has given rise to many differing techniques, each with advantages and disadvantages and each performing better in specific situations where others seem not to get the job done.

However, for the audio designer, regardless of how stereo is defined, the narrative functions of stereo are:

- Complete separation of sound elements
- Accurate placement of sound elements
- Division of voice from background
- Space/time orientation (of audience and imagery)

The narrative functions may be achieved either in recording or during postproduction processing. The chief methods that have evolved in recording are as follows:

- **Spaced pair:** two identical microphones spaced apart from each other facing the sound source and slightly pointed toward the left or right. Both get signals from all directions, but some right-side sound will be delayed by the distance differential to the left microphone, and vice versa. This time/phase difference should give a wide, spread-out stereo image. (Figure 10–5)
- **Coincident pair** (X–Y): Two microphones are placed as close together as possible in the horizontal and vertical planes in either of two modes:
  a. **Coincident:** elements placed at 90 degrees to each other. Right channel output is +6 decibels relative to left. (Figure 10–4)
  b. **Near-coincident:** barrels crossed at 90 degrees. Left channel is delayed and −6 decibels relative to right (Blumlein setup). (Figure 10–6)
- **M + S stereo:** The M or mid microphone is pointed directly toward the center of the source; it may be an omnidirectional, cardioid, or bidirectional pattern. The S or side microphone is normally a bidirectional element with its axis at right angles to the M. If the S is pointed toward the left, the

M + S will be acting like a cardioid. M − S will have an identical pattern leaning toward the right. The outputs of the two can be put through a plus and minus matrix to produce left and right stereo channels. The ratio of ambience to direct sound (stereo image) is a function of the relative proportions of M to S mix. MS stereo uses **intensity** cues only for stereo localization; phase differences are close to zero. The two microphones get the reverberant information at the same point in space, creating identical spectral content in both channels. (Figure 10–3)

- **Three-point system:** utilizes two matched pairs in triangular conjunction with a third dissimilar microphone, for instance, a pair of omnidirectional microphones spaced apart about 6 feet and a shotgun centered behind about 3 feet and 3 to 5 feet above to form an equilateral triangle. This obtains full coverage of the field with spaced-pair separation and a point source emphasis from the shotgun. Various versions of the three-point system will produce a unique background/foreground perspective dominated by the point source. A PZM microphone used, for instance, on a back wall in combination with two hypercardioid elements produces a very live, resonant spatial image. Experimental in nature, the system requires careful rehearsal for placement of the three microphones to avoid cancellation problems.

- **Single microphone with bipolar internal pattern for coincident-pair separation:** Behaves essentially like two microphones housed together (M − S stereo).

- **Multiple microphones:** two or more microphones positioned in such a way that the desired separation of important sound sources is achieved. This may involve wireless and PZM combinations, which tend to work very well together, recorded on a stereo Nagra.

One problem with stereo recording is that often a mono track must be derived from the master for broadcast or foreign track preparation. The MS system seems best in providing a mono track. When the left and right channels are folded together, the S microphone is cancelled out: (M + S) + (M − S) = 2M.

When creating stereo in postproduction, multichannel recording can provide the raw material for creating stereo in the mixdown. Each channel is kept acoustically and electrically from the others. The series of mono channels is then combined according to several techniques, including the keeping of each channel at least three times as for on the sound stage from the next channel as the microphones are from their respective sound sources (Lou Burrough's idea), and Eric Small's[1] advice to have at least 20 decibels of acoustic separation between channels.

M and S signals can be recorded straight from the microphones and matched to program material in the mix. When a scene widens to a long shot, the stereo

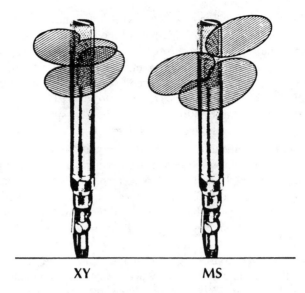

XY MS

Figure 10–2 XY and MS techniques using twin capsules in one housing.

imaging should be matched since the monaural signals remain available and unchanged at all times.

Since dialogue is generally always kept on a separate track for film on TV work to maintain continuity, trying to record pure stereo in production seems foolish and undesirable. However, using the stereo (two-track) recorder to generate the raw materials for creating stereo separation is a primary task for the audio designer. (See Figure 10–7)

Stereo microphone traditional setups are shown in Figures 10–2 through 10–6.

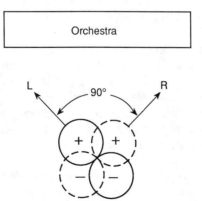

Figure 10–3 The Blumlein technique.

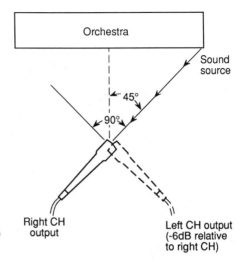

Figure 10–4 Coincident-pair technique. Cardioid mikes crossed at 90 degrees.

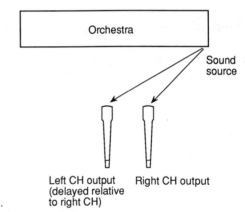

Figure 10–5 Spaced-pair technique.

Stereo Microphones

The mid-side (MS) intensity stereo technique appears to provide the best mono compatibility while affording alterable spatial localization. New systems like the Neumann stereo shotgun microphone (Figure 10–8) allow sizing the sonic image to the visual image while recording through its adjustable matrix. The ratios of the two signals, one from the directional condenser head and the other from the bidirectional capsule, are varied like a "zooming" of aural perspective without any phase differences. One element points directly toward the center of the sound source; the other (bidirectional) is oriented 90 degrees to the source, parallel to the width of the source. The Neumann sum and difference matrix varies the ratio of M + S, thus changing the usable pick-up pattern (stereo base angle).

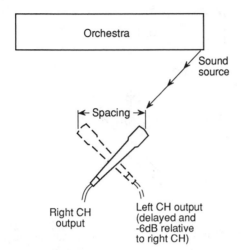

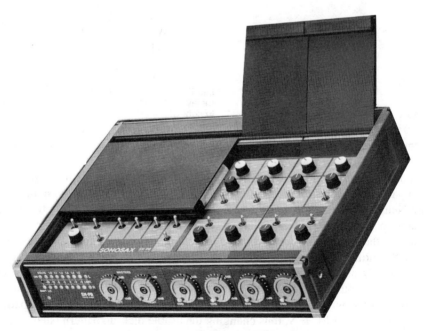

Right CH output

Left CH output (delayed and -6dB relative to right CH)

Figure 10–6 Near-coincident technique. Cardioid mikes crossed and spaced.

Stereo Field Recording Applications

The following are some applications of stereo recording.

1. Stereo two-track news gathering in high-ambient noise environments provides a master and protection backup track isolating noise from subject.

Figure 10–7   Stereo mixer: Sonosax SX-PR for use with R-DAT.

2. Stereo location recording isolates and allows for focus of specific performers while maintaining proper balance and perspective between speaking and nonspeaking subjects in complex scenes with movement. Sonic image of groups and crowds may be augmented. The Neumann RSM 1905 Stereo ''Shotgun'' employs MS system for ENG/EFP recording.

3. According to changes in the studio, stereo imaging may be ''spread'' or focused live or in postproduction.

4. There is a possibility of remote control of nonrepeatable stereo imaging at high sound pressure levels (134 decibels).

Figure 10–8 Tools of the soundperson's trade: lightweight, slightly flexible fishpole with shockmount or cueing device, 4–8 input portable (Sonosax) mixer, digital slate, miniature Nagra SN (the ideal backup recorder fits in the pocket), Neumann switchable stereo field shotgun with handgrip, and Porta-Brace field case. Fresh batteries are the most important item.

Figure 10–8   Continued

5. Hand-holding, close-miking techniques open up new creative options.
6. The Schoeps UMS 20 Universal Stereo Bracket is a device that may be mounted on a video camera or fishpole, as well as on stands and other fixed positions. Adjustable clamps allow for perfect spacing and angling with **sideways slew,** permitting microphones of 20 to 21 mm diameter to be arranged at two levels. (See Figure 10–9 (a)–(d).)

Stereo Sync Signal

The neopilotone technique consists of a dual push–pull head arrangement. Head gaps are perfectly perpendicular to tape travel. Head gaps are on line with the opposite polarity. The audio head spans the full width of the tape and reproduces two sets of impulses simultaneously, canceling each other and yielding no sync pulse upon transfer. Only the sync head can reproduce the sync pulse due to its dual-gap design.

Center Track Pilot/Cue

Two-track (stereo) recorders must have the sync signal deposited between the two tracks to prevent crosstalk. Since relatively low frequencies have a greater tendency to bleed into closely adjoining tracks, the Nagra uses a **carrier.**

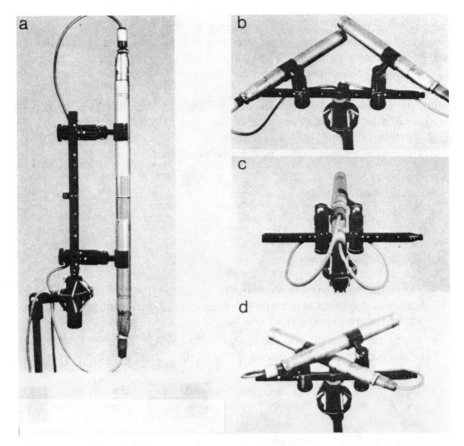

Figure 10–9   Schoeps twin-mike bracket-adjustable to four configurations: (a) intensity stereophony with microphones with lateral sound incidence (Blumlein, XY, MS); (b) intensity stereophony with microphones with frontal sound incidence (90 degrees − XY); (c) MS stereophony with lateral horizontal figure eight and a cardioid for frontal sound incidence; (d) stereophony according to the ORTF principle. Spacing, 17 centimeters; angle 110 degrees.

Two-track Method of Recording Vocals

Phase-related stereo, which utilizes two matched microphones placed at 45-degree axes to each other, creates overlapping patterns. The phase interrelationships create a positioning across the aural spectrum similar to the singer's relative position in the pick-up field. Components of voice exist on both tracks with:

1. Varying intensity
2. Time delay

Every point in the aural spectrum is affected by both microphones.

Phase-separated stereo, which uses two matched microphones parallel to each other, exhibits no overlap at an optimum point (six feet) apart. Each signal is concentrated at one point of the aural spectrum. This point may be moved by using the pan pot. There is no true "stereo" left and right, but rather two points (bimonaurally) in the field. The sound pressure level of each track is not a combination of two tracks since each mike does not affect every point in the aural spectrum. (Figure 10–5)

The goal of proper stereo microphone placement is to obtain:

- Localization accuracy
- Directional fidelity

Consider the following factors:

- The sensation of localization depends, in part, on the intensity differences between **all** systems in record and playback. A 20-decibel difference makes a sound seem to come from one side only.
- The farther to one side a sound source is, the greater the intensity difference between channels that it produces (the farther from the center it is reproduced).
- Image location depends on **signal time differences between loudspeakers.** A 2-millisecond delay is sufficient to give a sensation of one side only locality.
- With spaced-pair microphones, the farther a sound source is from the center, the greater the time difference between channels and the farther from the center is its reproduced sound image.

Summary for Stereo Miking

To summarize:

1. Angling cardioid microphones (coincident pair) produces **intensity** differences.
2. Spacing cardioid or omni microphones (spaced pair) produces **time** differences.
3. Angling and spacing cardioid microphones (near-coincident pair) produces both time and intensity differences.
4. As the microphone spread increases toward 90 degrees, the localization accuracy is altered.

Perimeter Recording

In 1881, Clément Ader, a French physicist, first demonstrated the concept of **stereo space.** This "grande illusion" was fostered by Blumlein in the first half of this century, and although various technological advances have been made, no theorist has advanced our knowledge of spatial acoustics beyond those initial fundamental musings. An understanding of the listening process is needed.

"Surround sound" and "quadrophonic" (ambisonic) recording and playback systems reflect an attempt to come to terms with the circular nature of the aural world. Since every pore of our body can act as a sound receptor, and considering the now well-known phenomenon of what I call **subpleural stimulation** (the use of low frequencies to affect the diaphragm by Hitchcock and others), it seems creatively more appropriate to think in terms of **boundary** or **perimeter** recording and playback, which emphasize the circuitous nature of the aural experience.

Various tests have shown that only two discrete channels may be sufficient to program the entire circumference of a given spatial continuum. Except in special cases, the viewer cannot locate images over the entire 360-degree sound sphere. The reproduction of natural ambience is improved when using a sur-

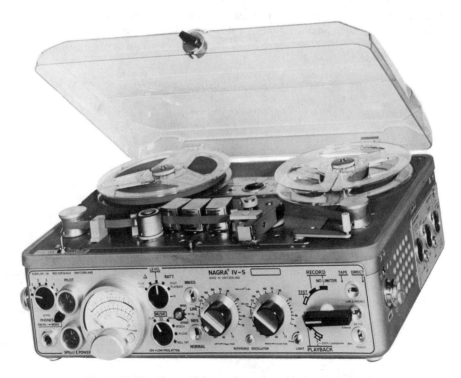

Figure 10–10   Nagra 4S Stereo Recorder with time code panel.

round-sound loudspeaker system. Microphone techniques for surround sound (perimeter) recording are no more complex than for conventional stereo, but they may not be ideal for stereo two-channel playback.

Endnote

1. Small, Eric, "Broadcasting Stereo in a Mono World," *Millimeter,* May, 1985.

References

BARNETT, STEVE, "Techniques for Preserving Sound Perspective in Film Production Recordings," *Recording Eng./Producer* (Aug 1980) pp. 54–61.

BARTLETT, BRUCE. "Stereo Microphone Techniques," *db* (Dec 1979) pp. 34–46.

FINNEGAN, P., "Tape Recorder Measurements," *db* (Mar 1978) pp. 9–11.

HOWELL, D., "SMPTE Time Code Applications in Film," *Millimeter* (Apr 1981) pp. 59–64.

SMALL, ERIC, "Broadcasting Stereo in a Mono World," *Millimeter*, May 1985.

SMITH, ARLEN, "The Lost Art of Recording," *db* (May 1978) pp. 37–41.

TANENBAUM, JIM AND MANFRED KLEMME, "Using Time Code in the Reel World," Los Angeles (Nagra Seminar Notes), 1987. (Sound Recording Services.)

11

DIGITAL RECORDING

Digital recording removes sound data
from the acoustic world, transposes it
to the mathematical domain, and then
recombines it into new structures
without background noise. This
chapter discusses the concept and
technology of digital audio and then
moves on to systems of sound
shaping that employ basic digital
hardware. MIDI, the link to
synthesized music composition, is
explored, as is the role of desk-top
audio, which employs the personal
computer as a means of control and
composition.

Figure 11–1 Digital recording. The greatest strides often take place in the
smallest windows of time. (ENCORE™ printout from PASSPORT)

Introduction

Every analog recording is limited by four primary problems: dynamic range limits, imperfect frequency response, relatively high harmonic distortion, and perceptible wow and flutter. Digital recording renders these problems inaudible and unmeasurable.

Since magnetic tape can only handle a limited signal, digital recording [using the pulse code modulation (PCM) method] requires only pulses and silences to be recorded.

Tape dropouts, on the order of $\frac{1}{5000}$ of a second, can affect the binary code, causing an error in the recorded signal. The digital processor utilizes cyclic redundancy check code (CRCC) for error correction. During recording, the CRCC system records a test word and a check word for every six words of musical/sound signal input. These are compared during playback, and any discrepancy triggers error-correcting words to reconstruct the proper word. The backup system shuffles the digital words before they are recorded. During playback, **de-interleaving** restores the proper order by interpolating the average values or preceeding and succeeding words around the dropout problem.

Digital components don't suffer from physical problems. A resistor has no noise. Inductors don't saturate their core. Op-amps have absolute gain accuracy. Capacitors have no leakage, no dielectric absorption, no voltage memory latency. Diodes have no voltage drop unless chosen. There is no temperature drift or aging, and phase characteristics are perfectly behaved.

It has been discovered that a sampling frequency twice that of the signal being recorded is sufficient to reconstruct the original signal. Many sampling frequencies have been considered, and since the practical audio-frequency range was found to be 20 hertz to 20 kilohertz, a sampling frequency of 44 to 50 kilohertz is being considered. The problem of standardization now begins. Some systems have been developed to translate the digital codes from one system to another, but the cost for such a device is high, and some degradation of signal does occur.

The advantage of digital recording is that the digital pulses can be recorded at a level below the saturation and above the residual noise level of the tape. Thus, the dynamic range is not limited by the parameters of the magnetic tape, up to a point.

In analog recording, a dubbing can add 3 decibels of noise; with digital recording in theory there is no degradation of the signal-to-noise ratio (the dub is as good as the master!). Also there is no print-through problem, because there is no high level recorded.

The signals are synchronized by a crystal-controlled oscillator, making wow and flutter virtually negligible. The digital editing system can analyze waveforms to be joined together for both amplitude and slope, making the splice inaudible.

A typical digital system made jointly by 3M and the British Broadcasting Company has a flat frequency response of ±0.3 decibel from 30 hertz to 15 kilohertz and ±3 decibels up to 20 kilohertz, the signal-to-noise ratio is 90 decibels or better, and the harmonic distortion is less than 0.03% at any frequency from 20 hertz to 20 kilohertz.

Some disadvantages of digital sound are **alias distortion** when the signal frequency beats with the sampling frequency to form products not present in the original signal; although some feel the distortion is audible, it has not yet been proved.

In analog recording, **drop-out** goes unnoticed (since our ears tend to fill in the gaps), but in digital it means an absence of pulses, which would be interpreted by the system as a different bit-code altogether causing distortion of the wave pulse. However, error-correcting codes have been developed to reduce this problem in some cases to zero!

In Japan the standard digital format is PCM (pulse code modulation). This system also has many advantageous points; the trick is, as always with new equipment, to make it compatible with other equipment (unless, of course, you are trying for a monopoly), to look ahead before the final choice is made on a sampling frequency (since the sampling frequency determines the maximum bandwidth), and to be sure that it doesn't become obsolete.

A digital recording must first be produced from any one type of analog audio format, either electric, optical, magnetic, or mechanical, which all bear a pattern in direct analogy to the original sound waves. These analog audio waves are examined at an accelerated rate, around 50,000 times a second. The waves produce a sequence of values that is translated into a numerical code, which is in essence the digital sampling of that particular sound wave. The more digits, or bits as they are called, used to describe a particular value in a sound wave, the more accurate the digital audio becomes, somewhat like the ASA rating of a film emulsion. A sequence of digital samples is then linked together like DNA molecules into a sequence of digits.

This sequence is the digital audio. However, in order to hear this array, it must be reconverted back into analog audio waves. By re-forming the digital information, and using it to control the output of a voltage generator, and then running these signals through a low-pass filter, analog waveforms are produced.

It sounds as if a great deal of clarity is to be lost by first converting and then reconverting the digital codes back into analog audio waves. However, if these reconstructed waves are initially sampled at faster than twice per cycle of the highest frequency and the low-level filter is ideal, then these waves will turn out exactly as the original. And since we are dealing with numerical codes that represent the qualities of the sound waves and since there are no numerical codes representing tape hiss or other noises, these noises are automatically lost in the transfer.

Digital audio today offers the most precise means of transmitting, processing, and recording sound. There is no distortion of any kind since the signals do not pass through many black boxes. Most digital systems are compatible, having numbers that represent a signal in the same form, so they can be processed mathematically to achieve any of the special effects that are attainable with analog systems.

The editing of digital tape is unique. The conventional way of editing tape by splicing is archaic for analog tape, let alone digital. Digital audio uses a system in which the tape is never cut, but copies are made of the digital data from one stage to another. All the juxtaposing of takes is done by a computer that has been programmed to find pre-selected cuts and copy information, while also playing back those cuts. The digital words are reconstructed from the tape into the computer's memory. All the various sound takes are stored on disc packs. The engineer, on hearing the takes, will push a button where he or she feels there is a precise spot for connecting the two takes. The computer then records the numbers at the precise spot for those two takes and then links them and plays them back. If the engineer is not sure, he or she can move the takes either forward or backward through the computer control or the engineer can view the waveforms of the two takes on a graphics display and, by visually examining them, determine where the cuts should be made. The original tape is never physically cut, no damage is ever done to it, and it can be "recut" as many times as needed.

Portable Rotary Digital Audiotape

Rotary digital audiotape (RDAT) is a relatively new format for field recording that provides studio-quality audio specifications in a small package. RDAT is a fully digital recording process with virtually zero wow and flutter and a sampling rate of 48 kilohertz, which translates into a frequency capability of 10 hertz to 22 kilohertz to 85-decibel signal to noise ratio. Sony, Panasonic, Fostex, and others have begun to release RDAT systems. The first-generation recorders have no provision for microphone powering, so they must be used with external battery packs. Inputs are mono phone jacks, but adapters allow for the use of Neumann, Sanken, Sennheiser, and Schoeps mikes. Unlike the PCM processors, which use videotape as the audio recording medium, RDAT uses a compact miniature cassette with emulsions closer to audiotape characteristics.

Recording technique is very similar to the use of the Nagra, except that RDAT is less tolerant of overmodulation.

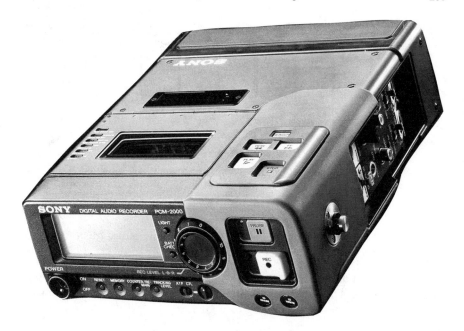

Figure 11–2 Sony PCM 2000 Digital Recorder for field use.

PCM Processor and VCR Combination for Field Use

The Sony PCM-2000 (see Figure 11–2) is typical of the new-generation digital audio recorders that may be linked to a field video cassette recorder for high-quality location sound on tape. Basic recording practice for digital audio requires:

- Strict adherence to 0 decibels on the VU meter for setting level. There is no headroom above 0 decibels.
- Leave 5 seconds of silence before and after each take.
- Minus twenty decibels appears to be a nominal working point for average sound sources. This allows for overrecording without the distortion (see Figure 11–3) caused by running out of digital "words."

Basic Terminology

Here is a list of basic digital recording terms:

Quantizing and quantizing noise: process by which analog signals are translated into digital code by dividing the range of values of the sampled amplitude into subranges, to each of which a value is assigned. The slight error between

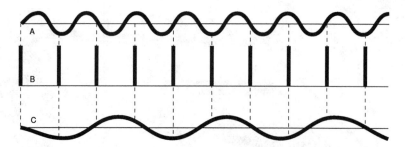

Figure 11–3 Alias distortion. It has a higher frequency than pulse train B, the sampling waveform. Sine wave C, of lower frequency than A, gives the same series of samples and appears in the output when samples are reassembled.

source signal and quantized value is heard as quantizing noise (distortion). (See Figure 11–4)

Sampling and holding: A circuit that measures an analog signal (sampling) and increases the duration of that signal (holding). With holding, a fixed period of time is needed to convert analog to digital.

Word: A group of bits that expresses a single quantizing value.

Algorithm: A prescribed set of well-defined rules or processes for solving a problem in a finite number of steps.

Baud: A unit of signaling speed equal to the number of discrete signal events per second.

Bit: A unit of information; contraction of "binary" and "digit."

Byte: A sequence of adjacent binary digits that is affected as a unit; usually shorter than a word; made up of 8 bits.

Interpolation: Technique of filling in missing information in a sampled system.

Nyquist rate: Maximum rate of transmitting pulse signals through a channel or bandwidth. If B is the bandwidth, then 2B is the maximum number of code elements that can be received with certainty (Nyquist sampling theorem).

Pixel: Smallest picture element with RGB values in television.

Figure 11–4 Low-frequency sine-wave amplitude equal to plus or minus one least significant bit is converted to a quasi-square wave by quantization. The effect resembles amplifier clipping and introduces gross distortion.

Characteristics of the Digital Sound Synthesis and Editing Processes

Digital Domain Versus Film Domain

The following are characteristics of digital recording:

- Replacing of sound is instantaneous. During a mix, should a sound be deemed inappropriate, a retrieval from the digital library can be made instantaneously without stopping the mix. In the film domain, additional cutting room and machine room time may be necessitated.
- The memory recorder function allows the sound editor to record real-time effects onto the track either in real time or after the fact; if they don't work, a simple punch-in on the track allows a new attempt without erasing the original hit list or changing the sounds chosen. Stereo pan movements may be rehearsed, previewed, saved, and then changed. Volume fades may be overdubbed and combined with stereo data, but the system allows punch-in onto a specific effect like the stereo pan without affecting the volume setting already programmed. (Discrete real-time affects editing.)
- Foley effects lay-in time is greatly reduced. For instance, the ability to access a library of stored foot steps and perform exact time editing is a basic function on the Synclavier. A Foley artist does not need to be retained for multiple takes of a scene. The discrepancies will be easily adjusted in real time, and the sounds may be sampled and reused in other scenes at different speeds, pitch, and duration.
- Atmospheric effects, background ambience, and nonspecific sounds (traffic) change as a result of action, or change as a result of edits, or remain continuous throughout a shot. In multiple atmospheric tracks, uniformity is important. Film uses loops or cartridge inserts and original production track ambience (room tone). On the Synclavier, sampled or real sounds may be played and fitted into the required time segments, with fades and crossfades overlaid. Stereo positioning of an atmosphere such as pan or movement left to right may be programmed into a sequence before the mix and loops are assigned to different areas of the same stereo spectrum within a shot (multiple atmospheric localization).
- Resynthesis creates complex sounds with a programmable time-varying harmonic spectra that plays like "natural" sound. The computer analyzes the harmonic content, pitch, and envelope structure of a sampled sound and synthesizes those elements by creating a series of frames that reflect the harmonic structure of the sound at any moment in time; it then plays back all frames in a linear fashion. The harmonic content of the frames can be altered, creating more new sounds.
- Digital filtering allows high-frequency resolution. Complex filters may be

constructed. For example, noise or room hum can be sampled, inverted, and used as a filter to eliminate those exact frequencies in a dialogue sample.

- Mix information and hit list data can be transmitted to the Synclavier workstations via modem. You can edit on-location dialogue in New York and send it to Los Angeles for combining with music and effects (from Australia), or mail an optical disk to your uncle editing in Rome. For a cost comparison see Tables 11–1 and 11–2.

- The Synclavier records and reads any SMPTE time code. This allows the system to strip off dialogue from the production (coded) track and separate it into many discrete sections, each assigned a separate sequence track and each with its SMPTE time code in sync with picture.

- No downtime for booking and waiting for transfer facilities and no studio time for premixing and recording effects.

TABLE 11–1 Comparison of Time Requirements for a Selected Sequence from *Apocalypse Now* with Complex Layered Tracks. (Estimated by New England Digital)

	Synclavier (hours)	Film (hours)
Auditioning and sampling of effects	4	4
Creating editor's hit list (events)	4	4
Recording, ADR fitting, wildtracks, laying	2	10
Laying effects,stereo imaging, effects creation	8	16
	18	34

TABLE 11–2 Film Stock Cost Comparison

	Film (ft)	Syn.(min)	Film	Syn	Savings
Sound rushes	87,000	875	$7000	$2105	$4185
Effects	30,000	333	3400	990	1410
Postsync	40,000	444	3200	1069	2131
Music	20,000	222	1600	666	934
Premix	20,000	n/a	3400	801	1599
Master mix	20,000	n/a			
M & E	20,000	n/a			
Transfer to optical	20,000	n/a		Total	$10,259

Let $20 = cost of 250 feet of 35mm film.

Fujitsu tape capacity is 18.7 minutes/cartridge at $45 per cartridge.

Kennedy tape capacity is 15 megabytes per cartridge at $30 per cartridge.

Narrative Function of Digital Sound

The significant element of digital sound is the relative lack of background noise. It is not perceived as silence. Silence has a background. What is the narrative meaning of the digital domain's noiseless acoustic void (shadow)? Explore this question.

The void must be assigned a function in the expressive order of aural impressions. It can have the same implications as voice and natural sounds that assert their individuality.

The capacity of digital sound systems to extend or shorten the length of a sound (and its perceived or felt duration) has yet to be fully explored for narrative purposes. The keyboard is the primary compositional tool, and several popular workstations employ it. High-powered synthesizer/sequencers like the Synclavier hold the key to the finite construction and manipulation of the sound track.

The Synclavier

The Synclavier is a powerful audio processor with solid-state memory (RAM). The system has 32 stereo audio channels for sampling and 32 for synthesis. Each channel is called a **voice.** A sequencer controls the voices by recording cue information fed to it by the keyboard or an alphanumeric terminal. The cues may be edited and moved in time; they can have volume or stereo pan data attached to them and can have different audio events assigned to them. Sections of audio or music can be treated like a paragraph in a word processor and copied or moved to another part of the sequence. Audio events are recorded onto sequencer tracks (200 tracks maximum).

Mouse sound editing. By dragging the cursor across the waveform with the mouse, the system will play back the sound file at any speed without changing pitch. The sound editor can preview the sounds in slow motion and make edits digitally by clicking the mouse. Sections of "buzz" or ambience can be looped and digitally copied from within the dialogue segment to the beginning and the end of the sound, providing overlays. The Synclavier is able to cut a section of ambience from the middle of a dialogue and (electronically) splice it onto the beginning or end of the sequence.

Synclavier ADR system. Up to 200 dialogue tracks may be stored in sync with a picture. Takes are instantly previewed; no rewind time is expended, and there is no transfer time or reload time for recording or selection of takes.

The delivery and inflection of dialogue may be altered using the **pitch wheel.** All takes are first generation.

The advantages of digital audio event editing are:

- High-speed
- Nondestructive: original sync plus edits always on-line
- Words can be stretched or reduced by changing the pitch with the pitch wheel tuning settings
- No transfer or rewind time losses
- No generation loss

Sound Effects Replacement

Some options available to the Synclavier operator as a Foley artist:

- Pressure can be set to adjust the volume of a sound so that the harder the key is pressed the louder the sound plays against the picture. (Creating waves crashing on the beach; the play volume changes as an editor sees them in real time.)
- SMPTE offsets for all 200 tracks and SMPTE editing for every event on the track.
- Ripple or deletion and/or insertion of frames within tracks; blank spaces can be inserted at any point.
- Each track can be shifted against the other tracks by a specified time, without changing the start time for any other track.
- Once a list is created, sounds can be interchanged onto the track without altering the *hit list* in any way (instant reassignment).

Sampling

In the digital domain, a note is an event referenced in time. The design provides the sound to the sampler through a microphone, a tape or compact disc, or from an R-DAT master. The sound sample is recalled at a faster or slower clock rate than its original, resulting in a pitch change similar to that effected by changing tape recorder speed.

Most musical instrument samples are shorter than the notes a musician would play; musical samples are looped electronically to provide an accessible duration of audio output.

The higher the sampling rate, the higher the frequency response. Therefore, accuracy should improve at higher rates. However, a typical sample is seldom longer than 30 seconds. It is also possible to use a sampler to process words of dialogue by cleaning up the heads and tails of selected words and then rearranging their sequence into a new line electronically.

Samplers are capable of multiple voices (the simultaneous playback of multiple sounds); therefore, a sampled background sound may be combined with a verbal sample to match the mix of sound on a master tape. Any bite will do; as little as $\frac{1}{2}$ second of clean background sound is sufficient to build on.

The Functions of Resampling

Resampling can provide the following adjustments:

- **Corrective equalizaton:** Unwanted low frequencies reduced by resampling through the high-pass filter (noise gate).
- **Equalization and vocals:** High-pass filter to emphasize breathiness while reducing formant band associated with specific vowels. Female vocal formants are approximately 17% higher than male. A parametric equalizer, aural exciter, or the like may be used to reprocess the sample. The aural exciter adds top end harmonics even where none exist! (See Figure 11–5)
- **Adding ambience and effects:** Reverberation and cyclic effects such as phasing and flanging as well as compression with altered variable attack times are possible. Effects pedals can provide fuzz, overdrive, and distortion effects to the sample.
- **Pitch correction:** Use a tuning source, the samples may be tuned to each other and remixed into the original series of samples.
- **Adjusting sample length:** Sampling at another pitch may force the sound material to occupy a smaller loop position.
- **Sampling chords and rhythms:** Both may be sequenced and resampled—rolled up or down, mimicked up or down.
- **Simulated stereo effects:** Layer one sound upon another and send each sample to its own output while aligning the start points to avoid phasing problems. Simulation is possible by experimenting with reverberation, auto-panning, phase-shifting/flanging, and chorusing.

Sounds sampled on a digital sampling keyboard can be transferred to the Macintosh, where up to three sound waveforms can be displayed and scaled to show the entire sound, edited, and rearranged, with an editing accuracy of 1/50,000 of a second. A "pencil" tool can be used to draw or repair waveforms in sampled sounds. Loop points may be assigned. A digital mixer can create hybrid sounds that crossfade from one sound to another. Sounds can be divided into hundreds of separate frequency bands. See Figure 11–6 for other options.

Once a cue list has been created, Q-Sheet (Figure 11–7) turns a Macintosh into a complete MIDI automation center. When synchronized to a video tape recorder, Q-Sheet can trigger sounds, automate outboard equipment, and mix down the entire soundtrack to two track.

Because of flexible random-access technology, no tape rewind time is utilized. As a comprehensive **workstation,** the Synclavier provides both **digital synthesis** and **sound sampling.** With the direct-to-disk system, multiple live vocal or instrumental tracks may be overdubbed for up to 1 hour of continuous recording time per track. As a digital multitrack recording system, the Synclavier

TURBOSYNTH

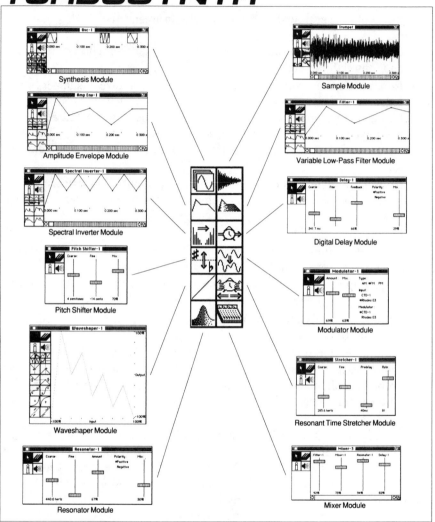

digidesign
1360 Willow Road, Suite 101
Menlo Park, CA 94025
(415) 327-8811

Figure 11–5 Digidesign's Turbosynth™ display program for sound design and generation. Used with Macintosh computer. (Courtesy of DigiDesign, Inc.)

SOUND DESIGNER™

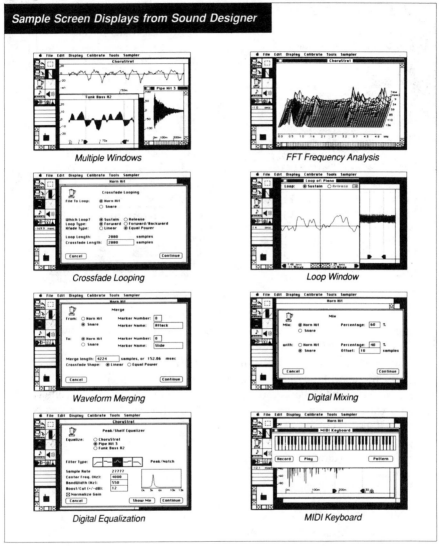

Figure 11–6 Sound Designer™. A Digidesign program that allows manipulation of the waveform, analysis, looping, and merging, interfaced with a Macintosh and digital sampler. (Courtesy of DigiDesign, Inc.)

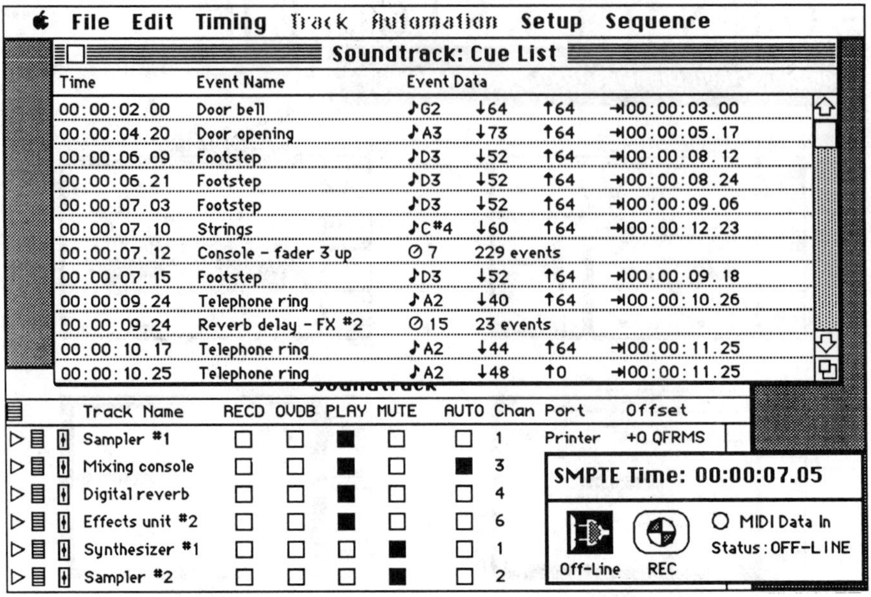

File   Edit   Timing   Track   Automation   Setup   Sequence

Soundtrack: Cue List		
Time	Event Name	Event Data
00:00:02.00	Door bell	♪G2 ↓64 ↑64 ⇥00:00:03.00
00:00:04.20	Door opening	♪A3 ↓73 ↑64 ⇥00:00:05.17
00:00:06.09	Footstep	♪D3 ↓52 ↑64 ⇥00:00:08.12
00:00:06.21	Footstep	♪D3 ↓52 ↑64 ⇥00:00:08.24
00:00:07.03	Footstep	♪D3 ↓52 ↑64 ⇥00:00:09.06
00:00:07.10	Strings	♪C#4 ↓60 ↑64 ⇥00:00:12.23
00:00:07.12	Console - fader 3 up	⊘7 229 events
00:00:07.15	Footstep	♪D3 ↓52 ↑64 ⇥00:00:09.18
00:00:09.24	Telephone ring	♪A2 ↓40 ↑64 ⇥00:00:10.26
00:00:09.24	Reverb delay - FX #2	⊘15 23 events
00:00:10.17	Telephone ring	♪A2 ↓44 ↑64 ⇥00:00:11.25
00:00:10.25	Telephone ring	♪A2 ↓48 ↑0 ⇥00:00:11.25

Track Name	RECD	OVDB	PLAY	MUTE	AUTO	Chan	Port	Offset
Sampler #1	☐	☐	■	☐	☐	1	Printer	+0 QFRMS
Mixing console	☐	☐	■	☐	■	3		
Digital reverb	☐	☐	■	☐	☐	4		
Effects unit #2	☐	☐	■	☐	☐	6		
Synthesizer #1	☐	☐	☐	■	☐	1		
Sampler #2	☐	☐	☐	■	☐	2		

SMPTE Time: 00:00:07.05

○ MIDI Data In
Status: OFF-LINE
Off-Line   REC

Figure 11-7   Sample cue sheet from the Soundtrack program display.

can create a musical score or Foley effects track locked to film or video with sync accurate to 1/80th of a frame.

Sound design capacity uses **additive synthesis.** A basic waveform created by setting the amplitude of 24 harmonics can be further modulated using a six-stage **FM envelope.** The computer can determine the harmonic content of a sampled wave form and then duplicate it through **resynthesis.** Elements controlled include:

Volume envelope

Vibrato

Portamento

Stereo and chorus effects

Real-time effects

Each note of the keyboard can be assigned a different sample in order to create unique sounds. A complete drum kit can be assembled by assigning a snare sample to one note, a kick drum to another, a cymbal to a third, and so on; these are then combined into one idiomatic expression. As many as four layers or **partial timbres** can be combined, and they may be sampled or synthetic. Each partial timbre corresponds to a **single voice** so that a system with 128 voices can sound 32 four-layer sounds at once!

Layering Tones

By layering partial timbres, a string sound can be created that consists, for example, of one layer of a sharply bowed attack, one of gently bowed swell, one sustained without vibrato, and one of general-purpose playing. These different layers can be activated by different keyboard articulations so that the sharp attack is heard when the keys are struck with force or gentle swell is brought out with **after-touch pressure.**

The programmable 78-note keyboard provides the basic real-time effects:

- Velocity and pressure sensitivity
- Pitch and modulator wheels
- Ribbon controller
- Breath controller
- Foot pedal
- Repeat
- Arpeggio
- Chorus
- Decay adjust (increase decay time of notes while in lower key)
- Tuning (whole tone to microtones)
- Keyboard envelope (assigns each layer of a sound to a different range on the board)

Sequencer

This feature records and plays back a series of **audio events**—musical notes, MIDI data, a sound effect, a Foley effect, dialog—occurring at a precise moment in time originating from any of 200 sequencer tracks or up to 16 direct-to-disk tracks. During playback, the sequencer triggers each of these events at the appropriate time.

Direct-to-Disk

The system functions like a digital recorder, providing 16 live tracks of sound material (project tracks). A **project** is a reserved work area on all tracks used for recording. A **cue** is a designated area of sound originating from a direct-to-disk track. These cues may be edited, synched to picture, placed in a sequence, and triggered by the sequencer.

Inputs/Outputs

The computer receives its information from an input device called a **control interface.** These interfaces include:

- Synclavier
- Direct-to-disk system
- Another synthesizer or sequencer via MIDI
- Roland GR guitar
- Microphone or tape
- Modem

The central signal processing unit (CPU) converts input to computer language. After processing, data are converted at the output terminals into sound signals, visual signals, or digital signals. Sound output is produced by **voices** (sampling voices or synthesizer voices). Storage devices include a floppy disk drive, Winchester drive, Kennedy tape drive, optical disk, and direct-to-disk (hard disk or tape drives).

When a sound is played on a Synclavier, it comes through a voice to the audio outputs. The number of voices installed in a given system represents the number of notes that can be simultaneously played back. Thirty-two polyphonic sampling voices are presently available or up to 32 stereo FM synthesizer voices can be installed. Each track in the direct-to-disk represents one voice.

MIDI interface makes it possible to place the Synclavier into a network of synthesizers, sequencers, rhythm machines, or other audio-processing equipment.

Software programs provide complete control over recording and editing sound. Each program has its own terminal displays. The sophistication of the program will depend to some extent on the complexity and power of the computer linked to the system.

Fairlight Features

The Series III Fairlight sound production system (Figure 11–8) uses a graphics pen to draw or alter sound waveforms, special envelopes, and function curves. Menu selections are made from the screen **icons** using the pen and an interactive pad. Musical notes displayed on the monitor can also be edited with the pen.

Sound is stored in 16-bit linear format with a sample rate of up to 100 kilohertz. The higher sample rates capture ultrasonic harmonics often present but unheard in many acoustic sounds. These harmonics become audible when played back at lower sample rates.

To eliminate **aliasing** (digital noises) when playing back sounds lower than the original pitch, the series III provides a proprietary, dynamically controlled tracking filter on each channel.

Through its independent **voice channels,** 16 different voices can be played simultaneously or a single voice can be played with **16-note polyphony.** Each voice can have up to 63 subvoices—a separate sample or sound for almost every key on the keyboard.

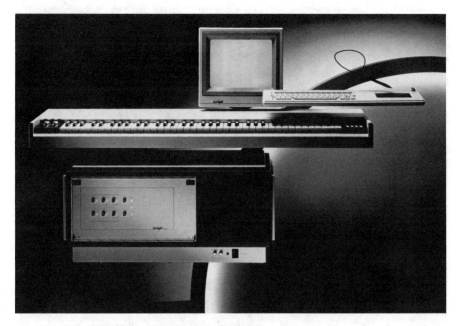

Figure 11–8 The Fairlight CMI Computer Music Instrument Series III. (Courtesy of Fairlight Instruments Corporation.)

Live performances can be recorded from Fairlight's own MIDI keyboard, which provides key velocity, eight variable controls, and five switches, each assignable on the effects page. Each voice has its own effects patch bay where various parameters enhance the performance.

A **real-time sequencer** (Figure 11–9) graphically presents 16 parts as individual lines across the screen. Each note records pitch, key velocity, and duration, as well as pitch bend and an auxiliary control. Patterns are displayed one at a time on the screen, typically one measure in length.

MFX Mix Console

The **cue list** is a time-code (SMPTE) based sequencer that will start from the correct point as soon as a valid time code is detected and execute any Fairlight function in sync with video. A music sequence may be "loaded" and played at a precise time while dynamic voice changes are orchestrated. Repeatable sound loops may be inserted through the **library file** function. Events can overlap in time (up to 30 events simultaneously).

Resampling can be accomplished in three ways: (1) feed the output of a sampler back into the sampler input, making certain there is sufficient level to preserve the transients; (2) record a sample on tape and then input into the sampler; and (3) use a specialized software package.

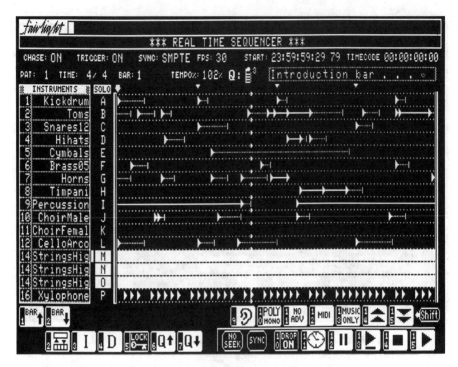

Figure 11–9 Fairlight's Real Time Sequencer program displays Fairlight's sequencer program for the allocation of subvoices; here 13 different subvoices are split up over the keyboard. (Courtesy of Fairlight Instruments Corporation.)

Applications of resampling include the following:

Corrective equalization
Creative equalization
Add ambience or effects
Pitch correction
Adjust sample length
Sample chords/rhythms
Simulate stereo samples
Save memory

Some disadvantages include:

Adding some digital distortion
Decreasing fidelity

MIDI Interface

The Musical Instrument Digital Interface (MIDI) was developed in 1983 as a protocol among five synthesizer manufacturers. The MIDI language is **gestural.** It does not communicate notes or sound but the gestures used to perform those notes or sounds: playing a key, striking a drum pad, how hard a note is struck, pitch, tempo, and other limited expressive aspects such as pitch bending and modulation wheel effects. These data may be transmitted to another keyboard or to a computer through the MIDI interface electronics, which convert **per-formances** into a special digital code, a rudimentary SMPTE cue trigger. The data can then be transferred from computer back to other synthesizers or sound systems to duplicate the performance parameters as previously recorded.

A MIDI **sequencer** is one of the basic playback systems that records as many gestures as instruments are capable of transmitting. It can also edit/ manipulate. It may be a stand-alone unit like a Roland MC500 or based around a PC that will store, manipulate, and recall MIDI data (but not sound). It is an electronic version of a player piano that uses coded rolls to play back a composition, but here the roll is a digital time code. As a transfer system, the sequencer receives data from a master keyboard and converts it to the correct channel for the **slave** playback instrument(s).

The basic difference between a sequencer and a recorder is that data are set against a metronone or click that can be set to any tempo. **Quantizing** is a process that corrects any timing problems by moving the beats to the nearest fraction of a bar, as selected by the operator. Completed data patterns (short musical lines or phrases) are then combined using a **song arrange** function. More sophisticated compositional techniques are available through the growing inventory of computer software programs. The basic melodic structure can be reworked and further manipulated, corrected, and reorchestrated and then stored on floppy disk. (See Figure 11–10)

Most MIDI systems allow for 16 discrete channels of data send/receive. As with cable, they are sent over the same line and tuned into at the receiving end. There are several modes of transmission: **omni on/poly** allows any data sent over any channel to be played by any synthesizer. Omni off/poly allows for different synthesizers playing separate channels of music polyphonically.

MIDI does not transcend equipment limitations or differences but merely enables them to communicate at their least common level. The second generation of MIDI instruments has the capacity for two mono modes to send individual note events through the channels for processing, orchestration, and storage, to be later synchronized with other tracks.

There are four categories of MIDI data: channel, system common, system real time, and system exclusive, each with their defined number of **status bytes** (commands and operations). These status bytes are distinguished from data bytes according to whether the most significant (MS) bit is set (1 = status) or reset

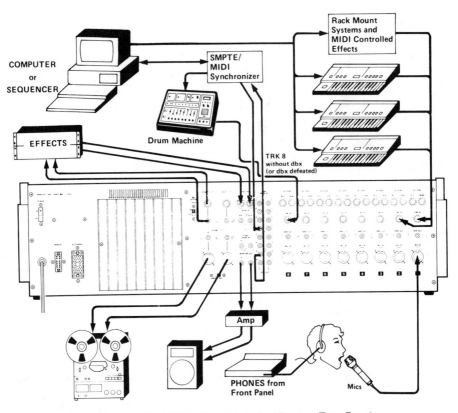

Figure 11–10   MIDI system interlock. (Courtesy Teac Corp.)

(0 = data). The data bytes identify keys going down (ON) and up (OFF), their on or off **velocities,** and the pressure or **after-touch.**

The four data categories are defined as follows:

System common: identifies song selections, measures numbers, and tunes requests for all units

System real time: synchronizes and performs reset functions

System exclusive: allows exchange of data to units conforming to the manufacturer's format

Channel: performs routine work

A motion picture or television composer/arranger, working with a state of the art digital audio synthesizer with MIDI interface, can create an entire sound design package—music, dialogue, and sound effects—in the same time it took an entire team working with full orchestras to score just the music.

"Stakeout" (*Touchstone*, 1988), composed and arranged by Brian Banks and Anthony Marinelli with a pair of Synclaviers, and Jan Hammer using a Fairlight Series III to score music for TV's "Miami Vice" attest to the new and limitless variety of sounds these systems provide. Microchip-generated melodies are here to stay, but they are simply another tool, not an end in themselves for the audio designer.

The basic hardware inventory all linked by MIDI includes synthesizers and electronic keyboards that create sounds, drum machines that create rhythms, and samplers that digitally record sounds.

MIDI language may control any electrical system. Stage lights, sound systems, and motors may be controlled and interfaced with robotic cameras and switchers. Live-music-based video presentations could be orchestrated from a single piano-style keyboard. This modern Lumigraph (see the work of Oskar Fischinger) could comprise light and color, set and camera motion, switching and special effects, and audio mix at the stroke of a note. We are looking at a time when "playing" a movie will be more than simply popping a tape into a VCR.

Technique of Additive Synthesis

The timbre of a sound is the final result of its harmonic series and the mix of its harmonics. Creating a sound requires a move backward, breaking down a given sound into its harmonic components.

A synthesizer waveform is like a guitar string. A perfectly pure tone may be represented by a sine wave. One cycle of the wave is the first harmonic. Two cycles within the same wave are the second harmonic, and so on. A square wave has all odd-numbered harmonics (first, third, fifth) mixed by taking an amplitude level of one over their harmonic number (the third harmonic is a third as loud as the fundamental). Mixing in different harmonics at different levels produces different **waveshapes,** just as they produce different timbres. The synthesizer has a wide selection of waveforms, each with a unique harmonic mix.

By adding together pure frequencies (sine waves), sound is created. By varying their mix and harmonic relationship, different timbres are produced. In theory, any sound may be reproduced by choosing exact harmonics and mix.

Individual harmonic identity is a function of three parameters:

1. **Frequency:** might be **detuned** from an exact integer multiple (such as 3.02 instead of 3 times the fundamental), giving a beating effect inside the sound.
2. **Amplitude envelope:** the mix of the harmonics changes over time, therefore changing timbre. Change may be slow or severe, fluctuating or undulating, before calming down; the amplitudes of some harmonics die away naturally; others tend to be emphasized.

3. Pitch-bend envelope: a harmonic may swing wildly during the attack before it reaches a stable state at a certain frequency, like horn "blips," where pitch quickly goes down and stabilizes.

Building a sound by setting the amplitude, pitch envelopes, frequency of each harmonic is a painstaking process. Multiple oscillators may be needed for detuning and filters for faking harmonic envelopes and pitch envelopes, giving control over every component of a sound.

Resynthesis

Breaking down and rebuilding a sound is called **resynthesis.** Between breaking down a sound and rebuilding, the waveform may be manipulated as follows: drop all the harmonics an octave while keeping the time evolution constant; boost or cut some harmonics; mix segments of upper harmonics of one source instrument with the lower harmonics of another source instrument; take a midsection of a sound and stretch it (frame resynthesis).

Once the sound is broken down, **performance controls** are attached to the components before assembly. Take any sound, a woodwind, for example, and have the velocity or pressure actually change the harmonic mix of the sound during the attack or while it is sustaining to create a unique "signature." The graphic display of a string signature appears in Figure 11–11.

Music Delivery Systems

A wide range of music is available on floppy disk. It may be modified through proprietary PC programs provided by the designer. The floppy disk of your personal computer is fast becoming a production medium.

The first MIDI CD (from Warner New Media and Passport Designs) is encoded to contain MIDI codes along with music that may be read by a new JVC CD player, decoded to standard MIDI, and fed directly into a sequencer.

Using a sequencer program, one may then plot sound against SMPTE frame numbers or hit the key on the keyboard as videotape plays. Graphics editing functions allow for the precise adjustment of a word or footstep or musical note to timing that was established against MIDI/SMPTE events. The completed bits may be mixed to feed the edited master directly or the master can be laid back to a multitrack ATR for sweetening.

The sequencer can adjust the tempo of a prerecorded sequence to make a tune fit a particular SMPTE time window. Because the pitch of the sequence does not change with its speed, compression or expansion is virtually unnoticeable.

Synthesizers cannot emulate the expressive vibrations produced by a finely crafted violin nor the subtle coloration of fingers against strings. While they can imitate musical instruments, synthesizers have their own unique **tone color**

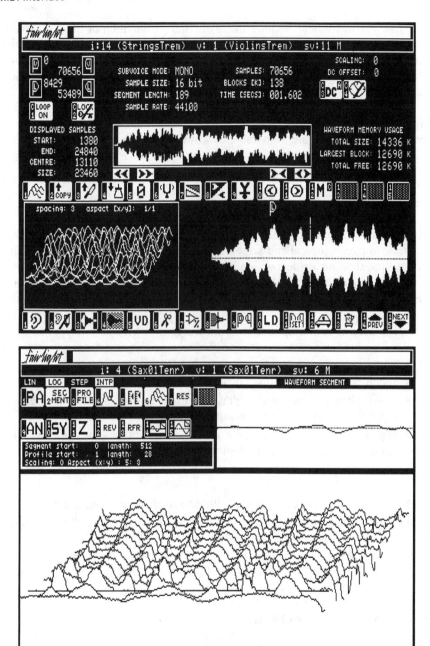

Figure 11–11   Waveform edit page from Fairlight displays a cross-sectional envelope of a string sample. Alternate 3-D waveform view. A graphic display representing allocation of subvoices; 13 different subvoices are split up over one keyboard.

and, like any instrument, require the talent and imagination of the **operator** to play a new key. While naturally produced sound fluctuates slightly in volume, synthetic sound exhibits constant-level output without background and transients. This superclean sound has its place in the audio spectrum, but is nothing more than another tool at the call of the designer.

Sampling instruments like the Emulator represent sound as a series of highly accurate, nondegradable **numbers,** rather than magnetic impulses on recording tape, which are vulnerable to wow, flutter, hiss, and high-hertz loss. Playback is distortion free.

The Editorial Function of Music

Music justifies the pace of action by providing a real-time "beat," which adjusts real time to psychological and screen time. Music provides a time scale against which "the rhythms of decoupage become concrete."

From standard musical practice, we have the sample devices shown in Table 11–3. The following are basic musicological terms helpful to the designer:

The uses of sound include the following:

- Sound is used as a bridge between shots that do not match.
- Sound is used to make the cut less noticeable.
- Sound elements are used to draw attention to details in the background in the same shot without necessitating the use of a close-up or insert.
- Sound is used to give a sense of the tempo of passing time within a sequence or series of shots depicting one or more events.
- Sound is used to reinforce the sense of movement within and between shots.
- Sound is used to create mood without visual or performance cues.
- Sound is used to control the overall sense of the pacing of the program while speeding up or slowing down action.
- Sound provides a bridge for leaps in time and space and changes in compositional elements within and between scenes.

Study Sources for Film Music

Miklos Rosza's score for *The Jungle Book* (1942) was the first preserved on a soundtrack album.

The following is a partial list of recorded film music sources. The primary source is *RTS/PR8*, Box 750579, Petaluma, CA, 94975.

London Records has repackaged many 1970s recordings (Phase-4 series)

TABLE 11-3 Elements of Musical Analysis

Beat (rhythm)	Duration, organization in time; with stress and accentuation.
Tune (melody)	Memorable succession of tones having a recognizable shape and contour (Nino Rota's Love Theme in *The Godfather*). Program music.
Countermelody	A melody of secondary importance heard simultaneously with the theme.
Ternary form	A three-part form of composition in which one of two melodies repeats.
Orchestral suite	Separate movements linked by a similar element (all dances, same theme, and so on). Aaron Copland's *Rodeo*.
Syncopation	A passage or melody in which stresses or accents fall in other than expected places. Anticipation, early stress, suspension, later stress; unexpected beat with stress. Charles Ives's *Putnam's Camp*.
Rhapsody	Exciting or exaggerated legend of melodies
Pizzicato	Plucked.
Lyric	Song to be sung; instrumental melody sounding like a song.
Sequence	Repetition of a melodic line at different pitch levels.
Motive	Shortest melodic pattern of memorable quality.
Meter	Regularly recurring accents indicated by time signatures ($\frac{2}{4}$, $\frac{3}{4}$, $\frac{4}{4}$); 2 beats = duple, 3 beats = triple.
Pedal point	Sustained tone persisting through changes in harmony and melody.
Counterpoint	Harmonious combination of two or more independent parts or melodies.
Fugato	Music treated as two or more counterpuntal voices that imitate each other in succession at the interval of the fifth.
Crescendo	Dynamics of a passage become louder. Opposite is diminuendo.
Canon	One melodic line imitated by one or more parts entering in such a way that the statements of the theme or melody overlap.
Chord	A combination of three or more different pitches heard simultaneously.
Polyphonic	Many voiced; melody pitted against itself or another in a counterpuntal manner.
Harmonic	Melody is accompanied by chords.
Choral	Harmonized hymns and secular songs for four voices.
Interlude	Contrasting phrase occurs in middle of larger work.
Pianissimo	Very soft. Opposite is fortissimo.

conducted by Stanley Black, Roland Shaw, Frank Chacksfield, and Bernard Herrmann. The collection is called Cinema Gala and includes compilations of classic film scores from many movies:

Warsaw Concerto	*The Big Country*
The Third Man Theme	*Moon River*
The Dream of Olwen	*Spellbound*
Things to Come	*James Bond 007*
Cornish Rhapsody	*Dr. No Theme*
Great Love Stories	*Goldfinger*
The Guns of Navarone	*Diamonds Are Forever*
Blood and Sand	*For Whom the Bell Tolls*
Gone with the Wind	*Sea Hawk*
The Alamo	*Victory at Sea*
Citizen Kane Suites	*Jane Eyre*
The Devil and Daniel Webster	*The Snows of Kilimanjaro*
Jason and the Argonauts	

EMI has a series of vintage sound tracks that include:

by John Barry:

Thunderball	*You Only Live Once*
Man With the Golden Gun	*On Her Majesty's Secret Service*
Moonraker	

by Bill Conti:	by Henry Mancini:
Rocky themes	*Revenge of the Pink Panther*
About Last Night	*Trial of the Pink Panther*
Absolute Beginners	*New York, New York*

Desktop Audio

The personal computer has become an integral component of the professional audio design system with the benefits of increased productivity and lower hardware investment costs. Desktop systems like the Apple Macintosh have the capacity for recording, storage, editing, equalizing, time compressing, and mixing controlled by SMPTE time code and interfaced through MIDI to a vast complement of electronic music hardware and ancillary processing gear.

The typical desktop digital workstation takes up little space, can be put together for under $8000 (but up to $40,000 for greater track and storage/manipulation capability), and can interface with CD storage systems.

Computer icons replace the traditional knobs and faders of analog audio hardware. Banks of interlock film transports (machine room) are replaced by the Compact or Winchester disk. A typical system (Digidesign) requires 5 megabytes of disk (Winchester hard disk) storage per channel of sound per minute. A standard 40-megabytes hard disk drive will store 4 minutes of stereo or 8 minutes of mono sound.

Record function is via the computer keyboard's record button icon or the icon on the computer screen. A visual representation of the sound is displayed on the screen taken from the hard disk. The entire sound recording may then be edited with accuracy up to 1/50,000 of a second with no pops or clicks at edit points! Other functions are performed by the capabilities of the particular software package: time compression, cross-fade, pitch shift, equalization, and so on. MIDI instruments and analog audio may be interfaced to complete the audio design desktop studio. But none of it helps without aural ideas and approaches to those concepts.

Workstations in Postproduction

A digital audio workstation integrates what were once separate audio processes: mixing console, multitrack recorder, patch bay, synthesizer, and signal processors.

The digital video signal is able to withstand repeated transfer between machines because the program content has been reduced to a series of ones and zeros; or, more clearly, the video and audio signals can be in only one of two states, off or on. In contrast, the analog waveform is electrically dynamic with regard to rate of change and amplitude. The magnetic imprint of an analog signal on videotape contains every variation of change and amplitude within the bandwidth of the recorder and tape response characteristics. After several analog generations, the timing of the electrical peaks and valleys begins to shift and blur, and the background begins to get noisy.

The ones and zeros comprising a digital video signal when retrieved from tape will pass through electronic memory, there to be properly timed and corrected, with flaws concealed by the substitution of appropriate values.

Moreover, higher-saturation magnetic heads have yielded the creation of higher-coercivity magnetic tape emulsions, allowing for a higher degree of short-wavelength recording. (The unit of measure for coercivity is the oersted, named for the Swedish experimental scientist who conceived of magnetic storage in 1819.)

Computer Editing

The first on-air use of video recording occurred in 1956, prior to which recording was chiefly intended as a means of network delay programming. Early editing (cutting and splicing) required the viewing of a series of latent magnetic video stripes running almost perpendicular to the length of the videotape. Splices were made between the stripes.

Electronic editing appeared in the early 1960s in which original material was played from one VTR and recorded onto a second VTR. This resulted in a second-generation assembled edit master ready for broadcast (with minor imperfections, which caused station managers nightmares). The system trade-name was Ampex EDITEC, 1963.

Assemble editing consists of making an edit that completely replaces all information on the edit master tape from the point of edit. New video, audio, and control tracks are recorded onto the master at each edit point.

Insert editing requires "preblacked" tape and allows for video only, audio only, or video/audio cuts. By 1967, EECO Corporation introduced the first time code edit control system that provided control over both source and edit machines. Later, CBS and Memorex married video and computer technologies to produce the CMX computer-assisted editor, unleashing several generations of automatic time-code-based editing systems.

Audio Computers

Optical disk technology weds multiprocessing computing to yield the audio computer, a device that allows for direct recording and editing on $5\frac{1}{4}$-inch optical disks, immune from erasure or wear. During the recording only the laser beam touches the surface of the disk, which is permanently encased in a cartridge that employs a Bernoulli aerodynamic effect to stabilize the record/play head on the disk at very low contact pressure.

Three recording speeds in mono or stereo provide 72 minutes of ultra-high fidelity stereo, frequency response (20 to 20 kilohertz with 88dB signal to noise) at the highest speed and up to 512 minutes of hi-fi voice recording at the slowest speed (double-sided disks). *PC SONICS* is one such system.

Simple one-keystroke editing commands allow entire recordings or any fragment to be copied, deleted, segmented, looped, or spliced. New edit lists may be assembled at any time from whole or edited sections. All edits are stored on the same disk as the original audio, allowing many different **playback sequences** based on identical source material. Full-screen editing of the audio is possible through an interface to an IBM PC.

Soundtracker

You've got a deadline to replace music and dialogue in a scene, but the music is off-speed and the playback ends up too long, while the dialogue ends too soon. Even if the time code is correct, the sound may not be what you need. The Soundtracker synchronizer is another computer-based editing tool that is a sound-matching playback speed controller. It enables audio, video, or film systems to automatically track and follow a sound whether live or prerecorded. It works by matching any two similar **line-level inputs;** one is designated the master and the other, the slave. Using real-time digital sound analysis, the system measures the difference in **tempo** between the sound elements and then outputs a speed-control signal to the slave player to make it sound-follow the master.

With dialogue replacement, actors no longer need perfect timing since the Soundtracker can vary the speed of their best attempt to make it fit the visual.

Optional editing software allows for visually finding and marking cut points while generating edit lists accurate to one-quarter of a SMPTE frame. Dubbing software allows for the auto sync of two phrases of dialogue in different languages for foreign language dubbing.

Because it responds to sound, the Soundtracker compares a program's soundtrack to the live version being produced by a performer, thereby providing the control for a film to follow, for example, the leader of a sales seminar or a music video to follow the tempo of a band.

Synchronizer modules like the Lynx SAL will accept external speed control from the Soundtracker synchronizer and use it to control a slave transport.

Correlation of sounds is performed in real time by a high-speed TMS digital signal-processing card in the host computer, using both **bandpass** and **envelope** measurements. There are 2 correlation modes:

1. **Prestored:** uses prestored spectral frames from one signal compared to the spectral frames from another input coming through the Soundtracker **live.** Anticipates future events up to 1 second ahead of the present moment.
2. **Split frame:** both signals are run through at once and correlated "on the fly." Speed control accuracy is within one-quarter of a video frame, $\pm 15\%$ of normal speed depending on the transport. The variable-speed SMPTE time codes used are 24, 25,29.97, and 30 fps. The variable tachometer pulses read 60, 360, 1200, 2400, 4800, and 9600 hertz.

Match-frame Editing

This technique relies on frame-accurate edit controllers. Each VTR in the edit system is independently synchronized by its own dedicated microprocessor to arrive at its designated in point precisely at the edit. A main microprocessor edit clock provides the edit in points. A match-frame edit is essentially a continuation of a scene, usually from the same recorder/TBC combination, a very linear concept of continuity.

The edit controller uses time code, and all source machines are capstan-servo locked to **house sync.** The controller does the bookkeeping through the edit decision list. The edit points may be shifted back to any point location in the previous edit numerically. When an audio match-frame edit is performed, the edit point is moved at least two frames earlier than the last edit-out point to eliminate edit-point popping. The match-frame technique decouples the edit points from the scene transitions, allowing for more creative freedom, but not much.

ACCESS

Digital audio recording and manipulating (sound shaping) methods, such as ACCESS, are based on taking analog sound and **sampling** it 50,000 times per second and then converting it into digital numbers that represent the voltage level of each sound at each instant in time. These digital language numbers are recorded on tape and during playback are converted to the corresponding voltage levels and then into audio signals.

Digital eliminates the possibility of faults found in analog waveform "pictures" of sound, which include noise, distortion, pitch shifts, print through, crosstalk, and wow and flutter. Transfer does not result in generation loss.

A computer memory allows for repetition and greater multifunction control for the designer.

ACCESS digitizes sounds and stores them on magnetic disk packs, and permits creating or modifying sounds electronically using computer control or computer-assisted control of a two-channel operations console. The audio designer can work on any portion of a reel and can build as many reels as desired in any order. All entries are error checked by the computer. Various printouts are furnished, such as final mix sheets and sound library inventory. The system can be synchronized to SMPTE code or can generate it, permitting the interlocking of external equipment for inputting or **laying off** of sound tracks.

Access Programs

Editor: Fetch and edit a sound. ID# from continuous display selected. Sound is monitored and/or modified. Two audio tracks are used on $\frac{3}{4}$-inch video tape.

Choice: Play, play previously modified sound, repeat sound continuously, edit.

Edit: Delays start of or shortens end of sound.

Prescript: Can create 19 tracks (10 minutes each). Assigns: reel number, track, start/stop, time code, sound ID, MOD number, chronology sequence. Show pack (42 reels) is maximum. Up to 80 show pack histories can be on one show history pack. (See Figure 11–12)

Play: Playback one of two tracks of same reel.

Tracks: Lay-off or record to external single or multiple-strip mag recorder.

Record: There are 6 output lines.

Update: Loads new sounds into library.

THELWALL (REVISION II)   REEL= 05

FX-01   FX-02   FX-03   FX-04   FX-05   FX-06   FX-07

             11.15   11.15   11.15
             QUIET GHETTO PRES.   TRUCK IN.IDLE   2ND TRUCK IN.IDLE

                                                                                        29.10
                                                                                        TRUCK DOOR OPEN
                                                                                        ----->> 31.02

             ----->> 40.08   ----->> 40.08   ----->> 40.08

                                45.00   75.00
                                <<OS TRUCK BY>>   <<OS TRUCK BY>>

                                ----->> 82.08

                                109.08
                                O/S TRUCK IN   ----->> 112.08

40.05
O/S QUIET GHETTO

                                                                                        123.02
                                                                                        O/S DOOR CLOSE
                                                                                        ----->> 124.09

----->> 144.04   144.02   ----->> 144.03   144.02

QUIET GHETTO PRES.
151.08   ------->> 151.09
O/S QUIET GHETTO

                         183.14
         ------->> 183.15   QUIET GHETTO PRES.   157.08
191.00   ------->> 191.02   O/S TRUCK IN
O/S QUIET GHETTO   200.04   ------->> 183.14
         ------->> 200.06   QUIET GHETTO PRES.   191.01
                                                            OS CROWD PANIC

FX-01   FX-02   FX-03   FX-04   FX-05   FX-06   FX-07
         QUIET GHETTO PRES.

FX-01   FX-02   FX-03   FX-04   FX-05   FX-06   FX-07
05-P2   05-P2   05-P2   05-P2   05-P2   05-P2   05-P2
         QUIET GHETTO PRES.   OS CROWD PANIC

216.15
O/S QUIET GHETTO
         ------->> 217.00

         ------->> 229.10   ------->> 229.10
229.08   229.08   229.08   229.08   229.08   229.08   229.08
O/S QUIET GHETTO QUIET GHETTO PRES. CROWD PANIC CROWD SCREAMS ANXIOUS CROWD CROWD PANIC

O/S TRUCK BY
         ------->> 151.10

Figure 11–12   ACCESS log of effects. (Printout)

Library: Displays or prints out data, cue sheets.

List: Displays inventory of effects.

A similar system, P.A.P. (see Figure 11–13 log) was developed by Glenn Glen Sound on the Paramount lot in Hollywood in the early 1980s.

Montage Picture Processor®

This electronic editor handles two sound tracks and one picture track. It creates instant sound overlaps and allows for temporary music or effects tracks or recorded narration. It uses word-processor technology with storyboard print-outs of digitized pictures of head/tail frames, user notes, and cut lists. The edit decision lists are frame-accurate and ready for electronic auto assembly of a 1-inch tape master and/or original negative conforming.

Glen Glenn
pap   SPOTTING SHEET   Page 1

CLIENT   SHOW   PROD#   EPISODE   R# V# NOTES

In	Out	Item	Action	Source	Track	Footage	
5:00:08:01	5:00:46:28	O/S CITY TRAFFIC	XFR	CART2	5	12-	70
5:00:08:01	5:00:46:28	O/S TRAFFIC	XFR	CART3	5	12-	70
5:00:08:01	5:00:46:28	O/S BIRDS	XFR	CART1	6	12-	70
5:00:10:29	5:00:33:16	O/S BASE BACKGROUND	XFR	CART2	7	16-	50
5:00:10:29	5:00:33:02	O/S MARCHING	XFR	CART3	8	16-	49
5:00:12:03	5:00:15:09	GATE OPEN	XFR	SRC1	3	18-	22
5:00:14:02	5:00:17:17	GATE OPEN	XFR	SRC1	1	21-	26
5:00:15:18	5:00:18:03	GATE LATCH	XFR	SRC1	2	23-	27
5:00:25:28	5:00:27:18	PADLOCK	XFR	SRC1	1	38-	41
5:00:26:06	5:00:27:26	HASP	XFR	SRC1	2	39-	41
5:00:26:25	5:00:27:29	TIN DO	XFR	SRC1	1	40-	41
5:00:27:17	5:00:31:08	BOMB TICK	XFR	SRC1	3	41-	46
5:00:42:19	5:00:46:16	WATER BED	XFR	SRC1	4	63-	69
5:00:46:18	5:00:55:04	CAR IN	XFR	SRC1	2	69-	82
5:00:46:28	5:00:59:02	CITY TRAFFIC	XFR	CART2	9	70-	88
5:00:46:28	5:00:59:02	TRAFFIC	XFR	CART3	9	70-	88
5:00:46:28	5:00:59:02	BIRDS	XFR	CART1	10	70-	88
5:00:48:00	5:00:49:11	TIRE SKID	XFR	SRC1	3	72-	74
5:00:50:18	5:00:52:07	CAR DOOR OPEN	XFR	SRC1	4	75-	78
5:00:51:00	5:00:51:28	CLEAN	XFR	SRC1	3	76-	77
5:00:51:29	5:00:52:19	SHIFT	XFR	SRC1	4	77-	78
5:00:52:00	5:00:57:24	CAR BACK	XFR	SRC1	3	78-	86
5:00:52:00	5:00:53:28	TIRE SKID	XFR	SRC1	5	78-	80
5:00:55:02	5:00:56:08	METAL SCRAPE	XFR	SRC1	6	82-	84
5:00:55:24	5:01:00:27	CAR OUT	XFR	SRC1	2	83-	91
5:00:55:25	5:00:56:09	SHIFT	XFR	SRC1	4	83-	84
5:00:56:00	5:00:57:20	TIRE SKID	XFR	SRC1	5	84-	86
5:00:56:22	5:00:59:02	HERO WIND	XFR	CART2	4	85-	88
5:00:59:02	5:01:00:25	BASE BACKGROUND	XFR	CART2	5	88-	91
5:00:59:02	5:01:00:25	MARCHING	XFR	CART3	6	88-	91
5:01:00:25	5:01:02:04	O/S BASE BACKGROUND	XFR	CART2	7	91-	93
5:01:00:25	5:01:02:04	O/S MARCHING	XFR	CART3	8	91-	93
5:01:00:25	5:01:02:04	GENERATOR	XFR	CART2	9	91-	93
5:01:00:25	5:01:02:04	BOMB TICK	XFR	SRC1	3	91-	93
5:01:02:04	5:01:05:02	HERO WIND	XFR	CART2	4	93-	97
5:01:05:02	5:01:06:10	O/S BASE BACKGROUND	XFR	CART2	7	97-	99
5:01:05:02	5:01:06:10	O/S MARCHING	XFR	CART3	8	97-	99
5:01:05:02							

Figure 11–13 PAP log is a version of the audio edit system developed at Paramount by Glen Glenn Sound.

Clips may be viewed (up to 4.5 hours of dailies), copied, lengthened, shortened, and played in any desired order in real time along with fades, dissolves, soft cuts, and wipes. For the designer, storage and retrieval of multiple versions of final cuts allow unlimited creativity.

The system behaves like a word processor, providing delete, close the gap, pull-out, and position functions. Repeat, copy, and rearrange modes go beyond traditional sequential video-editing limits, allowing for insertion of new program material with rerecording.

Computers control multiple tape transports (Beta format), and a terminal CRT and keyboard set the computer to perform various tasks: take a new input, dump out an edit decision list (EDL) onto floppy disk, print a storyboard made of visual clip (see Figure 11–14) information, and print data/display data (reel number, transition type, length, duration, code in and out numbers, and so on).

A lever/wheel system controls picture scrolling, the moving across seven pairs of small monitors of digital video images. The top monitor holds the first frame of the clip; the bottom holds the last frame of the clip. The initial function is to allow for **selection** and **arrangement** of the desired takes while storing unneeded takes in a **discard bin,** usable takes in a **pull bin,** and all previous and new takes in a **source bin.**

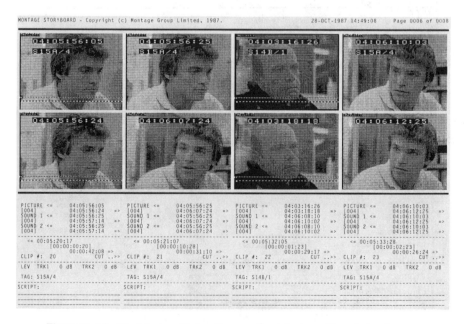

Figure 11–14 The Montage Picture Processor® printout provides aural and visual logs of each edit with the capacity to modify totally in the digital domain. (Courtesy of The Montage Group Ltd.)

The Montage can be programmed to perform wipes, dissolves, soft cuts, split ends, and keys. But its chief advantage is in its capacity to free the video editor to make both structural and narrative edit decisions.

Mu-Sync Tempo Editing Computer

This system controls the entire process of tempo and music editing for film and video. As a flatbed editor styled viewer with CRTs and computer assist, the Mu Sync gives a visual representation of the frames of the film, with action and music cues noted over each appropriate frame (like electronic click tracking). Move the cursor to a frame and the film will physically move to that point in the action sequence. Program in a tempo and the computer screen will mark the frames on which the beats appear, with different codes for downbeats. A third screen shows a conducting display, visualizing the exact placement of each beat and downbeat as well as the number of beats remaining in the measure. A metronome beep is also produced. The computer will assign tempi to coincide with important visual events and performs **accelerandos** and ritardandos between sections of different tempi.

The Mu Sync can be harnessed to control the Con Brio playback, resulting in frame-accurate, programmable electronic orchestration. The length and speed of a piece may be changed at any point by the Mu Sync, without altering pitch, to match the pacing of the program. Basically, picture is cueing and conducting the orchestra.

Other Systems

The AMS Audiofile system is a random-access digital audio tool that is used under real-time, on-line control of a CMX 3400 video editor/computer (at Multivision, Boston) with automated mixing console. Since two-, four-, and eight-track audio machines cue up more slowly than video decks, the change to digital cuts down on wait time. As editing proceeds, audio goes into the Audiofile and video goes to a 1-inch videotape; both remain in sync through the CMX. The Audiofile sits in the console and is then recorded through the console onto the 1-inch master.

New England Digital's Direct-to-Disk option to the Synclavier can be set up as a dubber in the film chain, running at 24 fps, 30 fps, or mixed, or can be used to store effects or design new ones.

The Con Brio ADS 200 digital synthesizer records an actual performance; the sequence in which keys are pressed, the nuances of performance in terms of timing and duration, and instrumentation changes are all stored as control voltages in the instrument. Any factor may be altered. Any note may be inserted, altered, or dropped out.

References

LEHRMAN, PAUL. "Computer Controlled Synthesis in the Studio," *Recording Eng/Prod.* (Dec 1983) pp. 109–24.

McLAUGHLIN, TOM. "Re-Sampling," *Music Technology* (Apr 1988) pp. 42–45.

MEYER, CHRIS. "All About Additive, Part 1," *Music Technology* (Apr 1988) pp. 22–25.

PATTERSON, RICHARD. "Musync: Computerized Music Editing," *American Cinematographer*, Vol 63 #8 (Aug 1982) pp. 783–86. This is another instance in which the prototype system reflects the needs of a composer (Basil Poledouris).

RONA, JEFFREY. "Recording Engineer's Guide to MIDI," *Recording Eng/Prod.* (Dec 1983).

SHARPLES, WIN JR. "The Aesthetics of Film Sound," *Filmmakers Newsletter*, Vol 8 #5 (Mar 1975) pp. 20–27.

STURHAM, LARRY. "The Art of the Sound Editor," *Filmmakers Newsletter*, Vol 8 #2 (Dec 1974) pp. 22–25.

WHITE, PAUL. "Studio 110," *Home & Studio Recording* (Jul 1988) pp. 89–91.

HYPERMEDIA

The medium (of storage) is the
message. Hypermedia provide an
overview of emerging technologies,
all of which promise to provide a
more stable distribution matrix for
audio information. Primary among
these is the laser disc, but part of the
future is hidden in the past, as the
sections on widescreen formats and
McLaren's early work illustrate.

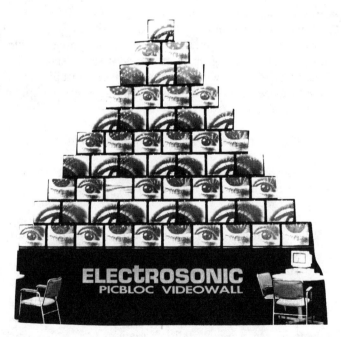

Figure 12–1   The real video space is outside the tube. As an "installation,"
whether in the home or museum, video makes more sense as a multiple window
on the world, interior or exterior. Multichannel design begs for spectator
interaction by its expanded view of both simultaneous, dissimilar, and alternative
parallel viewpoints. The subsegments may be organized rhythmically in
competitive and repetitive combinations, with stereo, multichannel aural links
creating sonic apparitions.

The Future Is Near: CD-IV

We have entered an age in which the scientist's "aesthetic feeling" about the way the universe ought to be has redefined his role from discoverer to artist. With compact disc interactivity, graphics, motion video, and audio can now be handled like an inventory of real-time digital effects. The early "color organs" and light/sound sculpting "instruments," like Oskar Fischinger's Lumigraph, are finding their spirit and substance demonstrated in the hybrid coupling of synthesizer, digital effects processors, the personal computer, and the audio mixing console, providing artists the opportunity to create a complete audio visual **hypermedia** track based on the capabilities of CD-IV technology.

CD-IV provides 660 megabytes of memory. It can carry still graphics and motion video as well as audio. Up to 32,768 colors are possible, with 2, 4, 8, or 16 channels of audio yielding up to 16 hours of stereo sound. CD-IV will likely be an analog/digital mix with full motion-video capabilities. Everything is in place. What we need now are designers with the desire to explore beyond the limits of the technology.

Compact Disc Formats for Film and Video

Consumer distribution has created several variations of the original laser videodisc that have found their way into video postproduction.

CAV: constant angular velocity type rotates at the same speed (1800 rpm), regardless of the pickup's position on the disc. Thirty-minute limit per side. Allows for still frame and "tricks."

CLV: constant linear velocity type varies speed from 600 to 1800 rpm. Larger outer tracks contain more than one video frame; no still frame or tricks.

CD: original 12-centimeter compact digital audio disc allows 72 minutes of stereo digital audio. Variations are:

CD-V: 20 minutes of standard CD at center, with room for 5 minutes of full-motion video at edges.

CD-ROM: records bits rather than audio; crams 550 megabytes on 12 centimeters. Retrieves data for personal computers but can't "write back" (read-only memory).

CD-1:   interactive. Stores hours of audio, video, or data under computer control.

CD-G: subcode space has medium-resolution graphics capability without impairing audio. Decoding tuner allows watch and listen.

DRAW: direct read after write ability; records still pictures or full-motion video (record once).

WORM: write once, read many; also an option for IBM PS/ 2 model 80 PC.

The Digital Harmony Graphics and Music Program

John Whitney sees the computer as a visual and musical calligraphic (temporalizing) instrument, and he has begun an exploration into the creative possibilities of digital sound married to digital image (see Figure 12–2). His present computer program allows him to compose, figure for figure, graphic action patterns and musical note patterns. Control functions affect speed, color, shape, position, and other qualities of abstract design, and these parameters, in turn, may be used to control pitch and the duration of musical tones.

The numbers that describe musical time and periodicity and that define computer graphic color and design have similar logic functions in computer circuits. Whitney's sample music/graphic compositions demonstrate just one approach, one probing into direct interactivity of music with color action patterns in the digital domain. Whitney's "Bagatelles" attack various aspects of the relationship between musical gesture and the actions of color, shape, and figuration. Tone and action combine to form new relationships. "With computers," he says, "we have begun to thaw temporal architectonic resonances in color, sound, space, and time." The process by which this is achieved is called

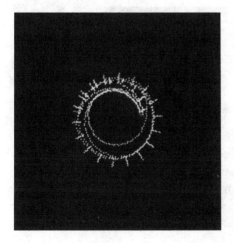

Figure 12–2 John Whitney and a frame sequence from one of nine short pieces dedicated to the arts of Native America. Whitney comments: "A solitary chord from a keyboard sonata by Mozart tells us very little about his tempo, just as one stroke of the brush of a calligrapher says little about his haiku talent. Just so I find that a few frames from any of these compositions (in time) says little or nothing about them." (Courtesy of John Whitney, © 1989. All rights reserved.)

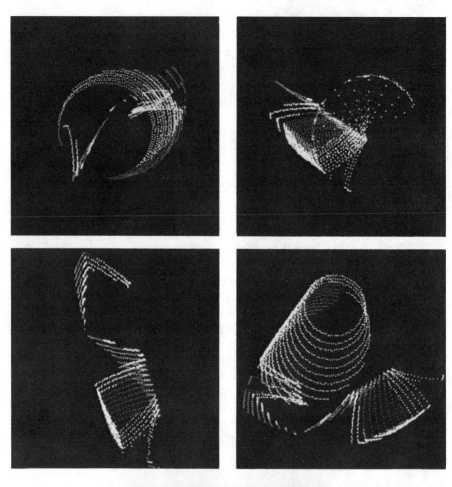

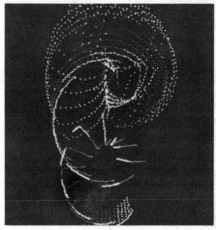

"temporalization," introducing structured rhythmic time and tone into formal dimensions of a new visual art.

Norman McLaren (see Figure 12–3) used the card system in which each template represents a band (tonal band). As the band widens, the pitch lowers. The system employs five parallel rows of 12 cards equal to one octave. The tonal range is precisely augmented directly on film. Cards are used like photographic mattes during exposure of the optical sound track.

E. A. Schlopo and Nicolai Rimski-Korsakov worked with the N. Voinov system of 87 drawings measured in semitones covering 7 octaves of the 12-tone chromatic scale. Tonal range is a function of geometric shapes. Pitch change is accomplished by camera close-up, volume by exposure changes, and harmony by double exposures. N. Voinov's "ornamental" *Animation in Sound* was fully developed with A. M. Avzaamov and N. Y. Zhelinsky by 1930.

Sound Design for Multiimage Audiovisual Presentations

Multiimage denotes polyphonic space–time structures. Multiple points of interest call for a speaker-dependent envelope around the audience and multitrack playback.

Two basic strategies may be helpful:

1. Vocal structures: the "guiding" voice or narrational approach with strong presence.
   - Musical; melodic
   - Synthetic; "Kabuki" style atonality
   - Natural; voice of the mother
2. Editorial structures: images and sound organized through:
   - Tonal cut on highs and lows
   - Directional cut on melodic flow and ebb
   - Formal cut on shape, contour, notes

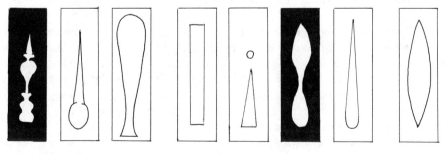

Figure 12–3 Waveforms drafted onto paperboard by Norman McLaren. Waveform manipulation.

The polyphonic (many-layered) space–time (moving) structures (patterns) allow for several approaches.

Director's Approach

Sergei Eisenstein thought of the plasticity of sound in terms of Japanese hieroglyphics, aural word pictures, which are to be built up from bits and pieces of auditory material. G. W. Pabst believed that background could make a comment upon action. The Ernst Lubitsch "touch" was his use of dubbing as the creative force behind his *The Love Parade* (1929).

Reuben Mamoulian exerted his will in converting the fixed set into an arena for motion. He was the first to employ two microphones (for separate characters) in *Applause* (1929). His *Dr. Jekyll and Mr. Hyde* (1932), narrated in the first person, boasts one of the initial experiments in synthetic sound. In his 1931 film, *City Streets*, he creates the sound "flashback" as a significant narrative element, while pioneering in his use of a moving microphone that follows action.

The master of shock, surprise, and revulsion, Henri-George Clouzot had a profound impact on narrative sound technique with his "sounds of terror," as demonstrated in only four films: *Le Corbeau* (the Raven) 1943, *Manon* (1949), *Wages of Fear* (1953), and *Les Diaboliques* (1955). Vivid realism is achieved with selected natural effects, magnified or focused.

Rene Clair composed his films with an overriding rhythmic structure through music, chorus, and effects asynchronously woven.

King Vidor's all-black, all-singing *Hallelujah* was devoid of "literal" sound. Shot silent, the film blended the black spiritual idiom, impressionistic atmospheric sounds, and sparse dialogue accomplished without sophisticated audio gear, but evoking intense mood and atmosphere. It was obvious that the cinema could not live on words alone. Vidor proved that the source was less important than the quality of a sound effect.

Weekend provided Jean Luc Godard with the ideal surface—visceral polysci—to indulge in audio closure, a design technique that distances the viewer from the event and forces him or her to listen to the film on the track as visuals interrupt.

Bernardo Bettolucci's *The Spider's Strategem* expanded the theme of "Dada politics" with an odd track that mingles the sounds of provincial Italy with the whispers and menacing melody of Facistic, mock-heroic melodrama.

Story of a Love Affair used sound very sparingly. Michaelangelo Antonioni discovered that the lack of the aural image is as compelling as its exaggerated presence. Sound becomes all the more expressive and effective when arriving infrequently in the audience's consciousness.

In *Before the Revolution*, Bertolucci uses aural separation, flicking back and forth from the realistic to the artificial, to prepare the audience for his volatile mix of romantic and antiromantic stylistics.

In *Le Chinoise* sound slaps the spectator in and out of Godard's fanciful political landscape until the only emotion left resembles inspired annoyance.

Quiet moments and long stretches of timed silences provide *Two or Three Things I Know About Her* with the sense of lived life that Andy Warhol strove for with his real-time mock-doc drama exercises. Godard, however, constructs a vision and a texture of a degraded social order without the shock of boredom and the boredom of shock.

Composer's Approach

In the early days, movers and shakers like Cecil B. De Mille insisted upon a "kinetic score," one that would alter the pace of the action and enhance editorial content; in short, make up for directorial deficiencies.

Then composers began taking an new interest in the medium as an avenue for new and stimulating forms of composition. Sound had become more important, and composers had definite approaches to the problem of film music.

Alfred Newman relied on the monothematic score in which a theme is stated and variations are used throughout (*Love Is a Many Splendored Thing*); the theme song becomes a way of attracting audience attention.

Dmitri Shostakovich developed the "6 minute movement" with hints of Tchaikovsky and French dance forms. He used basic musical forms like the scherzo, fugue, sonata, and waltz in films like *King Lear* (1970) and *Hamlet* (1964), both directed by Grigori Kozinstev. Selections are available on RCA CD 6003-2 and 77632.

Dimitri Tiomkin impacted audiences with his theme song for *High Noon* (1951). Lyrics soon became the way to make it "on the charts." In television, the Henry Mancini theme for "Peter Gunn" revolutionized the technique for creating strong audience identification with the show.

Alexander Scriabin experimented with the notion of a color and sound score for the film *The Poem of Fire*, but it was never exhibited.

Art Director's Approach

The sound track is a sonic landscape to be dressed. Preview the program landscape and find **moments** which could arise through denotative or connotative sound. Find or invent textures, little effects that describe the nature of things or people. For instance, the tinkle of glassware and bottles could denote that a refrigerator is full without having to see the inside.

Break down each texture into planes or levels of aural interest. The scene in *Citizen Kane* in which Kane speaks to his bankers employs three distinct planes of conversation: foreground, midrange, and background. These are polyphonic space–time structures.

Attempt to weave elements of sound together so that the audience "hears" sound in their mind, not on the track—suggest, imply, allude. This is the most experiential, intimate method; jostle the sense memory of the audience. True high fidelity has no medium of transmission save the mind.

The atonal clavier of the theme and variations introducing the dramatic intervals/interludes in "thirtysomething" presents an inherent incongruity: the simultaneous presentation of disparate ideas/emotions, the bitter/sweet of life. Like Dadist art, it seeks unexpected beauty in the irrational.

Words alone could not convey feelings in the intimate musicals of Fred Astaire. His dances were extensions of story, not interruptions.

The Semiotic Approach

Semiotics deals with communication modes as signs. Both the sign and the signifier are of importance. There are three fundamental categories in the semiotic system proposed by American logician, Charles Sanders Peirce:

1. **Icon:** a sign that represents an object by its similarity or likeness.
2. **Index:** a sign that forms meaning by its existential bond with an object, like the association of a sailor with his gait.
3. **Symbol:** a sign that lives in the mind of its user, like a figure of speech (metaphor), such as "scales of justice."

The primary design elements refer to the use of language in the program. Language can have metaphorical, magical, or mystical impact through:

* Articulation and intonation
* Color symbolism of vowels

The idea is to create a **factograph** (after Soviet filmmaker Sergei Tretyakov), a grid of images and sound whose creative geography has a synesthetic effect on the observer. Voice typage is very critical; the voice is an actor working against an artificial landscape of image/facts. A study of the works of Vsevolod Meyerhold and Kabuki Theatre is suggested.

Widescreen and Stereophonic Sound Formats

Widescreen exhibition converted sound from novelty to an element of narrative impact. An overview of past experiments in widescreen presentation may provide a basic groundwork for the anticipated revival of 65mm as a modern release standard. Showmanship has always been the hallmark of the motion picture industry in its efforts to withstand the mass media onslaught from television to home video and bring audiences back into the theaters. A brief history leads us into a discussion of current industrial "light and magic" widescreen systems, including IMAX,® Omnimax,® Showscan, 70mm six-track Magnetic and 70mm eight-perf digital Audio CD Pack playback.

Brief History of Widescreen

The industrial giants already involved in the telephone, wireless transmission, and the radio saw in the film industry a new market for emerging sound technologies. Both RCA and AT&T. (Western Electric) competed actively in research and development that applied radio technologies to the recording industry.

Subsequently, the film industry adopted the Westrex ''light valve'' optical recording system to standardize the production of the optical sound track. RCA, however, indulged in production/distribution/exhibition with its creation of RKO, and began acquiring most of the significant television patents for the new and emerging medium that would have an immediate impact on the way films were made and exhibited.

Taking a position in both camps, RCA, in a joint venture with Walt Disney, developed **Fantasound,** a separate, synchronized 35mm optical sound film for the release in 1940 of *Fantasia*. Involving Leopold Stokowski and the Philadelphia Orchestra, the recording took two months; 33 microphones were employed and about 420,000 feet of film were used.

The elaborate playback system was developed by RCA at a cost of $100,000. The system employed four optical sound tracks and 96 speakers in the theater. The additional 12 production Fantasound systems built for use in 76 theaters were never used again; RCA was enjoined by the federal government to cease production and turn its energies toward the war effort. This first commercial demonstration of optical stereophonic sound, astonishing as it was, would not again find an audience until well into the 1970s.

By the early 1950s, plastic base/ferrous oxide emulsions were introduced, replacing direct sound-on-film optical recording. Magnetic recording had been demonstrated as early as 1929 with steel (wire) tape, refined by the Germans with their introduction of the **Magnetophon;** its use was halted by the war and subsequently became one of its ''spoils.'' The magnetophon was the archetype magnetic tape recorder for motion pictures. With less cumbersome equipment and higher-quality sound, magnetic recording found its mass-market appeal through the efforts in 1952 of the newly formed Cinerama Corporation, which introduced the phenomenon of widescreen stereophonic movie spectacle. The new novelty married the greatest preoccupations of the industry: showmanship (natural magic), the commercialization of new technologies, and a viable audience magnet against the inroads made by television. Table 12–1 provides a list of widescreen movie ''firsts.''

This Is Cinerama (1952), the demonstration movie, and the subsequent theatrical (narrative) features, *The Seven Wonders of the World* (1952–53), *The Wonderful World of the Brothers Grimm* (1962), *How the West Was Won* (1963),

TABLE 12–1 Widescreen and Stereophonic Firsts

1941	*Fantasia*	Fantasound
9/1952	*This Is Cinerama*	First Cinerama
	Seven Wonders of the World	Cinerama
9/1953	*The Robe* (Fox)	First Cinemascope
10/1954	*White Christmas* (Par)	First VistaVision
12/1954	*Vera Cruz* (RKO)	First Superscope
1955	*Door in the Wall*	First Dynamic Frame
10/1955	*Oklahoma* (MGM)	First TODD A-O
1956	*Carousel* (Fox)	First Cinemascope-55
1956	*The King and I*	Cinemascope-55
1956	*Around the World in 80 Days*	TODD A-O
12/1956	*Monte Carlo*	First Technirama
1958	*South Pacific*	TODD A-O
1959	*Sleeping Beauty*	First Panavision-70
1959	*Big Fisherman*	Panavision-70
	Innocents Abroad	Ultra-Panavision
1959	*Ben Hur*	First Ultra-Panavision
1959	*Porgy and Bess*	TODD A-O
8/1960	*Honeymoon*	First Wonderama Arc-120
1960	*The Alamo*	TODD A-O
	Can Can	TODD A-O
1960	*Exodus*	Panavision-70
1962	*Mutiny on the Bounty*	Ultra-Panavision
1962	*Wonderful World of the Brothers Grimm*	Cinerama
1963	*How the West Was Won*	Cinerama
1963	*It's a Mad, Mad, Mad, Mad World*	First Ultra-Cinerama (Pan-70)
	Windjammer	First Cinemiracle

and *Battle of the Bulge* (1965), utilized three cameras to record images that were projected by three projectors side by side (seamlessness was always a problem) in the first peripheral vision spectaculars filmed in 35mm (see Figure 12–4).

The sound system was the first seven-channel, six-track stereo magnetic film played back in interlock with the three projectors. Five speakers behind the screen provided a **panning** sensation of highly localized sound, with a response of 15 hertz–15 kilohertz. Side speakers provided ''surround'' information in conjunction with one or two centrally located ''roving'' speakers in the rear, which fulfilled the expectation of multileveled, aural perspectives.

The immediate success of the spectacle mobilized Warner Brothers to refine the RCA Fantasound system: three audio optical tracks plus three superimposed control tones on a fourth track (to control playback levels) became **WarnerPhonic Sound,** separate magnetic four-channel stereo (plus an optical track on the picture print). Warners' 1953 release of *House of Wax* using this system was touted as the first ''All 3-D Movie'' with ''3-D Action! 3-D Color! 3-D Sound!''

By September 1953, Warners had attempted to standardize the widescreen format with its new **Cinemascope** release of *The Robe* (1953), which used four

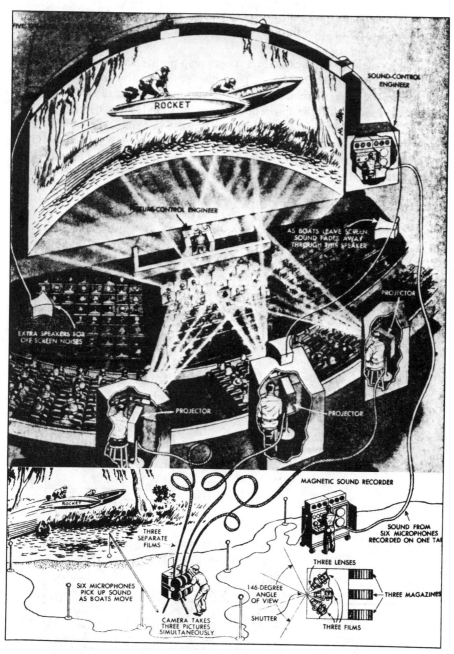

Figure 12–4 How Cinerama is projected on the screen. (*SMPTE Journal*, October 1982, p. 948.) Diagram oriented by Hazard Reeves.

combined magnetic tracks striped onto the 35mm print to provide four-track stereophonic reproduction through conventional speaker setups available in all theaters.

Not content to sit back and let others reap profits, Paramount and MGM tried **Perspecta Sound** (1954), a "poor man's" alternative to the glamorous, expensive Cinerama. Normal mono plus three superimposed subaudible control tracks were used to **shift** the apparent source of the sound between three speakers. This accompanied the **Vistavision** picture process in 65mm.

The overwhelming technical achievement came, however, with the TODD A-O 70mm six-track magnetic stereophonic sound process. (see Figure 12–5) *Oklahoma* (1955), based on the Richard Rogers and Oscar Hammerstein Broad-

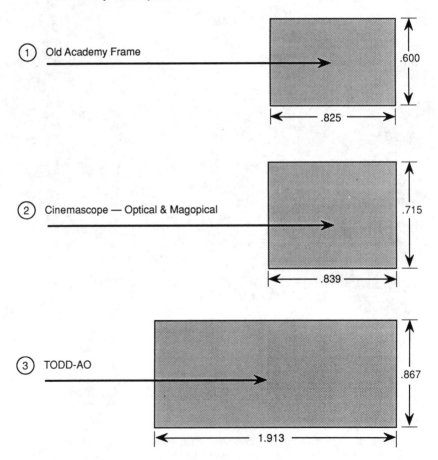

Figure 12–5 Comparison of projection apertures: Old Academy Frame, Cinemascope, TODD-A-O.

way musical, created a sensation with its hi-fi orthosonic playback. *Around the World in 80 Days* followed in 1956, winning an Academy Award for its score.

Warners followed the success of *The Robe* with *How to Marry A Millionaire* (1953) and *A Star Is Born* (1954). But TODD A-O 70mm had firmly established technical and creative superiority with a selection of family entertainment that included *South Pacific* (1958), *Sound of Music* (1965), *Porgy and Bess* (1959), *The Alamo* (1960), *Can Can* (1960), *The Agony and the Ectasy* (1965), *Hello Dolly* (1969), and *Cleopatra* (1963).

Sensurround, introduced in 1974, used high-power subsonic frequencies to physically vibrate the audience during suitable sequences. Control signals switched film sound and/or generated subaudible effects through an auxiliary low-frequency amplifier speaker system surrounding the audience. Both an optical track including control signals with dbx noise reduction and stereo magnetic prints with optical control track were used. Control tracks are carried on 70mm prints on tracks 2 and 4.

IMAX® and **OMNIMAX**® are horizontally projected widescreen presentations that use a separate six-track magnetic film. The IMAX image occupies a 60- to 120-degree lateral field and a 40- to 80-degree vertical field of view. OMNIMAX typically uses 80-degree of a true hemisphere, a lateral field at 180 degrees and vertical at 125 degrees. The 70mm, 15 perf frame is projected against a domed screen.

IMAX Projection System

The system employs a "rolling loop" technique. Film is advanced horizontally in a smooth, wavelike motion. Each frame is positioned on fixed registration pins, and the film is held firmly against the rear element of the lens by a vacuum.

Standard playback incorporates six-track magnetic interlock dispersed to the speaker systems as follows: audience left rear, screen left, screen center, screen right, audience right rear, and screen top. Sound channels are usually biamplified with at least 100 watts per channel. A sub woofer is used to enhance low bass. The IMAX Systems Corporation staff works with architects as new theaters are developed to ensure that each IMAX/OMNIMAX environment has suitable acoustics, noise control, sight lines, and entry and egress and lighting. (see Figure 12–8 & Figure 12–9(a))

High-definition Film and Sound System

Using the basic Kinoton high-speed projection system, Arriflex has developed a large-format exhibition system called HDFS. Synchronization of film and sound is through the ARRI-COMOPT time code procedure. Since Arriflex is also providing a 65mm version of its ARRI BL camera system, producers have a viable option to other widescreen processes, whose success is partially based on quality and availability of lenses and cameras. (See Figure 12–6)

The playback system operates as follows. The 65mm negative is used to cut a 70mm release print with optical time code. The code "excites" a compact disc player through a synchronizer interface. The sound tracks with time code playback from a compact disc are relayed by a cinema processor unit to the

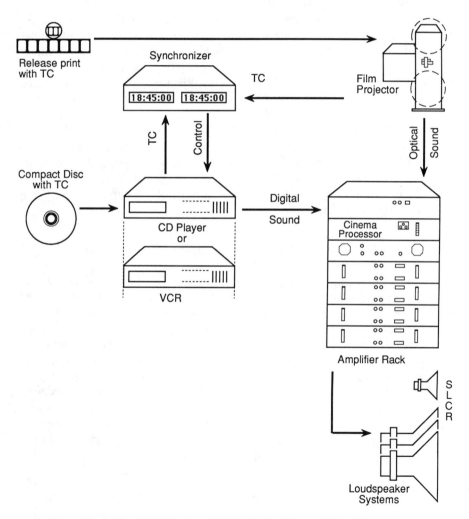

Figure 12–6   The ARRI-Kinotone High Definition Film and Sound Projection system uses the compact disc and digital technology to provide sound quality beyond the playback capacity of most older-styled theaters, which would require minor upgrading to take advantage of density and clarity of sound. (Courtesy of Arriflex, America)

standard amplifier/loudspeaker racks. Both time code and audio are digital, affording all the benefits of that domain. (See Figure 12–9(**b**))

Showscan™ uses 70mm film projected at a rate of 60 frames per second, providing 10 times the detail of standard 35mm feature film, thus heightening the physical "psychokinetic" experience in the theater. (see Figure 12–7)

The sound system employed is a five-channel magnetic stripe on film format. The kinetic illusion is further enhanced with the Dynamic Motion Simulator system, which employs programmable motion-controlled seating that moves in synchronization with the implied motion on the screen. Essentially, a theme-park attraction, the Dynamic Motion Simulator suggests a new approach to exhibition that utilizes sound and motion to provide a first-generation theatrical event close to reality. The audience sense of displacement is derived from both the allusion through sound placement and physical causation from the motion of the seats.

The Miracle of Wadi Rumm

It was as much Sam Spiegel's "miracle" as it was Sir David Lean's "labor of love." *Lawrence of Arabia* is one of the glowing examples of the collaboration of the last of the great "creative producers" and "Pantheon" directors of the old school, and it is the widescreen multichannel spectacle against which all modern attempts ought to be measured in both spirit and substance.

Spiegel had assembled an armada[1] of talent and resources along campsites beyond the Wadi Rumm near the border of Jordan and Saudi Arabia. Lean brought it all to fruition despite accounts of his obsession with perfection while on location in 120 degree heat. The reissue of *Lawrence of Arabia* in a new format is not only a victory for film preservation, but also a landmark entertainment event; its reintroduction (a "technical classic" ahead of its time in 1962) is now a fully reconstituted version closer to director Lean's original intentions, and it was exhibited, finally, in showplaces technically able to do justice to his craftsmanship.

Lawrence was shot in Super Panavision 70, a spherical 65mm system similar to TODD A-O, which yields 70mm prints with a screened aspect ratio of 2.2 : 1, and presented (in 1962) in striped four-track magnetic sound. The restoration of the exquisite visuals was no mean feat, but the real miracle was in the re-creation of the sound track.

Sitting in the balcony of the old Criterion Theatre in 1962, I was not aware of the grand experiment in widescreen multichannel exhibition about to unfold. Nor would I guess that in a short 25 years since its opening, *Lawrence of Arabia* reached a state of near irretrievable loss.

The spectacle that captivated audiences then was not the fully realized version director David Lean had envisioned. Forced to trim the presentation by 20 minutes to provide both a more comfortable screening experience and more

DYNAMIC MOTION THEATERS

▼ Dynamic Motion Theaters simulate action environments, such as roller coaster rides and car chases, by synchronizing the motion of hydraulically actuated theater seats with short Showscan process films projected in a theater environment. The seats, manufactured by Intamin Corp. Inc., are computer-programmed to produce vertical translation, roll, pitch and yaw functions. A fully automatic system allows for a constant change of film software without expense of a complete ride system installation.

► The Showscan Electronic Automated Projector

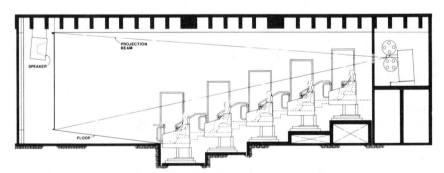

Figure 12–7   The Showscan (courtesy of Showscan, Inc.) process of high-speed, widescreen, multitrack film presentation, with dynamic motion system.

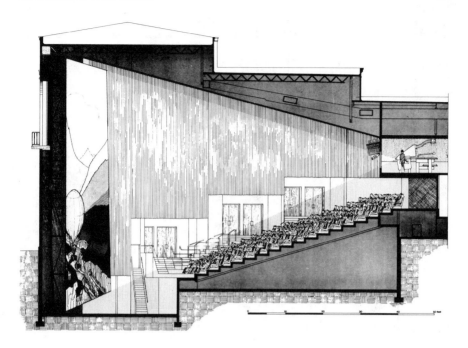

Typical IMAX® Theatre

Figure 12–8   The typical IMAX™ theater will soon offer the option of discrete six-track
magnetic playback or three-track-stereo compact disc playback of digitally recorded sound.
(Courtesy of IMAX Systems, Inc., Toronto.)

accessible scheduling for exhibitors, Lean provided a 220-minute original. A
1971 reissue was edited down to 187 minutes. But in the process, original
material was either lost or discarded, and the system of accountability for trims,
negatives, sound masters, and dupe prints (not to mention archival protection
copies) is notoriously poorly organized and managed chiefly through space and
budgetary limitations, management turnover, and simple neglect.

Filmmakers and archivists Robert Harris and James Painten of Davnor
Productions had worked on the reconstruction of Abel Gance's *Napoleon* (1928)
and had for some time harbored the modest desire to bring back another archetypal widescreen epic, Sir David Lean's *Lawrence of Arabia*. In the clutter
of gimmicky production, Hollywood hype, star-power politics, and competition
like *Advise and Consent*, *Gypsy*, *How the West Was Won*, *The Hustler*, *Jules
and Jim*, *The Longest Day*, *The Music Man*, and *Mutiny on the Bounty*, *Lawrence
of Arabia*, despite garnering 10 Academy Award nominations, was almost lost
in the proverbial shuffle for a place in the moviegoing sun. One hundred and
three films in widescreen format were released in the United States in 1962.
Most, like *Lawrence*, were never given a suitable venue for presentation. The

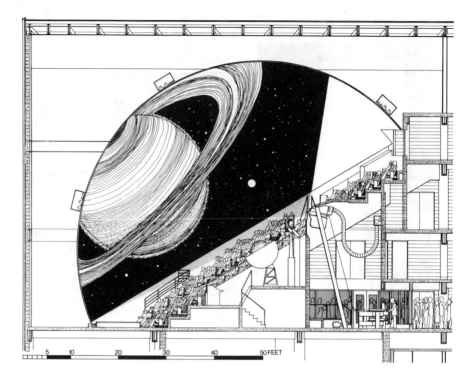

Typical OMNIMAX® Theatre

Figure 12–9(a)   The mammouth hemispherical OMNIMAX domed screen and theater allows for a truly "ambisonic" playback in which the finer techniques of "virtual mixing," which were developed by composer Michael Sterns, may be optimized. Using a Macintosh computer, Sonic Associates' DEQ-29 hardware, additional subbass speakers, and the TAC-86 (Theatre Audio Control) one-button sound operating boards, an "architectural" composition may be mixed directly in the theater. The mix remains fixed for all other theaters through encoded equalization available at the touch of a button. (Courtesy of IMAX Systems, Inc., Toronto.)

sound track for *Lawrence*, in particular, with its memorable use of Alford's "The Voice of the Guns" march (during a grand ironic turn in the film), its primal use of the Onde Martinot, an electronic instrument, to denote loneliness and the inexhaustible heat of the desert, its timorous cithara effects and its climatic gushing blast of a train wreck, may have never achieved its intended effect because it overreached the technical capacities of the theaters of the day.

Winston Ryder's superb and intricate four-track stereo magnetic sound track (presented by a multichannel system that was amazingly clean and quiet for a film before the era of Dolby noise processing) may now find an adequate screening space in its reconstituted six-track Dolby Spectral Recording version.

"Reconstruction" barely expresses the effort involved in saving the film.

1 STANDARD 16 mm

2 STANDARD 35 mm

3 STANDARD 70 mm

4 IMAX®

5 OMNIMAX®

Figure 12–9(b) Film format comparison. Three times the size of 70mm, IMAX totally immerses the audience with a sharp, clear audiovisual envelope. (Courtesy of IMAX Systems, Inc., Toronto.)

Harris and Painten were instrumental in convincing Columbia Pictures of the significance of the restoration of the epic to the director's original cut (221 minutes) with materials never before seen or heard! Even David Lean expressed marvel at Columbia's willingness to invest big money in the venture.

In poring over the more than 3 tons of material, Harris and Painten realized the plight that a new generation of studio management faces in the cost-effective preservation of our film heritage. (*Bridge on the River Kwai* faces a similar plight in that materials have been lost or discarded.)

With the blessing of Columbia's then president, Dawn Steel, Davnor Productions embarked on the search for missing shots and sound elements for this grand action/adventure/character study movie in which sound and image conspire to express the contradictory motives behind military heroism. To their chagrin, an initial search yielded no extant 35mm or 70mm Technicolor prints. (Release was in Eastmancolor printed by Technicolor Labs.) But the 19-month odyssey of film preservation resulted in an exquisite new 216-minute director's cut (the original Sam Spiegel production was shot in 18 months on location in Jebel Tubeiq, Saudi Arabia; Morocco; and Seville and Almeria, Spain).

Sand, wind, heat, and the massive 70MM Super Panavision rig made location sound recording nearly impossible. Sound editor/mixer Winston Ryder constructed a sound track with traditional location and studio recorded elements and with Maurice Jarre's music, a built-up four-track master with stereo effect and surround. However, in the 1970s, nearly $\frac{1}{2}$ million feet of original magnetic sound had been dumped. Moreover, the original four-track master mix on 35mm magnetic stock was in a state of advanced decay as oxide flaking had rendered the track useless. Bob Harris soon discovered that a complete rebuilding of many elements was required and set about locating available fragments from which to extract usable audio. Fortunately, the four-track printing master was found in London and it became the basis for the restoration master. However, one of the chief problems for postproduction sound supervisor Richard Anderson and Academy Award-winning mixer Greg Landaker was to dispel the leakage that had occurred of the 12 kiloherz cue tone on track 4 to track 3.

The first step was to make a ``4 to 4'' (track) protection copy onto 35mm full-coat magnetic film with the Dolby type A noise-reduction processing.

Since some scenes cut from the original release were now to be reinserted, some of the missing sound elements were replaced by transferring sections from Music and Effects masters [used for FLVs (foreign language versions)] to another ``4 to 4'' copy master. Some sound elements were also taken from old editorial trims, which are notorious for dust, dirt, and scratches.

Tracks were derived from the trims from an optical 35mm dupe located in London to cover new scenes (never before shown) whose tracks were missing. The 35mm dupe was a black and white positive sound print representing a fourth-generation sound element, a so-called ``slash dupe'' cut for editorial purposes only, of generally poor quality, which now had to substitute as a prime source to replace lost original masters. All audio was transferred to single-stripe magnetic stock for more precise control in the remixing.

The Anderson/Landaker Academy Award-winning team working at Samuel Goldwyn Sound of the Hollywood Warner Studios had the agonizing task of mixing fifth-generation materials with the widely differing background levels and noise of first-, second-, third-, and fourth-generation tracks, magnetic and optical derivatives, into a seamless and affecting new master track.

A good portion of the original dialogue track exhibited out-of-sync problems, bad cuts, physical damage, lost syllables, and generally unusable inserts. Harris drew dialogue from alternative sources—the trims left over from old work prints and the "sloppy dupe." The surviving outtakes became a valuable source for other support dialogue and missing fragments of words. However, it was glowingly apparent that some dialogue would have to be redubbed.

Director David Lean helped supervise the recording sessions. Twenty-eight years after the first take, Peter O'Toole, Sir Alec Guiness, Anthony Quale, and Arthur Kennedy consented and made arrangements to redub their lines. Jim Painten flew to Savannah, Georgia, with a sync Nagra to record Arthur Kennedy's lines, which were then transferred to 35mm full coat.

Maurice Jarre's original music suffered from masking by dialogue mixed over it on the composite. More mix magic was required to extract elements of the original score to re-lay over portions of the already reconstituted music master. The newly redubbed dialogue then had to be woven into the mix without masking portions of the old track. Masking occurs when certain resonant frequencies in the vicinity of their harmonics make it physically difficult for the ear to discriminate between them, resulting in a "masking" of the proximate frequency.

In the "officer's club" scene between Jack Hawkins, Peter O'Toole, Tony Quale, and others, for instance, music trims were cut back into the full mix mono dialogue master. The effects from the Music and Effects master had to be suppressed and the music layed in back over itself in a virtual line-by-line reconstruction process (like hand-painting technicolor frames). Often parts of words or full words and phrases had to be inserted from the newly redubbed dialogue to correct bad cuts and old faults in the original that had never been cleaned up. In addition, new Foley effects had to be generated to combine with new and never-used footage. This all had to be seamlessly mixed with sound from existing shots, a marriage that would have been doomed prior to the era of postproduction automation.

Goldwyn's state of the art technology includes a fully automated Harrison 64-input console, Magna-Tech dubbers, automated Foley, and full sound synthesis and effects gear.[2]

To enhance aural balance and maintain continuity between elements in the multigenerational mixdown, Landaker and Anderson created optical hiss loops that were blended in and out of selected track areas between, over, and under the plethora of trim inserts, new and old Foley, and new and old dialogue.

As a testament to the craft of Winston Ryder's original composite, most of the "stereo effects" (although some new stereo Foley was inserted) were usable and were enhanced to create a true "surround" track that essentially did not exist in the original release, save as an encoded ON–OFF surround track of the four-track magnetic striped 70mm release print (of which only one track apparently survives).

One bright spot according to Bob Harris was the fact that the musical overture (4 minutes long) and the intermission "entr'acte" together with "walk-out" music had been saved from the M&E masters. These elements were then used as his basis for a stereo remix for the 216-minute restoration master.

Greg Landaker supervised the final mix at Goldwyn Sound. The soup-mix included sound bites from six-track spectral Dolby, four-track non-Dolby, new and old Foley and ADR, insert loops, fifth-generation trims, and assorted fragments. The result is a miraculously crafty rebirth (line for line) of the master in a new six-track SR Dolby format free of distractions. The spectator will never realize what had been missed in 1962.

Davnor/Columbia's restoration provides ample proof that the time and effort are well worth it. The experience is totally new—more true to the substance and spirit intended by Spiegel and Lean. True sound localization with the heightened experience of widescreen (see Figure 12–10) (non-anamorphic) im-agery and stereophonic sound can now achieve its fullest appreciation with an exhibition technology that meets the challenge.

During the great Hejaz Railway train wreck scene, for instance, audiences will for the first time experience the effect at a level originally intended but never realized. All the density of detail is now present, the nuances of speech and ambience now audible from new 70mm prints, which provide a richness and aural depth of field incomparable to the 1962 version. A great film has been given a new life for a new generation of moviegoers unaccustomed to the grand showmanship that was the hallmark of film production and exhibition from 1955 to 1965.

So now we may reassess this filmic paradox of the self-promotion/self-abnegation of *Lawrence of Arabia*, who, as Christopher Isherwood has remarked, "suffered in his own person, the neurotic ills of an entire generation." On one level, the epic was a womanless,[3] imperialist wet dream of an "epicene young Englishman who proves himself as courageous, resourceful, strong . . ." whom the Bedouin Sheiks call "Destroyer," an agent provocateur whose "revolt in the desert" comes across like the archetypal CIA operative; Lawrence, who remarks when asked by a character in the fictionalized film, "What is it that attracts you personally to the desert?" retorts, "It's clean."

Lean's film, however, is not functioning on the literary/personalized his-torical level. He frames the theater of the Middle East in widescreen, where the center of attention is discovered by the audience in quiet contemplation. Exaggerated action takes place against the natural stage of wide expanses. The eye follows sound; all of Lean's aural objects are signposts for an intuitive grasp of what truth there may be in quasi-historical events and characterization. In the new six-track format, it is ever more evident that the track is the acoustic signifier of emotional content.

Early on in the politically insecure 1960s, the release of Columbia Pictures' *Lawrence of Arabia* was viewed as spectacle that nearly missed the mark. Reviews of the time discussed it in terms of grand entertainment, and even Bosley Crowther in his *New York Times* review of December 16, 1962, found

Figure 12–10 *Lawrence of Arabia*, 1962. Wide screen creates the impression of a sonorous envelope while opening up the prospect of no center. It is closer to acoustic reality, wherein sound must lead the eye in order to narrow the field of view, define movement, and isolate significant objects. On the large screen, edges tend to become invisible; the all-compelling sense of environment shatters the "window" effect so common in the narrower-gauge aspect ratios. Wide screen was a compositional format whose narrative specificity is defined by movement, not editing. (© 1988, Columbia Pictures Industries, Inc. All rights reserved.)

the production "vast, awe-inspiring, beautiful with everchanging hues, exhausting and barren of humanity." And to many other commentators of the day, the "huge and thundering camel-opera" failed to reveal the mystic and poet in the characterization of Lawrence as conceived by Sam Spiegel, David Lean, Robert Bolt, and the then unknown (to cinema) young Irish actor, star of the Royal Shakespeare Theatre, Peter O'Toole.

But O'Toole enjoyed critical acclaim, nevertheless, for his efforts (nearly a year on location, enduring great physical duress, and performing all his own stunts) and built a career around the success of his blue-eyed, enigmatic and somewhat androgynous role.

Twenty-five years hence, the film is not only an icon for preservationists but also an index of the political naiveté of the period. After all, it was a time in which victory in a land war in Asia was a popular myth, and the struggle for identity and survival in the Middle East heated up like the glowing vistas Lean so masterfully unfolded in his epic.

Although questions of purpose are best left to the province of historians, truth often reveals itself, despite the best obfuscation by the collaborative nature of filmmaking, and perhaps, this time around, the point will not be missed. With the reemergence of the grand spectacle, the widescreen canvas of backgrounds, humanity, and emotions, in the wide perspective of nature so dreadfully missing in home video,[4] comes the opportunity for reassessment and, more importantly, the occasion for the grand panorama to elicit a contemplative experience enhanced by an envelope of living sound and image.

Endnotes

1. Nestled in the area called Wadi Rhumm (wadi is Arabic for dry river bed) were a cast and crew numbering some 405 individuals often working 3000 feet above sea level and subject to severe wind and sand storms, extreme heat, and dehydration. Together with the more than 1400 camels assembled for the various desert scenes, the entourage required 35,000 gallons of water per day (which was trucked in; nearly one truck load of provisions was needed per person.) In the "Valley of Hell" water was not closer than 150 miles away at Aqaba, where Lean had built a headquarters site.

2. As an example of how new technology can alter the narrative effect of sound, Landaker utilized a Lexicon 480L digital reverberation unit to match background and levels and a DBX subharmonic "boost box" to create natural sounding horse rumble under the many action scenes. This, as well as other naturally directional sounds, did not exist or playback in the original 1962 exhibition because there was no true surround technology. Quad-panning, the ability to move sound elements across the screen, also did not exist. Without the new Urei Dip Filter, little of the 12K hiss could have been removed from the leakage into track 4. This enabled the option of also cutting a two-track stereo Dolby SR optical master with full surround encoded for playback in theaters with decoders.

3. The all-male cast also included Anthony Quinn and Omar Sharif. Several scenes called for some women, but in the Bedouin custom it was forbidden for Islamic women to be photographed (deemed as iconic possession of another man's wife), so Lean employed several of the local Christian females as extras.

Very little of the film harbors any directorial private conceit, for instance, Lawrence's masochistic scene in which he poker-faced slowly snuffs out a match in his fingertips. The autobiographical material is essentially extracted from Lawrence's lengthy *The Seven Pillars of Wisdom*, which details his philosophical and emotional development. But we might point to the 1919–20 film/lecture tour by Lowell Thomas entitled "With Allenby in Palestine and Lawrence in Arabia" for the inspiration that brought Spiegel and Lean to the project. Even Lawrence remarked that Thomas had transposed his life to myth (with the musical accompaniment of the Royal Welsh Guards Band!). Lawrence is so revered in the Middle East that King Hussein gladly cooperated in all the efforts to bring his life to the screen.

4. The videocassette was struck from the 65mm negative to ensure optimum sharpness and

released in "letterboxed" format, which preserves the correct widescreen aspect ratio through top and bottom black masks.

The six-track Dolby SR track will be decoded to Dolby type A noise reduction and released as a stereo two-channel format. Promised is a laser disk version, which may include ancillary production materials for the cineaste.

References

BORWICK AND ZIDE. "The Ambisonics System," *db* (Aug 1978) pp. 29–31.

CAMPANELLA, ANGELO J. "Getting the Message Through," *Sound & Video Contractor* (Jan 1988) pp. 32–48.

HAVER, RON. "Sound of Movies," *Video Review* (Aug 1988) pp. 45–7.

NIVER, KEMP. "Motion Picture Film Widths," *SMPTE Journal* (Aug 1968) pp. 814–18.

REEVES, HAZARD. "Development of Stereo Magnetic Recording for Film Parts 1 & 2," *SMPTE Journal* (Oct 1982 and Nov 1982).

SHAW AND DOUGLAS. "Imax and Omnimax Theatre Design," *SMPTE Journal* (Mar 1983) pp. 284–90.

13

AUDIOPLASTICS
FOR THE THEATER

Figure 13–1 To act is to locate oneself in a middle. Harold Rosenberg (*Act and the Actor*, University of Chicago Press, 1970, p. 6).

Audioplastics for the Theater.

Originally conceived by Brazilian composer/filmmaker Michel Fano, **audio-plastics** is the stylization of sound for a narrative purpose. There are five basic concepts which we have proposed:

Equal Presence: All sound components in the scene begin as equals. The ear discriminates with the aid of visual localization. Audio requires "channeling"—the separation of distinct elements isolated against background ambiance of a specific place. The designer must decide which elements should be emphasized.

Ambient Silence: The track exhibits a noise level even if blank. Sound elements are introduced into this aural field to a greater or lesser differentiation by the designer. Every acoustic space has a specific sound or ambiance. This may be recorded live or reconstructed. Coloration of ambiance is defined by its apparent source, size, and location (city-country).

Apparent Source: For every subject, there is a characteristic tonality or resonance which best suits it. This sound parameter is not narrative (emotive-psychic) but physical; corresponding to an implied sound-generating object. In the analysis of a space, the designer must choose an "apparent" source principle to the action or mood.

Aural Interference: Often a function of chance, this is the exaggeration, congruency or incongruency of auditory (and visual) space, time, or rhythm with the expectation of reality of the audience. One example is the alternate use of live and dubbed dialogue within one scene. The acoustic void behind an object-acoustic shadow is an interference phenomenon seldom utilized as well as aural foreshadowing, which is change in level from plane to plane within a scene.

Aural Analogies: Similarities and allusions organized into musical structures—"concert of sirens" in a police raid, for instance—can exhibit an organic interaction of effects and music or complete aural stylization via music. Sounds which are alike in some respects can be used to replace or comment upon each other. For example, rain can be perceived as applause.

As the audio designer looks at a specific sequence, these basic questions should come to mind:

1. What can be said (aurally) about the qualities/characteristics of the space?

2. What can be suggested about the characters?

3. What would give a hint as to the nature and significance of an object in the composition?

4. How can we make the action or event more specific?

The narrative function is performed if these questions are solved properly because sound here is not used as support but rather as an emotional or objective sign, which describes or adds something that cannot be better conveyed visually.

Other procedures which control and modify the action on the stage include:

- Jumps forward and backward in time:

  Alter orchestration—the choice of instruments and dominance of specific tonality gives an immediate sense of period, i.e., a Souza brass for a turn-of-the-century theme.

  Alter tempo—the rhythm and meter specific to an era can also be juxtaposed to inform the listener of a change. Modify an old song—the Tennessee Waltz set to a disco beat!

- Continuous temporal auditory event: Any event which is verbal, musical, measurable and/or uninterrupted constitutes temporal continuity.

- Spacial shift: Denotes changes in location, angle, distance, composition, or movement pictorially. The duration of the shift is variable. Interference of new aural data (sonic overlap) occurs. Background-to-foreground balance is disturbed and redistributed. New sound elements are added, others omitted.

- Musical devices: Include cliches of musical narrative such as rhythmic alternation, recapitulation (repetition in a shorter form), retrogression (reverse playback), gradual elimination, cyclical repetition (duplication of the first series), and serial variation (revision and modification of the atonal arrangement).

- Off-stage sound: Brings space to life. It:

  Conveys the vaguely possible.

  Uses silence as a value with various qualities.

  Orchestrates movement with direction and distance clues.

  Exhibits retroactive or deferred sense of scale.

- Centers of compositional focus: structural and plastic values.

  Contrast between ascending and descending movements.

Similarities of musical style.

Perceptible duration.

Tension via frustration—variation in tone or brilliance (sonogenics).

- The audible vs. the inaudible (the doors in *The Blue Angel*—various levels of sound are heard with each varied opening and closing of the doors. When they swing, sound takes on a stacatto rhythm.)

How to Make an Audio Design Scratch Track

A scratch track is a map created to provide a compositional template for a more complex and refined design plan. The most efficient method to create the scratch track is to work with scenes, one by one, from the entire program in proper final edit order. Preview the first scene or sequence.

Set up a simple workstation using a basic keyboard instrument—even a simple Casiotone will suffice, although a Synclavier would be nice. Set up a Nagra or other sync recorder with a uni-directional microphone aimed at the board. Run the print in a mixing studio or use a videotape setup for pictorial playback.

Sit at the keyboard. Assign relative values to the left, right and center of the keyboard. These values correspond to your intuitive feelings and responses to screen action, and require simple annotations as they are transcribed from the audiotape recordings made on each successive preview. Four previews should provide sufficient information in the form of cues or chordal landmarks. Even if you cannot play a piano, the keyboard may be used to record a simple design notation which serves as a kind of mix cue log to be further developed.

The first preview should be used to record the emotive flow of the scene or sequence. Any contrast between notes should denote some sort of emotive development. Be fluid and intuitive. Play along.

The second preview is used to annotate in order the rhythmic changes within each sequence and between scenes. For instance, you would assign a certain pacing of played notes to correspond to the level of action or inaction on the screen, movement within the shot and between shots, etc. If camera movement is significant, you will have to assign a certain octave or section of the keyboard to denote camera movement. For instance, quick pans left or right might be played as a quick succession of three notes near the middle of the keyboard, zooms could be assigned lower notes on the scale with fast or slow zooms conveyed by fast or slow play of those notes. Design a legend to describe the assignments you have made for yourself.

The third preview should convey the editorial content of the scenes or sequences. This would amount to some simple rendition of the transitions between shots (soft-hard; slow-quick; indefinite-precise) using certain notes to mark places where editorial "events" occur so they can be matched, later on, against the flow of other elements which you are tracking.

The final preview is to assess and indicate colors and changes in colors in preparation for paint-box or light-grid manipulation.

After each preview recording is transcribed, you would have a series of flow charts that look something like Table 13–1.

Read vertically, these charts provide the pattern for creating a multi-track master from individual pre-recorded elements other than dialogue which should then be worked into the overall design scheme step-by-step. The prospect exists for the hookup of a keyboard to a paint-box via MIDI, which would allow the designer to alter color via the keyboard (See Figure 13–2).

Deal with action first—it's the most direct approach. Animated sequences provide fine examples to discover process. Every action is a musical (aural) event which is composed of fragments in time that can be assigned musical values. Try to make a selection of notes or sounds to match the intervals of the mushroom man (See Figure 13–3).

TABLE 13–1   Sample Audio Design Scratch Track Display

Emotive

Rhythmic

Editorial

Tonal (Color)

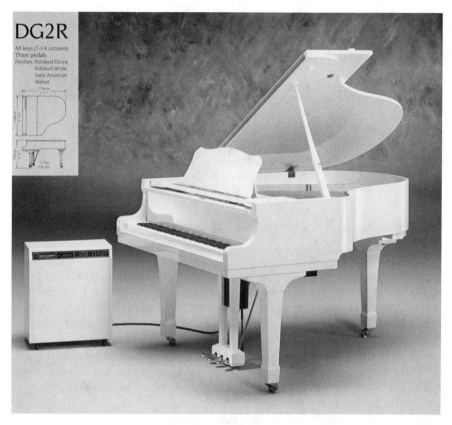

Figure 13–2 Yamaha model DG2R digital piano has an outboard hard disc drive that can play a pre-recorded floppy disc with music, music cues or enhancement cues. It can also record and store incoming signal data from the keyboard in a first step toward total sound-color-light automation.

Accidental "Au-tourism"

Digital recording formats lend themselves very adequately to the random elements of the aleatory techniques of serial or atonal music. The unpredictable can be planned. Stravinsky believed that within the limitations of the 12-tone scale there was great creative option. John Cage abandoned conscious control and found precision. John Whitney has carefully orchestrated a completely computer-controlled composition. The sound bite is a Marcel Duchamp "ready-made."

The musical elaboration of "open" works (the cinema verité documentary, for instance) uses chance as the prime technique. This improvisation with limits, with its multiplicity of musical forms, interchangeable movements and alternative variable modes of performance, provides a feeling of the untampered truth, musical revelation, sonic inter-invention that stagecraft demands.

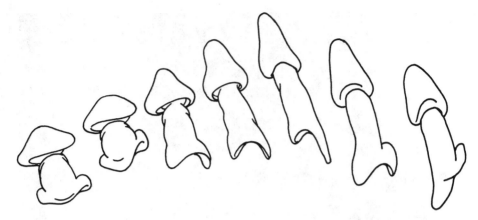

Figure 13–3 Precise analysis of locomotion leads to a precise synthesis of anthropomorphic realism.

The designer can pre-determine the plastic behavior of one element in the scenic composition. Through the use of multiple itineraries; such as re-edited versions, multi-channel reproduction and viewer-initiated interactive forms, (see "Hair, the Musical)" yet to be invented; the levels of authenticity and the many possible editorial matches all lead to a track which is "agent provocateur." See Jean Rouch's *Moi, un Noir* (1959) as an example of the "participatory" track.

The nonmeasurable rhythms of film and stage action favor serial music and digital composition. The ear must make an effort to decipher messages transmitted by the sound track.

Music is an organic and integral part of the overall formal texture of stage, film and TV because of its flexibility and suppleness (like Japanese classical music with its serial structure). Serial or atonal music composition is characterized by free flow, odd timbres, empirical use of silence and irrational structure. Tonal composition is characterized by a pre-determined form, strong tonal polarities, a range of homogeneous tone colors, musical synchronicity, an avoidance of silence and tyranny of the bar line.

In classical Japanese cinema and Kabuki theater, paramusical elements often replace sound effects. The Japanese are adept at organizing real-life sounds into musical structures. The closest western examples are the pneumatic train doors in *Trans-Europe Express* (Robbe-Grillet), dialogue in Polonsky's *Force of Evil* and the auditory patterns of von Sternberg's *Saga of Anathan*. Fuco's score for Antonioni's *Cronaca d'un Amore* integrates sax and piano intervals; it finds in blues jazz similar plasticity to the patterns in *Enjo* (Kon Ichikawa), *Fallen Flowers* (Ishida), and *The Crucified Lovers* (Mizoguchi).

The role of chance plays well in Boris Barnett's *Okraina* in which artificial sound is generated via the light and dark geometrical patterns of the optical negative; Fischinger and Norman McLaren have also experimented with this method of direct, "painterly" sound on film.

Dialogue is not exempt from the rule of chance. In Pinter's *"The Collector"* and Kurosawa's *The Lower Depths*, dialogue is musically orchestrated, the pace and rhythm of the spoken word conforms to musical patterns as in the German Singspeil form of musical recitation.

Observations from the rhythm of nature provide a reference for the design of a serial track. The Fibonacci theorem in mathematics was developed from observation of the seemingly random patterns of leaf growth on a plant. Closer observation yielded the basis for a precise arithmetic progression. In the media arts, every pictorial action is a musical (aural) event. Precise analysis of locomotion leads to a precise synthesis of anthropomorphic realism.

An exercise that may prove fruitful is as follows: Take a frame sequence of seven (more or less) units (see Figure 13–4). Assign a random selection of keyboard notes one to each frame. Reverse the selections and log both in the keyboard memory. Double the meter or raise the group one octave and log this series. Play back any two series together. Slowly chance yields a formal and workable progression. Devise another mathematical option.

An entire rhythm track could be manufactured with a synthesizer by the chance modification of the pitch of existing music tracks or fragments. This can also be accomplished by changing playback speeds of tracks and re-recording same onto a new master. The arithmetic progression is as follows (See Figure 13–5):

An electronic track sheet from which you can program output assignments and track volumes is from New England Digital's POSTPRO. The computer can become the instrument for chance re-composing of existing tracks and elements into a unified whole and cut automatically and precisely to each pictorial event. (See Figure 13–6)

The Audio Event Editor offers word processing-style editing control over live recordings (N.E.D.'s POSTPRO) (See Figure 13–7).

Composing for the stage need not be locked into melody as is the tradition of the American Musical Theater and its albeit great and much loved "show tune" from Richard Rogers to Stephen Sondheim. There is still room for experimentation.

The Row and Its Manipulation

Twelve-tone music begins with the selection of a basic row made up of any 12 tones of the chromatic scale. There is no hierarchy in the row. Every

Figure 13–4 Sample frame strand.

Changes in Film Speeds for Raising or Lowering the Pitch of Music Tracks
(*Bases*: A = 440 cycles per second; percents computed to the nearest tenth; film speeds computed to the nearest whole foot per minute.)

To Raise the Recorded Pitch—Read Up

Change in Musical Steps	Percent	Feet Per Minute
6 steps. Octave	100.0	180
5½ steps. Major 7th	88.8	170
5 steps. 7th	78.2	160
4½ steps. 6th	68.2	151
4 steps. Augmented 5th	58.7	143
3½ steps. 5th	49.8	135
3 steps. Augmented 4th	41.4	127
2½ steps. 4th	33.5	120
2 steps. Major 3rd	26.0	113
1½ steps. Minor 3rd	18.9	107
1 step. Major 2nd	12.2	101
½ step. Minor 2nd	5.9	95
0 step. Tonic	0.0	90

To Lower the Recorded Pitch—Read Down

Change in Musical Steps	Percent	Feet Per Minute
0 step. Tonic	0.0	90
½ step. Minor 2nd	5.6	85
1 step. Major 2nd	10.9	80
1½ steps. Minor 3rd	15.9	76
2 steps. Major 3rd	20.6	71
2½ steps. 4th	25.1	67
3 steps. Augmented 4th	29.3	64
3½ steps. 5th	33.3	60
4 steps. Augmented 5th	37.0	57
4½ steps. 6th	40.5	54
5 steps. 7th	43.9	50
5½ steps. Major 7th	47.0	48
6 steps. Octave	50.0	45

Figure 13–5   Changes in film speeds for raising or lowering the pitch of music tracks.

tone is equal. Next, the basic shape is formed. The row becomes a theme or shape when the tones acquire rhythmic relationships, or intervals.

Once a tone is sounded it is not repeated until the series has been completed. However, for reasons of sonority and rhythm one tone may be repeated under certain conditions. The row is used in four forms: Original, Retrograde, Inverted and Inverted Retrograde. The series can be used vertically or horizontally, as

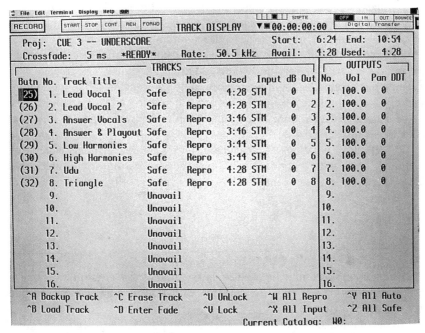

Figure 13–6   Inventories or logs serve to expand creative choices.

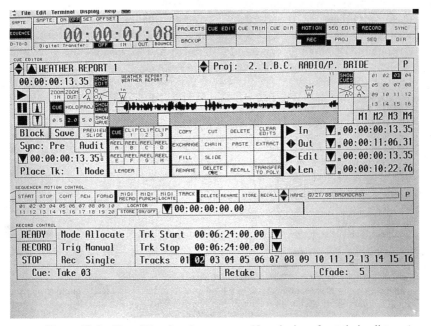

Figure 13–7   The editing function program. Note the in and out timing list.

melody tones, melody and accompaniment or as chords. The series may start at any point as long as the *sequence of intervals* is retained. Any tone of the row can be sounded in any octave. Endless variants are possible.

Abstract variations can be designed, for instance, a row made of variable measures—measures of varying lengths. Metrical modulation is created when the tempo has changed smoothly and accurately from one absolute metronomic speed to another by lengthening the value of the basic unit. Rhythmic patterns may be augmented or diminished by the addition or subtraction of fractional values like a quarter note:

Directions or notations for chance music require new symbols which must be defined, often with marginal notes for a scoring session. (See Table 13–2) Here is an example of augmentation by quarter value: A diminution by $\frac{2}{3}$ means that

The human voice may be used as an instrument. **Sprechstimme** is neither conventional singing nor recitation but pure intonation. Arnold Schoenberg made early use in his *Erwartung*.

In his manifesto of 1913, Luigi Russolo proposed a *music of noises* which suggests six families of sounds: booms, whistles/hisses, whispers/murmurs, screams/screeches, percussion, voices of animals and humans. **Musique concrete** of the post-WWI period used this futurist plan.

Microtonal music, proposed by Ferruccio Busoni, uses sixth tones and even smaller divisions of the octave, but conventional instruments except strings were incapable of playing such an idiom which had to wait for the electronics music industry to be invented. (See Figure 13–8)

Eric Satie (1866–1925) is credited for composing "Wallpaper" music free from expressionist fog whose precision, clarity and order seemed ideal for

TABLE 13–2 Notation for New Forms

1. "as fast as possible"	
2. a little shorter than the other notes	
3. loudness is indicated by the thickness of the dot (notes) in 6 degrees	• • • ● ● ⬤
4. sound duration	
5. hold to extinction	
6. velar click : the player simultaneously with a sound on his instrument, should produce a loud and very short click with the tip of his tongue on his (upper inside) gums	

Figure 13–8   Atonal composition.

narrative film and stage. His score for Rene Clair's *Entr' acte* (1924) was a model of emotional incongruity.

The basic row is simply a succession of tones without rhythmic differentiation. When shaped, intervals lend rhythmic relationships. In this example, the 16th notes do not change in speed; therefore, in the second measure, there are seven 16ths to the unit rather than four, so the pulse almost doubles in length. In the last measure, quarter notes have a slower value and tempo has changed smoothly from one absolute metronomic speed to another by lengthening the value of the basic note unit. (See Figure 13–8)

The Basics of Acoustical Treatment

Every set presents problems of soundproofing which take care and patience to solve. Listening is the primary method of analysis. A well-designed set visually may be comprised of too many hard reflective surfaces which will cause loss of vocal clarity on the stage.

A well-constructed set would comprise a balanced mix of reflective, absorptive and diffusing materials. Acoustic treatment of a room is essentially simple, but a theater stage presents a special problem. The set itself represents a real or imagined space, and that space sits within yet another acoustic environment—the theater envelope, which includes seats and the audience, rigging grids, lighting gear, the stage floor, and in classically constructed showplaces, the proscenium arch.

For the sake of clarity, we will have to assume that the theater envelope has been treated with tiles, carpets, drapes and soft seating. We can then focus our attention upon the set.

The quantity of movement around the set and the volume of the space must be calculated. Very few sets are designed with some sort of ceiling in mind—it's cumbersome and distracting of the action. However, it would be a good idea to construct several large (4–8 foot) panels of absorptive material which could be hung overhead just out of sight or as close to the set as possible without detracting from the overall design.

During a rehearsal with performers (and music, if any) notes should be taken of the offending noises or problems related to reverberation and reflection. Notes must be taken of the kinds and quantity (in surface square feet) of all the materials used for all the surfaces of the set, including floors.

Two methods could now be used to determine the kind and extent of acoustic treatment necessary. The first method calculating the RT60 value is more precise (and expensive). RT60 is an expression of the time in seconds it takes for a sound to delay 60 dB in level. The formula for RT60 is V × 0.05 ÷ S, where

$$V = \text{cubic volume of room (ft}^3)$$
$$S = \text{total available units of absorption (Sabins)}$$

Procedure:

1. Find cubic volume.
2. List the sound-absorption coefficients for the materials used. (Basic lists are available.)
3. Calculate the total square footage of each kind of material used in the set.
4. Multiply the total square feet of each material by its coefficient.
5. Using the formula, you can now find out how many Sabins you must gain to quiet the space.

For the second method, select sound-absorbing materials to be added to the set that offer high coefficients in the ranges of noise encountered on the set. Placement of these materials is critical.

Ideal placement means placing the materials opposite and adjacent to the offending surfaces. Use geometrical structures with oblique angles to break up the reflective uniformity of the stage. Props and furniture can play a significant role as prime diffusers. Remember that glass and mirrors will be difficult to handle. When possible, relocate opposite absorbers.

Natural fibers in the form of stuffing, bales, boards and hangings can be made inexpensively and shaped to needs. Where movement and dancing predominate, work with the performers' blocking diagrams to create paths of diffusing materials. Soundproofing can be a highly creative aspect of the overall stagecraft plan that enriches both the visual and aural experience for the audience.

Stagesonics

Stagesonics is the process of designing audio for theatrical presentation. The process consists of three basic stages.

The first, the breakdown of action, requires the logging during the rehearsal of mental as well as physical movement with reference to the set layout. The result is a basic list of sound elements needed to enhance the plot line.

The second stage in the process is the listing of sounds which enrich and extend characterization. This results in an inventory of aural elements associated with specific characters in the play.

The third stage requires the development of spatial and temporal sound elements which provide information relating to period, place, time of day, and so on; and development of aural projections—sounds that contrast, focus, colorize or otherwise make the audience aware of some event, person, element or thing (perhaps, for instance, the sound from a prop on the set).

Sound may also be used to create planes of perspective. The most obvious planes in the scenic design include: floor, foreground (upstage), backstage, overhead, optional levels—steps, ramps, balconies—and off-stage space. If this process of enumerating planes of activity is carried to completion, we have a complete 3-D psychoacoustical imaging of the set, including sense of movement, size and volume.

Playback and Sound Reinforcement

In order for any of the sound-design elements to have an impact on the audience, theater management must make an investment in top-quality playback equipment. The basic package includes

a source machine (stereo cassette deck, 4- to 16-track multitrack recorder/ reproducer, reel-to-reel deck, compact disc player or synthesizer

processors (filters or equalizer built into a mixer, reverberation and other effects gear, or noise reduction cards)

amplifier (40w–100w power rating)

speaker systems and clusters

soundproofing

The investment can be sizable ($100,000), but startling results can be obtained for under $5000. One set of carefully placed speakers and a basic playback tape deck and honestly-rated amplifier can provide results superior to the most expensive but poorly installed system. This brings up the prime issue of speaker placement in the theater.

To a certain extent, placement is limited by the kind of stage. The chief types of stage currently in use include:

fixed proscenium stage

open thrust stage

arena stage (see Figure 13–9)

amphitheater

stadium

small studio theater

The prime objective of loudspeaker placement is to isolate and localize fields of sound information for the entire audience. Ideally, the loudspeaker should not be heard; that is, no hiss or hum during periods of silence. Proper

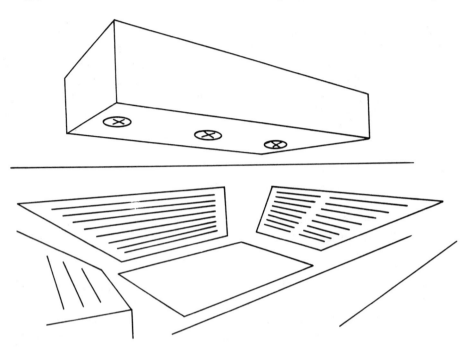

Figure 13–9 The open arena style theater space introduces the problem of multiple angles of view requiring true surround sound playback.

wiring, grounding and noise reduction are unfortunately rare in many theaters, but time and effort spent quieting-down speakers is well worth it.

Conventional placement techniques find speakers hung in the far reaches of the theater, usually left and right of the curtain and perhaps on the side walls.

Compact, high-efficiency speakers allow for placement in many more effective locations. For instance, there is absolutely no reason why a speaker cannot be disguised as a prop on the set (See Figure 13–10). This would provide exacting spatial enhancement. Floor mounting and ceiling suspension of speaker systems (see Figure 13–11) overcome the limitations of the small studio stage. A spaced array technique for the placement of speakers in the proscenium stage (Figure 13–12) takes into account a front and backstage reality as well as the traditional left-to-right arrangement. A further elaboration of this technique is the planar arrangement (Figure 13–13) that simulates aural projections through deep space as defined by the chapel-like set. Completely encircling the theater with speakers and speaker clusters provides uncommon spacial differentiation while enhancing the perception of loudness, intelligibility, and movement in planes.

Any arrangement of speakers presupposes proper angling of the speaker system (see Figure 13–14). Computer graphics systems allow for the precise previsualization of proper center-of-gravity mounting. But the quality of sound

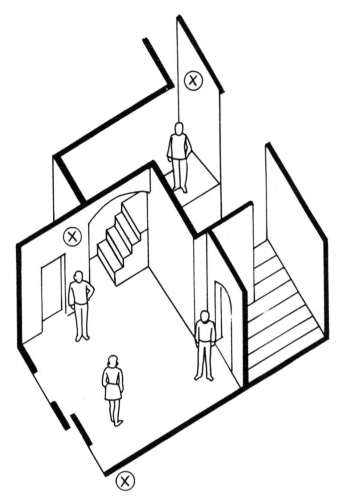

Figure 13–10 Abstract of a basic set. Sound reinforcement, proper choice and placement of speaker systems is as critical for an affecting aural experience in the theater as are the choices of aural elements. (⊗ = Speaker)

radiation depends on how well the system is mounted, how efficiently it is matched with its amplifier, how well the wiring is insulated and the class of its radiating element. Figure 13–15 shows three types of radiation: smooth balanced waveform (top), reflective (center), and directional with intensity greater at the center (bottom).

Many new speaker systems have been introduced in the sound reinforcement field; they have practical applications for the stage; they differ greatly from conventional speaker design (see Figure 13–16). They include **wavecannons, audioplates, surround clusters** and **soundspheres.**

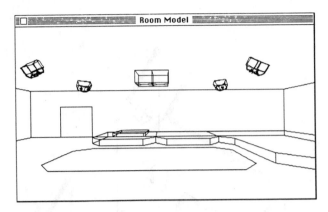

Figure 13–11   The limited room acoustics of the small studio stage can be overcome with overhead placement of multiple speakers.

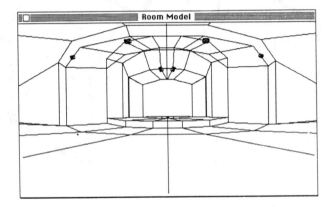

Figure 13–12   One possible solution to the lack of definition of sound playback in the proscenium arch stage.

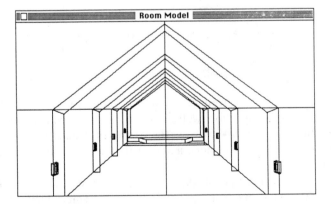

Figure 13–13   The room model presents layers of sound through planar arrangement of speakers.

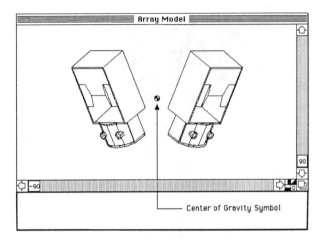

Figure 13–14   Center of gravity of a small loudspeaker array as displayed by computer monitor using Bose Corp's new SpeakerCAD Graphics Program vl. 1. Precise angling of the models is possible for a given space.

Audioplates

Barcus-Berry Audioplates

These transducers have very unique propagation characteristics. They provide extremely wide and uniform horizontal and vertical dispersion throughout their entire frequency range, which extends well above the normal limits of human hearing. With audioplate transducers, there are no "beaming" effects, even at the highest frequencies. Audioplates have no magnet, no voice coil, no moving diaphragm; they are rugged, highly shock resistant and insensitive to environmental conditions. In short, they are highly reliable.

In assessing the capabilities of a high-frequency transducer, its transient response characteristics should be carefully considered. If the high-frequency transducer section of a speaker system fails to respond accurately in real time to changes in amplitude and frequency of the input signal, the sound which the system produces will lack definition and seem "masked." The Audioplate transducers used in Barcus-Berry "Total Definition" speaker systems exhibit remarkable transient response; they effectively "unmask" the sound and make the systems incomparably articulate.

The Problem with Crossovers

The basic purpose of frequency-dividing networks is to protect transducers by allowing them to be driven only in their optimum frequency range. But crossovers also do many other things which they are not intended to do. They

Figure 13–15 Horns, tweeters, and subwoofers radiate sound differently.

are, in a word, troublesome. Most authorities will agree that the perfect speaker system would employ no crossover at all.

Now, such a design is a practical reality. Due to the extended range of the dynamic speakers used in the Model 6088, the need for a low-mid crossover is eliminated. And, by using Audioplate transducers which tend to reject low-frequency signals, the system also achieves a smooth transition in the upper region without a crossover and is, therefore, totally free of the sound-degrading effects normally introduced by frequency-dividing networks.

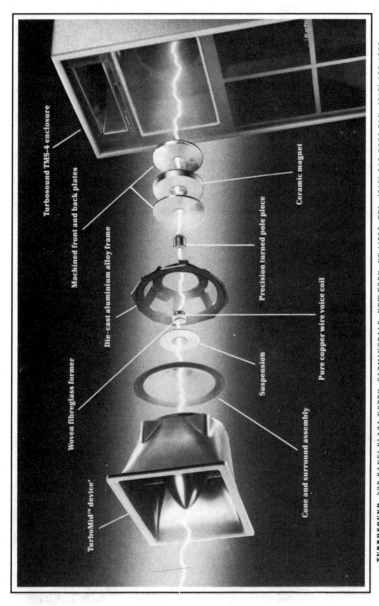

Turbosound TMS-4 enclosure

Machined front and back plates

Ceramic magnet

Precision turned pole piece

Die-cast aluminium alloy frame

Pure copper wire voice coil

Woven fibreglass former

Suspension

Cone and surround assembly

TurboMid™ device'

TURBOSOUND, 30B BANFI PLAZA NORTH, FARMINGDALE, NEW YORK, NY 11735. TEL: (516) 249-3660 FAX: (516) 420-1863
IN CANADA: OMNIMEDIA CORPORATION LTD. COTE DE LIESSE, DORVAL, QUEBEC, H9P 1A3. (514) 636-9971 FAX: (514) 636-5347
TURBOSOUND LIMITED, STAR ROAD, PARTRIDGE GREEN, WEST SUSSEX RH13 5EZ. TEL: (0403) 711447 FAX: (0403) 710155 TELEX: 87873 TURBO G IMC: TURBO UK
Turbosound Patent Information: Australia: 515, 535 Canada: 1,076,033 Japan: X113424/77 UK: 1,592,246 U.S.: RE 32,183 West Germany P2742600/2 Other patents pending.
'Turbosound Patent Information.

Figure 13–16 Here is a typical exposed view of a Turbosound loudspeaker. A speaker is only as good as its damping, isolation and suspension system.

The ideal audio design plan for the theater determines where listeners will hear certain sounds. During a live performance, the sound mixer can orchestrate and improvise within the limits of the rehearsed cues, the entire auditory program. The mixer becomes an active element in the performance activity. Automated sound systems with their repeatability and essentially fool-proof precision locked to performance cues provide a measure of security although the performers have the pressure of hitting the cues punctually.

Regardless of which approach is taken, silences are very important. The 3-dimensional psychoacoustic imaging that is now possible with software like Dan Lowe's **QSound,** a program for graphically displaying the layers of aural information in a track on a PC terminal monitor (see Figure 13–17), leaves little excuse for sound not being exciting and fun in the theater.

In terms of actual playback machine modes, we may elect to use one separate track on a multitrack machine for each speaker or select the basic two-track (stereo) playback format. When processed with the **QSound** system, sounds played on conventional stereo systems will be perceived to emanate from several distinct locations.

To summarize, the prime considerations in creating tracks for the theater are to:

Figure 13–17   Dan Lowe, creator of QSound, determines where listeners will hear various instruments, voices and sounds as analyzed and selected on computer and placed on a master recording.

- create on- and off-stage space
- focus attention
- enhance mood
- shock into recognition
- emphasize the significance of silences
- convey narrative information
- convey character traits

Although the tools of the playwright remain essentially the same, the tools of the designer (see Figure 13–18) now include digital recording, computer-assisted production and high-end playback equipment. Although the small stage production can hardly rationalize a budget for such luxuries, very great things can be accomplished with the simplest of materials if, and only if, both the

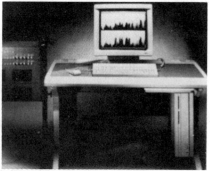

Figure 13–18 Tools of the trade: Multitrack digital recorder. a) Digital multitrack; b) workstation; c) monitor speaker.

playwright and the designer know exactly how they can manipulate the audience by virtue of the aural experience.

References

BERANEK, LEO L. "NOISE." *Scientific American*, Vol 215 # 6 (Dec 1966), pp. 44–58.

CLEGG, ALMON. "The Shape of Things to Come: Psycho-Acoustic Space Control Technology," *db* (Jun 1979) pp. 27–29.

DEUTSCH, D. "Auditory Illusions, Handedness and the Spatial Environment," *AES Journal*, Jan 31, (1983). pp. 607–18.

LEVIN, J. "The Acoustic Dimension," *Screen* (May–Jun 1984) pp. 32–40, 71–91.

PICKLES, J. O. *An Introduction to the Physiology of Hearing*. Academic Press, 1982.

SAVAGE, W. R. *Problems for Musical Acoustics*. London: Oxford University Press. 1977.

Articles

Stage lighting—design and construction

Touring. (lighting design) by Alice M. Hale, v21 *Theatre Crafts* Aug–Sept '87 p24(6)

Architectural acoustics—theater use

Acoustical design of multipurpose theaters; altering the balance between reflective and absorptive surfaces is key to the facility's flexibility, by John Gregerson, v29 *Building Design & Construction* Oct '88 p108(5)

Soundproofing—technique

Guidelines for building noise control enclosures, by Kenneth E. Carney, v41 *Plant Engineering* Dec 17 '87 p68(4)

Unwanted sounds. (Audio update) by Larry Klein v58 *Radio-Electronics* June '87 p78(3)

Sound designer (computer program)

Simpler Samplers: is it live or is it MIDI hex? (four MIDI sampler programs) (includes two related articles on a history of computer sampling instruments and a description of what a sampler is and does and an evaluation) by Tim Tully il v4 *MacUser* Oct '88 p. 148(9). Sampling is a procedure for recording, processing and playing back acoustic sounds with an electronic device called a sampler. When connected to a computer, sound waves can be represented in various graphical formats to let users manipulate them more easily. Four sampling software programs are evaluated. Blank Software's $495 Alchemy loads and edits digitally sampled sounds from most commercial samplers and produces a sample compatible with all of them but requires at least two MB of RAM to do this well. Digidesigns's $349 Turbosynth creates sounds from a sampler using modular synthesis techniques. Both of the programs are given top ratings for documentation, performance and value. Digidesigns's $295 Softsynth creates sounds for additive synthesis samplers, but downloading from the Mac to sample is time consuming. Digidesigns's $495 Sound Designer set the standard for editing samples on lower-cost samplers and vastly improves on sample editing abilities of the samplers it supports.

Theaters—sound effects

Sound reinforcement for the 90s: trends, techniques, technologies. (sound technology) by Michael S. Eddy, v23 *Theatre Crafts* Nov '89 p30(3)

MIDI and the theatre: a guide to software applications. (Musical Instrument Digital Interface) by Jim Roper v23 *Theatre Crafts* Oct '89 p70(5)

CD libraries: sound effects on compact discs. by Tom Clark, v23 *Theatre Crafts* August-Sept '89 p38(3)

Making a telephone ring. (theatre production) by Karl G. Ruling, v23 *Theatre Crafts* April '89 p92(4)

L. B. Dallas. (theater sound designer) by Bob Saturn, v22 *Theatre Crafts* Nov '88, p88(4)

Tony Meola: the sound designer of "Anything Goes" experiences months of creative "madness." by Robert Long, v22 *Theatre Crafts* Aug-Sept '88 p38(6)

Sinister sounds. (sound effects for the stage) (Murder, Mayhem, and Mysterious Events) by Ronn Smith v22 *Theatre Crafts* May '88 p49(5)

Aural Fixations. (Guy Sherman) by Susan Borney, v21 *Theatre Crafts* Oct '87 p42(7)

Theaters—stage setting and scenery

The play may be the thing, but it needs a friend in set design. (Leisure and Arts) by Frank Rich, 36 col in. v139 *The New York Times* Jan 18 '90 pB1(N) pC21(L) col 1

Tony Walton's daring set for a moody "Grand Hotel." (Living Arts Pages) by Mervyn Rothstein, 23 col in. v139 *The New York Times* Nov 20 '89 pB1(N) col 2

Turning restrictions into design benefits for "Grand Hotel." (set designer, Tony Walton) (Living Arts Pages) by Mervyn Rothstein, 15 col in. v139 *The New York Times* Nov 20 '89 pC13(L) col 4

Designfile: Walton show. (Tony Walton, American Museum of the Moving Image, Astoria, New York), v23 *Theatre Crafts* Nov '89 p16(1)

Set symbols: Jerome Sirlin projects Philip Glass and David Henry Hwang into the cosmos. (production of "1000 Airplanes on the Roof"—theater) by Patrick Pacheco, v178 *Vogue* Dec '88 p192(1)

Rigging in the 21st century. (theater rigging) by Mark Loeffler, v22 *Theatre Crafts,* Oct '88 p86(4)

Setting the stage: dramatic designs. (theater sets) by Paul Kunkel, v 121 *Harper's Bazaar* Aug '88 p82(2)

Murder, mayhem, and mysterious events. (includes related articles on staging mystery and detective plays) by Michael Sommers and Michele Larue, v 22 *Theatre Crafts* May '88 p29(9)

Svoboda & Vychodil: Czechoslovakia's two master scenographers. (Josef Svoboda and Ladislav Vychodil) by Jarka M. Burian, v21 *Theatre Crafts* Oct '87 p34(10)

Theater, open-air—noise control

Having a ball at the Bowl. (Hollywood Bowl; Festivals '89) by Richard S. Ginell, v109 Musical America May '89 pS16(4)

Theater of the Imagination: Radio Stories by Orson Welles and the Mercury Theater. (audio tape reviews) rev by Michael Rogers. A v114 Library Journal Nov 1 '89 p128(1)

APPENDIXES

Figure A–1a The original German Magnetophon. (Courtesy of Ampex Corp.)

Figure A–1b First Ampex audio recorder. (Courtesy of Ampex Corp.)

Figure A–1c First Bing Crosby promo for Ampex. (Courtesy of Ampex Corp.)

Figure A–1d Yamaha Electronic Instrument, piano/synthesizer.

A. Developmental History of Sound Recording

In 1857, a French scientist, *Edouard Leon-Scott* invented the **Phonautograph**. It was capable of making recordings of sound waves but could not play them back. In 1863, a German scientist, *Karl Rudolph Koenig*, completed an improved version of the Phonautograph by providing it with a parabolic-shaped horn, thereby extending the ability of the machine to collect and make graphic records of all kinds of sounds; but he did not provide any means of playing back the sounds it recorded. In 1860, an amateur scientist, *Charles Cros*, envisioned a machine that would record and reproduce sounds of spoken conversation so that they would be visible and readable by deaf mutes. However, nothing came of this idea at the time, and Cros was too impecunious to afford a patent. Finally, on December 15, 1877, *Thomas Edison* received a U.S. patent on his **phonograph.** Because of the above previous works, there was some doubt as to whether or not Edison had priority of invention; however, there is no doubt that his tinfoil phonograph of 1877 was the first talking machine that actually worked.

During 1885–1886, *Alexander Graham Bell*, *Chichister Bell*, and *Charles Sumner Tainter* invented the **Graphophone.** It worked on the same principles as the phonograph but improved on Edison's machine by having the sound impressions incised on the wax-coated surface of a cardboard cylinder, which was shipped on a rotatable mandrel; the latter did not move linearly as it rotated, but the recorder was moved along it by means of a feed screw. Meanwhile, another invention called the **Gramophone** was looming in the background. The Gramophone was a machine that played disks instead of cylinders and was the work of *Emile Berliner*. It was marketed during 1893, along with a seven-inch disk made of hard rubber.

During this time, various inventors were working on machines to make moving pictures. The most successful of these inventions was the **Kinetoscope.** It stood 48 inches high and resembled a closed-in casket. On the top of the box was an eyepiece. Inside the machine, approximately 56 feet of 35mm film circulated at 46 frames per second in an endless loop under a viewing lens, each frame briefly illuminated by a flash of light through a rotating shutter. Although credit for this invention should be attributed to a man named *Dickson*, Edison publicized it as his own invention and began making grandiose claims about it. In May 1893, he presented a combination of his two machines at the Colombian exposition in Chicago whereby he harnessed a Kinetoscope to a phonograph. He could photograph the face at the same time that one talks into the phonograph. By this method, the sound and the motion of the lips in producing it were accurately reproduced. However, synchronization was not accurate. So Kinetoscopes, although very successful, were all silent, and soon demands for the **Kinetophone** were driving sales for the Kinetoscope down. Edison's lukewarm interest in anything pertaining to moving pictures and the growing demand for a sound version of the Kinetoscope were probably the main motivations for abandoning further experiments and for marketing a machine as unsatisfactory as the Kinetophone. The only novelty that the Kinetophone provided was music, and it was seldom appropriate to the scenes it was accompanying.

In 1894, *Louis Lumiere* visited a Kinetoscope parlor in Paris. What he saw there suggested the idea of making an apparatus that could project films onto a screen so that many people could view them at the same time. In a few months, Louis and his brother Auguste had constructed a practicable machine that combined the function of a camera and projector. The **Cinematographe** premiered in Paris on December 28, 1895.

In the United States, the commercial premiere of the motion picture took place in New York on April 23, 1896, on this occasion by the **Vitascope,** a projector designed by *Thomas Armat* and manufactured and marketed by Edison.

However, during most of the years in which one disk system after another had come and gone, other inventors were exploring very different ideas for making sound movies, and none involved using the phonograph.

The evolution of sound on film involved three different techniques: the groove on film, magnetic sound, and optical sound systems.

In effect, groove on film was nothing more than a variation of sound on disk, with a track on the film performing the same function as the grooves on a record. Magnetic sound fared a bit better and was to eventually triumph over other methods. However, at the time it was demonstrated it was not a success. In terms of clarity, tone, and amplification, magnetic sound on film compared unfavorably with the leading optical systems.

The French inventor *Eugene Augustus Lauste* was the first to make a motion picture with visual images and a photographically recorded sound track on the same strip of film. He created the **Phonocinematophone** whereby sound waves were photographed upon **Kinemotograph** film by the simple action of light acting through it upon an electrically energized resistance cell. Unfortunately, Lauste's work was interrupted by World War I. In 1923 the Photocinematophone in its most perfected form was demonstrated by Lauste.

However, at the same time General Electric had a research team perfecting their own sound-on-film system called **Pallophotophone.** It used a single film for the images and sound track. A special feature of the recording process was the use of a mirror smaller than a pinhead. This mirror was made to vibrate by a fluctuating current from a radio microphone. It then threw a vibrating beam of light onto the edge of the unexposed film. The developed motion picture carried a photographic tracing of the sound vibrations in a zig-zag pattern 1/10 inch wide along the entire length of the film.

The Pallophotophone was later improved by employing a narrower variable-density sound track (1/16 inch wide) and was renamed **Kinegraphone.** As such, it attracted the attention of Paramount and in 1927 the studio took the option of using it to provide synchronized sound for William Wellmann's *Wings* on April 27, 1927, less than two months before *The Jazz Singer*. The sound effects and music were added after the film had been shot. There were no recorded dialogue scenes.

The decisive events leading to the coming of talkies occurred during the mid-1920s and involved the association of Warner Brothers Pictures with Western Electric and Bell Telephone laboratories. Some three years before the Warners came into the picture, a little-publicized experiment took place. In October 1922, *Edward B. Craft* demonstrated the synchronization of a phonograph record and a projected motion picture. The recording system was imperfect but aroused the interest of the researchers at Bell Telephone laboratories. The energies of the Bell people were concentrated on perfecting a sound-on-disk system.

Because Warner Brothers was growing at this time, they needed more studio space and equipment. These requirements were fulfilled by buying the ailing Vitagraph company. The immediate concern was to transport the heap of apparatus to their studio and get it working. The installation job was given to Western Electric. *Benjamin Levinson,* a radio expert, was in charge. Levinson visited the Bell labs in 1925 and saw one of the early sound films. Levinson convinced Warner Brothers to see the demonstration. If anything, they were more impressed than Levinson and ordered work to begin at their Vitagraph studio. By Spring 1926, short test films using the new sound system were being made regularly at Vitagraph. Before legalizing arrangements with Western Electric, the Warners decided to keep their venture into sound films separate from the silent ones and established a new company, Vitaphone Corporation, and named the sound system **Vitaphone.** Affirming their faith in Vitaphone, they began having their theaters wired for sound.

By 1928, four types of Vitaphone movies were being released: silent features with added sound, short subjects, part talkies, and 100% talkies. Within one year, talkies had taken over and the silent cinema was doomed. Warner Brothers and First National released a total of 67 sound pictures, Paramount released 49 and Fox 47.

The Vitaphone sound-on-disc system synchronized orchestral scores and sound effects to picture using a 6 ″ record. The road show movie *Don Juan* (1926) was followed closely by *Old San Francisco* and *The Better 'Ole* (1926) and *The First Auto* and *When a Man Loves* (1927). Shorts included vaudeville acts and opera arias. *The Jazz Singer*, however, was the first Vitaphone feature with talking and singing sequences.

By 1932 there were 8507 theaters capable of playing the limited range (50–5500 Hz) Vitaphone records. Warner Brothers had found a great way to save a fortune in musician fees and with the release of Lights of New York, presented the first 100% all-talking motion picture.

The Fox success with Movietone News and its sound-on-film process spurred Western Electric to promote more actively its variable-density light valve technology developed by Bell Labs. Via the new entity E.R.P.I. it offered the **Fox-*CASE* AEOlight** or the option of the Wente Light Valve system to exhibitors in and effort to compete with Vitaphone. David Sarnoff promoted via RCA (partly owned by GE) the *RCA* **Photophone system,** a variable area sound-on-film system which required less-precise projection equipment. Seeking outlets for the system, *RCA* bought the *RKO* chain of theaters and established *RKO RADIO PICTURES*; a thrust that lead to the development of the American musical idiom. (See Figure A–2.)

D. W. Griffith prophesized that sound film would become an ''eighth art.'' Mel Brooks' perspective is closer to the reality of the marketplace which produced the sound film. More than 60 years after the birth of the talkies Brooks quipped, ''Hollywood used to be *SHOW*business, now it's all show-*BUSINESS*.'' (to Tracy Ullman on the Tracy Ullman Show broadcast of 2–11–90.)

Developmental History of Sound

1857   Leon Scott constructs a Phonautograph sound-to-disc device.

1877   Thomas Edison invents the Phonograph, which records and plays back.

1878   Blake of Brown University invents Optisound optical recording.

1880   Bell develops selenium cells to detect sound by a modulating light source.

Figure A–2 The Gold Diggers.

1886   Bell finalizes variable-area and variable-density optical recording techniques.

1887   Dickson and Edison create the Phonokinetograph, a camera/recorder.

1898   V. Poulsen patents a magnetic recording device, the Telegraphone.

1901   Ernst Ruhmer invents the Photographophone.

1907   Poulsen and Pendersen patent DC biasing.

       E. Lauste perfects the rocking mirror and grate valve for a single system galvonometer.

       De Forest demonstrates the Audion tube.

1910   Gaumont produces its version of the Kinetophone.

       Messter produces a version of the Kinetophone.

       Wassily Kandinsky, painter, writes "On the Spiritual in Art," establishing the theoretical basis for nonobjective painting. His circle of influence grows to include painters and musicians. Early demonstration of painterly relationships of color to sound.

1912   Leopold Sturzwage (Survage) produces plates for *Colored Rhythm Designs*, but never films them. Visual music without sound; paintings that move. First of the painter/musicians.

1913   Edison patents the Kinetophone, a projector interlocked with a phonograph.

1916   H. C. Bullis and Jos. A. O'Neill suggest applying iron powder to film and creating sound films.

1918   J. Tykociner, University of Illinois, uses gas flame light source for optical recording.
       J. Kunz, University of Illinois, uses mercury vapor arc source for optical recording but both sources need amplification.
       Earl Sponable develops thalofide cell for single system.

1921   Max Kohl constructs a telegraphone with amplifier tubes (electron vacuum tubes) using a steel disc as the recording media.
       Viking Eggeling, a Swedish painter and pianist, produces a visual music film, *Diagonal Symphony*.
       Hans Richter, painter and pianist, produces *Rhythm 21*, visual music without sound film.
       Walter Ruttmann shows the first "sound painting," *Lichtspiel—Opus 1*, seen by Oskar Fischinger and critic Bernard Diebold in Frankfurt; announces, "The New Art, The Vision—Music of Films."

1922   Lazlo Moholy-Nagy works on a theoretical basis for the sound film and by 1933 has produced the codification, *The Sound ABC*, a film.

The Tri-Ergon (Josef Engel, Joseph Massolle, and Hans Vogt) demonstrate a photographic sound process in Berlin. Mike current is converted into variable light rays controlled via variable density or area.

Theo Case invents the helio vacuum tube.

A. G. Bell-Craft invents sound-on-film disc.

1926   Oskar Fischinger begins his work in animated sound and by 1932 has developed an "opto-acoustic notation" influencing composers Edgar Varese and John Cage, while creating a vast body of work.

Warner Brothers releases *Don Juan* using the Fox/Bell Labs non-voice sync Vitaphone system.

1927   Warners releases *What Price Glory* (January) with orchestral score.

January 21, Fox/Case sound-on-film demo of *MOVIETONE NEWS*

Warners releases *Seventh Heaven* (May) with orchestral score.

Stunning success of Warners *The Jazz Singer* (October) using the Vitaphone system, with lip-sync performances in a fiction film for the first time.

1927   Fritz Pfleumer devises magnetic oxide coating for tape. U.S. Navy's Carlson and Carpenter discover positive effects of AC biasing in recording.

Theo Case develops AEO Light recording system using a Western Electric amplifier (Radio Industry) with thalofide cell for reproduction.

Lee DeForest establishes Phonofilm.

Paramount releases *Wings* with music and effects via the Kinegraphophone.

ERPI (ATT) markets Western Electric amplifiers.

General Electric's C. A. Hoxie creates Pallophotophone sound on film.

RCA Photophone adopts variable-area recording standard.

Radio Keith Orpheum (RKO) bought by RCA; releases *The Perfect Crime*.

Walter Ruttmann's *Berlin, Symphonie of a Great City* premiered, with 15-minute sound montage recorded on film. Ruttmann was a painter, cellist, and violinist.

1928   Fox Movietone City built in Beverly Hills; adopts variable-density standard.

Paramount releases first 100% talkie *Interference*; the "talkie" introduces a "surplus" of reality.

1929   The crash keeps FOX from gaining total control of the industry.

Reuben Mamoulian's *Applause* is released, exhibiting a continuous, sustained use of sound. During this period, projection speed increases 50% from 60 feet per minute to 90 feet per minute, accommodating higher fidelity and greater image stability. Costs rise for exhibitors.

1930 Sound becomes a separate entity to be recorded and modified due to advances in magnetic recording (on wire).

Norman McLaren begins work on animated sound works: *Allegro*, *Dots and Loops*, and *Phantasy*.

1931 German firms AEG and I.G. Farben refine recorders and tape emulsions respectively (AEG + BASF).

Contract between Fritz Pfleumer and AEG.

1932 Dialogue and music can be **mixed,** creating more subtle and discrete entry into the screen experience.

Rudolph Pfenninger devises system of cards to be photographed directly onto optical sound tracks. *Tonende Handschrift*, cards of single pitch, are graded in semitones (sine curves) and sawtooth forms (variable area). Volume is controlled through exposure (variable density).

1933 *King Kong* demonstrates innovative sound utilization and some stylistic quirks, demonstrating that sound can be separated from film, modified, and recombined for greater creative control.

1934 Marvin Camras describes a new magnetic wire recorder.

1935 S. J. Begun flees to America to continue his work on recorders.

The Magnetophon joint effort by AEG and BASF is introduced at the Radio Exhibition in Berlin. It uses cellulose acetate film with carbonyl iron powder emulsion coating, (type C- "cellite") rust-colored; [(1943, Luvitherm, type L tape introduced), gamma ferric oxide coating.]

1939 Stereo steel tape machine by Bell Labs demo at World's Fair uses Vicalloy hard metal tape and a Mirrorphone monitor device.

Germans perfect the Magnetophon recorder for Radio Luxembourg. Runs at 30 ips.

1940 Brush Development and Bell experiment with paper tape. Weber and Braunmuhl use high-frequency premagnetization to reduce noise level (SN).

1941 John Whitney creates an optical sound track through the visual source of oscillating light waves in *Exercises*, direct animated sound. With his brother, he develops a technique using 12 pendulums of variable length linked by fine steel wire connected to an optical wedge. The wedge oscillates over a light slit by motion of the pendulum, producing a variable-area type of track exposure.

The frequency of each pendulum can be adjusted or tuned to conform to any scale by moving a sliding weight.

Studio sound recording practices create codified formula setups because sound leaves no room for error. Music relies on sourcebook cliches.

1943   Webcor of America builds recorders for the Navy.

1944   3M is invited by Brush to develop an oxide tape.

1945   Major Jack Mullins confiscates some German Magnetophons.

1946   Colonel Richard Ranger attempts to build a domestic equalivalent to the Magnetophon, the Rangertone recorder. Ampex's Lindsay designs a series 200 Ampex recorder based on the Magnetophon.

Magnacord formed by Boyers (Bell), Tinkham (Ampex), Parker (Filtors), and Landon.

1947   Model 200 Ampex recorder is demonstrated for Bing Crosby/ Philco, who had been using Mullins' Magnetophons at NBC. Crosby Enterprises orders 20 recorders and agrees to act as distributor.

First 3M black oxide magnetic tape (paper backed).

Crosby records a program of film and tape at WJZ, New York; it was transmitted by telephone to MUZAK, where it was recorded on tape. The disc was made by NBC and the film by RCA.

1948   ABC buys 12 Ampex machines.

Carson splicer for audio tape is introduced.

Magnacord creates first commercial stereo recorder.

Audio Devices sells paper and plastic red oxide tape.

1950   First synchronous record–reproduce system for $\frac{1}{4}$-inch tape.

1951   First demo of black and white video recording (Crosby).

JBL Paragon speaker system developed by Ranger.

First catalog of recorded tapes (Recording Associates).

1952   Ampex works on development of TODD A-O sound system for Mike Todd.

Cinerama widescreen and stereophonic sound introduced.

1953   RCA debuts a longitudinal video tape recorder.

Electronic data-processing systems (computers) become commercial with 3M 100-byte-per-inch tape.

1954   Reeves Soundcraft gets Oscar for magnetic sound recording for *The Robe*. Introduces Mylar-based audio tape.

1955   First color television signal transmitted from RCA to 3M.

1956   Two-inch-wide tape and Ampex quadruplex videotape recorder ordered by ABC, CBS and NBC.

George Gould, Telestudios, first independent video production house.

"Douglas Edwards and the News," CBS: first use of videotape for network delay.

1958   First communications satellite (Score).

1959   Ampex forms United Stereo Tapes with duplication rights of all phonographs from Verve, MGM, Warners, Mercury and London labels.

1960   Ranger develops a crystal-controlled device and first Sync-Selsyn Interlock system.

1961   RCA TR-22 fully transistorized compact VTR debuts.

1966   Ampex VR-1200 VTR demo. Videotape production standardized and VR-2000, used for multigeneration dubbing for syndication and advanced teleproduction techniques.

1967   VR-3000, Ampex's first battery-operated portable color VTR.
       IVC introduces 1-inch color helican scan VTR.

1970   IVC demonstrates first time-base corrector and the age of electronic news gathering expands.

B. Selected Films for Study

Steamboat Willie	(1928)	Ub Iwerks (Disney). Cinephone sound on film used; two beats per second rhythm.
St. Louis Blues	(1928)	Dudley Murphy (RKO). Musical form with Bessie Smith.
Applause	(1929)	Reuben Mamoulian (Paramount). Background and location effects.
Blackmail	(1929)	Alfred Hitchcock (British International). Part-talkie with dubbing and effects.
The Love Parade	(1929)	Ernest Lubitch (Paramount). Audience "eavesdrops" via cutaway camera.
The Blue Angel	(1930)	Josef von Sternberg (UFA). English and German versions: songs, sets, Dietrich and Jannings, background sound.
Westfront 1918	(1930)	G. W. Pabst (Nero-film). All natural sound, no music, bare dialogue.
Le Million	(1931)	Rene Clair (Tobis). Scored musical operetta with choral *singspeil* gestures + edit patterns = musical rhythm. Narrative connected by continuity of melodic line and the "complicity" of silence.

Monkey Business	(1931)	Norman McLeod (Paramount). Vaudevillian sound with Marx Brothers.
Road To Life	(1931)	N. Ekk (Mezrabpomfilm). Ideal of Soviet docudrama; natural sound to inform a mass audience.
Alexander Nevsky	(1938)	Sergei Eisenstein's unique aural collaboration with Sergei Prokofiev.
Time in the Sun	(1939)	Marie Seton: compiliation of Eisenstein's *Que Viva Mexico* footage into formalist documentary with effects and narration.

DeMille had a theory about film music. He was interested in telling stories and that's what he thought film music should do in a film. He was able to tell me in very exact terms that what he wanted music to do was to aid the story and the way in which he wanted the music to do it was to create themes for every individual, every important character in the film and every important force.   Elmer Bernstein

Chronological List of Films of Interest

In each instance, the film represents a unique directorial approach to both the technical and narrative functions of the track.

Ghosts before Breakfast (1928) Richter

The General Line (1929) Eisenstein

A Propos de Nice (1930) Vigo

A Nous la Liberté (1931) Clair

The Threepenny Opera (1931) Pabst

Rain (1932) Milstone

Story of a Simple Case (1932) Pudovkin

Ornamente Sound (1932) Fischinger

Composition in Blue (1933) Fischinger

Night on Bald Mountain (1933) Alexeieff

Zero de Conduité (1933) Clair

King Kong (1933) Cooper

Circles (1933) Fischinger

Deserter (1933) Pudovkin

Color Box (1935) Lye

Book Bargain (1936) McLaren

Rhythm in Light (1936) Bute

Rainbow Dance (1936) Lye

The Silence (1936) Bergman

"A man isn't dead just because you put him under-
ground." *The Third Man*

Orson Welles is the elusive, evil Harry Lime in Carol
Reed and Graham Greene's cold-war thriller *The Third
Man.*

Figure A–3 *The Third Man.* Carol Reed's exhaustive use of a whistled theme song and all its variations demonstrated the narrative role music could play. (Courtesy of New Yorker Films.)

Grand Illusion (1937) Renoir
Victory (1938) Pudovkin
Rumba (1939) McLaren
Allegro (1939) McLaren
Musical Poster—No. One (1939) Lye

Citizen Kane (1941) Welles
Fantasia (1942) Disney
Magnificent Ambersons (1942) Welles
Meshes of the Afternoon (1943) Deren
Five Film Exercises (1943) Whitney
Cabin in the Sky (1943) Minelli
Children of Paradise (1943–1945) Carne
Open City (1943) Rosselini
Ivan the Terrible (1943) Eisenstein
Spellbound (1945) Hitchcock
Color Rapsodie (1948) Bute
Dots (1948) McLaren
Forces of Evil (1948) Polonsky
Spook Sport (1949) Bute
Un Simple Histoire (1949) L'Herbier
Los Olvidados (1950) Bunuel
Momma Don't Allow (1952) Reisz
Forbidden Games (1952) Clement
All My Babies (1952) Stoney
Ugetsu (1953) Mizoguchi
Polkagraph (1953) Bute
Blinkety Blank (1954) McLaren
La Strada (1954) Fellini
Seven Samurai (1954) Kurosawa
Crucified Lovers (1954) Mizoguchi
Lola Montes (1955) Ophuls
Invitation to the Dance (1955) Kelly
Throne of Blood (1957) Kurosawa
The Cranes Are Flying (1957) Kalatozov
Touch of Evil (1958) Welles
Floating Weeds (1959) Ozu
Shadows (1959) Cassavetes
Scent of Mystery (1960) Castle (first ''Smellovision'')
Viridiana (1961) Bunuel
La Dolce Vita (1961) Fellini
Lawrence of Arabia (1962) Lean*

* Denotes films analyzed in main text.

Last Year at Marienbad (1962) Resnais
Blonde Cobra (1963) Jacobs
This Sporting Life (1963) Anderson
La Jetée (1963) Marker
Kwaidan (1964) Kobayashi
Blow-up (1966) Antonioni
Le Mistral (1966) Ivens
Wavelength (1967) Snow
Teorema (1968) Pasolini
2001 (1968) Kubrick
Rain People (1969) Coppola
The Spider's Stratagem (1970) Bertulucci
A Clockwork Orange (1971) Kubrick
Walkabout (1971) Roeg
Cabaret (1972) Fosse
Cries and Whispers (1972) Bergman
The Conversation (1974) Coppola
Spirit of the Beehive (1974) Erice
The Passenger (1975) Antonioni
Tommy (1975) Russell (first quad-Dolby)
Nashville (1975) Altman
Dersu Uzala (1975) Kurosawa
Sym of Dombas (1976) Vertov
All the President's Men (1976) Pakula
Close Encounters of the Third Kind (1977) Spielberg
Star Wars (1977) Lucas
The Deerhunter (1978) Cimino
All That Jazz (1979) Fosse
The Shout (1979) Skolimowski
Black Stallion (1979) Ballard
The Rose (1979) Rydell
Popeye (1980) Altman
Heaven's Gate (1980) Cimino
Raging Bull (1980) Scorcese
The Shining (1980) Kubrick
Raiders of the Lost Ark (1981) Spielberg
McCabe and Mrs. Miller (1981) Altman
Reds (1981) Beatty

Lili Marleen (1982) Fassbinder
Blade Runner (1982) Scott
Never Cry Wolf (1983) Ballard
Burden of Dreams (1984) Blank
Spend It All (1984) Blank
Fitzcaraldo (1984) Herzog
Dead of Winter (1987) Penn*
Empire of the Sun (1987) Spielberg
Stormy Monday (1988) Figgis
Tucker (1988) Coppola*
Darkman (1990) Raimi

Documentary Films for Study

Non-fiction programs selected have a diversity of renditions of reality with sound dominating the emotional landscape.

Nanook of the North (1922),   Robert Flaherty. Originally silent; Eskimo songs later added.

Lindbergh's Flight from N.Y. to Paris (1927),   Jack Connolly. 1927 marks the first of the Fox Movietone Entertainment Newsreels.

Granton Trawler (1934),   John Grierson. No narration; just live sound and the sea.

Man of Aran (1934),   Robert Flaherty. Barren daily existence reflected in the musically rhythmic structures of silence and editing.

Song of Ceylon (1934),   John Grierson. Directed by Basil Wright with sound echoing sense.

Night Mail (1936),   Harry Watt and Basil Wright. Alberto Cavalcanti is sound director, verse by W. H. Auden, music by Benjamin Britten. Intricate, extraordinary marriage of sound to "creative treatment of actuality."

The River (1937),   Pare Lorenz. Music by Virgil Thompson and poetic prose by Lorenz provide evocation of the awesome grandeur of an abused Mississippi. A plea for better management through the brilliant editing in parallel with the forward rush of water (and sound).

The Plow That Broke the Plains (1938),   Pare Lorenz. Music by Virgil Thompson. Uses repetitive blank verse and beautiful but simple visual shorthand to convey a massive social problem. Counterpoint/contradiction: Thompson's use of the hymn "Old Hundred" over images of "blown-out, baked-out and broke" Dust Bowlers.

The City (1939), Ralph Steiner and Willard Van Dyke. Music by Aaron Copland. A transition film in the development of documentary technique.

La Mer (1939), Ovady Julber. Early attempt at synchronized visuals and mood music by musician/composer/poet Julber. Rough and rhythmic.

The March of Time (1939), Louis de Rochemont. Narrated by Westbrook Van Voorhis, this first of the single-subject newsreels of national interest and importance prefigures network news programming and was affectionately parodied in *Citizen Kane*.

The Fight for Life (1940), Pare Lorenz. Simulation of actuality uses actors in a live location situation; fictional format dramatizes nonfiction social concern (prenatal care). Composer Louis Gruenberg wrote large portions of his score to the rhythms of maternal and fetal heartbeats; the score was the longest ever for a nonmusical feature. Visuals filmed to metronomic beats.

Power and the Land (1940), Joris Ivens. Stephen Vincent Benet's narration defines the film, reflecting the spirit and substance of rural American life, breaking into metered rhyme during a harvest scene; an emotional document leaving a lasting impression of heartland America.

The Land (1941), Robert Flaherty. Flaherty directed, wrote, and narrated "an epic poem" about the land and its people, poverty, and the force of mechanization.

Listen to Britain (1942), Humphrey Jennings. Evokes in the sounds of British life a tribute to the music of a nation.

Why We Fight (Prelude To War) (1942), Frank Capra. Harnesses the musical talents of Dimitri Tiomkin and Alfred Newman with narrators Walter Huston and Anthony Veiller in one of seven "orientation" films for the Army during World War II. Visual symbols, dynamic montage, stirring music support narrator and the need to boost morale.

December 7th (1943), John Ford. Moments of illusion have become the documentary reality. Simulation (in studio) of the Pearl Harbor events with music by Alfred Newman and extensive sound effects over rear-screen process cinematography.

Le Retour (1946),   Henri Cartier-Bresson. Liberation of French prisoners from Nazi camps.

Momma Don't Allow (1952),   Karel Reisz and Tony Richardson. At the edge of nonfiction, this British "kitchen sink" realistic portrayal of on-the-spot exploration of youth out for an evening of dancing.

Titticut Follies (1967),   Frederick Wiseman. Bold attempt to record the events in a mental institution; allowing inmates to express themselves in front of the camera was seen as an intrusion on their rights of privacy.

Films of the "Intimate Observer" (Free Cinema)

These early *realist dramas* make use of unprocessed location sound, dialogue and natural effects to depict the working class.

Blood of the Beasts (1949), Georges Franju (slaughterhouse)
O Dreamland (1953), Lindsay Anderson (amusement park)
Momma Don't Allow (1956), Karel Reisz and Tony Richardson (jazz club)
On the Bowery (1956), Lionel Rogosin (flophouses)

Leads to the British "Kitchen Sink" Fiction Film Movement

Primary (1960), John Drew and Richard Leacock (Kennedy/Humphrey)
Don't Look Back (1965), Richard Leacock and Don Pennebacker (Bob Dylan)
Titticut Follies (1967), Frederick Wiseman (revelation)
Salesman (1969), Albert and David Maysles (psych study)

Forerunners of the Documentary of Revelation

Phantom India (1968), Louis Malle (epic canvas)
Tokyo Olympiad (1964), Kon Ichikawa (aural close-up)

Commentary Becomes a Limiting Factor in "Ethnographic" Film

Sync sound speech brings back real-time sequence of events catching life *sur le vif*.

The Selling of the Pentagon (1971), Peter Davis (medium of conscience)
The Sorrow and the Pity (1970), Max Ophuls (catalyst)

Worldwide, the documentary becomes a medium of revolutions.

Radio Programs and Drama for Further Study

The following programs are available for study from the Museum of Broadcasting, East 53rd Street, New York, New York 10022. Phone (212) 752-7684 for appointments.

1938	The War of the Worlds	Mercury Theatre on the Air	Welles
1939	Private Lives	Campbell Playhouse	Coward
	Show Boat	Campbell Playhouse	Ferber
1940	H. G. Wells and Orson Welles	KTSA, Texas	
1940	Dinner at Eight	Campbell Playhouse	Ferber
	Vanity Fair	Campbell Playhouse	Thackery
	June Moon	Campbell Playhouse	Lardner
1944	Jane Eyre	Lux Radio Theatre	Bronte
	Break of Hearts	Lux Radio Theatre	Heerman
	Suspense	Donovan's Brain	
1945	Miss Dilly Says No	This is My Best	Pratt
	I'll Not Go Back	This is My Best	
1946	Moat Farm Murder	Mercury Summer Theatre	Corwin
	The Fred Allen Show		Fred Allen

Special Study Collection

1938 The Shadow
Dracula
The Thirty-Nine Steps
Sherlock Holmes
The Count of Monte Cristo
Rebecca
Magnificent Ambersons
A Christmas Carol

The classics of radio drama made the female voice an icon of imagination. Inflection, intonation, emphasis and pronunciation, not dialogue, per se, carried the narrative. (See Figure A-4)

C. Information Sources

Academy of Motion Picture Arts and Sciences   Historical resources
and The Margaret Herrick Library
8949 Wilshire Blvd., Beverly Hills, CA 90211

Figure A–4 *Lili Marleen.* The drama invoked the mythic power of voice and song (an anthem) to magnetically reinforce ideology. (Courtesy of New Yorker Films.)

American Film Institute Center for Advanced Film Studies 2021 N. Western Ave., Los Angeles, CA 90038	Foot in the door
American Institute of Physics, Niels Bohr Library 333 East 45th St., New York, NY 10017	Research
Association of Independent Video and Filmmakers 625 Broadway, 9th Floor, New York, NY 10012	Independent magazine
Audio Engineering Society 60 East 42nd St., New York, NY 10017	Recording arts and sciences
Audiophile Systems 6842 Hawthorn Park Drive, Indianapolis, IN 46220	Build-it-yourself
Barcus-Berry 15461 Springdale, Huntington Beach, CA 92649	Sound consultants
The Burbank Studios, Sound Department 4000 Warner Blvd., Burbank, CA	Audio for video

Cable Films/Video Country Club Station, Box 7171, Kansas City, MO 64113	Classic 1930s and 1940s videos
Cinema Audio Society P.O. Box 8337, Universal City, CA 91608	Professional society
CineScan-Newsreel Access Systems 150 East 58th St., New York, NY 10155	Documentary footage
Director's Guild of America Special Projects 7950 Sunset Blvd., Hollywood, CA 90046	Seminars and media events
Doheny Memorial Library University of Southern California, Los Angeles, CA 90007	Film study
Entertainment Effects Group (SHOWSCAN) Marina Del Rey, CA	Widescreen high-speed pix and sound
Frank Serafine (Synthesation) 426 S. Barrington Ave., Los Angeles, CA 90049	Pioneer audio designer
IATSE Local 695 11331 Ventura Blvd., Suite 201, Studio City, CA 91604	Sound union
The Independent Feature Project 21 West 86th St., New York, NY 10024	Production and critical studies
Iowa Acoustics Colloquium Department of Physics and Astronomy, University of Iowa, Iowa City, IA	Acoustics
James Webb, Soundman 15117 Hamlin St., Van Nuys, CA 91411	Prototype of the creative pro
Ken Wahrenbrock Sound 12115A Woodruff Ave., Downey, CA 90241	PZM pioneer
Larry Edmunds Bookshop 6658 Hollywood Blvd., Hollywood, CA 90028	Largest cinema book collection
Museum of Modern Art Film Department 11 East 53rd St., New York, NY 10016	Film study
Nagra Magnetic 1147 N. Vine St., Los Angeles, CA 90028	Nagra importer
National Association of Broadcasters 1771 N St. N.W., Washington, DC 20036	Television advocacy
N.Y. Public Library, Donnell Media Center 20 West 53rd St., New York, NY 10019	Film/video collection

Northeast Historic Film Blue Hill Falls, Maine 04615	Film technique; appreciation and preservation
Pacific Coast Studio Directory 6331 Hollywood Blvd., Los Angeles, CA 90028	Studio telephones
Paul Veneklasen & Associates 1711 16th St., Santa Monica, CA 90404	Acoustic architects
The Producer's Masterguide N.Y. Production Manual 611 Broadway, #807, New York, NY 10012	Basic source guide
Production Works (AICP Budgets) 35 East 20th St., New York, NY 10003	Budget software
Quad Eight Magnetics 11929 Vose St., North Hollywood, CA 91605	Manufacturer audio post
Research Video 4900 Vineland Ave., No. Hollywood, CA 91601	Vintage music and performance footage
Samuel Goldwyn Sound Warner Hollywood Studios, 1041 N. Formosa, Hollywood, CA 90038	Classic film mixing
Screen Actors Guild 7065 Hollywood Blvd., Hollywood, CA 90028	Union
Society for the History of Technology Georgia College of Technology, Atlanta, GA	Historical reference
Society of Motion Picture and Television Engineers 595 West Hartsdale Ave., White Plains, NY 10607-1824	Technical journal
Society for the Preservation of Film Music 10850 Wilshire Blvd., Suite 770, Los Angeles CA 90024	Publications and membership
Studio Pass/Harvestworks (Audio Arts Org.) 596 Broadway, # 602, New York, NY 10012	Audio for artists, facilities
Syn Aud Con Seminars P.O. Box 1115, San Juan Capistrano, CA 92693	Sound reinforcement
TODD A-O/Glen Glenn Sound, Inc. 1021 N. Seward St., Hollywood, CA 90038	State of the art

UCLA Film and Television Archives 405 Hilgard Ave., Los Angeles, CA 90024	Film preservation and study collection
Universal City Studios, Hitchcock Theatre 100 Universal Plaza, Universal City, CA	Acoustic standard for playback
Visual Music Alliance 8435 Geyser, Northridge, CA 91324	Audio design society

Film Composers' Laboratory

The Film Composers' Program is designed to promote higher standards for film composition, and greater interaction and planning between the composer and filmmaker. Participants are selected by invitation and are solicited from the industry, colleges, universities and schools of music.

The primary focus of the Lab is on communication—between participants and the professional resource-in-residence, between filmmaker and composer and between composer and the audience. Emphasis is given to the process of creating a musical theme and its subsequent development in enhancing the total film experience.

Deadline for application for the program is *April 15*. Application inquiries should be made to David Newman, Sundance Institute, Producer's Building 7, Room 3, 4000 Warner Boulevard, Burbank, CA 91522. (818) 954-4776. Please include a self-addressed stamped envelope.

Unique Sources for Cleared Music/Effects

Associated Production Music 888 7th Ave., 12th Floor New York, NY 10106	Provides sound on compact disc from the Bruton and other collections. File sample: a. Fanfares, links b. Jingles c. Sadness d. Pastoral, romance e. Children, animation
Audio Archive Films for the Humanities Box 2053 Princeton, NJ 08540	The BBC collection of theme music, broadcast news materials, historical events, and vast sound effects; lists generically organized. File sample: a. Airplanes: twin, prop, jet b. Birds: parrots, ducks, swans c. Farm sounds: bells, lambs, sheep d. Period: Paddle steamer, trolley
Capital Production Music 1750 N. Vine Los Angeles, CA 90028	Treasure trove of standard music and effects sorted according to tempo (fast, medium, etc.). File sample:

Figure A–5 Sound design is a craft of the eye, hand and ear. Eye follows ear. Sound either manipulates conditioned reflexes or stimulates thought. (Photo: Dennis Griggs.)

a. Bionic
b. Blues
c. Chase
d. Circus

CBS Sound Library
Columbia Special Products
51 W. 52nd St.
New York, NY 10019

Vast library of broadcast selections, mostly factual accounts. File sample:
a. Vietnam battle sounds
b. Macy's department store lobby
c. Auto carwash

Celebrity Licensing
P.O. Box 3731
Hollywood, CA 90028

Inventory of 1000 rerecorded hits from 1953–1979 with original artist performing the original hit, years after the original version. 2000 "Sound Alike" versions and many uncharted nostalgia pop songs. Legitimate owners located for rights negotiation. File sample: "Johnny B. Goode"

Celestial Harmonies
605 Ridgefield Rd.
Wilton, CT 06897

Direct metal masters made in Germany provide clean, crisp pressings, obviating the argument for digital or other low-noise recordings, which never stay quiet after the pressing. Offerings are metaphysical, melodic, meditative. File sample:
a. Astral trip
b. Russian church music
c. Descending moonshine
d. Dervishes

Dan Gibson Productions Ltd.
Box 1200, Post Station Z
Toronto, Ontario, Canada
M5N2Z7

Environmental sounds from lakes, mountains, streams, and wildlife, all done with his Stereo Parabolic Microphone system. File sample:
a. Dawn on the Desert
b. Gentle Stream

Library of Congress
Music Division
Recorded Sound Section
Washington, DC 20540

Public domain recordings, many by Alan Lomax (ethnomusicologist). File sample:
a. Afro-American folk tunes
b. American Indian
c. Michigan lumberjacks
d. American sea songs and shanties

Musication
1206 Bay Ridge Avenue
Brooklyn, NY 11219

Provides software for MIDI and computer-generated music systems compatible with Commodore, IBM, and Macintosh, interlocked with KORG keyboard systems. Many shelf and proprietary kits; OPCODE, SONUS. These programs are for music notation/editing processes and other functions, including create, copy, move, delete, transpose, and quantize. Basic packages include:
MIDI events
Edit mode
Score mode
Recording mode
Graphics mode
Library mode

National Archives
AV Records
Washington, DC 20408

Recorded music includes many public domain radio shows and historical works. File sample:
a. Federal Music Project, 1936–1942
b. Smithsonian ethnology, 1912–1941

        c. Gangbusters
        d. Fred Allen's Town Hall
        e. Kay Kyser's Kollege of Musical
           Knowledge

Thomas J. Valentino   Since 1932, this effects house has customized
151 W. 46th St.   selections by redoing library material or
New York, NY 10036   generating to order new "simulated" sounds.
                             File sample:
                             a. Cat's meow
                             b. Small pistol shot
                             c. Space ships

The compact disc is the preferred medium of storage and transfer of pre-recorded sound. Given the explosion of PC-based software for music and effects manipulation, the floppy magnetic disc is replacing tape as the production medium of choice. (See Figure A-6a—d)

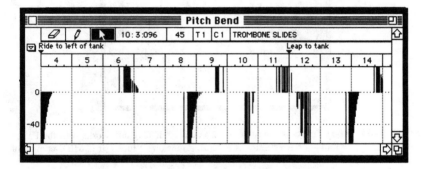

Figure A–6a Pitch bend display from Passport's Pro 4 Master Track program is a MIDI data window for the designer.

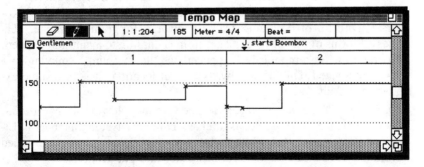

Figure A–6b The Pro 4 Tempo Map extends the limits of tempo within each beat. (Courtesy of Passport, Inc.)

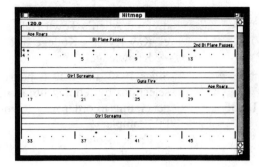

Figure A–6c The Hit Map represents aural landmarks in the composition and is used for timing at a bar-by-bar chart.

HIT	TIME	DESCRIPTION	BEAT	BT	OFFSET	+ -	TIME
0/00	00:00.00	Ape Roars	1.00	1	0	+0.0	0:00.00
3/11	00:02.47	Bi Plane Passes	5.93	6	0	+0.8	0:02.50
9/04	00:06.18	2nd Bi Plane Passes	13.37	13	♪ ♪	+1.6	0:06.25
14/10	00:09.73	Girl Screams	20.47	20	♪ ♪	+0.4	0:09.75
18/02	00:12.10	Guns Fire	25.20	25	♪♪♪	+0.6	0:12.12
22/05	00:14.87	Ape Roars	30.73	30	♪· ♪	+0.2	0:14.88
27/15	00:18.62	Girl Screams	38.23	38	♪♪♪	+0.2	0:18.62
36/04	00:24.15	Guns Fire	49.30	49	♪♪♪	-0.6	0:24.12
41/06	00:27.58	Description	56.17	56	♪♪♪	+1.0	0:27.62
45/16	00:30.65	Description	62.30	62	♪♪♪	-0.6	0:30.62

FILM[35MM]   Tpo = 120.00
-- 8 CLIX WARNING AT : - 6 ft 0.0 frms --

Figure A–6d Kong Tracks is a basic effects processor display and works with the Passport Clicktracks™ program—a powerful tool for scoring music to "hits." It is MIDI compatible.

Independent Film and Video Showcases in New York City

American Museum of the Moving Image, 34–12 36th Street, Astoria, NY 11106. Phone: (718) 784-4520. Rochelle Slovin, Director; Richard Kozarski, Director of Programs; David Schwartz, Program Associate. Features all forms of the moving image, from silent film to avant-garde video. Programming is temporarily suspended, as the museum is moving to a newly renovated building nearby its current location. It is to resume exhibition in May 1990.

Anthology Film Archives, 32–34 Second Avenue, New York, NY 10003. Phone: (212) 505-5181. Jonas Mekas, Director; Nadia Shtendera, Librarian. Reference Library by appointment only. Screenings were resumed in March 1990. Call or write for schedules and publications.

Artists Space, 23 West Broadway, New York, NY 10013. Phone: (212) 226-3970. Dan Walworth, Curator. Series of three film screenings per year: fall, winter, and spring. Occasional video/film/slide installations throughout the year. Continuous screenings of thematic video exhibitions in the Lower Gallery. Hours are Tuesday–Saturday, 11:00–6:00. Call for schedule.

The Brooklyn Museum, 200 Eastern Parkway, Brooklyn, NY 11238. Phone: (718) 638-5000, ext. 232. Deborah Schwartz, Manager of Public Programs and Media. Exhibits thematic film series on Sundays at 2:00, from October to May; and children's films on Saturdays at 3:00, from November to May. Guest lectures and panel discussions are held in conjunction with each series.

Collective for Living Cinema, 41 White Street, New York, NY 10013. Phone: box office, (212) 925-2111; administration, 925-3926. Jack Walsh, Executive Director; Robin Dickie, Program Director. Avant-garde and experimental film showcase. Filmmakers frequently present and discuss works. Regular programs from October through June, with special events, seminars and workshops. Performances and installations are often presented in conjunction with screenings.

Donnell Media Center, 20 West 53rd Street, New York, NY 10019. Phone: (212) 621-0609 (after 12:30). Marie Nesthus, Principal Film/Video Librarian; Fred Riedel, Film/Video Historian. Collection films are shown regularly from November to June. Tuesdays: *Featuring . . .* at 12:00 and *Collector's Choice* at 2:30. Thursdays: *Viewpoint* at 12:00 and *Films for Children* at 2:30. Spring and Fall series: *Meet the Makers*, independent film and video artists screen and discuss their work. Screening facilities available by appointment for 16mm film, $\frac{3}{4}$-inch, and VHS video (621-0611).

Film at the Public, The Public Theater, 425 Lafayette Street, New York, NY 10003. Phone: box office, (212) 598-7150; schedule recording, 598-7171; administration, 598-7166. Fabiano Canosa, Film Program Director; Stephen Soba, Film Program Coordinator. Presents premieres, rediscoveries, retrospectives and festivals. Open daily except Mondays, year-round. Free documentary series on Saturday and Sunday afternoons.

Film Charas, Teatro la Terraza, El Bohio Community and Cultural Center, 360 East 10th Street, Between Avenues B and C, New York, NY 10009. Currently showing films every Tuesday night at 8:00 P.M. Admission is $2.50.

Film Exhibition Series presents films by independent filmmakers at the Clocktower (109 Leonard Street, 13th Floor, 212-233-1096). Call numbers for film and video schedules.

Film Forum I, (Call for new location). Phone: box office, (212) 431-1590; administration, 431-1592. Karen Cooper, Director. New York City premieres of independent animation, avant-garde, narratives and documentaries made in this country and abroad, daily and year-round. Film Forum II screens repertory films year-round.

Global Village Video Study Center, 454 Broome Street, New York, NY 10013. Phone: (212) 966-7526. John Reilly, Executive Director; Julie Gustafson, Director. Independent film and video makers present and discuss their work in the *Endangered Documentaries and Other Species Series* during the fall, and the *Annual Documentary Festival*, during the spring, which is presented in conjunction with Joseph Papp and the Public Theater. Produces independent documentaries.

The Institute for Art and Urban Resources, Inc.: Project Studies One (P.S. 1), 46–01 21st Street, Long Island City, NY 11101. Phone: (718) 784-2084. Tom Smith, Film Curator; Matthew Geller and Barbara Osborn, Video Curators. Presents experimental and/or multidisciplinary film and video programs. Film and video installations are presented in two exhibition spaces at P.S. 1, by artists who incorporate video as part of a total environment. Exhibition hours are Wednesday–Sunday, 12:00–6:00.

International Center for Photography, 1130 Fifth Avenue, New York, NY 10128. Phone: (212) 860-1777. Lori Zippay and Kathy Rae Huffman, Consultants. Presents *Video-Feature*, an ongoing series of documentaries and artists' videotapes, during gallery hours.

The Jewish Museum, 1109 Fifth Avenue, New York, NY 10128. Phone: (212) 860-1863. Jean Bloch Rosensaft, Assistant Director of Education; Erika Sanger, Program Assistant; Ronnie Parker, Acting Director, National Jewish Archive of Broadcasting. Independent film and video are regularly presented in public programs organized in conjunction with the museum's regular exhibition schedule.

The Kitchen, 512 West 19th Street, New York, NY 10011. Phone: (212) 255-5793. Barbara Tsumagari, Executive Director; Robin O'Hara, Video Distribution. Exhibits all forms of media art, including single and multichannel video and video installations, 16mm and Super-8 film. Distributes video tapes. A video viewing room with a monthly schedule is open and free to the public. Evening screenings of film and video on a regular basis.

Millennium, 66 East 4th Street, New York, NY 10003. Phone: (212) 673-0090. Howard Guttenplan, Director. Millennium is a nonprofit media arts center with four major programs: equipment access; film workshop classes; the *Personal Cinema* series, an exhibition of new avant-garde and independent films presented and discussed by filmmakers; and the *Millennium Film Journal*, a tri-yearly publication dedicated to avant-garde film theory and practice.

Museum of the American Indian, Broadway at 155th Street, New York, NY 10032. Phone: (212) 283-2420. Elizabeth Weatherford, Associate Curator, Film and Video Center; Emelia Seubert, Assistant Curator, Film

Figure A–7 The Arriflex 35BL4 is the premiere quiet 35mm sync sound portable production camera.

and Video Center. Presents a Native American Film and Video Festival in December to exhibit new works about Inuit and Indians of North, Central and South America. Film and video makers attend most screenings to introduce their work. Film and Video Study Center open by appointment. Call or write for screening schedules.

The Museum of Modern Art, 11 West 53rd Street, New York, NY 10019. Phone: (212) 708-9400. Contact Adrienne Mancia or Larry Kardish for film; Barbara London for video. Independent film series include: *Cineprobe*, filmmakers presenting their films; *New Directors/New Films*, emerging and established filmmakers present new works; *What's Happening?*, films of current political and social interest; occasional American independent retrospectives; and films from the archives. Video is shown regularly in the galleries, and in *Video Viewpoints*, a series where videomakers present and discuss their work.

Museum of the Staten Island Institute of Arts and Sciences, 75 Stuyvesant Place, Staten Island, NY 10301. Phone: (718) 727-1135. Robert A. Haller, Film and Video Curator. (The museum is a five-minute walk from the Staten Island Ferry Terminal.) Presents independent films and videotapes monthly, as well as classic films. All programs are on Sunday afternoons at 1:30. Call for schedule.

The New Museum of Contemporary Art, 583 Broadway, New York, NY 10012. Phone: (212) 219-1222. William Orlander, Curator. Presents video programs, and often includes video in other installations. Hours are

Wednesday, Thursday, and Sunday, 12:00–6:00; Friday and Saturday, 12:00–10:00.

20 West, Home of Black Cinema, 20 West 120th Street, New York, NY 10027. Phone: (212) 410-2101. Jessie Maple, Director. The only permanent facility in the United States which showcases independent Black and Third World films and video. Call, write or visit for calendars. Films are exhibited Tuesday–Saturday at 8:30. Film programs are shown in two-week periods.

Whitney Museum of American Art, 945 Madison Avenue, New York, NY 10021. Phone: (212) 570-3617. John G. Hanhardt, Curator; Lucinda Furlong, Assistant Curator. Presents *The New American Filmmakers Series*, exhibitions of independently produced films, videotapes, and audio, film and video installations, from October through June. Closed Mondays. Museum hours: Tuesday, 1:00–8:00; Wednesday–Saturday, 11:00–5:00; Sunday, 12:00–6:00.

Glossaries

*Sound Editing Glossary**

This list is not complete due to the fact that terminology varies from studio to studio and from one group of sound editors to another.

Background: A continuous general sound that is indigenous to a given area where a film sequence is shot. Can be anything from traffic to surf or birds or crowd walla.

"B" dialogue: Or *Dialogue #2*. This is a second dialogue track prepared by the sound editor that contains all dialogue that needs special electronic treatment during dubbing. It may have to be filtered or reverbed or simply held down in volume for an off-screen effect. It may also contain loop lines or wild line dialogue.

Beep: Sometimes called a *pop*, a *tone pop*, a *bleep*, or a *sync pop*. A one-frame high-frequency tone cut into either the dialogue or sound effects track at a specified footage at the beginning and end of each reel. It is recorded on the negative sound track and assists the negative cutter to synchronize that track to the negative picture for the laboratory process in making a composite print.

Bump: See *smooth*.

Butt patcher: A small table film splicer for cutting and patching sound tracks

* Prepared by the *Motion Picture Sound Editors*.

together. A self-sticking tape manufactured to the exact specifications of the film for which it was intended; used to hold the two butt ends of film together.

Composite FX: Or *pre-dubb*. A rerecording of multiple sound effects tracks to a single track. This is advantageous for two primary reasons: it aids the sound effects dubbing mixer where there are too many sound effects tracks to handle at once, and it frees playback machines for other sound units.

Composite print: Picture and sound on the same strip of film.

Cue the picture:

1. The procedure of making detailed notes as to the placement of sound effects, repairing or replacing of sound tracks, and any other vital information the sound editor needs to prepare a picture for dubbing.
2. The process of placing cueing tape or punch marks or other form of cues on the picture as a guide for the dubbing mixers to indicate where certain sounds occur or are to be eliminated.

Cue track: The original production sound track used by sound editors as a guide for setting up loop lines and matching backgrounds and effects for dubbing.

Distortion network: See *filter*.

Double system: Used exclusively in major film editing in which the sound track and picture are separated for the purposes of editing and dubbing. It is not until the negative has been cut and assembled and gone through the laboratory process that picture and sound end up on the same strip of film.

Dubbing: See *rerecording*.

Dubbing log: Also called *rerecording log*. A columnar and lined sheet of paper used by the sound editor to indicate to the dubbing mixer the different sound effects and the footages at which they occur in the reel to be dubbed.

Dubbing room: Also called *dupe room* or *dubbing stage* or *rerecording room*. The sound stage where all pictures are put through the rerecording process. (See *rerecording*.)

Dubb track: Also called *composite track*, *composite dubb track*, or *putt track*. This is the final rerecording track that will be added to the picture to make a composite print.

Dummy: A rerecording playback machine on which a reel of sound track is placed for feeding into the dubbing panel for mixing purposes.

Dummy room: Also called the *MACHINE ROOM*. An area close to the dubbing room where all the playback machines are located. All these machines can be interlocked with the projector and run synchronously during dubbing. Each machine is capable of carrying one sound track reel or one loop. There are some machines set up for $\frac{1}{4}$-inch tape reels.

Dupe picture: A reversal print of the edited work picture. It is used when a music and sound editor must work on the same reel at the same time. In TV films, where time is a premium, it frees the work picture so that the assistant editor and negative editor may complete their work without interfering with the music and sound editors.

Electric pencil: A pencil-like magnetic tool for demagnetizing the sound track. It does the same work as using carbon tetrachloride or a razor blade for physically wiping off a portion of the sound track in *smoothing* backgrounds.

Fill: A piece of sound film used to fill or cover a gap or hole in the master dialogue track. This gap might occur because the sound editor cuts a director's voice or a noise alien to the scene, such as a squeaky floor, or an overlap of dialogue cue lines. A hole will cause a noticeable drop-out of sound. This process is called "making a fill" or "filling the track" and is often done by using reprints of sound tracks of those takes that need filling.

Filter: *Distortion network* or *futz* or *squawk*. This is the electronic method of altering the quality of a sound, principally dialogue, as though it were coming through a telephone receiver, a radio, or some similar audio instrument.

Flash: A method by which production sound effects can be electronically eliminated from the rerecorded dialogue track and recorded on another sound track (usually the FX stripe of the three-stripe) without having to do it physically. In this way, "minus dialogue" tracks are created for foreign versions. Some studios use a "notcher" or punching device that perforates the edge of the film and triggers the mechanism that throws the sounds to another recording channel. Other studios use a metallic or silver-coated adhesive tape, which is placed on the underside of the sound track a specified number of frames from the sound effect, and this electronically triggers the mechanism.

Foley: See *sync*. This term is used at Universal and named for the man who originated the procedure there. (*Effects recording*)

FX: Sound effects.

Impact sounds: These are sounds that hit hard in quality at the beginning. Gunshots, doors closing, thuds, socks, and other types of hits fall into this category.

Loop: A piece of sound track spliced together to form a circle of continuous sound. Used for traffic, birds, wind, or similar types of sounds.

Loop lines: Also called *postsync*. Dialogue recorded after production to replace unwanted production dialogue. Loop lines are necessary if words were indistinguishable; if the reading of the actor was poor; if the dialogue was overridden by some extraneous sound; or if the background sound is alien to the sequence (e.g., an airplane overhead during a western scene). The original production track and its corresponding picture are made into loops. The actor watches himself and listens to his dialogue over earphones and repeats the dialogue, trying to synchronize to lip movements. The sound editor takes the newly recorded dialogue and with the aid of previously indicated sync marks can, more or less easily, replace the old dialogue with the new. In some studios, the picture is dispensed with, but a piece of leader the same length as the line to be recorded is made a part of the loop. The actor hears himself and then repeats the line during the dead area caused by the leader.

Machine Room: See *dummy room*.

Magnetic film: There are two types. *Stripe* has a clear base with a 300-mil magnetic iron oxide stripe on one side. This type of magnetic film is used most often in editing. The second type is *full coat*. The entire surface of the film is coated with iron oxide and can be utilized for multiple track recordings. See *three stripe*.

Make and sync: Or "M and S." See *sync*.

Master dialogue: See *work track*.

Mill: See *movement*.

MOS: Means "without sound" or "silent." No one knows for certain where this definition came from, although the story is that a German assistant film editor used to refer to silent scenes as being "*mitout sound*t."

Movement: A general movement of shuffling indistinguishable in nature. *Safari*, *scuffle*, and *mill* are similar in that they represent certain types of movement, such as footsteps but horses, but with varying types of impacts.

Moviola: A film editing machine with a sound-pickup head and a small picture screen, for double system editing. Each has a separate motor, with the sound-head motor set at a standard 90 feet per minute and the picture motor at variable speed. Each can be run independently of the other or interlocked so that picture and sound can be run in synchronization. A moviola enables a sound editor to determine the exact frame at which a sound effect should start.

MX: Music.

Post sync: See *loop lines*.

Predubb: See *composite FX*.

Production track: The sound track recorded during filming of picture.

Rerecording: The process of recording and combining all sound elements (dialogue, sound effects, music) onto one single sound track. Also called *dubbing*.

Reverb: An echo effect. If it is dialogue, it will be removed from the master track and transferred over to a second dialogue track for proper handling by the dubbing mixer.

Room presence: Or *room tone*. A nondescript background noise indigenous to any room or sound stage. It is almost like a gentle hiss and has no specific characteristic.

Safari: See *movement*.

Scuffle: See *movement*.

Smooth: The procedure of balancing the level of background sound from cut to cut. For example, the sound picked up on location varies in relation to the distance of microphone from the action and from the source of background noises. Thus, when an editor cuts the picture, there is a definite bounce or bump between cuts as the level changes from close-up to long shot to medium shot. Smoothing can be accomplished in several ways: (1) By extending a piece of the loudest background over the area where it is softest, by loop or reprint; (2) By physically scraping or wiping off, on an angle, a portion of the sound track leading to or from the splice on the loudest side; (3) By using an electric pencil to eliminate part of the sound.

Sound effects: Abbreviated FX. Any sound or noise important to the action or background of a scene. They come from four sources: (1) production (those recorded during filming); (2) sync effects; (3) wild tracks; and (4) a library of sound effects saved over a period of years and kept in stock for reuse.

Sync FX: Also called *M and S*, or *make and sync*, or *Foley*. Sound effects recorded live to picture utilizing the same technique as for loop lines. Sound editors follow the action on a screen and make all footsteps and extraneous movement in synchronization. Sync marks later enable him to easily cut the sound effects into his units in sync with the picture. This is established procedure at major studios. Sound editors who work for small independent companies do not have this luxury and must depend entirely on library effects.

Sync Loop: A loop of sound, often containing distinguishable sounds, on which a sync mark is placed corresponding to the start mark of the picture. The specific sound on the loop then can be dialed in and recorded on cue.

Three stripe: Also called *3 H master*, *triple track*, *triple stripe*, or *three head*. This is a full-coat magnetic film on which three separate sound tracks have been recorded. In feature filming, sound effects, music and dialogue are separated. In television filming of laugh shows, sound effects and music are on one stripe, laughs on another, and dialogue on the third.

Transfer room: An area where all sound transfers are made from one recorded medium to another. Various types of recording and playback machines are located here. These include magnetic and optical film recording, acetate disc recording, and tape recording.

Walla: Any type of low conversation from a crowd. It is unintelligible but usually contains the characteristics of that particular type of crowd, such as theater, sports, night club or party.

Wild lines: This is dialogue recorded without picture and is used in much the same way as loop lines, except that there is little attempt made at synchronization during recording.

Wild track: A sound track recorded without picture. It is more often a sound effect that might have occurred during filming, and a wild track was made of it for the sound editor.

Wipe: The process of literally taking away part of the sound track. See *smooth*.

Work picture: The final edited picture, which is used by the sound and music editors and all concerned in preparation for dubbing and negative editing.

Work track: Also *master dialogue* or *master track*. The final edited sound track corresponding to the work picture, used by the sound and music editors in preparing for dubbing and in the dubbing process.

Selected Equipment for Editorial Functions

Audio swabbles: Tight-knit cotton tips for cleaning magnetic heads with solvents.

Blooping ink: Black ink applied to optical negative track to create opaque areas for silence.

Blooping tape: Opaque masking tape of various mil widths placed over the splice at the edge to eliminate noise as film moves over head.

Bloop punch: Makes a 16mm wide triangular cut at the frame edge, eliminating the rough cut of the splicer.

Bloop tones: Prerecorded 1000-hertz tones in tab form placed opposite the #2 of the academy leader during tonal matching before the mix and during dubbing and other stages.

Cue punch: Available in several diameters for each gauge. Used for punching printing start marks.

Demagnetized scissors: Brass scissors for silent cuts.

Dust-off: Compressed air used for dusting the optical negative during conforming stage.

Freon TF: A fluorocarbon used for cleaning mag track.

Markers: Easiest to clean from track; grease markers if used on base side; otherwise, Sharpies or Neumade Fiesta.

Music cue punch: Characterized by three rectangular in-line punches for cueing music tracks.

Splicing tabs: Precut and perforated splicing tabs for the mechanical series of audio splicers made by Quick-Splice, Editall, and Kodak.

Stop-n-Cue: A metallized sensing tape used to mark at edge for sync cueing of audio tapes; also for automatic start and stop in certain cassettes.

Videotape Transfer

Balance: Equality of level in the red, green, and blue images that produces neutral blacks and clean whites. When levels are out of balance, the blacks or whites may exhibit unwanted color, and color values in the picture may be distorted.

Banding: Evenly spaced horizontal bars or bands across the picture that differ in brightness or color saturation from the rest of the picture.

Blanking: The electronic black border surrounding the picture on all sides. On occasion this border may intrude into the picture area, thereby covering up picture information.

Camera match: Shot-to-shot picture fidelity. Improperly matched cameras may exhibit differences in level, balance, colorimetry, or defects that will cause the picture quality to change from shot to shot.

Chroma level: Color saturation. Low chroma level produces pastel, "washed out" color. High chroma level produces heavy, saturated colors.

Clipping: An electronic limit usually imposed in cameras to avoid overly bright or dark signals. When improperly applied can result in loss of picture information in very bright or very dark areas.

Colorimetry: The accurate analysis, processing, and reproduction of all colors. Some television cameras do not reproduce all colors accurately. The most noticeable colorimetry errors occur in the red area of the spectrum.

Compression: Lack of separation in signal levels. Commonly called *black compression* or *white compression*, indicating a lack of detail or gradation in the very dark or very light areas of the picture.

Control track: A synchronizing signal on the edge of the tape that provides a reference for tracking control and tape speed. Control tracks that have heavy dropouts or are improperly recorded may cause tracking defects or picture jumps.

Drop outs: Small bits of missing picture information usually caused by physical imperfections in the surface of the videotape.

Edge curl: Edge curl usually occurs in the outside $\frac{1}{16}$-inch of the videotape. If the tape is sufficiently deformed, it will not make proper contact with the playback heads, resulting in a loss of cue track or control track.

Edit errors: A normal edit will produce a change of picture without disturbing any of the synchronizing pulses or the video signal. A bad edit may produce a momentary flash, color hue shift, horizontal picture shift, video dropout, or geometrical distortion of the picture at the edit point.

Enhancement: A form of signal processing that artificially sharpens an image by accentuating the transitions or edges within the picture. This edge sharpening can produce unwanted ringing and noise if not carefully and sparingly applied.

First line error: Velocity error (color hue difference) confined to single scan lines evenly spaced down the picture.

Hum: 60-cycle power-line frequency that has interfered with the video signal. This may occur in the camera sweep circuits, causing a slow-moving wobble or warp to the picture, or it may affect the video level, appearing as a slow-moving horizontal line or bar rolling up the picture.

Lag: Comet tail. Under some lighting conditions, camera pickup tubes will exhibit image retention in bright areas of picture causing these areas to form "comet tails" or smears when the camera is moved or panned. As no two tubes will react exactly the same, lag often appears as a color trail—green, red, or blue, or any of these in combination.

Level: Loudness. A quantitative measure of a video signal. Low level indicates the dark portions; high level indicates the bright.

Microphonics: Video level distortions caused by sound or physical vibration picked up by sensitive camera tubes or other video equipment. These appear as flickering horizontal lines and bars across the picture.

Moiré: The effect produced when one frequency is superimposed over another frequency. This may be observed when a man wearing a pinstriped suit is recorded through a television system. When the camera is close enough to resolve the stripes, the suit will flicker and show larger stripes of light and dark. False colors or a rainbow effect is produced when the stripes in the suit approach subcarrier frequency. In some 1-inch recorders, moiré is produced by the carrier frequency overlapping the color subcarrier.

Noise: Unwanted random signals dispersed throughout the video, usually more evident in dark areas. Very similar in appearance to film grain.

Overdeviation: Commonly called *bearding*. Caused by an excess of chroma or video level, which is too high for the tape to handle. Appears as a black "frying" in overly bright picture or overly saturated color.

Phase: Hue. Color signals in correct phase will reproduce color as the camera saw them. Signals that are out of phase will exhibit hue shift, which is most noticeable in flesh tones, giving rise to magenta or green faces.

Registration: The alignment of the red, green, and blue images precisely on top of one another. When one or more of the images are misaligned, color edge images are visible at sharp transitions.

Resolution: Sharpness. The ability of a system to reproduce fine detail and clean, sharp edges.

Ringing: An edge effect that is commonly seen on sharp black-to-white or white-to-black transitions. Ringing appears as a secondary edge (or ghost edge) usually on the right-hand side of the transition. When excessive enhancement has been used, ringing may appear on all sides of a sharply defined object or the lettering in a title or graphic.

Safe title area; safe action area: Geometrical boundaries set up as a guide to avoid the placement of important action or titles at the edges of the picture that may be cut off on home receivers.

Scratches: Videotape scratches appear as an evenly spaced series of dropouts forming a diagonal line across the picture.

Shading (field): More commonly called color purity. Unevenness in level in one or more of the red, green, or blue images, producing overall color variations across the picture. On occasion the picture appears brighter in the center than at the edges (commonly called *porthole*).

Shedding: A condition in which the oxide, which forms the recording surface of the videotape, has begun to separate from the base. This loose oxide clogs the video heads, resulting in loss of picture.

Smearing: An electronic defect that causes bright object to flare or trail off toward the right-hand side of the picture.

Streaking/clamp: An unwanted level change in the portion of a picture, directly to the right and left of a very bright object, continuing all the way across the screen.

Sync: Synchronizing pulse. A pulse included in the signal that provides a synchronizing reference for each frame and scanning line of the picture. Defects in this pulse may cause jumping, rolling, or breakup.

Telecine: A motion picture projector and a television camera specifically set up to convert the film image to video signals while also converting the 24-

frames-per-second film to 30-frames-per-second television. Problems common to telecine are black-and-white compression, shading problems, and colorimetry errors.

Time base error: A variation in the relationship between the picture information and the sync pulse, the color information, or the reference burst that cannot be corrected in normal playback. This problem is normally associated with substandard tape formats, such as 1-, $\frac{1}{2}$-, and $\frac{3}{4}$-inch tapes.

Tracking: The process by which the video head on a playback machine follows exactly the same path as the video head that recorded the signal. Loss of tracking is evidenced by picture breakup or loss of video in segments of the picture.

Transients: Unwanted disturbances in video signals that travel or come and go causing small flaws in the picture.

Velocity error: Evenly spaced horizontal segments of picture that exhibit hue shift from top to bottom. This defect might be described as a color "venetian blind" effect. Velocity error is always more severe on the right side of the picture.

Wrinkles: A physical deformity of the video tape. Any crease or wrinkle in the video tape may produce dropouts or loss of picture information.

Videotape Recording

AB roll, A-B roll: *n.* 1. A technique by which information is played back from two tape machines *rolled* sequentially, usually for the purpose of *dubbing* the sequential information onto a third tape. 2. A recording thus produced.

Anhysteresis: *n.* Magnetization by means of an unidirectional field upon which is superposed an alternating field of gradually decreasing amplitude.

Assemble: *v.t.* To join together successive program segments so as to form a continuous program tape. *v.i.* To direct or carry out such joining. *adj.* Of a recording apparatus, pertaining to that mode designed to carry out such joining.

Audio buzz: *n.* A low-frequency disturbance in the reproduced audio signal from a VTR, especially that disturbance noted when the video tracks have been rerecorded and the prior audio information has been retained.

Azimuth: *adj.* Pertaining to the angle between the direction of head travel and the *pole-tip gap*. (For optimum *interchange*, this angle is usually 90°.)

Band-by-band correction: *n.* An automatic correction method wherein the errors of an entire head band are sensed and an average correction applied. (The parameter most often corrected by this method is the chroma amplitude error).

Breakup: *n*. A picture fault characterized by a complete scrambling of the reproduced picture. The effect is often caused by servo unlock. *v*. Of a VTR, to produce such a picture fault.

Buffer: *n*. 1. In a VTR, an apparatus capable of storing at least a TV line of the reproduced picture, and functioning as a *TBC*. 2. A device on a tape *transport*, usually pneumatic in operating principle, that can store a variable length of moving tape as it passes over the transport. 3. Any device capable of storing but not processing a signal.

Channel: *n*. An isolated signal path, especially a signal path dedicated to the conveyance of signals to or from a single record/playback head.

Chroma noise: *n*. 1. Noise appearing predominantly in that portion of the spectrum conveying chrominance information. 2. The picture fault resulting from such noise. 3. A picture fault characterized by unwanted hue and chrominance shifts, usually at a scan line rate. Often called *streaky noise*.

Clinching: *n*. The tangential slippage between tape layers occurring when a loosely wound *reel* of tape is subjected to high rotational acceleration or deceleration. This inter-layer slippage results in physical distortion of the tape, manifesting itself as a series of buckles, creases, or folds in the areas that have slipped.

Contact print: *n*. A copy of a magnetic recording made by placing the tape to be copied in close contact with the blank tape that is to become the copy and exposing the tapes to some process such as the *anhysteretic duplication* process, designed to accomplish the transfer of the flux patterns to the blank tape.

Contouring: *n*. The action by which the shape of a video head's tape-contacting surface slowly adapts itself to the tensions and pressures of the tape it is contacting. The result of such action is normally an improvement in the intimacy of head-to-tape contact and, hence, better performance.

Countdown: *n*. 1. A signal recorded just ahead of the desired program, providing an aural and visual indication of the number of seconds remaining before the start of the program. 2. That portion of a tape containing such a signal.

Cue, cuetone: *n*. A tone recorded on the *cue track* or *audio track* marking the point at which the tape is to be cued.

Cue channel: *n*. That portion of a videotape recording machine devoted to the recording and replay of the cueing information or time code signals relating to the video. 2. By extension, the signals in such a channel or the output of the channel.

Cue track: *n*. The area reserved on the tape for audio information relating to production requirements, electronic editing information, or an ancillary program signal.

Cue up, cue: *v.* To prepare a tape and machine for playback by positioning the tape in the transport at a point just prior to the beginning of program.

Dropout compensator: *n.* 1. An apparatus that detects the presence of a *dropout* and acts to minimize its visibility in the reproduced picture. 2. An apparatus that accomplishes the foregoing by replacing the missing information with statistically similar information from another part of the signal (e.g., from the preceding scan line).

Edit: *v.t.* To alter the content of a prerecorded tape, either by selectively erasing a portion of the tape and recording new material, or by appending new material in the previously unrecorded section at the end of the earlier recording, or by physically cutting out a section of the tape and inserting another segment of prerecorded tape. *v.i.* To direct or carry out such an operation. *n.* 1. A point or location in a tape at which such an alteration has been made. 2. The program material in the immediate vicinity of such an alteration.

Edit code: *n.* 1. Generally, any pulse train used as a code to facilitate or aid the tape editing process by locating the program segments on a tape. 2. Specifically, the SMPTE Edit Code as described in American National Standard (ANSIV98.12). 3. The magnetic pattern on a tape representing such a code. Also called time and control code, time code, or time and location code.

Edit pulse: *n.* 1. A pulse derived from and occurring during the vertical interval of the even field of the TV signal and recorded on the *control track*, originally to facilitate mechanical editing procedures and, in later equipments, to control *electronic editing* equipment. Occasionally called *editing pulse*. 2. The magnetic pattern recorded on tape representing such a pulse. 3. The pulse replayed from such a magnetic pattern. (The preferred term for Defs. 1 and 2 is *frame pulse*; equipment descriptions often distinguish between Defs. 1 and 3 by calling the first *frame pulse* and the second *edit pulse*.)

Flagging: *n.* A picture fault characterized by a random left-and-right motion of picture elements near the top of the picture. Also called *flag-waving*, *broomsticking*, and *hooking*.

Hardbanding: *n.* 1. A tape fault characterized by either a non-constant thickness or non-constant elasticity across the width of a tape. 2. The variation in the recovery of the RF signal caused by such a fault. 3. The picture faults such as *chroma banding* or *velocity errors*, which are caused by such a fault.

Digital Recording

Additive synthesis: The process of creating a sound or timbre by adding harmonics to a sine wave.

Aliasing: Sharply noticeable inaccuracies in the rendering of any line or surface caused by too low a sampling rate.

Amplitude modulation: Periodic change in volume with tremolo effect or repeated emphasis of same sound.

Analysis: Computer measurement of a sampled waveform to synthesize or resynthesize.

Animatics: A video or animation simulation of a special effect used to fill in scenes in a work print until the final shot is completed.

Attack: Beginning of a sound.

Audio still frame: Commentary, music, or effect accompanying a single still image, recorded by audio compression.

Backing up: Saving copies of a file or sequence to a disc during processing for permanent storage.

Breath controller: Enables a player to express sound parameters with breath pressure via a mouthpiece device.

Chorus: Addition of a duplicate sound, sometimes at a different pitch, to single partial timbres or whole timbres.

Click: Digital metronome used for tempo and rhythm reference during recording.

Compressed audio: System of recording and transmitting audio data in a highly compact form by encoding and decoding analog signal digitally or by audio-to-video conversion.

Configure: Setting up system software to recognize existence and nature of all hardware components.

Cross-fade: Fading one sequence, timbre frame, or sound file out while another fades in gradually.

Cue: A section of a recording identified by in and out points.

DAC unit: Digital-to-analog converter transforming binary code to audible sound waves.

Decay: A selected amount of time change between events in a harmonic or volume envelope. Initial decay is the period between the peak volume level of attack and the volume selected for sustained portion of the envelope. Final decay is the period between key release at the sustained volume level and zero volume at the end of the envelope.

Dynamic envelope: A partial timbre setting that allows sounding or no sounding of the timbre.

Event: An audio occurrence placed in a sequence and triggered by a sequencer.

Frequency modulation: Additional harmonic components produced when a sound wave interacts with a second wave.

FSK signal: A frequency shift key signal to syncronize recording components.

Genlocking: Process of aligning the data rate of video images with that of a digital device to digitize the image and enter it into memory.

Harmonic envelope: A series of times and values controlling the addition of frequency modulation to a partial timbre. Delay, attack duration, peak volume, initial decay, sustain, and final decay may be controlled.

Justification: Repositioning of notes of a sequence to exact or nearest beat or beat subdivision.

Keyboard polyphony: Number of notes playable simultaneously defined by number of voices in system, each partial timbre requiring one or two voices for each note played.

Layering: Combining different sounds to make a complex timbre.

Looping: Continuous repetition of a section of a sound file or sequence.

Monophonic: Having one voice (chords are not possible).

Mouse: A hand-operated controller allowing remote control of a display cursor and its operations.

Offset: Difference between the time SMPTE starts and the time selected for a sequence to begin.

Overdubbing: Recording additional tracks of a sequence or recording additional notes on the same track.

Overwrite: To store a file or sequence over another of the same name, erasing the original data.

Polyphonic: Multiple voices defined by the number of polyphonic voice samplings in the system.

Resynthesis: Digital analysis of a sampled sound is used to create a synthesized sound that matches the analysis.

Reverse compiler: Program changing recorded sounds in Memory Recorder or Music Notation Display to a format for editing.

Sampling: Process of recording measurements of a sound wave a number of times (40,000 per second). The measurements can be used by the computer to reproduce the original signal or modify it by digital synthesis or by changing the sampling rate.

Sequence: A series of audio events that can be triggered by a sequencer.

Sequencer: Digital recording and playback device.

Soloing: Selecting a track or partial timbre to be heard or changed by itself or with selected tracks.

Timbre frames: A series of segments of a synthesized partial timbre, each of which can have different harmonics, delay times, volume, pitch, and splice characteristics. As the series of frames is played, a sound with a changing waveform is created.

Transpose: Change the pitch of a sound or sequence.

Tuplet: The notation of an irregular number of note values per beat or subdivision. Triplets or quintuplets in common time are examples.

Velocity/pressure keyboard: Keyboard unit that senses the velocity of the keystroke and the applied after-touch pressure. The sensed values can become expression parameter controls.

Voices: Sound generator units. One note sounded requires at least one voice.

Volume envelope: A series of times and values controlling the volume of a partial timbre over time.

Write: To save or store a file or sequence on disc.

Figure A–8   Cinema Pathe: the meaning of precision is clarity.

Figure A–9 The Edison phonograph turned the home into a concert hall.

Bibliography

Film Music

APEL, WILLI, ed. *Harvard Dictionary of Music,* 2nd rev. ed. Cambridge, MA: Harvard University Press, 1969.

ATKINS, IRENE KAHN. *Source Music in Motion Pictures.* East Brunswick, NJ: Fairleigh Dickinson University Press, 1983.

BAZELON, IRWIN. *Knowing the Score: Notes on Film Music.* New York: Van Nostrand, Reinhold, 1975.

BEHLMER, RUDY. "Erich Wolfgang Korngold," *Films in Review* (Feb. 1967), pp. 86–100.

BERG, CHARLES M. *An Investigation of the Motives for and Realization of Music to Accompany the American Silent Film, 1896–1927.* New York: Arno Press, 1976.

BEYNON, GEORGE W. *The Musical Presentation of Motion Pictures.* New York: G. Schirmer, 1921.

BUCHANAN, LOREN G. "Art of Composing Music Scores for Films" *Motion Picture Herald,* (Oct. 13, 1965), p. 38.

BURTON, JACK, *The Blue Book of Hollywood Musicals.* New York: Century House, 1970.

COLPI, HENRI. *Defense et Illustration de la Musique dans le Film.* Lyon: Serdoc, 1963.

DEARING, JAMES W. *Making Money Making Music.* Cincinnati, OH: Writer's Digest, 1982, 305 pp.

DOLAN, ROBERT E. *Music in Modern Media.* New York: G. Schirmer, 1967.

EISLER, HANNS. *Composing for the Films.* New York: Oxford University Press, 1947.

———. *A Rebel in Music.* New York: International, 1978, 223 pp.

Elesevier's Dictionary of Cinema Sound and Music. New York: Elesevier Publishing Co.

EMBLER, JEFFREY. "The Structure of Film Music." *Films in Review* (Aug–Sept. 1953).

EVANS, MARK. *Soundtrack: The Music of the Movies.* New York: Hopkinson and Blake, 1975.

FAULKNER, ROBERT R. "Music on Demand." NJ: *Transaction,* 1983, 281 pp.

Filmmusic Notebook, Elmer Bernstein's Film Music Collection, Vol. 1 (1974–), Elmer Bernstein Society, Calabasas, CA.

GAGNE, C. AND T. CARAS. *Soundpieces: Interviews with American Composers.* Metuchen, NJ: Scarecrow Press, 1982, 418 pp.

GALLEZ, DOUGLAS W. "Satie's Entr'acte: A Model of Film Music," *Cinema Journal* (Fall 1976), pp 36–50.

GAMMOND, P. AND R. HORRICKS. *The Music Goes Round and Round.* London: Quartet, 1980, 183 pp.

HAGEN, EARLE. *Scoring for Films.* New York: Criterion Music Corp. 1971.

HERRMANN, BERNARD. "Contemporary Use of Music in Film: Citizen Kane, Psycho, Fahrenheit 451." Cambridge, MA: University Film Study Center, 1974 Newsletter, Vol. 7 No. 3.

HOFFMAN, CHARLES. *Sounds for Silents.* New York: Drama Books Specialists, 1970.

HURST, W. E., AND D. RICO. *How to Sell Your Song.* Los Angeles CA: 7 Arts, 1980, 95 pp.

HURST, WALTER E. *How to Be a Music Publisher.* Los Angeles CA: 7 Arts, 1979, 74 pp.

KREUGER, MILES. *The Movie Musical from Vitaphone to 42nd Street as Reported in a Great Fan Magazine.* New York: Dover, 1975.

LANG, EDITH, AND GEORGE WEST. *Musical Accompaniment of Moving Pictures* (1920). Reprinted by Arno Press, New York, 1970.

LIMBACHER, JAMES L. *Film Music: From Violins to Video,* Metuchen, NJ: Scarecrow Press, 1974.

———. *Keeping Score, Film Music 1972–1979:* Metuchen, NJ: Scarecrow Press, 1981, 510 pp.

———. *Four Aspects of the Film.* New York: Brussel & Brussel, 1968.

LONDON, KURT. *Film Music: A Summary of the Characteristic Features of Its History, Aesthetics, Technique and Possible Developments.* London: Faber & Faber, 1936.

MANCINI, HENRY. *Sounds and Scores: A Practical Guide to Professional Orchestration.* Northridge, CA: Northridge Music, 1967.

MANVELL, ROGER, AND JOHN HUNTLEY. *The Technique of Film Music.* New York: Hastings House, 1975.

MCCARTY, CLIFFORD. *Film Composers in America.* New York: Da Capo, 1972, 193 pp.

MCNEEL, K., AND LUTHER, M. *Songwriters with a Touch of Gold.* Los Angeles: Martin, 1976, 222 pp.

MCVAY, DOUGLAS. *The Musical Film.* New York: A. S. Barnes, 1967.

PRENDERGAST, R. M. *Film Music, A Neglected Art.* New York: Norton, 1977, 268 pp.

RAPEE, ERNO. *Encyclopedia of Music for Pictures.* (1925). Reprinted by Arno Press, New York, 1970.

———. *Motion Picture Moods for Pianists and Organists: A Rapid-Reference Collection of Selected Pieces.* New York: G. Schirmer, 1924. Reprinted by Arno Press, New York, 1970.

SABANEEV, LEONID. *Music for the Film: A Handbook for Composers and Conductors.* London: Pittman, 1935.

SHARPLES, WIN, JR. "A Selected and Annotated Bibliography of Books and Articles on Music in the Cinema," *Cinema Journal* (Spring 1978), pp. 36–67.

SHEMEL, S., AND KRASILOVSKY, M. W. *This Business of Music.* New York: Billboard, 1979, 596 pp.

SIEGEL, ALAN H. *Breaking in to the Music Business.* New York: Cherry Lane, 1983, 274 pp.

SKILES, MARLIN. *Music Scoring for TV and Motion Pictures*. Philadelphia, PA: TAB, 1976, 261 pp.

SKINNER, FRANK, *Underscore*. New York: Criterion Music, 1960.

Documentary

BARNOUW, ERIK. *Documentary: A History of the Non-Fiction Film*. New York: Oxford University Press, 1974.

BARSAM, RICHARD M. *Nonfiction Film: A Critical History*. New York: Dutton, 1973.

JACOBS, LEWIS, ed. *The Documentary Tradition: From Nanook to Woodstock*. New York: Hopkinson & Blake, 1971.

LEYDA, JAY. *Films Beget Films*. New York: Hill & Wang, 1964.

ROTHA, PAUL, EDMUND SINCLAIR AND RICHARD GRIFFITH. *Documentary Film*. New York: Hastings, 1952.

SNYDER, ROBERT. *Pare Lorenz and the Documentary Film*. Norman: University of Oklahoma, 1968.

WRIGHT, BASIL. *The Long View*. New York: Knopf, 1974.

Recent Readings in Media

1. *The Acoustic Mirror,* Kaja Silverman, 1988, 257 pp.

   The female voice in psychoanalysis and cinema.

2. *The Art of Creative Writing,* Lajos Egri, 1985, 224 pp.

   Guide for the development of fiction, plays, TV and radio scripts.

3. *The Battle of Brazil,* Jack Matthews, 1987, 228 pp.

   Details what can go wrong with a feature like Terry Gilliam's *Brazil*.

4. *Child of Paradise,* Edward Baron Turk, 1989, 495 pp.

   Marcel Carne and the golden age of French cinema.

5. *Encyclopedia of Television,* Vincent Terrance, 1986, 480 pp./volume.

   Series, Plots and Specials documented year-by-year. Vol. 1, 1937–1973, Vol. 2: 1974–1984, Vol. 3: Who's Who in TV 1937–1984.

6. *Film Language,* Christian Metz, 1974, 268 pp.

   A collection of essays on the nature of cinematic discourse.

7. *Film Sound: Theory and Practice,* E. Weis and J. Belton, 1985, 462 pp.

   Anthology of essays on the significance of sound stylistics.

8. *Film Sound Today,* Larry Blake, 1984, 56 pp.

   Articles about technical innovations in sound.

9. *Grammar of the Film Language,* Daniel Arijon, 1976, 624 pp.

   Thorough explanation of narrative structures of storytelling.

10. *Hanns Eisler: A Rebel in Music,* Hanns Eisler, 1978, 223 pp.
    The composer writes about the functions of film music.

11. *The Hollywood Studio System,* Douglas Gomery, 1986, 213 pp.
    Analyzes the studio process as a business.

12. *Invisible Storytellers,* Sarah Kozloff, 1988, 167 pp.
    Voice-over narration in American fiction film.

13. *Keeping Score,* James Limbacher, 1981, 510 pp.
    Credit lists.

14. *The Melody Lingers On,* Roy Hemming, 1988, 400 pp.
    The great songwriters and their movie musicals.

15. *Mindscreen: Bergman, Godard, and First-person Film,* Bruce Kawin, 1978, 241 pp.
    Mindscreen is the visual and aural field that presents itself as the product of the dreamstate of film.

16. *Narration in the Fiction Film,* David Bordwell, 1985, 370 pp.
    The historical poetics of cinema.

17. *Narrative, Apparatus, Ideology,* Philip Rosen, 1986, 549 pp.
    Influential writings on film theory.

18. *The Origin of Consciousness in the Breakdown of the Bicameral Mind,* Julien Jaynes, 1976, 466 pp.
    Discusses the origin of language and being.

19. *The Psychology of Composition,* Sergei Eisenstein, 1988, 120 pp.
    Reprint of an older translation of one of Eisenstein's theoretical papers.

20. *The Quantum Self,* Danah Zohar, 1989, 268 pp.
    Human nature defined by the new physics.

21. *Signs and Meaning in the Cinema,* Peter Wollen, 1972, 175 pp.
    Covers important structural issues in constructing the narrative.

22. *The Silent Scream,* E. Weis, 1986, 200 pp.
    Explores Hitchcock's use of the sound track in films like *Vertigo* and *Psycho.*

23. *Soundtrack: The Music of the Movies,* Mark Evans, 1975, 303 pp.
    Historical tracking of careers and compositions.

24. *Thinking in Pictures,* John Sayles, 1987, 315 pp.
    A director details the decision process in the making of *Matewan.*

25. *Unheard Melodies: Narrative Film Music,* Claudia Gorbman, 1987, 190 pp.
    The theory and analysis of the functions of music in narrative cinema.

26. *Wide Screen Movies*, Robert E. Carr and R. M. Hayes, 1988, 502 pp.
    History of widescreen with attention to sound systems.

Pamphlets

American Cinema Labs Manual, ACL Association, Bethesda, MD.

ASCAP, The Facts, ASCAP, New York.

Harry Partch, B.M.I., 1968, Broadcast Music Inc. New York.

Instruments of the Orchestra, Pickering & Co., Plainview, NY.

Magnetic Sound Recording, Eastman Kodak, Rochester, NY.

Magnetic Tapes and Powders, Electrodes. BASF, by Paul Zimmerman, Vol 4. Archives
    of Badische Anilin & Soda Fabrik AG, Munich, 1969.

Microphones, G. Bore, Georg Neuman & Co. (Gotham Audio), New York.

Microphones, An Anthology of Articles, AES Reprint, 1953–79, New York.

Motion Picture Projection and Theatre Presentation Manual, SMPTE, White Plains,
    NY.

Nagra 4.2 Manual, Nagra Magnetic/Kudelski, New York and Geneva.

Nakamichi Live Recording System, Nakamichi Research, Santa Monica, CA.

Phonograph and Sound Recording, Audio Engineering Society Reprint, Vol. 25, No.
    10/11, 1977, the Society, New York.

The Time Code Book, EECO, Santa Ana, CA.

20 Years of Video Tape, 3M Center, St. Paul, MN.

Periodicals and Journals

Technical

dB: The Sound Engineering Magazine

Journal of the Society of Motion Picture and Television Engineers

Journal of the Audio Engineering Society

Journal of the Acoustic Society of America

Recording Engineer/Producer

Mix

American Cinematographer

Electronic Musician

HyperMedia

Critical

Film Comment

American Film

Screen

Sight and Sound

Cinema Journal (Society of Cinema Studies)

Films in Review

The Independent

Boxoffice

Animation

Millimeter

Video Review

The Film Journal

Music Writer's Guides*

Range and Transposition Guide, Robert Bornatein
Standardized Chord Symbol Notation, C. Brant and C. Roemer
Principles of Orchestration, Nicolai Rimsky-Korsakov
Music Arranging and Orchestration, John Cacavas
Arranged by Nelson Riddle, Nelson Riddle
Basic Harmony and Theory, Dick Grove
Scoring for Films, Earl Hagen
Harmony from the Science of Acoustics, Charles Koff
Music Theory Dictionary, William F. Lee
Sounds and Scores, Henry Mancini
The Art of Music Copying, Clinton Roemer
Music Notation Primer, Glen Rosencrans
Contemporary Arranger, Don Sebersky
Click Track "Minutes and Seconds," Knudson

Directory of Selected Manufacturers

Acoustical Products

Crown International, Inc., 1718 W. Mishawaka Rd., Elkhart, IN 46517; (219) 294-8000.

Nakamichi America Corporation, 19701 South Vermont Ave., Torrance, CA; (213) 538-8150.

QSC Audio Products, 1926 Placentia Ave., Costa Mesa, CA 92627; (714) 645-2540.

RPG Diffusor Systems, 12006 Wimbleton St., Largo, MD 20772; (301) 249-5647.

Tannoy, 300 Gage Ave., Unit #1, Kitchener, Ontario, N2M 2C8, Canada; (519) 745-1158.

Automation & Control Systems

Audio Kinetics Ltd., Kinitec Center, Theobald St., Borehamwood, Herts WD6 4PJ, U.K.; (01) 953-8118.

Fostex Corporation of America, 15431 Blackburn Ave., Norwalk, CA 90650; (213) 921-1112.

---

* Available from Crosscountry Film/Video, P.O. Box 145, Hoboken, NJ 07030

Harrison by GLW, 437 Atlas Dr., Nashville, TN 37211; (615) 331-8800.

Lexicon, Inc., 100 Beaver St., Waltham, MA 02154; (617) 891-6790.

Computer Hardware & Software

Altec Lansing, 10500 West Reno, Oklahoma City, OK 73125; (405) 324-5311.

Akai Professional, P.O. Box 2344, Fort Worth, TX 76113; (817) 336-5114.

Bose Corporation, The Mountain, Framingham, MA 01701; (508) 879-7330.

Digidesign, 1360 Willow Rd., Suite 101, Menlo Park, CA 94025; (415) 327-8811.

Electro-Voice, 600 Cecil St., Buchanan, MI 49107; (616) 695-6831.

Opcode Systems, 1024 Hamilton Ct., Menlo Park, CA 94025; (415) 321-8977.

Passport, 625 Miramontes St., Half Moon Bay, CA 94019; (415) 726-0280.

Yamaha Corporation of America, 6600 Orangethorpe Ave., Buena Park, CA 90622; (714) 522-9312.

Digital Workstations

AKG Acoustics, 125 Walnut St., Watertown, MA 02172; (617) 924-7697.

Digital Audio Research, 6363 Sunset Blvd., Suite 802, Hollywood, CA 90028; (213) 466-9151.

New England Digital, 49 North Main St., White River Junction, VT 05001; (802) 295-5800.

Solid State Logic, Begbroke, Oxford OX5 1RU, U.K.; (0865) 842300.

Studer Editech, 1370 Willow Rd., Menlo Park, CA 94025; (415) 326-7030.

Microphones

Audio-Technica, 1221 Commerce Dr., Stow, OH 44224; (216) 686-2600.

Beyerdynamic, 5-05 Burns Ave., Hicksville, NY 11801; (516) 935-8000.

Bruel + Kjaer, 185 Forest St., Marlborough, MA 01752; (508) 481-7000.

Gotham Audio, 1790 Broadway, New York, NY 10019; (212) 765-3410.

Milab, 30B Banfi Plaza North, Farmingdale, NY 11735; (516) 249-3660.

Schoeps/Posthorn Recordings, 142 West 26th St., New York, NY 10001; (212) 242-3737.

Sennheiser Electronic Corporation, 6 Vista Dr., Old Lyme, CT 06371; (203) 434-9190.

Shure Brothers, 222 Hartrey Ave., Evanston, IL 60202; (800) 257-4873.

Sony Corporation of America, 1600 Queen Anne Rd., Teaneck, NJ 07666; (201) 833-5241.

Music Products & Midi

Korg USA, 89 Frost St., Westbury, NY 11590; (516) 333-9100.

Kurzweil Music Systems, 1600 Broadway, Ste. 1000A, New York, NY 10019; (212) 957-9100.

Roland Corp US, 7200 Dominion Circle, Los Angeles, CA 90040; (213) 685-5141.

R-Dat

Digital Audio Technologies SA/Stellavox, Puits-Godet 20, CH-2000 Neuchatel, Switzerland; (038) 244-400.

Panasonic/Ramsa, 6550 Katella Ave., Cypress, CA 90630; (714) 373-7277.

Signal Processing

Altec Lansing, A Mark IV Company, P.O. Box 26105, Oklahoma City, OK 73126; (405) 324-5311.

Dolby Laboratories, 100 Potrero Ave., San Francisco, CA 94103; (415) 558-0200.

Furman Sound, 30 Rich St., Greenbrae, CA 94904; (415) 927-1225.

Klark-Teknik Electronics, Inc., 30 B Banf. Plaza North, Farmingdale, NY 11735; (516) 249-3660.

UREI, 8500 Balboa Blvd., Northridge, CA 91329; (818) 893-8411.

Speakers & Monitors

Eastern Acoustics Works, One Main St., Whitinsville, MA 01588; (508) 234-6158.

JBL Professional, 8500 Balboa Blvd., Northridge, CA 91329; (818) 893-8411.

Meyer Sound Labs, 2832 San Pablo Ave., Berkeley, CA 94702; (415) 486-1166.

Peavey Electronics, 711 A St., Meridian, MS 39301; (601) 483-5365.

Tape Recorders

Mitsubishi: distributed exclusively in America by Neve, Berkshire Industrial Park, Bethel, CT 06801; (203) 744-6230.

Otari Corporation, 378 Vintage Park Drive, Foster City, CA 94404; (415) 341-5900.

Studer Revox America, Inc., 1425 Elm Hill Pike, Nashville, TN 37210; (615) 254-5651.

Tascam, 7733 Telegraph Rd., Montebello, CA 90640; (213) 726-0303.

Further References

BRANWELL, NIGEL. "Ambisonic Surround Sound Technology for Recording and Broadcast," *Recording/Eng/Prod.* (Dec 1983) pp. 72-80.

LEWIS, JOHN R. "J. T. Tykociner: A Forgotten Figure in the Development of Sound," *J.U.F.A.* Vol 33 # 3 (Summer 1981) pp. 21–27.

LUTZ, E. AND TED UZZLE. "Illustrated Guide to Loudspeaker Health Care and General Sound System Well-Being," *Boxoffice* (Nov 1982) pp. 61–67.

ROGOFF, ROSALIND. "Edison's Dream: A Brief History of the Kinetophone," *Cinema Journal* Vol 25, #2 (Spring 1976) pp. 58–68.

ROMEO, S. "Surround Sound, Overlooked but not Overheard," *Boxoffice* (Feb 1984) pp. 25.

INDEX